WORLD WAR II

WORLD WAR II

CRUCIBLE OF THE CONTEMPORARY WORLD:
COMMENTARY AND READINGS ■ LOYD E. LEE

M.E. Sharpe, Inc.
Armonk, New York
London, England

Library of Congress Cataloging-in-Publication Data

Lee, Loyd E., 1939–
World War II : crucible of the contemporary world :
commentary and readings / Loyd E. Lee
p.   cm.
Includes bibliographical references and index.
ISBN 0-87332-731-4 — ISBN 0-87332-732-2 (pbk.)
1. World War, 1939-1945.
I. Title.
II. Title: World War 2
III. Title: World War Two.
D743.L45   1991
940.53—dc20
90-25544
CIP

Printed in the United States of America

MV   10   9   8   7   6   5   4   3   2   1

For Nancy and Philip, Ed and Jenifer

Contents

Preface

Even as the postwar era recedes into memory with the unification of Germany and the collapse of Soviet hegemony in Eastern Europe—the key symbols of the demise of the Cold War—the Second World War, *the* mythic event of our century, still retains its appeal in the popular imagination. At the same time, however, as the youngest participants of that global conflict reach retirement age, the passions informed by their lived experiences give way to analytical inquiry from different perspectives about how the war came to be fought and what its continuing impact on the world is. The past does not stay in the past. It becomes present. Each age recreates its own past.

Though accounts of the war will probably long sustain a steady supply of villains, it was inevitable that the sharp contrasts of good and evil, of virtue and justice against the forces of oppression, tyranny, and racial extermination would yield to subtler views on the meaning of the war years. But not entirely. While Hitler has been depicted as an ordinary man, a twentieth-century politician and statesman dressed in an ordinary business suit, his name will long head the list of unprovoked aggressors, butchers of humanity, and perpetrators of unspeakable crimes. It is notable that nearly five decades after the end of the war, few voices, if any, suggest that overall the war was not a just war on the Allied side; that in some way, the world is not better because the Allies won it and not the Axis.

Nonetheless, we now know too much about the silence of those whose moral and political courage took second seat to indifference and complacency, opportunism and expediency, to place full responsibility on the Axis for all that went wrong. Was "appeasement" necessary or advisable? Was it proper to disregard the treatment of minorities within other countries? Perpetrators of crimes and bystanders who knew but did nothing were there in plenty, not only in Germany, but also throughout Europe and the rest of the world. The atomic bombs dropped on Japan (as well as "conventional" Allied bombing campaigns) leave lingering doubts about the wisdom of that decision. And what of the Atlantic alliance? Did it have a noble purpose? Did the Allies win the war and lose the peace? The racially-inspired mania of Hitler, the bombastic warmongering of Mussolini, and the imperious claims of Japanese militarists in East Asia soon became anachronisms after 1945, but how different were they at root from the motives of the victorious great powers?

Not only have the moral certainties of the wartime era come under scrutiny, but other evaluations of the significance of those years also command attention. As we learn more about secret operations, espionage, and codebreaking, the course of the war is seen in a quite different perspective. Or, to choose a very different field, war, modern total war, exacted its costs, but it also transformed the societies that passed through its fiery blasts. Did the Second World War so distort social and economic developments that nations have become, ineluctably, warfare states? Is the drive toward racial and gender equality actually a product of war? If so, what does that mean for understanding the world today? Questions abound.

Though the Second World War lasted a mere six years, those years were burdened with portents of a postwar future. What the globe would have looked like without the war we can never tell. The task of determining how our present world was shaped by war is in itself a difficult task. The intent of this collection is to stimulate the reader to look at the Second World War and its impact in a new way. The war did not determine the present, but without an understanding of the war, much of the present will be obscure and less intelligible.

A Brief Chronology of Events Relating to World War Two

1931

18 September   Japanese Kwantung Army begins taking of
                          Manchuria

1933

30 January   German President Paul von Hindenburg names
                          Adolf Hitler Reich Chancellor
14 October   Germany withdraws from the League of Nations

1934

19 September   Soviet Union admitted to the League of Nations

1935

16 March   Germany introduces universal male military
                          service
3 October   Italy invades Ethiopia

1936

17 July   Francisco Franco begins a civil war against the
                          Spanish Republic
25 October   Germany and Italy form Berlin-Rome Axis

1937

7 July	"China Incident" begins with Japanese attack on Chinese troops

1938

12 March	Germany annexes Austria
28 July	Russo–Japanese conflict begins in Manchuria
29 September	"Sudetenland" given to Hitler in Munich Agreement

1939

15 March	Germany violates Munich Agreement by occupying Czechoslovakia
28 March	Three-year Spanish Civil War ends
31 March	Chamberlain announces support for Poland against Germany
7 April	Italy invades Albania
22 May	German–Italian Pact of Steel signed
20–26 August	Red Army trounces Japanese at Nomonhan
23 August	Soviet–German Non-Aggression Pact signed
1 September	Germany invades Poland
3 September	Britain, France, Australia, and New Zealand declare war on Germany
15 September	Russo–Japanese cease-fire agreed on
17 September	Soviet troops invade Poland
3 November	U.S. Congress modifies the Neutrality Acts by passing "Cash and Carry" permitting belligerents to purchase U.S. arms for cash if carried by non-U.S. shippers
14 December	Russia expelled from the League of Nations for invading Finland

1940

12 March	Finland cedes territory to the Soviet Union and ends Winter War
30 March	Wang Jiangwei (Wang Chingwei) forms pro-Japanese government in China
9 April	Germany invades Denmark and Norway
10 May	Germany invades the Netherlands, Belgium, and France

10 May	Winston Churchill becomes Prime Minister of Great Britain
26 May–4 June	British and French troops evacuated at Dunkirk
10 June	Italy declares war on Britain and France
15–16 June	Soviet Union occupies Lithuania, Latvia, and Estonia
22 June	Vichy government under Pétain signs armistice with Germany
27 June	Soviet Union annexes Bessarabia and North Bukovina from Romania
26 July	U.S. places partial embargo on trade with Japan
15 August	Battle of Britain (Eagle Attack in German) opened by Luftwaffe
3 September	U.S. lends fifty destroyers to Britain in return for 99-year leases on naval bases in the western Atlantic and the Caribbean
16 September	U.S. Selective Service and Training Act authorizes first American peacetime draft
22 September	Japan occupies French Indochina
27 September	Germany, Italy, and Japan sign Tripartite Pact
28 October	Italy invades Greece
5 November	U.S. President Franklin D. Roosevelt reelected for third term

1941

6 January	Roosevelt delivers his Four Freedoms speech
22 January	British take Tobruk for first time
11 March	Lend-Lease Act becomes law
3 April–30 May	Rashid Ali heads pro-Axis coup in Iraq
6 April	Germany invades Yugoslavia and Greece
13 April	Russia and Japan sign a ten-year Neutrality Pact
6 June	German High Command issues Commissar Order to kill Soviet political commissars upon capture
8 June	British and Free French seize Syria
22 June	Germany opens war on the Soviet Union in Operation Barbarossa
25 June	Roosevelt issues Executive Order 8802 establishing a Fair Employment Practices Committee

4 July	Italian Army invades British Somaliland
5 July	U.S. occupies Iceland
14 August	Churchill and Roosevelt issue Atlantic Charter
25 August	British and Soviets occupy Iran and replace pro-Axis Shah
13 September	Italian Army invades Egypt
16 September	Syria declares its independence, with Free French approval
11 October	General Tojo replaces Prince Konoe as Prime Minister of Japan
31 October	German U-boat sinks American destroyer U.S. *Reuben James*
6 December	Red Army opens counteroffensive against Germany
7–8 December	Japan attacks Pearl Harbor, the Philippines, Hong Kong, Malaya, and other bases in the western Pacific
8 December	U.S. Congress declares war on Japan
10 December	Germany and Italy declare war on U.S.
11 December	U.S. Congress declares war on Germany and Italy
25 December	Hong Kong surrenders

1942

1 January	Twenty-six countries join in the United Nations Declaration
20 January	Wannsee Conference on the "Final Solution to the Jewish Problem"
15 February	Singapore surrenders, ending four centuries of European control of the Straits of Malacca
8 May	Battle of Coral Sea
20 May	Japanese Army conquers Burma
26 May	Anglo–Soviet Treaty signed
3–6 June	U.S. Navy defeats Japanese in the Battle of Midway
21 June	Rommel's Afrikakorps retakes Tobruk
7 August	U.S. Marines land in Guadalcanal
9 August	Indian Congress Party opens civil disobedience campaign
16 September	German Army opens Battle of Stalingrad

8 November	British–American Operation Torch invades North Africa
13 November	British regain Tobruk

1943

11 January	U.S. and British sign treaty abandoning extraterritoriality in China; Japan follows suit the same week
14–23 January	Churchill and Roosevelt meet at Casablanca Conference
2 February	German Sixth Army surrenders at Stalingrad
19 April	Warsaw ghetto rises up against Germans
12 May	Anglo–American forces drive Axis from North Africa
24 May	Doenitz withdraws U-boats from Battle of the Atlantic
5 July	Battle of Kursk on German–Soviet front opens
3 September	Britain and U.S. invade Italy
8 September	Italy surrenders
14 October	Philippines declare independence with José Laurel as President under Japanese auspices
28 November– 1 December	Stalin, Churchill, and Roosevelt meet for first Big Three summit at Tehran

1944

17 April	Japan opens Ichi Go offensive against China
6 June	Operation Overlord begins Normandy invasion (D-Day)
13 June	Germans use first V–1 bombs
19 June	Battle of the Philippine Sea begins
22 June	Red Army launches summer offensive against Germany
1 July	Bretton Woods Conference on postwar international economy begins
1 August	Polish Home Army rises up against Germans in Warsaw
21 August	Dumbarton Oaks Conference to plan for United Nations opens
25 August	Paris liberated

8 September	Germans use first V–2 rockets
20 October	Red Army and Yugoslav resistance liberate Belgrade
	U.S. invades Philippines
21 October	Battle of Leyte Gulf begins in the eastern Philippine Islands
7 November	Roosevelt reelected to fourth term
24 November	U.S. B–29 bombers open air war on Japan
16 December	Germans launch last offensive in Battle of the Bulge

1945

12 January	Russia opens winter offensive against Germany
17 January	Red Army takes Warsaw
4–12 February	Big Three meet for Yalta Conference in the Crimea; decisions made to divide Korea and Germany for military occupation
13–15 February	U.S.A.A.F. and R.A.F. bombing of Dresden
9 March	U.S. begins intensive incendiary bombing of Japanese cities
22 March	Arab League formed
5 April	Suzuki Kantaro becomes Prime Minister of Japan
12 April	Roosevelt dies; Harry S. Truman sworn in as President
23 April	Red Armies enter Berlin
25 April	United Nations founded at San Francisco Conference
	American and Soviet troops meet on the Elbe River in Germany
30 April	Hitler commits suicide
2 May	German army in Italy surrenders
7 May	Germany surrenders unconditionally
8 May	French battle Algerian Nationalists in Algeria, killing more than 1000 at a cost to themselves of 88 dead
21 May	French troops attempt to reassert control over Lebanon and Syria
16 July–2 August	Stalin, Truman, and Churchill meet at Potsdam Conference

16 July	First atomic bomb exploded at Alamogordo, New Mexico
26 July	U.S.–British Potsdam Declaration to Japan
	Labour Party wins by a landslide in British elections; Attlee replaces Churchill at Potsdam
6 August	First atomic bomb dropped on Hiroshima
8 August	Soviet Union declares war on Japan
9 August	Second atomic bomb dropped on Nagasaki
14 August	Japan surrenders
17 August	Achmed Sukarno proclaims Indonesian independence
2 September	Japan signs surrender terms
	Hejiminh (Ho Chi Minh) proclaims Vietnamese independence
23 September	Egyptians demand British military withdrawal
16 October	Pan-African Conference meets in Manchester, England

WORLD WAR II

General Introduction

War is father of all and king of all; and some he made gods and some men, some slaves and some free.

—Heraclitus, Greek philosopher of the fifth century B.C.[*]

In spite of many major regional and national armed conflicts throughout the world in the half century since 1945, the Second World War, whatever its name in different parts of the globe, remains stenciled in the minds and language of men and women everywhere as "the war." It overshadows the Great War, the term English speakers originally gave to the First World War. Statistically, there is justification for this. The Second World War took more human lives—perhaps six times as many—destroyed more property, and cost more to finance than any other war in history.

Few would challenge the idea that the war was the worst man-made disaster ever. But that alone does not account for the hold it has on human memory. The key to the hold lies in the war's impact on all areas of human experience. For many societies, the advanced industrialized as well as the less-developed ones, and for individuals, the war marked a watershed. Whether for citizens at the front or at the factory and farm, whether in the ways governments related to their civilian populations, or

---

*Cited in Milton C. Nahm, ed., *Selections from Early Greek Philosophy* (New York, 1947), p. 91.

how people responded to their environment, the war shaped the meaning of life for such large segments of the world that the war years became a benchmark against which events before and after are measured.

The many ways the Second World War changed our contemporary world becomes ever more apparent in the daily swelling torrent of books, articles, films, expositions, and displays based on those years. Some of this is only the most visible part of a psychic and social iceberg, the bulk of which is not widely known. Historians, when writing about the past, may sometimes pursue obscure byways. On the other hand, they reflect a vast common interest in the war in all its aspects. Laymen, war buffs, and experts agree on the momentousness of the war years. Can we agree on their singular centrality for understanding the world of the 1990s? An underlying assumption of this collection of essays is that we can.

Thinking about the past is more complicated than it appears at first. We know how events turned out: the allies won the war; the Red Army occupied Eastern Europe, and so forth. Such knowledge inevitably shapes our outlook. No literary skill in creating suspense in order to tell a good story and no artistry in describing crucial turning points can obscure that fact. At the same time, the men and women whose lives we are trying to understand did not have that knowledge. To become aware of them as real people making real decisions at a specific place and time, we must attempt to suspend our present perspectives. Then we can gain insight into the origins of the present.

On the other hand, do we really know how the war turned out? And what its meaning is? Is such knowledge permanent? It is sometimes jokingly said that Germany and Japan won the war. What is meant, presumably, is that the years of occupation brought on a social renewal, economic reinvigoration, and demilitarization within the framework of a growing world market. The defeated Axis partners could devote themselves to trade and commerce and save the costs of burdensome military establishments. Though they lost the war in 1945, they surged ahead. In 1945, however, nothing seemed more unlikely.

This simplistic example contains an important truth. After nearly half a century, we are still discovering the meaning of World War II. Participants in the war, now a rapidly shrinking minority worldwide, only experienced some aspects of it. The events they shared were their war. Like the fabled blind men each examining his part of an elephant, other individuals and other nations lived different wars. National and global sharing of those experiences take time to mediate. The historical processes by which we enlarge and alter our vision of the war depend on many things. Political decisions play their part. Not too long ago, official Soviet histories ignored the role of the Normandy invasion in the liberation of Western Europe in 1944–45. Americans often viewed the same campaign as the key to Nazi defeat. German veterans have long shared reunions with their former enemies as they commemorate a common struggle in battle. Civilians and political leaders have yet to incorporate the Axis countries into their common memories.

Delayed consequences of war also change perspectives. The Second World War is widely credited with loosening the bonds of colonialism. Great Britain granted India its freedom in 1947, and African nationalist independence movements began to sweep the continent during the next decade. In the United States the civil rights movement of the 1950s and 1960s and the growing pressure for gender equality in recent years have both been traced, in part, to pressures and opportunities opened up by the war. Though science and technology are often thought to have an internal dynamic development of their own, developments such as radar, jet planes, computers, atomic weapons, and other post-war marvels were either the consequence of war or were rapidly propelled into existence in response to its demands.

The Second World War might be more appropriately called the Second Era of World War. Between 1939 and 1945, to choose the narrowest definition of the war years, several conflicts, each with separate origins, engulfed different regions of the globe. Depending on one's views of the origins and meaning of the conflicts, the first date can be pushed back to 1937, the beginning of the "China Incident," or to 1931, when Japan attacked Manchuria. Or perhaps the war was simply a twenty-years armistice beginning in 1919, and thus a continuation of the 1914 war. And when did it end? With the conclusion of the Chinese civil war in 1949, or with the creation of NATO and two separate German states the same year? Or did it finally end in 1990 with the reunification of Germany, the dispatch of German troops abroad for the first time in more than four decades, and the support by former Axis countries of the UN-Iraqi war?

The term "Second World War" began its own history in the 1920s,[1] but became current, especially among Americans, in the early 1940s.

---

[1]Visions of future wars have a long history in Europe. See I.F. Clarke, *Voices Prophesying War 1763–1984* (London, 1966).

For Britain and France the conflict was initially the War of 1939. For citizens of the Soviet Union, it is still the Great Patriotic War. The Japanese often refer to it as the Pacific War or as the Fifteen Year War (for those who include China), while the Chinese see it as the Anti-Japan War. Among Solomon Islanders it is known, appropriately enough, as the Big Death. Again, definitions and the words themselves reflect a people's perspective, an interpretation of the meaning of those years.

Should we then see the Second World War as a series of wars and not one war? There is certainly some justification for that. In late 1940 and early 1941, during the early stages of the European war, the Japanese-Chinese conflict involved no power outside of Asia until Japan attempted to resolve it by extending its empire into Southeast Asia. With motives different from the Japanese and however reluctantly, Great Britain and France declared war on Germany in September 1939, to thwart German expansion. The Soviet Union, having no mutual defense treaty with any power, entered the war only when attacked by Germany in 1941. The United States found itself at war on a Sunday in December 1941 with unclear goals. But it had no intention of saving the British Empire, nor of rescuing communist Russia, nor of realizing the aims of any power other than itself. Swirling around these major wars were those of lesser powers. Italy declared war on France and Britain in June, 1940 in order to have a seat at the peace table. The Soviet Union and Finland fought no fewer than three wars, each related to the larger conflict, but each about regional issues. Bulgaria declared war on the United States and Britain, which had no prospects of invading that country, but not the Soviet Union, which did invade in 1944. And so on.

Though interesting and instructive, to see the war as only myriad simultaneous conflicts misses the basic fact that the focal point, the fulcrum of the war lay in Europe because it was still the center of world affairs. This is not a Eurocentric judgment, but recognition that the main keys of world finance, global communications, and military influence resided in London and Paris. World War I had weakened the French and British grip, but American isolationism and Russian retreat in pursuit of a separate path to industrialization and modernity removed these two nations from the center of world affairs. Aside from the United States, Russia, and the Axis powers, the rest of the world, including Latin America, was still in thrall to Europe.

In the following essays the reader will find examples of the complexities surrounding the war. The course of military events will not be ignored, but since they are better known than other developments and are, in general, less subject to continued controversy, they will yield first place to other aspects associated with the war.

The Second World War ended in the defeat of an aggressive, brutal, racist empire in Europe. On that, all minds agree. Japanese imperialism, however understandable in comparison with its European predecessors, also arouses little sympathy. Need we say more of Mussolini's dream of restoring the Roman Empire? Though aggression and tyranny are not a thing of the past, in themselves they are not traceable to the war. Other hallmarks of our age are.

The Second World War produced tectonic changes in global relations. The United States moved into center stage as the world's major capitalist and military power. The Soviet Union extended communism into a weakened Eastern Europe and for half a century waged a proxy campaign against the industrialized capitalist countries for the hearts and minds of what, in the 1950s, came to be called the Third World. European imperialism began to expire, first for Britain and the Netherlands, but soon for Belgium, France and Portugal. All that remains is to sweep up the remnants such as Hong Kong and Macao, which will come in 1997, though many small island territories will probably continue to remain under European sovereignty.

The Second World War ushered in the nuclear age, along with rockets, jet travel, computers, and military-industrial complexes. While market economies survived and in some ways were strengthened, no country after 1945 returned to the *laissez-faire* systems of an earlier time. The age of big government arrived worldwide during the Second World War. That was one reason the prospects of world war struck fear into conservatives throughout the western world in the 1930s. Total war had taught them that the costs could not be measured only in men killed and resources wasted. It also required concessions to labor unions and a fairer or at least a more equal distribution of the gross national product. Women might respond to the call to help out—they might even, as it turned out, demand the right—but that had its social costs to patriarchy as well.

War meant revolution not only in the industrialized nations but also in their colonies. In India, for example, Gandhi and the Congress Party had long demanded independence. They launched their greatest civil disobedience campaign in 1942, and Britain promised self-determination, but only after the war was over. Meanwhile, British purchases of raw materials and manufactured goods spurred growth in the Indian economy. London's cash shortage led to the sale of British investments to Indian capitalists. The Japanese attracted many Indian nationalists to their side, including some 40,000 to Subhas Chandras Bose's Indian National Army. And the Americans, whose voices could not be ignored, supported decolonization. This is an exceptional case, but the Second World War did encourage anticolonial nationalists throughout Africa, the Arab world, and Asia.

From the enormous literature on the Second World War, one anthology can bring together only a representative sampling. In this instance, the criteria for selection has been to choose significant issues while also illustrating the variety of topics relating to the war. The readings deal with subjects important to contemporaries and to the present generation. The best English-language scholarship to date is presented. Though each part of the anthology contains a select bibliography, consideration has been given to choices that will make the issues discussed accessible to the undergraduate who may be beginning his or her study of the war. For this reason scholarly review articles have not been included. Controversy for its own sake is shunned, while readings that stimulate discussion and challenge received ideas have priority.

In all cases, complete essays or chapters have been reprinted so the reader can examine the author's ideas directly, without relying on the editor's opinion as to what is and what is not important. (The original footnotes have, however, been omitted.) From this introductory exposure to a topic, readers can go on to study the issues more fully.

General Bibliography

A brief list of general one- or two-volume histories of the Second World War:

Calvocoressi, Peter, Guy Wint, and J. Pritchard. *Total War: Causes and Courses of the Second World War*. London, 1972, rev. ed., 1989.
Keegan, John. *The Second World War*. New York, 1989.
Kitchen, Martin. *A World in Flames. A Short History of the Second World War in Europe and Asia, 1939–1945*. London and New York, 1990.
Lee, Loyd E., *The War Years: A Global History of the Second World War*. London and Boston, 1989.

Liddell Hart, Basil H. *History of the Second World War*. New York, 1971.
Lyons, Michael J. *World War II: A Short History*. Englewood Cliffs, NJ, 1989.
Michel, Henri. *The Second World War*. New York, 1975.
Stokesbury, James L. *A Short History of World War II*. New York, 1980.
Wright, Gordon. *The Ordeal of Total War*. New York, 1968.

Part I

The Road to the Last European War and the Advent of World War

Except for the history of strategy, campaigns, operations, and combat, no aspect of the Second World War has received more attention than its origins. In many textbooks the background and causes of the war often even eclipse consideration of the military course of the struggle. This is to be expected. Most people hate war; there is a sense that wars should, one way or another, be avoided. The catastrophic death, suffering, and destruction requires at least an explanation as to what went wrong. Perhaps some lesson for the present can be learned.

There are many approaches that can be pursued. Is the fault in the structure of international relations that transcends the actions of individuals? Perhaps the mere existence of independent, sovereign nation states, each attempting to maximize its own self-interests, makes war likely, if not inevitable. Is it in the nature of political ideologies and economic systems, so that monopoly capitalism, or imperialism, or fascism are the causes? If so, removing these from the historic stage would remove the cause of war. Perhaps the tragedy originates in the national character of a nation. Are the Germans innately belligerent, rabidly nationalist, and cravenly obedient? Is it a Japanese trait to be duplicitous and blood-thirsty, willing to subordinate all for the collective good as the government defines it?

Some wish to locate the responsibility for war in the primary decision makers. After all, in the final moments, countries go to war because orders are given, generals obey, armies march, ships sail, and planes take off to find their targets. Determining individual responsibility may show some to have been cowards, others to have been unimaginative or ignorant, and still others to have been guilty of conspiring and planning wars of aggression.

The difficulties in determining answers to questions regarding the origins of any war are complicated by the entrance of propagandists who, as soon as war breaks out, do their part in winning the psychological war: confirming their citizens in the rightness of their cause, wooing the uncommitted to their side, and undermining the determination of their opponents. They conjure up towering forces for good, however defined, which valiantly oppose equally powerful energies for evil. At every level, war is a terrible simplifier. There is no place for complexity and ambiguity. Caricature replaces subtle analysis, leaving a legacy in every society's consciousness that takes generations to defuse.

After hostilities cease, detached inquiry faces additional difficulties, even as the immediate passions of war abate. Objective history requires documented sources and careful, reasoned investigation to legitimate the historian's account and persuade the reader. For any of the approaches to understanding the origins of war noted above, that is difficult. Relevant documentary sources are not always easily accessible. To show that monopoly capitalism was the culprit would require massive documentation if it is to disprove the counter-documentation of the idea's critics. This is not to claim that capitalism, however defined, played no role. It is only to suggest that proof is not documented in such a way as to be persuasive among those who do not already believe.

Similar comments could be made about the other interpretations. This leads some to despair of knowing any truth about the origins of the war or about any historical event. Henry Ford said "History is bunk. . . . It is one damned thing after another." Such agnosticism, however, is unwarranted. It denies the human desire to understand and know, however imperfectly. One approach has had more success: that of examining the attitudes, decisions, and actions of the men (and they were all men) at the top, their subordinates, and their advisers. Documentation comes from diplomatic archives. Those of the Germans were captured at the end of the war; elsewhere they have been or are becoming available—even, as a consequence of glasnost, in the Soviet Union. In this approach, the sheer mass of material to be combed through and the formidable linguistic requirements made on the researcher create problems, but they are easier to manage than those with broader, less specific questions to ask. In addition, they make for dramatic narrative stories of real people, interacting in real situations with real, though calamitous results. That the end of the story is known in advance only heightens the interest in its telling.

On the question of who was most responsible for the origins of the European war, Allied wartime opinion remains confirmed. Adolf Hitler, alone among the world's heads of government, wanted, indeed insisted upon, war; undoubtedly, not the war he actually got and not in accord with any carefully laid down schedule of successive acts of aggression (as Allied propaganda portrayed it), but war. When the distinguished British diplomatic historian A.J.P. Taylor noted in 1962 that the historiography of the origins of the Second World War, unlike that of other wars, had not yet gone through a revisionist phase, he questioned not only the received wisdom about the path to war in Europe, but also the idea that Hitler shared direct personal responsibility for its outbreak. With impeccable professional qualifications and a well-known aversion to the course German history had taken in the previous centuries, Taylor was listened to. His conclusions were soundly questioned, though the effect was to open an international debate on the genesis of the war. The results have upturned many earlier judgments, but after twenty-eight years, there is still overwhelmingly unanimous opinion that Hitler was determined on war.

Though in his early years he did not foresee such a conflict during his lifetime, Hitler probably anticipated a future global war beyond the one unleashed in Europe in 1939. Whatever hesitancy he had about turning the European conflict into a global one, he did not draw back in December 1941. With remarkable alacrity he welcomed a worldwide struggle by declaring war on the United States after Japan attacked European and American bases in the Pacific. The decisions which made the European maelstrom into a global one, however, were taken in Tokyo and Washington, rather than in Berlin and elsewhere.

Revisionist historiography of the origins of the Pacific war has gone beyond that of the origins of the European war. As wartime propaganda yielded to a search for evidence and reasoned debates replaced self-serving, defensive justification, more diverse interpretations emerged. The histories of Japan, China, and the nations of East Asia could not be easily integrated into diplomatic accounts written wholly from a western point of view. The perception of the Japanese invasion of Manchuria in 1931 as the opening salvo of an Axis offensive against western democracies became ludicrous, not only because it ignored specific Sino–Japanese factors, but also because it flew in the face of evidence that the Japanese and Germans did not coordinate their policies and strategies. To be sure, along with Italy, Hungary, and other nations, Germany and Japan were unhappy with the structure of post-World War I relations. Both countries opposed communism and shared hostility to the Soviet Union, but Japan made no specific military agreements with Germany. Even the Tripartite Pact of September 27, 1940 came after German victories in Europe, when many thought Germany might win the Battle of Britain. Germany, for example, did not withdraw its military advisers and aid to the Chinese Nationalist government under Jiang Jieshi (Chiang Kai-shek) until May 1938. Italian–German relations were constantly strained by conflicting motives and interests. The Axis was an alliance without much substance.

If Japan, Italy, and Germany were not co-conspirators against Great Britain, the United States, the Soviet Union, and other Allies, then what was the origin of Japan's war? The Sino–Japanese War, the "China Incident," the Anti-Japan War, whatever its name, was a continuation of earlier conflicts between the two countries over Korea and Manchuria going back into the 1890s. It erupted in 1937 with an armed confrontation at the Marco Polo bridge in Beijing (Peking). Japan's aggressive stance in East Asia had its impact, especially in breaking up a long period of Anglo–Japanese cooperation and in stretching British naval power. The same is true of Japanese relations with the Soviet Union, which resembled those with China. The skirmishes and battles between the Red Army and Japan's Kwantung Army along the Manchuria–Outer Mongolian border are little known and are too often subsumed into the Axis offensives in Europe. The Japanese war in East Asia and the Pacific had specific Asian and American origins. It influenced the European conflict, but was neither an extension of that war nor a direct consequence of it. In the case of the European war, it is doubtful, given Hitler's determination to have war, that it could have been avoided. In the Pacific, that is not so clearly the case. For this reason, the origin of the Pacific war raises questions about American and Japanese perceptions of one another, of their interests, of their national goals, and their mutual relations that transcend a judgment of responsibility for the events leading up to December 7, 1941.

1

Gerhard L. Weinberg

Munich after 50 Years

A half century after the event, the Munich conference remains for many in the West an unparalleled example of unnecessary, cowardly appeasement of an openly aggressive dictator, that not only made general war more likely, but also made that war more diffi-

Reprinted by permission of *Foreign Affairs* (Fall, 1988). Copyright 1988 by the Council on Foreign Relations, Inc.

cult to win. The opening of archives, especially those of the British and French, and the renewed debate after Taylor's challenge to our understanding of the events of the summer of 1938, have raised new questions and have led to new interpretations of appeasement. Revisionists have modified the postwar stereotypes of Chamberlain. But many other aspects of British affairs have also been subjected to scrutiny: the state of British public opinion, military planning for war, and London's relations with the Commonwealth nations, the colonies, and other nations. More informed studies on the role of the secret services and intelligence as well as secondary figures in the diplomatic service have also contributed to our understanding. American and French policies have also been scrutinized again.

The result has not been agreement among historians. Professor Weinberg, author of a two-volume study of Hitler's foreign policy, authoritatively puts this recent research in a wide ranging perspective. Not everyone may agree with his analysis and the conclusions he draws, but no one who is interested in the topic, and in periodic comparisons of the Munich agreement with contemporary foreign policy problems, will fail to be challenged.

Half a century after the Munich conference, that event lives in the public memory as a series of interrelated myths. For most people, Munich represents the abandonment of a small country, Czechoslovakia, to the unjust demands of a bullying and powerful neighbor by those who would have done better to defend it. It is believed that the Allies, by the sacrifice of one country, only whetted the appetite of the bully whom they had to fight anyway, later and under more difficult circumstances. The "lesson" derived from this widely held view is that it makes far more sense to take action to stop aggression at the first opportunity.

This view, not surprisingly, is especially influential with those who personally experienced the events of the late 1930s and who thereafter found themselves and their countries involved in the costliest war in history. Many came to hold a view of the proper conduct of U.S. foreign policy, the so-called domino theory, which asserted that if drastic action were not taken to halt aggression at its earliest occurrence, the countries in the path of an encroaching power would fall like dominoes, with the fall of each only hastening that of the next. Once prominently put forward as a justification for American intervention in Vietnam, this thesis was temporarily discredited by second thoughts about U.S. policy there. More recently, however, it has been revived in connection with Nicaragua. Some believe that a Sandinista regime, once fully consolidated, will surely topple the adjacent "dominoes," this time in Central America.

Neither scholarship nor time is likely to shake the firm hold that the symbols of Munich maintain on those who remember a time when the city's name connoted more than good beer or bloody Olympic games. The umbrella that British Prime Minister Neville Chamberlain carried with him to Munich in the fall of 1938 came to represent not common sense in the European autumn but cowardice in the face of danger. The exclusion from the conference of Czechoslovakia, the country whose boundaries and fate were at stake, is considered by those even vaguely familiar with the history as a particularly revolting aspect of the affair. On his return to London, Chamberlain held in his hand an agreement stating that all questions concerning Anglo-German relations would be solved by consultation between the two countries, so they would never again go to war with each other. His famous comment that he, like Prime Minister Benjamin Disraeli sixty years earlier, had brought back from Germany peace with honor and "peace in our time," has provided superb copy for every parody of British policy in the 1930s.

II

Three aspects of the Munich conference that developed more fully afterward, or on which we are now better informed, suggest that this traditional interpretation warrants a closer look.

In the first place, it was after all the same two Allied leaders who went to Munich, Chamberlain of Great Britain and Edouard Daladier of France, who one year later led their countries into war against Adolf Hitler's Germany, something no other leader of a major power did before his own country was attacked. The Italians, who under Benito Mussolini thought of themselves as a great power, joined with Hitler in June 1940 in what Mussolini saw as an opportunity to share the spoils of victory. Joseph Stalin was sending the Nazis essential war supplies until a few hours before the German invasion of June 1941 awoke the Kremlin from its confidence in an alignment with Hitler. Franklin D. Roosevelt, who had repeatedly but vainly warned the Soviet leader of the German threat, had worked hard to rouse the American people to the dangers facing them; but until confronted by a Japanese surprise attack and by German and Italian declarations of war, he had hoped that Americans might be spared the ordeal of war.

Only Britain and France went to war with Germany out of calculations of broader national interest instead of waiting to be attacked; and it is perhaps safe to argue that without the lead from London, the French government would have backed off in 1939 and awaited a German invasion of its own territory. It is rather ungracious, especially for Americans whose country would not take action to defend either Czechoslovakia or Poland, and which had provided by law that it would not help anyone who did, to condemn as weaklings the only leaders of major powers who mustered up the courage to confront Hitler on behalf of another country.

A second factor that prompts us to take a new look at the 1938 crisis is the view that Hitler, the man usually thought to have triumphed at Munich, is now known to have held of it. The opening of German archives and the new availability of important private papers provide a picture rather different from the one commonly held.

We now know that Hitler had never been particularly interested in helping the over three million people of German descent living inside Czechoslovakia, but only in the ways they might help him in his project to isolate Czechoslovakia from outside support, create incidents that would provide a pretext for the invasion and destruction of that country, and thereafter provide manpower for additional army divisions. The new divisions, in turn, he considered useful for the great war he planned to wage against the powers of Western Europe as the prerequisite for the quick and far easier seizure of enormous territories in Eastern Europe.

Hitler believed that German rearmament was far enough advanced by late 1937 and early 1938 to make this first little war against Czechoslovakia possible. While spreading propaganda on behalf of the ethnic Germans of Czechoslovakia, Hitler was counting on the threat of Japan's advance in East Asia and Italy's support in Europe, and the reluctance of France and England to fight another great war, to isolate Czechoslovakia from outside support. It is understandable in this context that the successful and peaceful annexation of Austria in March 1938 (which left Czechoslovakia even more vulnerable than before), followed by a dramatic reaffirmation of Germany's alignment with Italy during Hitler's visit to Rome, produced Hitler's decision in the second week of May 1938 to go to war that year. We are not ever likely to know whether his belief that he was suffering from throat cancer contributed to his haste; he was certainly a man with a mission in a hurry who would explain later in 1938 that he preferred to go to war at the age of 49 so that he could see the whole issue through to resolution!

But there proved to be inner flaws in his strategy. The prospective allies he had selected turned out to be reluctant. The Japanese at that time wanted an alliance against the Soviet Union, not against the Western powers. Poland and Hungary both hoped to obtain pieces of Czechoslovakia but wanted them without a general European war. The Italians, furthermore, were not as enthusiastic as Hitler thought. Mussolini had given a hostage to fortune by committing large forces to the support of Francisco Franco in the Spanish Civil War, forces certain to be lost in a general war in which they would be cut off from their homeland.

III

The basic miscalculation of the German government was, however, of a different type: it was integrally related to the issue that Hitler deliberately placed at the center of public attention, the Sudeten Germans living in Czechoslovakia. The purpose of this focus was obvious. The constant attention in both publicity and diplomacy to the allegedly mistreated millions of Germans living in Czechoslovakia was designed to make it politically difficult, if not impossible, for Britain and France to come to Czechoslovakia's assistance when it was eventually attacked. How could democracies contest the principle of self-determination that they had themselves proclaimed? Would they act to turn a small war into a huge one on the unproven assumption that a big war inevitably would come anyway?

But there were aspects of this program that might, from Hitler's perspective, cause problems. One was that the continued diplomatic focus on the Sudeten Germans, which was needed to assure the isolation of Czechoslovakia, might eventually make the transition from diplomacy to war more difficult. The other was that, despite the number and significance of the Germans inside the Czechoslovak state, there were obviously far more Czechs and Slovaks. If ever the real as opposed to the pretended aim of German policy became clear, the very same concept of self-determination that worked against support of Czechoslovakia as long as its German-inhabited rim was under discussion would shift in favor of Prague once the undoubtedly non-German core came into question. It was in this regard that the crisis of the end of September 1938 came to be so dramatic and its resolution, in Hitler's eyes, so faulty.

We now know that Hitler had originally planned to stage an incident inside Czechoslovakia to provide Germany with a pretext for invading that country with the objective of destroying it all rather than merely annexing the German-inhabited fringe. He was influenced by the experience of 1914, when Austria-Hungary had taken the assassination of the Archduke Francis Ferdinand as an excuse to attack Serbia.

In Hitler's opinion there had been two deficiencies in Austria-Hungary's behavior, and Germany would on this occasion remedy both. The first was the plainly accidental timing of the assassination. If one waited for others to act, the most appropriate moment might easily be missed: Hitler had long held that the Central Powers should have struck well before 1914. The obvious solution to the problem of timing was to arrange for the incident oneself, and at the optimal moment. Hitler originally thought of staging the assassination of the German minister to Czechoslovakia, Ernst Eisenlohr; then he shifted to the idea of having incidents staged by the German military inside Czechoslovakia. Finally he resorted to the creation of special squads of Sudeten German thugs who—since it was not thought safe to entrust them with the secret date for the scheduled invasion—were simply assigned quotas of incidents to stage each week in each sector of the borderlands. This process would continue until the time had come for Berlin to announce that the most recent example of Czechoslovak wickedness (in responding to the latest provocation) obviously merited Germany's taking the drastic action of invading the country.

The second defect of Austria's action in 1914, in Hitler's view, was that Vienna had dithered for weeks during that summer while the shock effect of the original incident wore off. This time, Hitler reasoned, it would be very different indeed.

Since the decision to invade would precede rather than follow the incident selected as a pretext, the German military would move swiftly and in accordance with carefully prepared plans. The German dictator was confident that his army would obey the order to attack, in spite of warnings of dissent from some in the military hierarchy. Early in February 1938 he had replaced the commander in chief of the army, Werner von Fritsch, a great admirer of the National Socialist state but an independent thinker, with Walther von Brauchitsch, a man without backbone or scruples who was also the recipient of special secret payments from Hitler (apparently the beginning of a huge and never fully explored program of bribing most of the highest-ranking German generals and admirals).

Hitler had also, at the same time, assumed the responsibilities formerly assigned to Minister of War Werner von Blomberg. Furthermore, he had recently replaced the chief of the general staff of the army, Ludwig Beck, a vehement critic of the war plan, with the more complaisant Franz Halder. Although there were skeptics among the military—and there are some analysts of the 1938 crisis who believe that an order to attack would have touched off an attempted coup from within the army—it seems to me that Hitler's confidence in the response of the military to his orders and those of its new commander in chief, von Brauchitsch, was fully warranted.

What, then, went wrong? Why was there no transition from propaganda and diplomacy to war?

The constant emphasis on the Sudeten Germans in Nazi propaganda brought too late a response from the government in Prague, which until August left the initiative to Berlin. And this in spite of a formal and explicit, but confidential, warning to Prague from the French government in July that under practically no circumstances would it come to the defense of its Czechoslovak ally. Keeping this message undisclosed—and it was one of the few secrets that did not leak out in the Paris of the 1930s—was of course essential to the official French pretense that it was the British who were holding them back from full support of Prague, a pretense that turned to panic when the British position hardened and could no longer provide a fig leaf for French unwillingness to act.

The centrality of the nationality issue also created a terrible dilemma for London. Canada, Australia and the Union of South Africa (as it was then known) all made it absolutely clear to the British government that they would not go to war alongside Britain over the Sudeten German question. The British chiefs of staff strongly argued against the risk of military action. If war were to come, it would have to come under circumstances that made the issues clear to the public in Britain and the dominions, and, as the British learned in September 1938, to the French.

It was under these circumstances that on September 13 Neville Chamberlain decided to fly to Germany, originally planning not even to tell Berlin that he was coming until after his plane had taken off. The Germans were startled enough even when notified in advance, and they were trapped by their own propaganda that there were nationality issues to discuss. Moreover, those who genuinely believed in the fairy tale of the "stab in the back"—that Germany had not been beaten at the front in World War I, but had instead lost the war because of the collapse of the German home front—could not risk starting a second war unless German public opinion could be convinced that such a war, with all its costs in lives and treasure, was everybody else's fault.

So the British prime minister had to be received at Berchtesgaden. All he could be told, of course, was the official public line that something had to be done for the poor Sudeten Germans. While Chamberlain set about getting the agreement of France and Czechoslovakia to having the German-inhabited portions of Czechoslovakia ceded to Germany, Hitler began plotting other ways to arrange for war in spite of the meddlesome Englishman. When at their second meeting, on September 22 at Bad Godesberg, Chamberlain offered Hitler an Allied capitulation to his ostensible demands—the French, Czechoslovak and British governments had all agreed to the transfer of the Sudeten territory—the German dictator was dumbfounded and raised new and obviously preposterous conditions for a peaceful settlement.

IV

It was at this point that the issue shifted conspicuously from the fate of the Sudeten Germans to that of the Czechs and Slovaks. Here Hitler was indeed trapped by his own strategy. He now had either to risk a war with Britain and France as well as Czechoslovakia or pull back, call off the planned invasion, and settle for what Prague, London and Paris had already agreed to.

It was not only Germany's military and diplomatic leaders who urged caution on the Nazi dictator. Troubled by the prospect of a general war when the German people gave every sign of being unenthusiastic about it, Hitler's closest political associates, Hermann Göring and Joseph Goebbels, argued for a peaceful settlement. The prospective allies of Germany in this crisis were hesitant, now that war was a real and not merely a theoretical possibility. The Poles certainly wanted a piece of Czechoslovakia, but not at the risk of breaking completely with their French ally and Great Britain. The Hungarians were watering at the mouth over the possibility of realizing their extensive territorial demands: all of the Slovak and Carpatho-Ukrainian portions of the Czechoslovak state and a few additional pieces if they could get them. The authorities in Budapest, however, were very conscious of having only recently begun their own rearmament; they were also fairly certain that Britain and France would go to war over a

German invasion of Czechoslovakia and that such a general war would end in a German defeat.

Hitler never forgave the Hungarians, whose resolution, in his eyes, was not commensurate with their appetite, but he was even more astonished by the defection of his most important ally, Italy. Mussolini's urging him to settle for the German-inhabited fringe of Czechoslovakia instead of attacking that country as a whole—when Hitler had expected encouragement to go forward, along with a full promise of support—appears to have played a major part in his decision to recall the orders for war, already issued, and instead agree to a settlement by conference at Munich.

Precisely because he had not tested the predictions of those who had warned against an attack on Czechoslovakia, Hitler was then and ever after angry over having pulled back. He projected his own reticence onto others, denouncing as cowards those whose advice he had followed instead of testing his own concept in action, and despising the British and French leaders before whose last-minute firmness he had himself backed down.

If the Munich agreement, which others then and since have regarded as a great triumph for Germany, appeared to Hitler then and in retrospect as the greatest setback of his career, it was because he had been unwilling or unable, or both, to make the shift from propaganda and diplomacy to war as he had always intended. He had been trapped in a diplomatic maze of his own construction and could not find the exit to the war that he sought. In the last months of his life, in 1945, as he reviewed what had gone wrong and caused the dramatic descent from Germany's earlier heights of victory, he appears to have asserted that his failure to begin the war in 1938 was his greatest error, contributing to the eventual collapse of all his hopes and prospects.

In the intervening years he was most careful not to repeat what he considered were the great errors of 1938. A massive campaign was begun to rally the German people for war. As Hitler put it on November 10, 1938, meeting with the German press, the peace propaganda designed to fool others had carried in it the risk of misleading his own people into thinking that peace, not war, was intended. Thereafter, Hitler would sometimes postpone but would never again call off an attack on another country once ordered, and he would never again allow himself to be trapped in diplomatic negotiations.

In 1939 German ambassadors were kept away from London and Warsaw; they were in fact forbidden to return to their posts. The incident the Nazis had planned as the pretext for war against Poland—an assault on a radio station inside Germany—would be organized and managed directly from Berlin. Furthermore, as Hitler explained to his military leaders on August 22, 1939, he had things organized so well that his only worry was that at the last minute some *Schweinehund* would come along with a compromise and again cheat him of war. The allusion to Chamberlain and Munich was unmistakable. And it ought to be noted that his "lesson" of Munich remained with him. When the Soviet Union made desperate efforts in 1941 to avert war with Germany, by volunteering the most extensive concessions, by offering to join the Tripartite Pact and by soliciting diplomatic approaches from Berlin, Hitler once again claimed to be worried about only one thing: a last-minute compromise offer that would make it difficult for him to continue on the road to yet another extension of the war.

As for the remainder of Czechoslovakia, he was even more determined that it be destroyed. The German government devoted itself in the months after Munich to accomplishing that objective, never realizing that, in the face of universal relief over the avoidance of war, the violation of the agreement just signed would make any further step by Germany the occasion for war. In 1939 no one listened to Nazi tales of persecuted Germans in Poland; the Germans themselves had demonstrated to everyone that such propaganda was merely a pretext for actions with entirely different objectives. And when soundings were taken in London before the invasion of Poland, the answer was that Czechoslovakia must have its independence back first before any negotiations; similar soundings after the German conquest of Poland were answered with the demand that both Czechoslovakia and Poland be restored to independence. Since Hitler and his associates had not been interested in the fate of those who had been used as propaganda instruments, they never could understand that others had taken the issue seriously—but only once.

V

A third facet of the Munich agreement as we look back on it from the perspective of fifty years is the light shed on events by the opening of wartime archives and the progress of research. The account of German policy presented here is in large part based on materials that became available after World War II. The British archives have also been opened and show a government hoping against hope for a peaceful settlement, but prepared to go to war if there were an invasion of Czechoslovakia in spite of all efforts at accommodating what were perceived as extreme but not entirely unreasonable demands. We now know that Chamberlain was correctly reported as willing to contemplate the territorial cession of the German-inhabited portions of Czechoslovakia in early May 1938, and that the British knew that there was no serious French military plan to assist Czechoslovakia—the only offensive operation planned by the French if war broke out was into Libya from Tunisia. It is now also known that in June 1938 Winston Churchill explained to a Czechoslovak official that it was essential for Czechoslovakia to work out an agreement with Konrad Henlein, the leader of the Sudeten Germans, and that although he, Churchill, was criticizing Chamberlain, he might well have followed the same policy if he had held the responsibilities of power.

It is also clear that there were serious doubts within the British government—which may or may have not been justified—about the ability of Britain and France to defeat Germany, and a determination that if war came and victory were attained, the German-inhabited portions of Czechoslovakia would *not* be returned to Prague's control.

The question of whether or not Britain and France would have been militarily better off had they gone to war in 1938 will remain a subject for debate for historians. Most would agree that the defenses of Czechoslovakia would have proved more formidable in 1938 than those of Poland in 1939, but then the question remains whether, since there was to be no attack by the French in the west in 1938, a somewhat longer Czechoslovak resistance would have made any significant difference. It can be argued that the Germans used the last year of peace more effectively than the British and the French, but it must also be recalled that new British fighter planes and radar defenses would not in any case have been available to meet a German onslaught in 1939 as they were for the Battle of Britain in 1940. And the excellent Czechoslovak tanks Germany acquired must be weighed against Poland's essential 1939 contribution to breaking the German Enigma-machine code.

There are other factors to be considered, including several most difficult to assess. What, for example, would have been the evolution of U.S. attitudes toward a European war in which Canada remained neutral, as it might have done had war broken out in 1938? Certainly there was in 1938 great doubt about the economic and fiscal ability of Britain to sustain a second great war within a generation, at a time when financial support from the United States was prohibited by Congress. In an age of determined American isolation, no one anticipated the lend-lease program on which Britain would later prove so dependent.

The other side of this coin is the clarity of British policy, whether one agrees with it or not, in the year after Munich. If this Munich pact were broken, it was agreed, then the next German aggression that was resisted by the victim would bring on war. It is from this perspective that the pairing in internal British government discussions of Holland and Belgium with Romania and Poland must be understood: the key issue was *any* further step, not its specific direction or victim. With this determination came a resigned recognition of the likely, perhaps unavoidable, cost of a new war for a weakened empire. In August 1939 Foreign Office official Gladwyn Jebb, years later the British representative at the United Nations, was told by an official of the German embassy in London that in a general war in which, as the Englishman predicted, all in the end fought against Germany and eventually smashed it, there would be only two victors, the Soviet Union and America. The German then asked Jebb, "How would England like to be an American dominion?" Jebb replied that "she would infinitely prefer to be an American dominion than a German *Gau*."

The opening of French archives has suggested to some a rather more charitable view of France's policy. Efforts to rehabilitate the French leadership of the 1930s have focused on the deficiencies of British policy, the terrible weakening of France as a result of World War I and the social and political cleavages of the postwar years. Certainly the view of most scholars on French policy in the immediate post–World War I years has changed substantially: France is now viewed as weakened and frightened rather than combative and assertive, while the peace treaty of 1919 is increasingly seen as far more favorable to Germany than either German propaganda or subsequent popular views in the United States and Great Britain have pictured it.

Nevertheless, the archives demonstrate even more hesitation in French policy than was previously believed. In the terrible civil war in Spain (still raging at the time of the crisis over Czechoslovakia) it now is clear that the initiative for the policy of nonintervention came from Paris, not from London as was long believed. More immediately relevant is the revelation, previously cited, that in July 1938 the French government secretly warned Prague that French military assistance could not be expected. The publicly advanced argument that France could not commit itself in the absence of a British promise to help was a sham; but in response to a plea from the Czechoslovak government, this deception was kept secret. When the French government learned that the British were indeed serious about fighting if Germany invaded, the ensuing panic [French officials opposed fighting Germany, fearing they would lose] in Paris helped precipitate the decision of Chamberlain to fly to Berchtesgaden.

The new light shed on French policy in 1938 also clarifies the extraordinary evolution of French policy in World War II; first the insistence on trying to conduct the war in Scandinavia or the Caucasus, and, after the collapse of France in 1940, the Vichy French willingness to fight the English, other Frenchmen and the Americans, but under no circumstances the real enemies of France: Germany, Italy and Japan.

The archives of the Soviet Union remain closed to scholars, though lately there are signs that this might change. New light on Soviet policy has been shed, however, not only by Soviet documentary publications but also by material from the files of other powers. A new perspective on Soviet policy comes as a result of our knowledge that throughout the 1930s Stalin, who regarded Britain, not Germany, as the Soviet Union's main enemy, was trying to arrange an agreement with Hitler; the policy reversal that led to the Soviet-German Nonaggression Pact in 1939 was made by Berlin, not Moscow. Furthermore, Jiri Hochman has now demonstrated on the basis of material from the Romanian archives that Moscow deliberately rejected the option of sending land and air forces across Romania to assist Czechoslovakia in case of war in the 1938 crisis. These factors help explain why the Soviet Union was the only major power outside the Axis that recognized the legality of the disappearance of Czechoslovakia in 1939 and urged the Western powers to follow this example.

Americans have learned from the experience in Vietnam that a democracy should only enter a major war if its people see and feel the issues as so important to themselves as to warrant a sacrifice of blood and treasure. Few, if any, in this country urged the defense of Czechoslovakia against invasion in 1968 or action against its occupation since then. Perhaps someday this thought will make it easier for people to understand the reluctance of the dominions to rush to the defense of Czechoslovakia thirty years earlier, and why they implored the London government not to do so either. There are many objectionable acts committed in international affairs that are not necessarily perceived as so threatening to the national interest of third parties as to warrant calling on many to risk their lives to stop them. If a nation is to undertake the costs of war, what is needed is a popular recognition of its necessity, not the hurling of slogans.

What about the people most immediately affected? The Germans had entrusted their fate to a leader who had promised to establish a one-party state as had been instituted in the Soviet Union and Italy and to lead them "whither they must shed their blood." He certainly kept *these* promises, and by doing so led them to ruin.

For the people of Czechoslovakia, he brought other great disasters; first the end of their independence, and then their subservience to the Soviet Union. As for the Sudeten Germans, he brought a fate that included the return to Germany they had shouted for, but in a way they had not anticipated. Here is a lesson others might ponder. If you shout for something long and loud enough, you run the risk of getting it. Having tried to settle the problem by moving the boundary, the Allies decided, after Germany had broken that arrangement, to let Czechoslovakia move the people. The Sudeten Germans are no longer ruled from Prague, but that is because they were driven from their homes into post–World War II Germany. They have indeed come "Home into the Reich" as their slogan required. Those in other parts of the world who prefer not to live under a government they consider inappropriate for themselves might want to think about the risk of expulsion as a concomitant of the hope for new borders.

In the United States, the "lesson" of Munich may well remain that appeasing aggressors, by making concessions to them or merely verbally condemning their actions, only encourages them and makes them more willing to take greater risks. There is without doubt substance to this view, but only in a context in which the alternatives and prospects and costs are assessed soberly. As leaders contemplate the prospect of war, they would be well advised to make sure that their people, or at least a very large number of them, are prepared to make the relevant commitment and are ready to pay the price of sticking to it.

In 1938, in neither Britain nor France—to say nothing of the United States or the Soviet Union—were the masses clearly willing to run the risk of war unless Germany committed the most obvious and direct outrages. And the British dominions had made clear their determination to stay out. The following year Britain and France and the dominions acted in response to the German attack on Poland. On the first occasion in World War II in which a British army decisively defeated a German army—at El Alamein in 1942—the majority of the divisions in the British Eighth Army had come from the Commonwealth to fight alongside the soldiers of the United Kingdom. At a time when New Zealanders appear to some observers to be inclined to opt out of their alliances, their great share in that significant battle deserves to be recalled as a part of the lesson of Munich for societies in which, by whatever mechanism, the public's preferences control the policies of the state.

Those commitments, policies and alliances that can reasonably be expected to involve a country in a great war must be clearly articulated, understood at least in general by the public and perceived as truly essential to the nation's security. In an age of nuclear weapons that might be a useful "lesson" of the Munich conference.

2

AKIRA IRIYE

The End of Uncertainty

Revisionism has also affected the study of the origins of the Pacific war; in this case the issues are different. Though the League of Nations ineffectively dealt with the Japanese invasion of Manchuria in 1931, not to speak of the 1937 war between Japan and China, those events are no longer seen as part of a continuum of concerted Axis aggression and Allied appeasement. Instead, study has been focused on internal political struggles over Japan's long-term role in Asian and world affairs, and on what steps should be taken to achieve that country's rightful place. Concerning Japan's external affairs, scholars have closely investigated Japan's rela-

Reprinted by permission from *Power and Culture: The Japanese–American War, 1941–1945,* by Akira Iriye, Cambridge, Mass.: Harvard University Press, Copyright © 1981 by the President and Fellows of Harvard College.

tions with the United States and other powers in the context of
Nazi Germany's headlong plunge into war and its dramatic victories in 1940 and in the first half of 1941. The German threat
weakened European empires in Asia, and opened opportunities
for Asian nationalists as well as for Japan and the United States to
expand their spheres of influence.

Frustrated in its inability to resolve war favorably in China,
Japan had to pick its way through the shoals of a transformed and
uncertain international order, especially after Germany and Russia signed a Nonaggression Pact in August 1939, merely days
after Soviet troops had trounced a Japanese army at Nomonhan in
northeastern Outer Mongolia. The occupation of the Netherlands
and the fall of France severed the link between these countries
and their extensive colonies in Southeast Asia. The plight of the
British fighting alone against the Germans left Asia and the western Pacific a military vacuum. The main restraint on Japanese
aggression was American, but it was isolationist in mood and the
United States pledged to extend independence to its Philippine
colony by 1946. Its naval power was limited to the eastern Pacific and its leaders were preoccupied with the Anglo–German
war and the struggle for control over the Atlantic trade routes.

Out of this complicated welter of events, observers have
reached varied and contradictory opinions about the origins of the
Japanese–American war. By declaring war on the United States,
Hitler honored his commitment to Japan and the European and
Asian theaters were merged into a global struggle. In the following selection, Akira Iriye, a prominent American historian, examines the origins of the Pacific war without focusing primarily on
the issue of responsibility. An advocate of a new *international
history* that attempts to go beyond traditional diplomatic history
to look at relations among nations in broad cultural patterns, Professor Iriye holds all sides in view in his sweeping examination of
Japan's road to war. Not everyone will agree that his fair-handed
liberality adequately allows for the will to expansion on the part
of Japan's elite, but those who think of Japan as single-mindedly
conspiring to war will have to reconsider their judgments.

The eruption of war in the Pacific on December 7 (December 8 in
Asia), 1941, was preceded by several years of "cold war" between the
United States and Japan. As in the more famous Cold War after 1945,
the relationship between the two countries had frequently been expressed in terms of fundamental conflict, impending doom, and total

confrontation between opposite political and cultural systems. But much as the United States and the Soviet Union later avoided direct armed hostilities, Washington and Tokyo had managed to preserve a relationship that left room for negotiation. More important, despite mutual denunciations and war scares, the two peoples had not severed all ties; on the contrary, belligerent rhetoric concealed an undercurrent of shared interests and outlooks that both sides viewed as largely compatible. However, the very persistence of these outlooks created a sense of uncertainty, because they were at odds with the rapidly deteriorating governmental relations across the Pacific.

War came fundamentally because Japan's military leaders and their civilian supporters decided to close the gap and put an end to the "cold war." They wanted to bring unity to their national experience, so that war would define all political as well as cultural activities. In so doing, they were determined to part, once and for all, from an earlier definition of national life that had underlain Japan's external affairs since the Meiji Restoration. They had been characterized by an effort to integrate the country into the world economy and to achieve rapid industrial development, conditions considered essential for collective survival. In order to achieve these goals Japan had adopted a gold standard, regained tariff autonomy, pushed its export trade, encouraged emigration and colonization, and otherwise tried to act like a member of the community of advanced industrial nations. The task had not always been easy, and there had been occasional friction with other powers, but at least until the 1930s there had been a unified perception by the country's leaders; as a modern industrial state, Japan should cope with its external problems through the framework of multilateral agreements with the other advanced nations, according to the formula of "international cooperation."

In the 1920s the country avidly accepted the framework of international cooperation embodied in the League of Nations and the Washington Conference treaties and led by the United States and Great Britain. The Japanese eagerly turned to Anglo-American ways, adopting the tenets of Woodrow Wilson's "new diplomacy" as guides to their own international behavior. The Japanese economy was fully integrated into the world capitalist system, and the country enjoyed world-power status as the only non-Western member of the Council of the League of Nations. Japan's problems in Asia and elsewhere were legion; in China civil war endangered the safety and interests of foreigners, and in Asia anti-colonial movements were developing, in part inspired by the Bolshevik Revolution and supervised by Comintern operatives. Still, Japan coped with these problems as one of the advanced, colonial, and "treaty" powers through continuing consultation with the United States and Great Britain. Although neither Japan nor the Anglo-American powers were above negotiating separate advantageous deals, the framework of cooperation through economic interdependence with the other industrial nations provided the stable point of reference for Japanese diplomacy.

The world economic crisis that began in 1929 ushered in a period of confusion and uncertainty in international affairs, in long-range perceptions as much as in day-to-day relations among nations. Japan was one of the first countries to decide that the familiar economic order of unrestricted international trade and monetary transactions was being replaced by far more particularistic arrangements and by the division of the globe into autarkic units. In diplomacy as well, the Japanese saw a trend away from internationalism and toward regionalism, with a few nations establishing control over wider areas. There would still be "cooperation," but in the form of efforts to maintain equilibrium among these autarkic powers, as exemplified by the "cooperation" between Britain and Nazi Germany during the mid-thirties.

Compared with the situation before 1929, the new pattern was more conducive to uncertainty because there were fewer fixed points of reference; the League of Nations, the Washington Conference treaties, and most important, the world monetary order based on the gold standard and stable rates of exchange—all were losing their effectiveness as devices for defining international relations. The nations of the world were more determined than ever to effect economic growth, maintain domestic order, and promote national welfare, but they were more willing to use force and to act unilaterally to carry out these objectives without regard for international cooperation. Global interdependence, cooperation, and peace were no longer the prevailing rhetoric; more particularistic conceptions—new order, have-not nations, *Lebensraum*—emerged to provide ideological underpinnings for foreign policies. The assumption that domestic economic development required a peaceful external environment and vice versa, which had sustained the international system of the 1920s, gave way to uncertainty about the relationship between domestic and external affairs and that between power and nonmilitary aspects of foreign relations.

Japanese policy during the 1930s was intended to overcome this uncertainty, but the attempt was only partially successful. At one level there were programs for economic development and for population resettlement in Manchuria and north China under Japanese control. The plan was that "pioneers" from the Japanese mainland would settle in Manchuria and transform the economy to better serve the interests of the expanding empire, especially through increased agricultural output. A twenty-year plan worked out in 1937 called for eventually establishing one million households, totaling five million Japanese, in the area. About half a million Japanese actually migrated to Manchuria during 1931–1945, including some 250,000 farmers who left their villages in Japan to engage in agriculture and dairy industry in the state of Manchukuo. Even teenagers were recruited, 50,000 of them scattering in the frontier regions. The recent arrivals, along with the South Manchuria Railway and the "new zaibatsu" (industrial-financial concerns), hoped that industrialization would go hand in hand with agricultural development, that Manchuria would provide space for Japan's surplus population and also produce enough raw materials, foodstuffs, and manufactured goods to enable Japan to be more self-sufficient.

After 1935 northern China was considered an extension of this scheme. The South Manchuria Railway sent study missions to survey the area's potential resources and needs, and the Boxer Protocol Army (the so-called Tientsin Army) began to exploit the region's mineral resources. The Government in Tokyo formally sanctioned these moves, and in 1936, the cabinet drew up a plan for the economic development of north China under the supervision of Japan and Manchukuo. After the outbreak of the Sino-Japanese War in 1937, north China became an important source of supply for the Japanese expeditionary forces, so the newly created Planning Board undertook a special study of economic opportunities there. One result of this planning was the establishment of the North China Development Company in 1938. Capitalized at 350 million yen, of which the government provided half, the semipublic corporation was to engage in transportation, communication, electronics, iron mining, and other enterprises.

In the meantime Japan promoted intraregional trade with Manchukuo and China—the "yen bloc." Exports to Manchukuo and China increased from 25 percent of Japan's total exports in 1936 to over 40 percent in the first half of 1938, and imports from these countries rose from 14 percent to over 22 percent of the total. The concept of a new

East Asian order, enunciated in November 1938, was meant to be far more than an empty slogan, it was actually an ex post facto rationalization of Japan's policy of close supervision of economic affairs in Manchuria and north China, calculated to meet the nation's needs as much as possible within the area.

At another level the pan-Asianist doctrine gained influence within and outside the Japanese government. Publicists expounded on the doctrine of Asian solidarity, cooperation, and resistance to Western imperialism (including Soviet communism). Some were traditional right-wing nationalists who felt they had to justify the aggression in China in the name of a holy war against Western influences. But scores of others who were not simplistic chauvinists were genuinely convinced that the nation needed a new ideology under which it could unite in prosecuting the war. They believed that Asian unity was the antithesis of nationalism, individualism, liberalism, materialism, selfishness, imperialism, and all the other traits that characterized the bankrupt Western tradition. Instead, the pan-Asianists stressed themes such as regional cooperation, harmony, selflessness, and the subordination of the individual to the community.

The intensity of this propaganda campaign is, paradoxically, evidence of the tenacity of Western influence in Japanese thinking; author after author found it necessary to stress the supreme importance of liberating one's mind from unconsciously following familiar Western patterns of thought. As Uda Hisashi wrote in his influential 1939 treatise on cultural policy toward China, the Japanese had for too long looked down on things Oriental and dismissed Chinese culture as anachronistic. Outside of the army, few had known much about China or the rest of Asia. Now, however, Japan should "totally put an end to the long period of dependence on and copying after the West." The war in China must be sustained through a new cultural ideology for the new age, beginning with the recognition that Western-oriented scholarly and cultural activities had not served the nation. The country's cultural and intellectual leaders must overcome their past infatuation with Western liberalism and individualism and return to "Japan's innate intelligence." Only then would they be able to grasp the significance of the war in China. The Sino-Japanese War was seen in part as an inner war to cleanse the Japanese mind of Western influences and modes of thought, not just as an action to bring the recalcitrant Chinese to their senses. Once they recognized their past mistakes, the Japanese could proceed to rebuild the world order on the basis of pan-Asianism.

During the late 1930s Japanese propaganda laid tremendous stress on rebuilding, regenerating, reawakening, and rebirth, indicating their self-consciousness about ending Western-dominated patterns and restoring Asia to its past greatness. The East, Japanese writers pointed out with monotonous regularity, had had a tradition of cooperation, harmony, mutual respect, integration, and communal unity, quite in contrast to the West's egoism, constant rivalry, friction, and imperialism. Japan was attempting to recall that proud tradition. As the legal scholar Takigawa Seijirō noted, the new Asian order would be based upon the negation of Western concepts and the foundation of Asian cultural precepts. Japan, as the depository of traditional Asian virtues, was in a position to take the lead in this task. China, as Japan's closest neighbor, was destined to be its first partner in reconstructing the region's affairs. All of Asia, however, was one, as writers repeatedly asserted, quoting Okakura Tenshin, the turn-of-the-century pan-Asianist. All agreed that economic development was necessary for Asian liberation from Western domination, and cultural unity should ensure that this would not lead to excessive nationalism and imperialism as had been the case in Europe and America.

Despite this rhetoric and the military exploits in China that it sought to rationalize, Japan's external affairs lacked consistency and coherence through most of the decade. Although they talked of a pan-Asianist new order, the Japanese were never successful in making systematic plans to implement their vision. Because Manchukuo and north China were able to supply only a portion of Japan's essential needs, the country continued to depend on sources outside the yen bloc for commodities like cotton, wool, petroleum, rubber, and wheat. The bulk of these commodities came from the United States and from India, Southeast Asia, and Oceania, areas that were tied to sterling and other European currency systems, which maintained protective tariff walls against Japanese imports. Thus Japan almost always suffered a trade deficit with the European countries and their colonies. The United States continued to be Japan's most important trade partner, in spite of the confusion of world depression and the enmity generated by Japanese aggression in Manchuria and China. During the first half of 1938, the United States supplied goods worth 460,000,000 yen, of Japan's total imports of 1,394,000,000 yen, primarily cotton, petroleum, iron, and machine goods. These were essential for the prosecution of the Sino-Japanese War, and no rhetoric of pan-Asianism could enable Japan to do without them.

The Japanese were well aware that their dependence on extra-Asian markets and sources of supply made them vulnerable to foreign economic pressures. As Saitō Yoshie, a former Foreign Ministry official and confidant of Matsuoka Yōsuke, stated in 1938, sustained boycotts by a Western power would damage the national economy severely and ruin its plans for rapid development. Saitō asserted that fully integrating the economies of Japan and China was the only feasible way for Japan to lessen its dependence on other countries. But the very fact that Saitō had to argue his case in a 400-page volume, printed for confidential circulation within the government, indicates the absence of a blueprint for a pan-Asian economic system.

In fact, lack of adequate knowledge about Asia, let alone a systematic plan of action for the region, was so acutely felt within the government that in September 1938 the Planning Board established a Tōa Kenkyūjo (East Asian Institute) to study ecological, economic, and ethnographic conditions in China, Southeast Asia, and the southwestern Pacific. These surveys were far from completed when the war against the Anglo-American powers began. Within the Foreign Ministry, in the meantime, a planning committee was organized to analyze the effect of world economic trends on Japan's Asian policy. A product of the committee's research was a 500-page volume, which was made available for limited circulation in April 1939. Again the standard clichés were reiterated: the world economic order was being reorganized on the basis of regional blocs, which were stifling Japan's expansive energies everywhere except in Asia. It was incumbent upon the nation to build a new order of economic self-sufficiency in Asia through the cooperation of China and Manchukuo. Japan must expand commercial activities in these countries and promote their industrialization, enabling them to raise their standards of living and contribute to economic growth. Then if there should be war, Japan would be in a much stronger position.

Even this apparently clear-cut assertion contained seeds of uncertainty, however. Japan's bloc policy was justified as a defensive response to the development of regional blocs elsewhere. The implication was that while Japan would go along with present global trends, it would not hesitate to return to the pre-1929 system of more liberal transactions among capitalist countries, if that system were re-established. Moreover, the East Asian bloc was not truly self-sufficient; Japan, the study noted, still had to obtain oil, rubber, nickel, tin, copper, and other materials from Europe, America, and their colonies in Southeast Asia. Therefore Japan could not be as free of dealings with these countries as pan-Asian policy might dictate. Even as late as 1939, in other words, Japanese foreign policy was not consistently pan-Asianist. An undercurrent of Western-oriented sentiment arose from time to time, as if to warn the nation that a completely autonomous pan-Asianist order was not likely to be realized. Officials recognized the nation's economic dependence on non-Asian countries and knew that dogmatically anti-Western diplomacy could bring about Japan's isolation and not much else.

If anything, the need for some degree of understanding with the Western powers, in particular the United States, seemed to increase as the war in China bogged down. For one thing the military were becoming anxious about their state of preparedness toward the Soviet Union, and the battle of Nomonhan (May 1939) seemed to prove the superiority of Soviet air power and mechanized ground forces. To cope with the crisis, Japan would have to terminate hostilities in China through political means, but that might require the good offices of Britain and the United States. The government in Tokyo was particularly solicitous of America's goodwill and was chagrined when the U.S. State Department announced in July that it was going to abrogate the commercial treaty between the two countries. Instead of driving the Japanese to reduce their dependence on America, however, this announcement made them all the more determined to placate the United States. The growing importance of the American issue belied all the official rhetoric about a new order in East Asia and pointed up the ambiguity and uncertainty underlying Japanese policy.

If little was being implemented in the economic and political realm to implement pan-Asian regionalism, even less was being done about cultural unity. In the late 1930s the only tangible movement to unite Japan and China culturally was the Hsin-min Hui (the People's Renovation Society) in north China. The society was founded under Japanese auspices in December 1937 to bring together occupied China's prominent educators, journalists, and students under the banner of "hsin-min chui-i" or "the principle for the renovation of people," a concept adopted from the Chinese classic *Ta Hsüeh* (Great Learning).

From the Japanese point of view, the purpose of this movement was to provide an intellectual and ideological underpinning for the actions of the army of occupation, giving them historic and cultural meaning by stressing the ideal of Asian rejuvenation. From its headquarters in Peiping, the Hsin-min Hui issued newsletters, trained Chinese personnel to establish local branches, opened schools and agricultural experimentation stations, operated radio stations, and otherwise tried to reach out to the Chinese people as an alternative both to the Kuomintang and to the Communist party.

The movement was marred from the start, however, by its close identification with Japanese military policy in China. Several of the Japanese leaders of the society had worked in positions of influence in Manchukuo, and they collaborated with Chinese politicians like Miao Pin and Wang K'o-min, who had parted company with Chiang Kai-shek and chosen the path of reconciliation with the Japanese as the only way to restore peace and advance their own personal interests. These Chinese leaders parroted Japanese slogans about Asian renaissance, economic development without the excesses of Western capitalism, and harmony of all countries. Since most of these ideas could be found in the Chinese classics, the Chinese persuaded themselves that they, rather than the Japanese, were the ideological leaders of the new movement. In any event, the Hsin-min Hui was dedicated to awakening the Chinese people to the dangers of the Kuomintang and the Communists, both of whom looked to the West, whether capitalist or socialist, for inspiration and support. These parties, according to the society's propaganda, were really betraying China by tying its destiny to the interests and ambitions of outsiders. Japan, on the other hand, was the true savior of China, politically, economically, and culturally.

Because the Hsin-min Hui was financially and ideologically tied to the Japanese army of occupation, it did not become an effective movement for cultural pan-Asianism. The Japanese intellectuals and publicists who were active in the movement were mostly right-wing ideologues like Takigawa Seijirō and Fujisawa Chikao. Those who had arrived at pan-Asianism through exposure to the modern Western critique of capitalism and imperialism—men like Miki Kiyoshi, Rōyama Masamichi, Hirano Yoshitarō, and Ozaki Hotsumi—were never enthusiastic about the Hsin-min Hui and groped for other ways to promote their utopian schemes. Several of them gathered around Prince Konoe Fumimaro, hoping that he would provide the focus for a nationwide movement for Asian cultural awakening. Viewing the Chinese provisional regime in north China as a mere puppet of the Japanese army, they also looked to Wang Ching-wei and other prominent Kuomintang officials who might be persuaded to stop resisting Japan and work to save Asia from Western interference. Even here, however, the alleged union of Japan and China, politically, economically, and culturally, was not necessarily presented as a particularistic proposition. In fact Miki, Rōyama, and others took pains to show that their conception of the new Asian order was not founded merely on the region's geographical and ethnic identity but on some universal principles. The idea, Miki wrote, was to create a more " open Asia." According to Rōyama, it must aim at industrial development, popular welfare, and the advancement of science and technology—a construction hardly distinguishable from a liberal Western order.

Other Japanese who were more centrist were equally concerned with the need for a national movement in close contact with official policy. One such group, Kokusaku Kenkyūkai (the Society for the Study of National Policy), representing middle-ranking bureaucrats, lawyers, businessmen, and academics, held frequent meetings to discuss current affairs, but their discussions tended to be reactive to events and failed to generate an extensive Asian cultural movement. The group included liberal economists and businessmen as well as nationalistic bureaucrats, but it never succeeded in devising a comprehensive scheme for solving national problems. This seems to have been characteristic of the age. Although the Japanese felt compelled to react to world events in some coherent fashion and were beginning to embrace various shades of anti-Western, pan-Asianist ideas, they had no systematic approach to the problems of national defense, development, and identity.

Uncertainty and inconsistency continued to characterize Japanese policy and thinking after 1939, when they were influenced more than ever by events beyond their control. Despite all their talk of a new order in East Asia, they found that developments in Europe were the most important factor in determining Japanese relations with the United States and China. If the government in Tokyo had established a firm framework for carrying out a pan-Asianist policy, it would not have been so shocked by the Nazi-Soviet nonaggression pact or by the outbreak of the Second World War. Prime Minister Hiranuma Kiichirō's self-deprecating remark that trends in international affairs were truly "beyond comprehension" aptly reflected the confusion and ambiguity in Japanese policy. From then on the Japanese began thinking of ways to take advantage of European events to bring about their ideal of an Asian empire. The inherent instability of that ideal was nowhere more graphically revealed than in the Japanese infatuation with Germany, which grew into an article of faith, so that soon the government and military were convinced that only a German alliance could bring about the new order. Few bothered to ask how a pan-Asianist scheme established through the help of a European power could be free of Western influence. At first even fewer realized that Japan's destiny would be even more closely tied to the policies and strategies of Germany's actual and potential adversaries, above all, the United States.

The twelve-month period between the outbreak of the European war and the signing of the German-Japanese-Italian alliance revealed such a logic of events with stark reality. The Japanese army, frustrated by its inconclusive campaigns in China and shocked by the superiority of Soviet forces at Nomonhan, began to use its perception of "fundamental changes in the international situation" as a guide to strategy. Some top army officials became captivated by this vision and believed the country should take advantage of the European civil war to solve its Asian problems. By encouraging German and Italian victories over Britain and France and keeping the European powers divided, Japan could reduce their interference in China. Also, if Russia and America were compelled to divert their attention to the European conflict, they would be that much less willing to antagonize Japan and might even be prepared to persuade the Chinese to end their resistance to Japan. At the same time it would be easier to extend Japanese influence to areas south of China to obtain much-needed raw materials from the European colonies.

Presumably these developments might have enabled the Japanese to push ahead with their project for an Asian empire, but the reality was far different. Instead of reducing the influence of outside powers, Japan in effect ended up asking for their interference, which came about through two decisions. First, the high-level decision to approach Germany for an alliance was made on the assumption that Adolf Hitler would successfully crush his European enemies, whose colonies in Asia would then be easy prey for Japanese exploitation. Just before he became foreign minister, Matsuoka Yōsuke, who more than any other civilian official was responsible for concluding the Axis alliance, wrote that both the settlement of the war in China and the establishment of a new order in East Asia depended on events elsewhere. The destiny of Japan and Asia was intimately bound up with that of the whole world. More specifically, he urged that Japan take advantage of Germany's certain triumph in Europe to "construct a new order in East Asia," as he wrote in a memorandum to Konoe Fumimaro when Konoe organized a new cabinet in July 1940. This goal had been reiterated time and again after 1938, but little had been accomplished; now Matsuoka proposed to achieve the objective through an alliance with Germany and Italy. Obviously, an Axis alliance was an expedient tactic, based on a temporary faith in German success. Thus Japan's allegedly firm long-range policy depended on the vicissitudes of a war far away from Asia.

Second, even as they hoped for German victories in Europe, the Japanese wanted to redefine their relations with the Soviet Union and the United States, the two Western powers not yet involved in the war. Matsuoka hoped that these powers, not wishing to be involved in armed hostilities in two separate regions of the world, would want a period of stability and peace in Asia. In his grand design, Japan would establish supremacy in Asia on the basis of an understanding with Russia and the United States. However, such a design necessitated negotiating with these countries, which would enhance their roles in calculations of Japanese strategy. This was borne out by events subsequent to the conclusion of the Axis pact in September 1940. Both the army and the government in Tokyo needed at least a temporary peace with the Soviet Union, so Foreign Minister Matsuoka hastened to Moscow. The result of his trip was that Japanese policy in China and Asia was tied to fluctuations in Japanese-Russian relations, making the country paradoxically more dependent on Soviet behavior than when the army had considered Russia a hypothetical enemy.

The United States also began to loom large as a determinant of Japan's destiny, as Japan sought to reformulate their relationship to accommodate changing world conditions. Konoe, Matsuoka, and other civilian leaders believed that peace in the Pacific could be preserved if the United States pledged not to interfere with Japan's building of a new Asian order. But "noninterference" did not mean inaction or nonintercourse. Japanese officials took it for granted that the two countries would continue to trade and maintain diplomatic relations. Moreover, America might play a role in the settlement of the Chinese war, an idea the army was particularly attracted to in the winter of 1940–41. The army felt that only the Chinese Nationalists' blind faith in American support was keeping them recalcitrant; if the United States interceded to halt the conflict, the Chinese would give up their hopeless cause and begin to cooperate with Japan. These fanciful ideas provided the background for negotiations in Washington between the State Department and the Japanese embassy, beginning in the spring of 1941. The paradox was that Japan was courting American involvement in Asian affairs even while it was bent upon constructing a pan-Asian order. But the Japanese did not perceive this as a paradox—another indication that their policy was more opportunistic than dogmatic and more ambiguous than systematic. The German alliance, far from ending the uncertainty, further confounded the situation. The sense of aimlessness was numbing.

By the spring of 1941, Japanese dissatisfaction was pervasive. Despite Matsuoka's bold strategy, Japan's position had not visibly improved. It was still dependent on the United States for petroleum, and the navy's reserve of fuel oil would last only two years. The neutrality treaty with the Soviet Union, signed on April 13, temporarily assured a status quo in the north, but that was meaningless without an assertive operation in the south to establish a self-sufficient Asian empire. Yet both the army and the navy hesitated to take that step, basically because there was no comprehensive strategic plan for it. Japanese policy was not consistent toward either Germany or the United States. Tokyo politely but persistently refused Berlin's pleas for bold action in Southeast Asia, including an attack on Singapore, to demolish one corner of the British empire. At the same time, the Japanese embassy in Washington tried to convince American officials that the Axis alliance did not really infringe on United States interests or prerogatives in Asia. Still, Japan was determined to settle the Chinese war to its satisfaction and obtain more mineral resources in Southeast Asia, so it would be less dependent on the United States. With all these themes being pursued simultaneously, some concerned officials began calling for a more sharply defined national policy and a more comprehensive strategy to carry it out.

For Ambassador Ōshima Hiroshi in Berlin, the drift and indecision at home were utterly disconcerting. He believed that Japan either had to honor the Axis pact consistently and wholeheartedly, which might mean war with Britain and, probably, the United States, or it had to seek rapprochement with the United States and revert to pre-Axis alliance diplomacy. Ōshima urged the Tokyo government to give up all efforts at reconciliation with the United States. Such efforts would only weaken Germany's resolve to defeat Britain completely, because Germany would not be able to count on Japan to tie the United States down in the Pacific. A German rapprochement with Britain and even with America would mean the failure of Tokyo's policy of keeping the West divided, and Japan would be faced with a united and hostile coalition of Western powers. To prevent this possibility, Japan must do its utmost to assist Germany. "Please have complete confidence in [Germany's] capacity to carry through the war to total victory," Ōshima telegraphed Foreign Minister Matsuoka.

The army was also coming around to this view. Its hope of persuading the United States to play a mediatory role in China had been frustrated by the apparently inconclusive talks in Washington, and sentiment for ending these negotiations was becoming stronger, abetted by the growing conviction among navy staff officers that conflict with the United States was sooner or later inevitable and that negotiations were worthless. That view resulted not from a thorough review of Japanese strategy, but primarily from their unhappiness with the indecisiveness of the civilian government. The navy believed that its position relative to that of the U.S. navy would further decline with time. Either Japan should reach a basic agreement with the United States or it should plan seriously for war. With the first possibility apparently fading, the logical alternative was war in the near future.

Despite such pressures, the Tokyo government continued to court American goodwill, at the same time assuring the Germans that there was no departure from the spirit of the Axis pact. This indecisiveness reflected Japan's continued reliance on external events as a guide to policy as well as its inability to achieve anything through its own initiative. It was symbolic that even the commercial talks at Batavia to secure fixed quantities of East Indies goods ended in failure. Japan was not willing to use force in Southeast Asia, but neither was it ready to dismantle the edifice of Axis diplomacy.

Japanese foreign relations before mid-1941 consisted of an unsuccessful attempt to establish a new framework of Asian politics on the ruins of the old order. There persisted a serious gap between the avowal of an anti-Western, pan-Asian system and the reality of continued dependence on Western economic resources, diplomacy, and military vicissitudes. This weakness fortified the American policy of opposition to the Axis alliance and to Japan's moves in China and elsewhere in Asia. From Washington's point of view, Japan was not the enemy that Germany was likely to become—especially if the two powers could be separated. The best way to do this, and to frustrate Japanese ambitions, was to ignore Japan's pretensions as the definer of a new order in Asia and try to compel it to mend its ways and resume its earlier role as a responsible member of the international community.

The United States arrived at this stance, however, only after going through years of frustration in its external affairs. Although not a member of the League of Nations, the United States had in fact been the key to postwar international relations. Its capital, technology, and commodities sustained the world economic system throughout the 1920s, and other capitalist economies looked to America as the financial, business, and political center of the world.

The United States took the lead in ending armament competition, alliances, and ententes as mechanisms for peace and stability. Instead, it continued the Wilsonian policy of encouraging international cooperation among the industrial powers and with the underdeveloped regions. Central to this policy was the concept of "development," which went back to the nineteenth century. "Commercial and industrial development," as many officials, publicists, and intellectuals noted after the 1890s, was being promoted not only among Western countries but also in the rest of the world. And in the words of Benjamin Kidd, the English anthropologist, the Americans "will be the leading representatives of definite principles in the development of the world." These principles were defined by men like Elihu Root and William Howard Taft variously as interdependence, international fraternization, self-control, and peaceful expansion. America should use its resources for internal economic development and also to link the regions of the world closer together through its goods, ships, merchants, and businessmen. This, Taft once remarked, would "bring peoples and governments closer together and so form bonds of peace and mutual dependency."

Wilsonian foreign policy, the basic statement of United States policy until the 1930s, was built upon these concepts and further systematized them. Woodrow Wilson not only accepted the tenets of international economic development, he sought to establish a political framework for it throughout the world. To achieve this end, he believed the advanced industrial countries must refrain from making selfish, particularistic arrangements and from dominating the undeveloped countries, which for their part would need to avoid unstable domestic conditions and irresponsible foreign transactions. They must aspire to "development of ordered self-government," Wilson said. If all the peoples of the world joined in this peaceful, orderly transformation of the globe, they would share equally in the fruits of economic development. Wars, alliances, and armaments would be unnecessary.

Wilsonianism did not disappear immediately after the onset of the depression, but it was severely challenged by the unilateral acts of Japan and other countries and by the rising sentiment of nationalism and unilateralism in America. There was a reaction against Wilsonian internationalism as the United States, like virtually all other countries, became preoccupied with solving the severe economic crisis through price stabilization, devaluation, exchange control, and other measures, which were taken with little regard for their impact upon the international monetary system or world trade. Collective international action fell into disrepute in an environment of economic nationalism and of suspiciousness toward businessmen and bankers that emerged during the depression. The Wilsonian faith in friendly and peaceful relations among nations through economic interaction gave way to indifference to world problems. As Charles A. Beard expressed the prevailing view, national security was derived from attaining "minimum dependence upon governments and conditions beyond [the nation's] control" and developing "its own resources to the utmost."

This nationalistic view was a sharp break from the past, but the administration of Franklin D. Roosevelt accepted it with equanimity, having come to power on the ruins of the Hoover administration's heroic but vain attempt to solve the Manchurian crisis through international cooperation. That experience left American officials shaken, frustrated, and pessimistic about further attempts to preserve the postwar system of international relations. As Japan disregarded the principles underlying that system and as other countries undermined its economic foundation, Wilsonian internationalism became a hollow shell and no longer provided a point of reference for the conduct of American diplomacy.

For a while after 1933 United States foreign policy lost its sense of direction, although it was not altogether inactive. It enunciated a good-neighbor policy in the Western Hemisphere, recognized the Soviet Union, endorsed the League of Nations' embargo of goods to Italy when that country invaded Ethiopia, and enacted neutrality legislation. These steps, however, did not amount to a coherent policy; they were mostly reactive, not creative, responses to changing conditions outside the country. In the mid-thirties the United States sought to stabilize its relations with other nations primarily by recognizing the new realities, including Japan's control over Manchuria and Germany's revisionist thrusts, which aimed at more acceptable boundaries in Central Europe. America was willing to live with these developments simply because it saw no other alternatives. Thus for a while the United States was prepared to maintain some form of stable relations with Japan, refraining from overt support of China or from any action that might give the impression of penalizing or isolating Japan.

Despite the depression and the abandonment of internationalist diplomacy, however, American officials did not give up the idea of economic growth through industrialization. Equally important, economic nationalism did not imply stopping all activities overseas. If anything, the need for oil, rubber, tin, and other raw materials was increasing because of the worldwide trend toward autarky, with each power trying to limit shipments of materials to others outside its own trade bloc. The government in Washington encouraged private firms to continue investing in oil fields and rubber plantations in Southeast Asia and Latin America. In China, despite difficulties caused by the Japanese invasion, American capital investments amounted to $40 million in 1941. In that context, Japanese action in Manchuria and north China was seen as having a negative effect on China's economic development by discouraging the infusion of foreign capital and technology. But because Japan's Asian policy was never consistent, the Americans hoped that in time, Japan would go back to playing its traditional role as a promoter of development through cooperation with Western nations.

When this did not happen, and when the Japanese government in late 1938 enunciated the doctrine of a new order in East Asia, the United States was compelled to clarify its stand and reenter the international arena. Having survived four years in office, President Roosevelt and his aides were finally persuaded that they would have to reformulate the country's foreign policy instead of making ad hoc responses to events. At first, this took the form of trying to restore the framework of international cooperation. For instance, in June 1937 Roosevelt invited

Prime Minister Neville Chamberlain to Washington to discuss British-American cooperation, which had all but disappeared after 1933. Shortly afterward Under Secretary of State Sumner Welles proposed an international conference to lay down some basic principles for the guidance of all nations. One such principle, Welles suggested, might be "equal access to raw materials" throughout the world—harking back to the Wilsonian tradition. In October 1937 Roosevelt called for quarantining lawless nations to prevent the disease from spreading to the rest of the world. The idea of an international conference was revived in January 1938, and during the remainder of the year Roosevelt repeatedly appealed to Hitler and to Benito Mussolini to solve international disputes peacefully, more evidence that the American government again considered itself a factor in world affairs and that it wanted to reestablish some system of international cooperation. The Munich settlement of October 1938 fit into that framework, and Sumner Welles characteristically welcomed it, saying, "a new world order based upon justice and upon law" had been established.

This emerging internationalism, which was sometimes called "appeasement," was an effort to stabilize international politics through an understanding by all the major powers—Germany and Japan as well as Britain and the United States—looking to the reopening of the globe to economic activities. In such a scheme the major military powers, which were beginning to come out of the global economic crisis, would have to cooperate with one another and with lesser nations to reduce armament, promote economic interdependence, and settle outstanding disputes peacefully. It was a Wilsonian agenda. That the State Department under Cordell Hull and Welles was the major supporter of this agenda was not surprising, for they continued to formulate their policy statements in the language of international cooperation and interdependence. More notable was President Roosevelt's strong, if transient, interest in such a scheme during 1937–1939. He was sufficiently impressed with an internationalist solution that even after Germany annexed the rest of Czechoslovakia in March 1939, he talked of convening an international conference to obtain the powers' nonaggression pledges and to work out a formula for solving economic problems. Undoubtedly he believed that the American people would oppose any overt act that increased the chances of a war in which the United States might become involved. Also he apparently felt that they would prefer the administration to take some internationalist initiative to prevent war rather than to persist in complete inaction. As late as the beginning of 1940, Roosevelt consented to Under Secretary Welles's peace mission to Europe which, reminiscent of Colonel E.M. House's trip in the early summer of 1914, was designed to assert American interest in internationalism.

Just as the realization of Japan's new order in Asia hinged on events elsewhere, the implementation of American Wilsonianism depended upon events over which the United States had little direct control. Roosevelt's internationalist diplomacy was given a jolt in August 1939, when Nazi Germany and Stalinist Russia signed a nonaggression pact, precipitating the German occupation of Poland and the British-French declaration of war on Germany, thus bringing the world another European war. Although the State Department, much like Wilson and House in 1914, saw America's role as that of objective mediator, the reaction of President Roosevelt and most of his aides was more decidedly one-sided and forcefully interventionist. They did not give up their commitment to internationalist principles, but their overriding concern was to maintain the balance of power in Europe which depended on the survival of Great Britain. If the United States did not support Britain, they reasoned, Europe might become united under Germany and confront the Western Hemisphere. Starting with the repeal of the arms embargo in November 1939, official United States policy became more and more interventionist, hoping to ensure British survival without actually getting involved in the war.

This was clearly a power-political approach to foreign affairs, not an internationalist strategy. Although the Roosevelt administration couched its policy in idealistic language to appeal to public opinion, and although the State Department preserved a strain of internationalism, considerations of armament, balance of power, and strategic planning became the major factors in policy. Very often power considerations overshadowed ideological factors as in the decision to maintain official ties with the Vichy regime of conquered France. Likewise, at first the United States did not dispute Britain's particularistic economic policy of according preferential treatment to the members of the Commonwealth. President Roosevelt refrained from condemning the Soviet Union's invasions of Poland, the Baltic states, and Finland. A main objective of American diplomacy during 1939–1941 was to persuade General Francisco Franco's fascist regime to remain neutral instead of joining Germany.

Toward Japan the United States continued what may be termed a neo-Wilsonian approach, hoping it would in time give up its Asian policy and join the other powers in restoring a more open world. Certainly some of the internationalist principles the United States presented during 1938–1939, such as equal access to raw materials, were meant to appeal to Japan no less than to Germany. At the same time, the Roosevelt administration continued to view Japan as vulnerable to economic pressures and to external influence. In July 1939 the United States announced that it would abrogate its treaty of commerce with Japan after January 1940, which was rather out of character with the administration's generally cautious diplomacy at that time. But the announcement can also be taken as an expression of optimism that the United States could compel Japan to renounce regionalism and return to a framework of international cooperation.

This optimism persisted after the outbreak of the European war. The basic need was to prevent Japan from assisting Germany, but officials in Washington continued to believe that Japan was an inferior nation, vulnerable to outside pressures because of its lack of vital resources. They thought it would be relatively easy to restrain Japan through selective economic sanctions and to persuade the Japanese not to commit themselves to the Axis side. When Tokyo, in September 1940, went ahead with the Axis pact, Washington's reaction was predictable. The United States tried to nullify the effect of the German-Japanese alliance by exhorting China, Indochina (under the Vichy French regime), and the Dutch East Indies not to succumb to Japanese imperialism; by preventing Japan from accumulating large oil reserves; by working out joint strategy with British, Chinese, and Dutch authorities in Southeast Asia; and by telling the Japanese that the German alliance was the major obstacle to understanding in the Pacific. At the same time, the Japanese were told that if they renounced the pact, amicable and cooperative relations would be restored. The Japanese, it was pointed out, would gain far more from such an arrangement than they would from the German pact.

This was a delicate policy. The United States did not wish to drive Japan totally to the German side without being prepared for a two-ocean war. American strategic planning in the winter of 1940–41 was based on the premise that the country could conceivably become involved in a war in Europe and the Atlantic. Diplomatic talks and economic sanctions in the meantime were expected to keep Japan powerless to move, but the United States did not think it necessary to offer Japan specific inducements to stay out of the European war. At bottom was the fact that American relations with Japan were considered much less significant than relations with Germany, whose menace was clearly recognized as formidable. It did not seem that Japan would dare challenge the United States to a war that would be tantamount to national suicide.

Clearly, in the spring of 1941 the United States was not in a position to ingratiate itself with Japan, as had been envisioned by officials in Tokyo. Far from aiding Japan to consolidate its gains in China, America reminded Japan of its obligation to restore China's territorial integrity. Instead of ending uncertainty in the Pacific, the United States played upon that sentiment by persisting in inconclusive talks and stepping up aid to China.

China was becoming important to American strategy because of the European situation. It was obviously desirable to keep Japan mired on the Asian continent to weaken it as an ally of Germany. This necessitated actively supporting China, which had not been done in the past. Before the Sino-Japanese War, most State Department officials had not regarded the Chinese Republic as a principal factor in Asian politics. It had been important more as a test-case of postwar internationalism; the Western powers had been concerned not so much with China as with preserving a cooperative framework for settling international disputes.

Even after 1937, the initial American reaction to the Asian war was to try to settle it through third-party mediation or multinational talks like the Brussels Conference. But the mounting crisis in Europe compelled redefinition of America's Asian policy. China's continuing struggle with Japan could be used to frustrate German ambitions in Europe. Far from being a purely Asian matter, Japan's proclamation of a pan-Asianist new order had implications for the rest of the world. If Japan were allowed to carry out its regionalist scheme while Germany was doing the same in Central Europe, the relative position of Great Britain and hence of the United States would diminish, especially if the European and Asian blocs should combine. If Japan succeeded in controlling the Chinese economy, and China's several hundred millions joined Japan's advanced technology, the whole continent of Asia could become hostile to the West. It was thus imperative to encourage Chinese opposition to the Japanese scheme. More specifically, the United States condemned Chinese collaborators like Wang Ching-wei who appeared ready to accept the Japanese definition of Asian order. If Chiang Kai-shek developed into another Wang, China would become an even greater menace to peace and stability than Japan. The United States must therefore do everything possible to assist the Nationalists politically and economically, especially with capital and technology to aid war-torn China's industrial and agricultural development.

Thus China was becoming the key to America's Asian policy. It should be recalled, however, that at this time aid to China was in no way as important as the European conflict; Asia was still subsidiary to Europe. Whereas America was determined to defend Britain until the menace of Nazi Germany was removed, it had no intention of destroying Japan or of building China up as the major power in East Asia. Some officials in Washington, such as Stanley K. Hornbeck of the State Department and Henry Morgenthau, treasury secretary, urged stern measures to check Japan. They wanted to use economic sanctions and even military force to reduce Japanese power in Asia, but most of Roosevelt's advisers did not agree. They believed in using economic and political pressures to keep the situation uncertain, to keep the Japanese guessing and worried about American policy.

This state of uncertainty, a product of Washington's policy of calculated risk, was as frustrating to the Chinese as to the Japanese. To be sure, only a few Chinese officials and publicists openly sided with the Japanese army of occupation and its propaganda about the new cultural order. For most Chinese, pan-Asianism was a thin disguise for Japanese ambitions, and the Japanese themselves were uncertain what it meant. However, waging an all-out war of resistance against the Japanese was not such a clear-cut alternative as it appears in retrospect. Instead of engaging in open confrontation, the Chinese troops, guerrillas, and popular organizations would disrupt law and order in occupied areas and mobilize public opinion against defeatism. Most groups agreed that the best strategy was not to devastate the country through fighting but to wear the Japanese out, at the same time maintaining a high level of production and strengthening unoccupied regions. To obtain essential foodstuffs, raw materials, and foreign exchange, Chinese officials often connived at commercial dealings with the occupied areas. They also resorted to strange diplomatic maneuvers, with emissaries going back and forth between their headquarters and Japanese posts to engage in peace talks. Most of these talks were merely devices by both sides to gain time, but occasionally the Chinese used negotiation instead of fighting to tie the Japanese forces down. Some efforts at peacemaking were genuine, as when Wang Ching-wei and his aides left Chungking to deal directly with the Japanese government. The fate of these collaborators, mistreated by the Japanese and denounced by their compatriots, was a cruel one, but the significance of their effort lay in the symbolism of collaboration; since the war was inconclusive, the Chinese would try to reduce Japanese pressures in every possible way, even negotiation for something less than naked imperialism.

The Chinese were not sure that the war could be prosecuted through conventional means or even that it was a conventional war. To be sure, the presence of the Japanese was humiliating, and the arrogance of the occupation forces and the civilian administrators in coastal cities convinced the Chinese that ultimately they would have to drive out the invaders. But the Japanese military objectives were not always clear. Each new cabinet in Tokyo called for "settling" the "China incident." The Japanese seldom mentioned complete victory, and their officers in China seemed willing to leave much to Chinese administrators. Over the years personal ties and friendships had developed between Chinese and Japanese, and these were not completely broken even after 1937. The Chinese belief in nationalism did not mean that they were necessarily against associating with the invaders.

Chiang Kai-shek himself made frequent nostalgic references in his speeches to his experiences as a young cadet at a Japanese military academy and recalled the discipline, dedication, and frugality of Japanese soldiers. Although he denounced the Japanese invasion and rejected any compromise short of restoration of Kuomintang rule in occupied China, he often pictured the two countries as basically compatible. He had no fondness for Western-style democracy or private enterprise; his vision was of a China combining the traditional virtues of a great culture and the amenities of modern industrialization and bureaucracy. China had to be developed economically, but not necessarily on the Western model. Chiang's insistence on traditionalism and his recognition of the need for industrialization did not put him automatically on the side of the Western countries against Japan.

The Communists rejected Chiang's vision as reactionary, but their outlook was no more Western. Mao Tse-tung pictured China as a "new democracy" that would identify itself with worldwide victims of imperialism. China would lead the less advanced countries in the struggle against colonial oppression, an idea that was congenial to the Nationalists as well. The main difference between the Nationalists and the Communists was in their attitudes toward the Soviet Union. The Communist leaders closely followed the Comintern interpretation of world affairs, and in early 1941 they were still defending the Soviet policy of accommodation with Nazi Germany and neutrality with Japan. The Nationalists were more critical of Russia precisely on these counts and were particularly bitter about Moscow's apparent willingness to mollify Japan at the expense of China. The Soviet Union's selfishness, they thought, was one more reason why the Chinese should not rely too heavily on Russian goodwill or assistance, because it might result in the substitution of Soviet for Japanese domination.

The Chinese leaders found it extremely difficult to make long-range plans, because the Western powers were preoccupied with the European situation, and their willingness to assist China fluctuated with the circumstances of the British war with Germany. There was always the possibility that they would choose to concentrate on the Atlantic Ocean, avoiding armed involvement in Asia. The negotiations between the Japanese and the Americans in Washington were no less disconcerting to the Chinese than to the Germans. The Chinese suspected that if the United States had to choose between war against Japan to protect China or some understanding at the expense of Chinese interests, it would opt for the latter. Then the Chinese would be back where they were earlier in the decade, at the mercy of external powers for their salvation and development. The situation would in fact revert to the conditions of the 1920s.

In the spring of 1941, the future of the Asia-Pacific region depended almost entirely upon events outside the area. Japan's quest for Asian autonomy, never entirely consistent, had made its fate less predictable than earlier. The United States now had a definite policy in Europe, but its Asian strategy hinged on the course of the war between Britain and Germany. The Chinese were divided between submission to Japan and hope for Western assistance. In this situation, it is not surprising that Asia's next chapter opened with another major shift in the European war: Hitler's attack on the Soviet Union, launched on June 22.

The Japanese for once saw distinct alternatives: to join Germany in invading the Far Eastern territories of the Soviet Union or to honor the neutrality treaty with Russia. A further question then was whether to take advantage of the German-Russian war by attacking the European colonies in Southeast Asia, thereby bringing the ideal of Asian empire a step closer to fulfillment. Some officials argued for the first course of action, saying that a Japanese assault on the Soviet Union in conjunction with the German offensive in the west would quickly put an end to the Bolshevik regime and remove a menace to Japanese interests in Manchuria and the rest of Northeast Asia. This evidence of German-Japanese cooperation would strengthen the Axis pact, which would weaken the position of the Anglo-American powers and make them respect Japan's position in Asia. As Ambassador Ōshima cabled from Berlin on June 22, "the outbreak of war between Germany and Russia gives us a perfect opportunity to remove, once and for all, the menace in the north and to settle the China incident." If Japan adopted a wait-and-see policy, Ōshima warned, it would lose Germany's trust and damage its own prestige.

Minister Tsutsui Kiyoshi in Bucharest telegraphed Tokyo to express his confidence that Germany would destroy the Bolshevik regime in Russia "at least by the beginning of October." The Soviet Union would disintegrate, and a new government would come into existence in what was left of European Russia. If Japan did not join in attacking the Soviet Union, Germany would owe nothing to Japan and would decide Russia's future with no thought for Japan's desires. To prevent such a disaster, Japan should assault and acquire the Siberian provinces to remove their threat to Japanese interests in Northeast Asia. Of course, such action would violate the neutrality treaty, but Tsutsui believed that the Bolsheviks had already contravened the agreement by supporting anti-Japanese forces in China. Japan was not opposed to Russia and its people but was only determined to overthrow the Bolshevik government, he continued. Once that objective was achieved, the new Russian government would cooperate with Germany, Italy, China, Manchukuo, and Japan in a common struggle against the Anglo-Saxon countries.

Foreign Minister Matsuoka agreed and pressed his cabinet colleagues to sanction yet another shift in Japanese policy. Like Ōshima and Tsutsui, he thought that successful military attacks on Russia would release Japan's armed forces for a move south after the Russian war to capture the rich colonial areas. By that time both Germany and Japan would be so strengthened that American intervention would be unlikely. "We should first go north and then turn south," was the foreign minister's recommendation.

The military leaders in Tokyo, having abandoned hope of American mediation to settle the war in China, agreed that the German invasion of the Soviet Union finally gave Japan an opportunity to act resolutely and end the indecision and tentativeness that had characterized its relations with other countries. But the military did not agree to "go north" first, in part because they needed time to prepare for war against Russia. Twelve divisions of the Kwantung Army, totaling about 350,000 men, were stationed in Manchuria at that time, compared to the Soviet Far Eastern army, which reportedly numbered 700,000. An additional 500,000 Japanese soldiers would have to be mobilized. Realistically, preparations would not be completed until around August 10, and war could not be started for another month thereafter. The military authorities in Tokyo were willing to make such preparations, and at the crucial July 2 meeting of the cabinet ministers and military leaders in the presence of the emperor, it was decided to "solve the northern problem by force" if developments in Europe favored such action. However, the meeting also endorsed penetrating Southeast Asia by force "in order to consolidate the base of our national existence and self-defense." The army would occupy southern Indochina first, at the same time preparing for the anti-Russian offensive. The reasoning was that this would involve comparatively little risk. General Sugiyama Gen, army chief of staff, confidently expressed his view that occupation of southern Indochina would irritate the Anglo-American countries but would not provoke them to war. The navy believed such action would prevent Britain and the United States from taking advantage of a possible Japanese-Russian war. After October, moreover, the rainy season would make it difficult to build airfields in Indochina. Thus, despite Matsuoka's pleas to concentrate on the northern strategy first, Japanese troops began their invasion of southern Indochina on July 28.

If Japan had postponed the southern advance until the beginning of September, when the offensive against Russia was to have started, the subsequent history of the Second World War might have been drastically different. By early August, officers of the Japanese General Staff were losing confidence in a quick German victory over Russia. If Japan had then decided not to cooperate with Germany, the Axis alliance might have been seriously damaged, which in turn might have been conducive to reopening serious negotiations between Japan and the United States, as Prime Minister Konoe wanted. He reasoned that the German attack on Russia without consulting Japan was in effect a violation of the spirit of the Axis alliance and that therefore Japan had a right to repudiate the intent, if not the letter, of the alliance and seek an understanding with the United States. Konoe argued that the German alliance had lost its usefulness and that Japan should seek accommodation with the only power that was in a position to determine the future of the Asian conflict. He wanted to ask the United States to stop its hostile policy in China, help Japan come to a settlement there, and supply Japan with raw materials it would otherwise have to obtain in Southeast Asia. However, the military, while not opposing resumption of the talks in Washington, were convinced that chances for American mediation were slim.

Thus the events of June and July again revealed Japan's tendency to adopt policies in response to external developments. These responses were varied, including preparedness against Russia, occupation of southern Indochina, and resumption of talks with the United States; there still was no coherence in Japanese strategy.

It was in this context that the United States facilitated Japan's search for a coherent policy by speedy retaliation against the occupation of Indochina. On July 24 the U.S. government decided to freeze Japanese assets and on August 1 all export licenses for shipping petroleum to Japan were revoked. The Dutch authorities in the East Indies followed suit and refused to issue export permits without proof of exchange licenses—thus virtually stopping the shipment of oil because payment had to be made in dollars, which were blocked in the United States. After August 5 oil was no longer reaching Japanese shores from either the United States or the Dutch East Indies. Japan could produce about 400,000 kiloliters of oil a year, but the navy easily consumed that much in a month. The reserve, estimated at 9,400,000 kiloliters, would be exhausted in two years unless the nation obtained fresh supplies of oil by some means.

The oil embargo had a tremendous psychological impact upon the Japanese. The ambivalence and ambiguities in their perception of world events disappeared, replaced by a sense of clear-cut alternatives. Hitherto they had not confronted the stark choice between war and peace as an immediate prospect and had lived in a climate of uncertainty from day to day. Now, with the United States resorting to decisive measures, that phase passed. Any wishful thinking that America would tolerate the invasion of southern Indochina was dissipated; either Japan would stay in Southeast Asia at the risk of war with the

Anglo-American countries or it would retreat to conciliate them. The military judged that it was too late for conciliation; Japan would now have to consider the likelihood of war, with the United States as its major adversary.

The sense of inevitable crisis was shared by officials in Washington. As Secretary of State Cordell Hull told Secretary of War Henry L. Stimson in July, the United States had "reached the end of possible appeasement with Japan and there is nothing further that can be done with that country except by a firm policy." From this time on it was assumed that there would be war in the Pacific unless the Japanese made drastic changes in their policy. The only question was the timing.

A series of decisions made simultaneously with the oil embargo and the freezing of Japanese assets indicated a dramatic stiffening in Washington's attitude. A Far Eastern command was organized under General Douglas MacArthur, using the Philippines as a strategic base in case of war with Japan. Fighter planes and heavy bombers were to be placed there, a move designed to turn the archipelago into a bastion of U.S. air power and a deterrent to further Japanese aggression. Talks were held with British, Dutch, and Chinese authorities to exchange information and coordinate their defenses in the Pacific. Lend-lease assistance to China started, and the American volunteer air corps, the Flying Tigers, under Claire Chennault obtained aircraft from the United States and Britain to train Chinese pilots and even engage in military action against the Japanese air force. The United States was clearly determined to prevent Japanese domination of Asia.

Although this policy was dictated by power considerations, it is important to note that these steps were coupled with an assertion of certain internationalist principles, indicating Washington's perception that Japan's new Asian order was threatening to become more than mere rhetoric and therefore must be opposed by alternative ideas of international order.

The nature of that order was outlined in August at the Atlantic Conference of President Roosevelt and Prime Minister Winston S. Churchill. The enunciation of the Atlantic Charter complemented the evolving Anglo-American strategy against Axis aggression by defining certain principles for international peace. In the first of the charter's eight points, the United States and Great Britain asserted that they sought no "aggrandizement, territorial or other." Second, they "desire no territorial changes that do not accord with the freely expressed

wishes of the peoples concerned." The third point, a compromise between the American doctrine of self-determination and the British regard for empire, expressed the desire "to see sovereign rights and
self-government restored to those who had been forcibly deprived of
them." Those peoples who had not been independent presumably
would not have their "sovereign rights" restored. Fourth, in an obvious
allusion to the Axis propaganda about the rights of "have-not" nations,
the charter supported the principle that all nations, victor or van-
quished, should have access "on equal terms, to the trade and to the
raw materials of the world which are needed for their economic prosperity." The next four points further spelled out the ideal world that the
Anglo-American allies hoped to bring about after the war, a world in
which there would be "the fullest collaboration between all nations in the
economic field," where all peoples would "live out their lives in freedom
from fear and want," enabling "all men to traverse the high seas and
oceans without hindrance," and in which "all nations of the world" would
seek to lighten the "crushing burden of armaments."

These principles approximated Wilsonian internationalism, indicating that Wilsonianism was again providing ideological underpinnings
for American foreign policy. The older concepts of peace and stability
through economic development, prosperity, and interdependence had
survived the turmoil of the 1930s and would define the world order
after the Axis menace had been removed. Thus the Atlantic Charter
was an ideological complement to the concern with balance of power,
which had guided Roosevelt's foreign policy since the late 1930s.
Great tension remained between the internationalist language of the
charter and the more power-oriented strategy, but for the first time
since Roosevelt came to power the United States had a sense of direction in its external affairs: essentially a return to Wilsonianism and to
the pre-1929 system of international relations in which extensive economic exchanges had been the norm as well as the presumed path to
world peace. Some of the problems inherent in that decade would have
to be confronted and overcome, such as excessive protectionism and
immigration restriction, but it was assumed that internationalism was
as viable for the 1940s as it had been for the 1920s.

The Atlantic declaration was a challenge to the Japanese to return to
that system and promote their own well-being in cooperation with the
United States or else to face the latter's wrath awaiting their path of
aggression. Because Washington had already taken decisive steps to

curb Japanese expansion, the charter in effect defined for the leaders in Tokyo a world order that would be theirs if they mended their ways. The Americans felt that the Japanese had gone astray, but they could still rescue themselves from their own folly. All they had to do to regain American understanding was to remember the 1920s and reject the militaristic course they had chosen in the subsequent decade. American faith in Wilsonianism grew stronger after August, even as war seemed more and more imminent, and this feeling provided the setting for White House and State Department talks with Japanese envoys in Washington. Hesitation and uncertainty were replaced by conviction. The famous "Hull note" of November 26 expressed the same doctrine. Presented to Ambassador Nomura Kichisaburō, it enumerated ten points, including the conclusion of a multilateral nonaggression pact among Japan, the United States, Britain, the Netherlands, China, the Soviet Union, and Thailand; Japanese withdrawal of all forces from China and Indochina; negotiations for a new trade agreement "based upon reciprocal most-favored-nation treatment and reduction of trade barriers"; and the stabilization of the dollar–yen ratio. As Secretary Hull noted then and afterward, he was not demanding that the Japanese give up their right to exist as a vigorous and viable nation; he was inviting them to go back to the peaceful and interdependent world of the 1920s, where there had been ample room for Japanese interests and self-respect. The Asia pictured by the Hull note represented his image of what the region would have turned into but for the world depression, Japan's militaristic moves, and the various nations' particularistic trade and monetary policies.

The United States was clearly forcing the Japanese to make a choice, whether to continue the process begun in 1931, even at the expense of war with America, or to return to the framework of the 1920s on the basis of accommodation with the Anglo-American nations. As Ambassador Ōshima said in his September 4 message to Foreign Minister Toyoda Teijirō, "There are only two possible attitudes we can take: either to preserve the spirit of the Tripartite Pact and cooperate with Germany and Italy to construct a new world order, or to abandon the alliance, submit to the Anglo-American camp, and seek friendly relations with England and America." For Ōshima it was only a matter of time before Germany established hegemony over Europe, the Middle East, and Africa. It would be supreme folly for Japan to cut its ties with Germany and seek good relations with the United States.

Even if that resulted in settlement of the China war, it would only "cause Japan to be despised and isolated abroad, bring about a loss of hope and the atrophy of the national spirit at home." Rapprochement with the United States was essentially a backward step, to recapture the atmosphere of the 1920s, which was no longer workable. It would be much better for Japan to identify its fate with Germany's.

Ambassador Ishii Itarō at Rio de Janeiro disagreed. On September 2 he cabled his superiors in Tokyo, urging them "to perform a major operation, even if that means turning to other countries for assistance." He believed that Japan's destiny was bound up with that of the Anglo-Saxon countries and that the United States, especially, and Great Britain would retain an influence in Asian affairs no matter what the outcome of the European conflict. What Japan needed most was a stable and peaceful Asia, even if that meant sharing the continent with these other powers. War with them would devastate Asia, would seriously damage Japan, and would not solve the long-lasting conflict between China and Japan. It was regrettable but essential to settle the Chinese war by negotiating with Britain and the United States. Ishii was aware of the almost insurmountable problems this course of action would create in Japanese domestic politics, but he saw no alternative to "removing all obstacles in the way of solving the war and establishing peace in Asia."

At the fateful meeting in the presence of the emperor on September 6, Tokyo's leaders tried to see if a middle position was possible. They decided, on the one hand, to continue the talks in Washington to induce the United States to resume normal trade and desist from augmenting its forces in the Pacific. However, if there was no satisfactory settlement by the beginning of October, Japan was to be ready for war at the end of the month. Although the Japanese leaders decisively favored Ōshima's resolute stand vis-à-vis the United States, they wanted to make one final attempt to avoid war through negotiation. They clearly did not accept Ishii's recommendation for cooperation with the Anglo-American powers. Given the strengthening of the American position in the Pacific and the stiffening of Washington's attitude, the September 6 decisions could only mean war.

As the October deadline came and went without war, and the indecisive talks in Washington continued, Ambassador Ōshima and those who shared his views grew impatient. In Tokyo, Konoe was succeeded as premier by General Tōjō Hideki. Tōjō shared the fatalistic view of Japanese-American relations and believed that war in the Pacific was inevitable, but he was under pressure from the emperor and the court to try again to preserve peace. His was a thankless task, since nothing essential had changed in the two countries' relations, and Wilsonian cooperation was no more appealing in October than it had been earlier. To the exponents of pro-Axis strategy, the 1920s symbolized a discredited pattern of old-fashioned internationalism that had benefited only the United States. As Ōshima cabled to Tokyo on October 29, further delay in going to war would strengthen Japan's potential antagonist. Since the success of Japan's Axis diplomacy hinged on decisive action to take advantage of the relative weakness of the Anglo-American powers, last-minute negotiations with the United States made no sense; they would give the Americans more time and sow seeds of mistrust in the minds of the Germans. A new order in Asia was possible only if Japan seized the historic opportunity presented by the collapse of the British empire. "This is our last chance to consult with Germany so that we can coordinate action in east and west in order to secure southern regions rich in important resources. . . . We shall be leaving cause for regret for a thousand years if, instead of having a definite idea about the course of the [European] war, we are to adopt an opportunistic attitude."

Some resisted such thinking to the very end. Kamimura Shin'-ichi, chargé d'affaires in London, sent a strongly worded telegram to the Foreign Ministry on November 21, urging restraint in view of the growing ties between Britain and the United States, a formidable combination in the event of a break in relations with them. Noting the increases in United States aid to Britain and the consequent growth in British confidence of victory in Europe, Kamimura wrote that British leaders might even desire to crush Japan's strength in Asia, which would be good for British interests after the war. It would be folly to provoke both countries to war at this time. "It is an extremely dangerous situation that we have to start war when our resources have been used up in the Manchurian and China incidents." The best strategy was to be patient and try to reconstruct the nation's strength so it could grow in the future. Japan must accept temporary humiliation and concessions and be ready to resolve the China incident through negotiations with the United States.

Kamimura was waging a losing battle. Adopting his recommendations would necessitate a complete reorientation of Japan's military strategy, foreign policy, and, above all, domestic politics. It would mean going back to the premilitaristic stage of party politics, civilian supremacy, and business culture. The leadership in Japan in the fall of 1941, especially the cabinet of General Tōjō, was not prepared to do this. They believed the only choice was to go forward in search of a pan-Asianist solution. Attacks upon American and British possessions in Asia and the Pacific at dawn of December 7 (8 in Asia), 1941, would be the final step in that direction.

The Japanese-American war, then, involved more than just a clash between aggression and resistance or between militarism and peace. Such simple dichotomizing, while undoubtedly accurate at one level of generalization, conceals a far more interesting development: the degree to which the conflict revolved around the question whether a return to the past was possible and desirable. American officials believed the 1920s still provided the basic framework for comprehending international relations. That framework assumed that an international order of stability and peace could be built on economic interdependence among the industrial nations and their cooperation to develop other regions of the globe. The Japanese disagreed and instead opted for a pan-Asianist regional order. This did not mean, however, that they were rejecting all vestiges of Western civilization. They were, after all, as concerned with economic development and prosperity as other peoples, and the new Asian order was by no means defined as a preindustrial one. As commentator after commentator noted on the eve of Pearl Harbor, Japanese policy was aimed at the development and ultimate industrialization of Asian countries. They had in fact already been partially Westernized, one of them noted, and Japan's task was not to de-Westernize them but to "Asianize the Europeanization of Asia." Such a proposition was placed in opposition to what the Japanese regarded as American and European imperialistic domination of the region. The Americans, on their part, believed that the Japanese scheme was intended to put an end to all Western interests and influence in the East. Both sides exaggerated their differences, but the subsequent years showed that the legacy of Japanese-American interdependence was stronger than the tenuous edifice of pan-Asianism.

Further Reading for Part I

Baumont, Maurice. *The Origins of the Second World War*. New Haven, 1978.

Bell, P.H.M. *The Origins of the Second World War in Europe*. London and New York, 1986.

Carr, William. *Poland to Pearl Harbor: The Making of the Second World War*. London, 1985.

Crowley, James. B. *Japan's Quest for Autonomy: National Security and Foreign Policy 1930–1938*. Princeton, NJ, 1966.

Dallek, Robert A. *Franklin D. Roosevelt and American Foreign Policy, 1932–1945*. Oxford, 1979.

Douglas, Roy. *1939: A Retrospect Forty Years After*. Hamden, CT, 1983.

———. *The Advent of War, 1939–1940*. New York, 1981.

Fuchser, Larry William. *Neville Chamberlain and Appeasement: A Study in the Politics of History*. New York, 1982.

Hillgruber, Andreas. *Germany and the Two World Wars*. Cambridge, MA, 1981.

Iriye, Akira. *The Origins of the Second World War in Asia and the Pacific*. London and New York, 1987.

Martel, Gordon, ed. *'The Origins of the Second World War' Reconsidered: The A.J.P. Taylor Debate After Twenty-five Years*. Winchester, MA, 1986.

Morley, James W., ed. *The China Quagmire, Japan's Expansion on the Asian Continent, 1933–1941*. New York, 1983.

Murray, Williamson. *The Change in the European Balance of Power, 1938–1939: The Path To Ruin*. Princeton, 1984.

Robbins, Keith. *Appeasement*. New York, 1988.

Rock, William R. *Chamberlain and Roosevelt: British Foreign Policy and the United States , 1937–40*. Columbus, OH, 1988.

Sked, Alan. *Crisis and Controversy. Essays in Honour of A.J.P. Taylor*. London, 1976.

Taylor, A.J.P. *The Origins of the Second World War*. New York, 1962.

Watt, D. C. *How War Came. The Immediate Origins of the Second World War, 1938–1939*. New York, 1989.

Weinberg, Gerhard L. *The Foreign Policy of Hitler's Germany: The Diplomatic Revolution in Europe, 1933–1936*. Chicago, 1970.

———. *The Foreign Policy of Hitler's Germany: Starting World War II, 1937–1939*. Chicago, 1980.

Part II

Life under Nazi Occupation: Collaboration and the Holocaust

The precipitous German takeover of Western Europe from Norway to the Pyrenees in the late spring of 1940 shook western civilization to its core. It also brought on an unexpected new phenomenon of apparently willing cooperation with the enemy. Resistance to the Germans that summer was sporadic and easily contained. Commentators quickly refurbished the neutral word *collaboration* to let it now signify shameful cooperation with the enemy. This meaning soon established itself in most European languages and in popular usage. Collaboration and *resistance,* which at about the same time also took on a new connotation as an organized, covert opposition to German rule, became the twin poles of response to the German occupation.

Certainly, cooperation with the enemy was not new—how else could one explain the growth of the European territorial states throughout the last few centuries as they incorporated new populations into previously foreign regimes? What was new was that in an age in which nationalism reigned supreme, collaboration spread so rapidly and settled in almost naturally as the norm, at least in Western Europe. Moreover, the Germans were greeted by vocal fascists and racists whose enthusiasm for Nazism was exceeded only by their own ambitions for a New Order at home. That this ideological commitment to a fascist Europe, which was largely compounded from the illusions of an odd assortment of local, radical rightists, played no important part in German plans suggests that the phenomenon of collaboration reflected a deep malaise in European society. When coupled with its opposite, the resistance, it supports the notion that the Second World War was in some respects a civil war within European nations as well as a struggle against the occupier.

Not all collaboration was the same. As Jan Gross explains below, it is safe to exclude the speculators, the opportunists, and others who intended to take advantage of new circumstances. In a provocative essay on collaboration in France (cited by Gross, see bibliography at the end of this part), Stanley Hoffmann distinguished between collaboration with Germany for reasons of state—based on the presumed necessity to make the best deal possible with the occupier—and collaborationism, an ideological sympathy with National Socialism. Although everywhere individuals can be aligned on a continuum between the two, such a division applies to most occupied countries in Europe and Asia.

Collaboration is usually associated with Germany and political leaders and movements within its new Thousand Year Reich, but it also existed under Italian and Japanese rule. Although the term has generally been reserved to describe those who cooperate with fascist regimes, both of Hoffmann's definitions of collaboration could be applied to postwar Europe, in the East under Soviet occupation as well as in the American-dominated West. Italian instances have not been as thoroughly studied as have those in Asia, where collaboration with Japan's Co-Prosperity Sphere flourished from Manchuria through the Philippines, Indo-China, the Netherlands East Indies and Burma.

Though few historians would now characterize the wartime Japanese regime as fascist, collaboration may have been more extensive and important for the future of the region than it was in Europe. Collaborationists with Japan found no fascism to attract them, though Japan did have its own self-styled fascists. Instead, they saw in Japan's challenge to the West an opportunity to throw off their colonial yokes. The options for nationalists in Asia were to cooperate with the European imperialists, who offered little scope for indigenous leadership and at best only uncertain promises of national self-determination, or to test the Japanese offer to lead an Asian coalition against Western domination. That Asians generally perceived nothing shameful in the latter is illustrated by the examples of Subhas Chandra Bose, Achmed Sukarno, and José Laurel. Bose recruited the Japanese-backed Indian National Army which fought the British in Burma. Killed in an accident in 1945, he was exonerated after the war and became a minor national hero. Sukarno worked with the Japanese and emerged in 1945 as Indonesia's first President. He led the resistance to a Dutch attempt to reestablish their Southeast Asian empire. Laurel became the president of the Philippines under Japanese occupation during the war; he was charged with treason, but his trial was never completed. He is counted as the country's first president, not Manual Roxas. Roxas also worked with the Japanese and was elected in the country's first election after independence in 1946.

Collaboration must be looked at from the viewpoint of both the occupier and the occupied. What did the occupying country hope to accomplish? What were its long-term goals? What were the limits of the cooperation it could expect? It is remarkable that such questions are easier to ask than to answer. Though the Nazis projected an image of efficiency and thoroughness, the regime's administration was haphazard and anarchic. Hitler intended world dominion, but developed no specific plans for the administration and political control of occupied territories before occupation took place. There was talk of *Lebensraum,* which meant territorial expansion eastward and plans for German resettlement and colonization. Foreign sympathizers were cultivated and shown the domestic triumphs of the Third Reich, but these triumphs were intended more to overawe and to impress the visitor with German vitality and military strength, than to build the basis for cooperation and a united coalition of fascism against its enemies.

This German indifference from the top to the future of foreign fascist movements came as a surprise to ideological collaborationists. Vidkun Quisling, a young, brilliant former General Staff officer and defense minister, led the Norwegian *Nasjonal Sammling.* Modeled on the German prototype, the party had close contacts with leading Nazis. But Quisling was shut out of participation in the collaborationist government until 1942, by which time a victory for Germany looked distant and Berlin needed to exploit Norway's economy more intensely than before. Hitler preferred to curb local fascists and to seek collaboration among other circles. The story is similar in Denmark, the Netherlands, Belgium, France, and to a limited extent, in other parts of Europe. Though Jan Gross's article below deals with a country where ideological collaboration with Germany was hardly an option, since the Nazis intended to eliminate the Polish state and society, what he has to say about the kinds of collaborators the Germans might look for applies throughout Europe.

While the motives of fascist-inspired collaborationists and their tarnished ideas find few sympathizers today, it is easier to appreciate the predicament of those who collaborated for reasons of state. In 1940 German domination of Europe for the next generation seemed assured. Ineffective parliamentary government, socially divided nations racked by political scandals, economic depression, and a lack of purpose turned minds toward new choices. Perhaps more authoritarian forms of government, disciplined by the German example, could be turned to national advantage. What can we make of the aged, World War One hero Henri Pétain, answering the call of France in its hour of humiliation by acceding to head the state? Is there any idealism in his National Revolution, in which "work, family and fatherland" replaced "liberty, equality, and fraternity" as the national motto? Did he act as an effective buffer between the arrogant, demanding Germans and the mass of French citizens? And what of the thousands of government officials, police, judges, business leaders and so on who followed in the same path?

German occupation of Europe also meant a war against the Jews. While controversy still continues on many aspects of the war, it remains beyond dispute that the killing of two-thirds of Europe's Jews singled them out as the most important target of German policies. Only Poles and Russians experienced massacre on a comparable scale. Approximately 5,900,000 Jews were killed, or 67 percent of European Jewry; 5,480,000 Poles, or 15 percent; 9,500,000 Russians, or 5.6 per cent. While extermination of the Jews became German state policy, supported by civilian and military bureaucracies, it cannot be too strongly emphasized that the murder of so many people, especially of west European Jews, required collaboration among the governments of occupied countries. It is not simply that national governments went along; they anticipated German demands by passing restrictive, anti-Jewish legislation on their own and smoothing the road to the Auschwitzes of the New Order.

The course of the Holocaust poses questions for our understanding similar to those for collaboration, albeit in more extreme form. How can societies engender so much energy for such sinister purposes? How can a whole civilization lose its way? How can so many fail to see the consequence of their actions? And not choose a different course? Are we witnesses to atavistic, irrational and antimodern powers which spent themselves in a rage of destruction? Or did the Holocaust open a new era in human history where genocide becomes the norm? The essays which follow do not answer these questions. Like many of the critical questions in life, they may never be answered. But they do contribute toward defining the problem of understanding by anchoring our questions in specific examples of life under Nazi occupation.

3

JAN THOMASZ GROSS

Collaboration and Cooperation

Among the large numbers of books on collaboration or even of occupation, there are few in English on the German occupation of Poland. Jan Gross's study of wartime Poland, however, stands out because of his careful sociological analysis. The selection which follows is from chapter five of an engrossing examination of all aspects of German–Polish interaction within a context in which one agent, Germany, exercises extraordinary degrees of control and domination, and the other, Poland, is robbed, not only of recourse to even a semi-independent, sovereign government, but also of *any* claim to nation and statehood altogether. By terms of the secret protocols of the Soviet–German Nonaggression Pact, Poland was divided between the two and ceased to exist. The Germans usurped the Polish state whose outlawed but shadowy authority continued from Paris and later from London as a government-in-exile. Denied nationality and assigned the role of servile labor, Poles had few opportunities to collaborate along the lines of the west Europeans. Ideological collaboration was ruled out.

In these extreme conditions, it is possible to detail the boundaries of cooperation and resistance in ways which other "milder" forms of occupation obscure. As throughout his study, Gross proceeds here by first carefully defining the terms of the questions to be answered and establishing a model of social and political interaction reminiscent of master–slave relations. From that vantage point, he then looks at the historical record, both to test the model and to bring the historic experience into focus. The reader may wonder whether this approach leaves room for moral considera-

Jan Gross. *Polish Society Under German Occupation: The Generalgouvernement, 1939–1944*. Copyright © 1979 Princeton University Press. Excerpt reprinted with permission of Princeton University Press.

tions. Is his last sentence one that can command assent? Might it
be that the Polish example, which has many similarities to that of
the Jews, is so extreme that it sheds little light on the phenomenon
of collaboration in general?

Traditionally, the subject of the interaction between Poles and Germans during the occupation has been obscured by the considerable
emotional involvement of the contemporaries who reported on it. All
contacts across group boundaries, particularly when the groups involved have different goals and openly hostile perceptions of each
other, take place in an atmosphere of suspicion of outsiders and moral
censure of the group's own members against whom the charge of
treason is not infrequently raised. My purpose in this chapter is to
formulate the principles on which such contacts can be established and
to point out the various forms they may assume. The following discussion rests on the premise that an occupying power, in its official,
institutionalized contacts with a subjugated society, will seek three
kinds of "goods" necessary to rule the country, and that its official
relationships with that society will therefore take a form that is related
to its ability to satisfy its need for: authority, expertise, and manpower.
When dealing with authority, we shall speak of collaboration; in discussing the latter two goods, we shall speak of cooperation.

Before we present hypotheses about the sociology of collaboration,
it may be useful to reflect on the meaning of the concept itself. Only
recently has it acquired a peculiar connotation of an uneven distribution of power, an uneven partnership in which one party operates under
duress or, even worse, betrays the interests of its own group. In the
past, the word *collaboration* was employed only as a synonym for
cooperation, specifically in reference to collective work in artistic
areas.

I think it is important to make a distinction between cooperation and
collaboration with the enemy, since under the civilian occupation of
Poland, which lasted several years, the surface of interaction between
occupier and occupied was very broad. It is inconceivable that all
reactions by the occupied group were acts of resistance, but this does
not mean that they were, necessarily, acts of collaboration. For the
purpose of clarity, I believe it would be useful to limit the application
of the term *collaboration* to the area of politics.

Someone who acquires a business and prospers with the silent blessing of the occupiers (who would typically be in for a cut of his income) should be called a profiteer or a speculator rather than a collaborator, so long as he limits his sphere of activity to profit seeking. Nor would I designate as a collaborator a confidant of the occupier's police (whom I would instead call a renegade or something other to the point) who gives his services out of personal vengeance, for the money, or because he is blackmailed. Additionally, I would not cite as a collaborator an expert who works in an organization that performs services for the local population. Thus, employees of the city administrations or, for example, of the Bank Emisyjny would not fit into this category.

I would label as collaborators those who are prepared to grant the occupier authority, rather than merely to provide expertise or information. Accordingly, collaborators include those who would make the occupier the beneficiary of the trust vested in them by the population that had elected them to positions of authority, or those who are ready to accept posts that are traditionally vested with authority in a given community. By deliberately narrowing the meaning of the word, we should be able to distinguish among different attitudes, because everyone who lived for five years under the occupation *had* to "collaborate" in some way with the occupier.

But of course one cannot easily compartmentalize the continuum of variations of human behavior. Stanley Hoffmann, in an admirable essay on collaboration in France, tried to solve the problem by introducing two concepts: collaboration (that is, with Germany), and collaborationism (that is, with the Nazis). However, even this division did not seem precise enough to distinguish between the different kinds of behavior that fit into the general category of political collaboration. Hoffmann therefore subdivided collaboration into voluntary and involuntary collaboration, and collaborationism into servile and ideological collaborationism. But he showed convincingly that these attitudes constitute a continuum; that one can move imperceptibly from involuntary to voluntary *collaboration d'état,* and from there to collaborationism; that the difference between the two terms is often obscure; that collaboration and collaborationism are united in a peculiar dialectic:

> there was no clear yardstick to indicate where reason of state ended and folly began.... The Laval of 1943 needed a Darnand as a bloody collaborationist cover behind which he could more easily pursue the laborious rearguard action of mere involuntary *collaboration d'état.* But

Darnand himself, stubborn soldier and simple mind, found in *collaboration d'état* an invitation to collaborationism.

The Sociology of Collaboration

Collaborationists in Europe in 1939–1945 came predominantly from within the prewar power establishments. At first glance this phenomenon is puzzling and contrary to what we might expect, since it means that collaboration was not simply engineered and implemented by local fascist movements supporting the Nazi invaders. In fact, French fascists were kept at bay by the Germans in Paris, while the Pétain government was retained in "power" at Vichy; Czech fascists were not allowed to challenge Hacha effectively; Quisling's relationships with the Reichskommissar in Norway, Terboven, were difficult, and indeed, the Norwegian Supreme Court and the civil service, two important segments of the prewar power establishment, were able to curb Quisling's zeal successfully and set the pace of collaboration themselves. This pattern of collaboration calls for explanation, if only because it contradicts what one would think should most probably happen: namely, that the majority of collaborators should be recruited from the groups that previously had been alienated from the power establishments in the subjugated countries.

Clearly, in order to understand the phenomenon of collaboration we must first study the form of government that existed in the occupied country prior to its defeat and identify the groups and/or individuals that the occupier might possibly approach. Let us not forget that in seeking collaboration he is looking for authority, and it is only from an examination of the operation of the government that he could tell which groups command this authority. Let us examine two cases.

First, let us assume that large and/or important segments of the population in a given country perceive the government as illegitimate and imposed at the expense of groups excluded from power. Where, in the context of illegitimate government, would future addresses of offers of collaboration be found? Among the groups excluded from power?

In the first place, those groups are not all equally attractive to the occupier from the point of view of commanding authentic support in the society. It is quite probable, and perhaps even inevitable, that among the excluded groups under authoritarianism (or totalitarianism) one would find some unpopular ones, whose isolation and destruction is often presented by the rulers as precisely the need that justifies authoritarianism. Thus, not every victim of illegitimate or authoritarian government is fit to inherit power from a deposed ruler and then proceed to exercise authority.

On the other hand, a quasi- or nonlegitimate government can rule only when it performs well and/or is capable of using the apparatus of coercion effectively. When it performs poorly and its ability to coerce has to be curbed, by the occupier for example, it is better for the latter to look for allies elsewhere. After the country has been conquered, its preconflict quasi- or nonlegitimate government can hardly make an acceptable offer of collaboration to the occupying power. What little loyalty it commanded in the past most certainly will not survive total military defeat.

Finally, social forces and leaders that were illegitimately excluded from power under prewar authoritarianism may be approached by the occupier with an offer of collaboration. But it is very unlikely that collaborators can be found among them. These leaders apparently were not willing to compromise with local authoritarianism before a military defeat; therefore one must be skeptical about their readiness to compromise with a hostile and ipso facto authoritarian foreign invader.

Let us, then, examine the case in which the prewar government in a given country enjoyed strong legitimacy. Where should the occupier search for collaborators now?

It is very unlikely that collaborators who are able to command some authority can be found outside the prewar establishment. By virtue of its legitimacy, only marginal, unimportant groups or groups recognized by the majority as hostile remain outside of the system. It would not be worth the occupier's time to seek their support because there would be a negligible difference in the cost of keeping the country under control with or without these groups' support.

On the other hand, it should be very profitable for the occupier to obtain in some form the support of the preconflict government. To be sure, interest in collaboration would be mutual. The help of the native central administration might be so valuable to the invader that he would be willing to grant large concessions in order to secure it, offering conditions under which the former government, or some part of the government structure, could cooperate without too much embarrassment. At the same time, the defeated government might want to minimize as far as possible the adverse consequences of its defeat; as a legitimate government, it has the capacity to absorb defeat and humiliation that a nonlegitimate government lacks. Thus it could function under conditions of limited sovereignty without losing the allegiance of its people in the process. It could afford, to a certain degree, to collaborate.

We may summarize the preceding discussion as follows: it is easiest, and at the same time, most rewarding, for the occupier to find collaborators within the political establishment of a country that enjoyed legitimate government prior to military defeat and occupation. Conversely, there is no immediately suitable candidate for collaboration in a country that did not have legitimate government prior to defeat, with the exception of formerly repressed minorities with irredentist sympathies. Such minorities, however, cannot command the obedience of the majority nationality in a given territory. A highly probable development in such a case would be territorial secession and establishment of a new satellite state in the areas populated by the ethnic minority.

This discussion posits as an assumption that the occupier enjoys perfect flexibility in choosing collaborators. In reality, this rarely will be the case, particularly in modern times, when conquests are no longer motivated primarily by greed but instead are justified in terms of some ideology that precludes the possibility of strictly pragmatic calculation in the choice of allies. Ideology imposes restrictions on rationality of choice. Typically, therefore, some groups living in the conquered territory will be a priori excluded from consideration as candidates for collaboration. For example, the functionaries of the Polish "bourgeois" state were summarily rejected by the Russians in the part of Poland they occupied in 1939, or, as already mentioned, the Jews would never be considered by the Germans in the territories they occupied. Such "ideological" considerations help to explain a choice of collaborators that would not follow from the paradigm we have established.

It follows from our paradigm that there was no suitable structural framework for collaboration in the Generalgouvernement. What made it even less likely that the occupiers would sponsor a collaborationist government was that the model of occupation, based on the principle of unlimited exploitation, specifically prohibited the Germans to contemplate granting any concessions to the subjugated populace. The logic of unlimited exploitation imposed no limits on the quality of sacrifices that could be requested of the subdued population, nor did it allow for justification of any delay in fulfilling them. To the extent that collaboration means that the occupying power seeks to employ in its service those local institutions that wield authority, the institutions must be allowed—on terms specified by the occupier—to exercise that authority. Within the unlimited exploitation model, they could not have this opportunity.

Nonetheless, perhaps because the logic of their own rule in the East was never stated definitely or, probably, even understood by the Nazis themselves, they made some half-serious explorations into the possibility of sponsoring a collaborationist government in the GG. Since the presence or absence of such government was a crucial factor for the plight of the occupied countries in Europe during the Second World War, I think that we should briefly describe these attempts to find collaborationists in Poland (even though we know that they were doomed to failure), for there was a certain internal logic in them.

"Sovereign" Poland

One possible solution for the Polish problem envisaged in the early days of the occupation by the Germans was the creation of a "token Polish state," a *Reststaat*. Two groups in Polish society were queried about their willingness to help in such a project.

In March 1939 the Germans had tried to get in touch with peasant leader Wincenty Witos, who at the time was in exile in Czechoslovakia after having lost his appeal in the Brześć trial. Witos immediately informed the Polish authorities about this incident and, partly as a result of German approaches, decided to come back to Poland, although he knew that he could be sent to prison on his return.

When the hostilities ended in October 1939, Witos was arrested shortly after being found by the Germans, along with many other Poles who had played prominent roles in public life before the war. The Gestapo sent him to the prison at Rzeszów, where he was apparently approached again with an offer of collaboration, which he refused. He also rejected a proposal that he write an "objective" history of the peasant movement, suspecting that such a work would primarily serve as a directory to ferret out all activists of the movement who had not been arrested thus far. In spite of his refusal to cooperate, the conditions of his confinement remained, to say the least, very liberal. In March 1941 he was permitted to return to his house at Wierzchosławice, where he remained until the end of the war, with the authorities periodically checking on him. Although this treatment was highly unusual, we should not attribute too much significance to Witos's fate. His survival was due, in all probability, more to some lucky coincidence than to a carefully designed policy. Nonetheless, it is worth noting that he was spared from death, the usual fate of members of the Polish leadership stratum and, indeed, of several other prominent leaders of the peasant movement itself.

It seems quite apparent—and Witos's fate is also indicative in this respect—that it was among the peasantry that the Germans were initially willing to look for collaborators. The *Völkisch* ethos naturally designated the peasants as virtually the only social class uncontaminated with either bourgeois or revolutionary influences. Also, it was in the countryside that the German armies were received with the least hostility. German officials must have taken this attitude into consideration when they prepared the internal memorandum stating that only with the support of the peasantry would Germany be able to set up a collaborationist regime in Poland.

Another group approached by the Germans with propositions for collaboration were prominent patricians and aristocrats with openly conservative views and a political tradition of loyalty and collaboration with the Austro-Hungarian monarchy before the First World War. Professor Stanisław Estreicher, the most prominent *Stańczyk,* was reported to have been contacted by the Germans. The names of Princes Zdzisław Lubomirski and Janusz Radziwiłł and that of Count Adam Ronikier were mentioned as other candidates consulted after Estreicher's refusal.

Thus the Germans approached a representative of the Polish peasant movement, the least hostile, from their point of view, of the three main political movements alienated from the Second Republic. They also appealed to conservative aristocratic elements, and were justified in doing so on two grounds: first, this class had a tradition of collaboration; second, the traditional ethos of noblesse oblige stresses the responsibility of the aristocracy for "its people" when in need and its obligation to protect them. One must take into account this attitude of the aristocracy in order to understand why Prince Janusz Radziwiłł, Counts Ronikier, Potocki, Plater-Zyberk, and Pusłowski, Countess Tarnowska, and others participated in the formation and works of the Rada Główna Opiekuńcza (Main Welfare Council).

The Sociology of Cooperation

Finding collaborationists and setting up a collaborationists' regime in an occupied country requires not only that there be candidates available for that task but, first of all, that a major political decision be made by the occupier. It is necessary for the occupier to recognize the sovereignty, however truncated, of the conquered nation and to maintain such conditions in the occupation that the population recognizes that this "sovereignty," even within its limits, is the lesser evil when compared with what could be. Otherwise, collaborationists become a liability instead of an asset. Rather than placating their people so that they will willingly give the occupier what he wants—to spare him the cost of taking it by force—they will require from the occupier protection from the wrath and contempt of their own people. In this case collaboration becomes absurd, the contrary of what was intended. But with or without collaboration, the newly acquired territory must be administered in some way. Whether or not the politicians are ready to make the major decisions, they must cope with the daily tasks of administration.

When we leave the political dimension, we move from problems of collaboration to problems of cooperation. The occupier, its own population mobilized for total war, simply lacks the personnel to effect and supervise the exploitation of conquered territories. He needs *manpower,* to assure the sheer physical presence of his "agents" wherever necessary, and *expertise,* as some tasks can be fulfilled only by people possessing special skills. In order to find qualified administrators, he must staff the ranks of the auxiliary administration with the local population.

The pattern of cooperation of the Polish auxiliary administration during the occupation appears to have differed according to whether the administration was required to provide expertise or manpower. This functional differentiation overlapped closely with division into urban and rural administration. In the countryside the Polish administration had little to do except to supervise the collection and delivery of the agricultural quotas set by the occupier. No special skills were needed to accomplish this assignment. On the other hand, city administrations were entrusted with the complex tasks of running large bureaucracies (the Warsaw city administration, for instance, had over 30,000 employees) and maintaining at an adequate level the numerous services indispensable to an urban population. Consequently, urban administration had to be staffed by "experts."

Depending on whether the auxiliary administration was retained to serve the German need for manpower or for expertise, its relationships with superordinates (the Germans) and subordinates (the local Polish population) were different. In the cities the administration was able to retain some degree of independence from the Germans, and because it provided services, it was not perceived by the local population as an unequivocally hostile transmission belt of German exploitation. In the countryside administrators did not enjoy either advantage. They were not entrusted with distribution of any kind of services to the rural Polish population but were instead charged with the supervision of German exploitation. As no expertise was required for this activity, the personnel in the administration was perfectly exchangeable and, therefore, totally susceptible to German control.

Employment in Local Administration

Immediately after the war was lost and the Polish state officially dissolved, all former employees of the public sector found themselves without sources of income, and in many cases without qualifications for anything but administrative jobs. An underground report on the activities of the occupation authorities between September 1939 and November 1940 notes that unemployment affected government employees more severely than any other workers. Employees of the local administration were considerably better off, the report states, because only 30 to 40 percent of them were jobless.

Such was the situation at the beginning of the occupation. Ultimately, however, and surprisingly, considering that there was no collaborationist government, a high number of "brain workers" (as they are called in Polish statistics) found employment in the public sector. At Nuremberg, Hans Frank testified that about 280,000 Poles and Ukrainians were employed as "government officials or civil service in the public services of the GG." This estimate is reasonably accurate.

In comparing the 280,000 employees in the public sector of the GG with the 385,000 before the war, we must remember that not all of Poland was under Frank's administration. Only half of Poland was in German hands before June 1941; the westernmost part of the country was incorporated into the Reich, and the GG originally included only about one-third of the former Polish territory, with about 45 percent of its former population. Even after the district of Galicia was added to the GG, considerable parts of Polish eastern territories were still not under Frank's administration, but under the Ostministerium. Given these facts, and keeping in mind that not until 1944 were 280,000 people employed in the auxiliary administration, we must recognize that, in spite of the dissolution of the Polish state in September 1939, the majority of those who in various capacities had served the state in central and local administration eventually found employment and were discharging public functions.

City Administration

The nation-state, its institutions and its structure, is, in Talcott Parsons's words, an "institutionalized normative culture." One of the universals of this normative culture—no matter how different its content might be from one nation-state to another—is that its citizens owe loyalty to its institutions. When a state is forcibly dissolved by some external agent, a threatening insecurity enters the lives of its citizens. They lose the concrete formulations of their normative orientation, the source of authority, and the specification of appropriate behavior in many of their interactions outside the most intimate circle of "meaningful others." Typically, the population has an additional burden to bear: a last moment appeal from the former authorities that they do not surrender to force, that they not recognize the authority of the occupier, that they continue to fight against him. How does one who wishes to follow such an appeal know what behavior is expected of him? Soldiers know that when captured they are to give personal information, serial number, and outfit, and that they do not have to answer any other questions. Later, when they arrive at a POW camp, they find clear and detailed sets of regulations that they have to follow. *But there is no comparable "defeat code" for civilians.*

Since people, naturally, want to live, preferably in peace, the dilemmas of two Weberian ethics come to the fore. Should one, for instance, accept the position of mayor in the local administration if it is offered by the occupier? Should people employed in the administration yield to pressure that they sign a statement swearing that in obedience to the occupier's administration they will conscientiously and faithfully discharge their functions and that they no longer consider themselves bound by their earlier oath of loyalty to the Polish state? Should members of the professions agree to sign such statements in order to obtain licenses to practice?

With the legitimate source of authority absent, and with a patently illegitimate authority demanding that people formally (by accepting positions offered to them) or symbolically (by signing oaths of allegiance) declare their recognition of its right to command, Poles faced with such decisions experienced dramatic conflicts. Furthermore, normlessness did not end even if one received approval from, say, the underground, and was allowed to acquiesce in initial German requests. Indeed, his new problems might be more subtle, difficult to handle, and frustrating, as they required that he, while on the job, constantly evaluate specific German requests and decide whether compliance was justified. The chief representative of the Polish underground in the country, the Government Delegate Cyryl Ratajski, reported to London on March 13, 1941: "Normalization of opinion in the society: "Normalization of opinion in the society: this is one of the most difficult tasks. Different social groups ask for my opinion in matters related to their professions—railmen, artists, doctors, employees of city administration, etc., and they demand that I inform them *what are the admissible limits of their cooperation with the occupier*. Through various social organizations I try to answer their queries, keeping in mind than an overhasty decision, which could not be complied with by the society, would harm the prestige of the office of the Delegate."

Normative void was one of the most painful consequences of the dissolution of the Polish state. People did not know how to behave when they were forced to interact with the occupier; they could scarcely be expected to make decisions on their own. They sought advice frantically, looking for others who indirectly could share responsibility with them, or simply for someone who would tell them what to do. But where could they turn for consultation and advice? Only during the latter part of the occupation did the underground become so firmly institutionalized that various groups and individuals had relatively easy access to its highest echelons.

It is important to note here that in these circumstances the Polish auxiliary administration in the cities was able to cope with the apparent normlessness better than many other professional groups in the society. How did this come to be so? In my opinion, it was an unanticipated consequence of the German policy of granting exemptions from labor conscription to those who worked in enterprises related to military production and in various agencies of the local government. Those persons caught in a roundup who could show an *Ausweiss* proving their employment in these organizations had (at least in the first few years) a good chance of being released instead of being sent to work in Germany or to a concentration camp. Consequently, employment in German-sponsored institutions, the source of good "identification papers" and therefore of relative security, was used for cover by the underground. The employment of members of the underground in the local administration and the consequent opportunity for the heads of that administration to be in permanent consultation with civilian underground authorities helped to reduce the normative ambiguity of that institution. It was very significant that those people who knew well priorities and requirements, stemming from their active participation in an organized collective effort to eventually regain independence, worked in agencies of the local administration. There they could engage in large-scale activities of dubious legality that depended on the knowledge and active support of relatively large numbers of employees. Both Julian Kulski and Stanisław Rybicki, the Polish mayors of Warsaw and Częstochowa, respectively, testified to the integrity and courage of their administrations.

Because certificate of employment in local government resulted in relative security, another social initiative developed that further contributed to strengthening the ability of the local government to cope with normlessness. Since the intelligentsia was threatened with extinction, Poles already serving in the city government created many new positions calling for "experts" and manual workers and tried to inflate the ranks of administration in order to provide not only income but also the valuable *Ausweiss* for members of the intelligentsia. As a consequence, local government, which had a direct and important impact on the functioning of the German occupation, was staffed with personnel unusually skilled, flexible, versatile, and ingenious. The very jobs that in normal times were performed by unimaginative clerks and bureaucrats were in wartime held by university professors, lawyers, politicians, officers, and high civil servants, who were by training and experience able to react promptly to unexpected and unusual events.

This pattern of recruitment helped to reduce the normative ambiguity experienced by employees of the local administration, who were exposed to contradictory pressures of the occupier's demands on the one side, and the population's needs on the other. In addition, as people like Kulski, Ivanka, and Rybicki testified, the high quality of professional services and expertise of the administration gave it a certain degree of independence, a certain prestige and power, vis-à-vis the Germans. By realizing that power within bureaucracies rested with "experts," they anticipated by some twenty years Crozier's analysis of the bureaucratic phenomenon. Thus, curiously, it seems as if the pressures of occupation made the Polish society adjust in a manner that Mancur Olson singled out as the most economical when he argued that the most critical commodity that permits a social system subject to unusually severe strains and shortages to survive is neither food nor raw materials but "skilled and versatile people."

The Auxiliary Administration in the Countryside

The reception given the invading German army in the countryside has not been a very fashionable theme in Polish historiography, which has tended by and large to picture the war period as one of heroic struggle by a united society against the "Hun invasion." Nonetheless, even in official published sources we find acknowledgment that the invader was not received in the same manner throughout the country, and that not all strata of Polish society participated in the underground struggle with equal zeal. Several sources specifically state that the German victory was received with joy by the peasants in certain areas and that the entering German army received a friendly greeting from the population in many ethnically Polish hamlets and villages. Of course, this warmth did not represent the predominant mood, but rather an extreme form of an attitude unique to the countryside, which stemmed from the peasants' alienation in prewar Poland. On the other hand, the occasional friendliness of the rural population was visible enough to have been reported in memoirs written several years later, against the general trend of "heroic" interpretation of the war period.

The Germans encountered few problems in their search for pliant local Polish administrators. Many farmers of German origin were will-

Table V.1

Nationality of Wójts and Mayors in the Generalgouvernement as of January 5, 1944

District	German	Polish	Ukrainian	Belo-russian	Gorale	Unknown	Total
Galicia	6	3	346	0	0	27	382
Cracow	36	188	59	0	5	81	369
Lublin	24	120	55	3	0	43	245
Radom	59	237	2	0	0	3	301
Warsaw	19	169	1	0	0	26	215
Total	144	717	463	3	5	180	1,512

Source: Madajczyk, 1970 v.1:222.

ing to join the DVL. In addition, many *Volksdeutsche* were recruited from families who had been forcibly resettled in the GG from the western parts of Poland that were incorporated into the Reich. These refugees usually knew German and therefore were assigned to intermediary positions as translators and auxiliaries between the German apparatus and the Polish population. After their resettlement they owned nothing but their jobs, and thus their livelihood depended on their ability to keep them. It is not difficult to understand how this dependence could have fostered servility toward the new masters. Local people frequently saw the newcomers meeting with the Germans—because they could speak to each other—which intensified their hostility toward them. In some areas this anger toward their countrymen was stronger than their hostility toward the Germans. Finally, the Gestapo not infrequently found confidants among the local population, and personal feuds, particularly disputes involving partitioning of inherited land, occasionally led people to denounce their kin or neighbors to the police.

Except when they wanted to promote ambitious new *Volksdeutsche* in the area, the Germans would usually leave the old *soltys* (village head) in his post, and he was smart enough to become aware that many candidates were eager to take his place. Therefore, he made sure that his performance satisfied the Germans. In fact, 73 percent of the *wójts* (chief administrative officers at the *gmina* [township] level) and mayors in the GG (excluding the district of Galicia) were Polish (see Table V.1).

The Polish administration in the countryside was caught in a very difficult situation. First, local government officials were totally visible to the Germans and fully replaceable, as no special skills were needed to run a rural hamlet. They could not disappear and hide, except in forests, leaving behind family and possessions. They were therefore totally dependent on the mercy of the local German gendarmerie and administration officials. Second, the only tasks assigned to local administrators involved exploiting the local population rather than rendering any service. They were only the last tool in the German system of imposing and collecting quotas of various articles from the Poles.

The alienation of Polish officials from the local population was increased when they were granted discretion on the village level in allocating the individual share of the imposed quotas that each farmer had to deliver. Thus, although they were powerless when it came to imposition of the total quota itself, local Polish officials possessed full power to help anyone on an individual basis. However, since they could not help everyone, it was easy for the population to perceive them as refusing to help anyone. To make matters worse, they were personally charged with selecting the people who were to go to work in Germany after the administration imposed "human quotas" on rural communities. Consequently, though powerless, the sołtys wielded *visible* power on the local level. Their position subsequently became more important—and more hated—as the German-imposed quotas were increased and the material conditions and security of life in the countryside worsened.

As we can easily imagine, this deterioration was largely blamed on the local Polish administration. It was not uncommon for a sołtys and his cronies to form a closely knit clique that exploited the situation for their own advantage, using their power to set each individual's share in the quotas to extract favors and bribes. Indeed, in numerous memoirs it is recorded that wealthier farmers, who could bribe the local administration, were exempted from making compulsory deliveries of foodstuffs and from being sent to Germany to work. Frequently, the local Polish administration on the gmina level imposed higher quotas than those actually set by the Germans in order to make sure that the real quota was fulfilled on time, and to leave room to make a profit by accepting bribes in exchange for lowering the quota set for individual villages or farmers. Delegate Jankowski mentioned these facts to a visiting courier from London, indicating that he intended to begin a campaign against abuses, as well as against other forms of demoralization among the Polish population that could be traced to the conditions of life under the occupation. With their function as administrators for the Germans confined to collections from the local population, and with delivery of services prohibited, the Polish auxiliary administration was increasingly viewed as a hostile force that had to be deceived and/or placated through bribes.

In a closely knit, intimate rural society, the local administration was in an excellent position to blackmail and extort favors because it knew precisely what resources each individual possessed. At the same time, peasants who fell into disgrace or were threatened could not simply change address and disappear in the street. So it was natural for the individual to sever his ties with the local community in order to make it more difficult for the Germans to extract information about himself and his affairs. One was now much less willing to share one's surplus with neighbors who suffered a shortage; one could no longer expect reciprocity, nor be sure that today's surplus would not be tomorrow's scarcity. The future was totally unpredictable—anyone at any moment could become the victim of a gendarme, a quota-collector, an angry neighbor making a denunciation, a bandit. Indeed, it was best, safest, to keep away from others. Mutual suspicions and mistrust developed, as did relationships based on immediate reciprocity: one had to "pay" on the spot. Mutual mistrust, however, generated some relief: since everyone was evading regulations, people hesitated to denounce one another because they were themselves vulnerable to denunciation.

I stated at the beginning of this chapter that one is likely to encounter a great variety of behavior in a society under occupation. It should be clear by now, however, that this variety is not unlimited. It is of particular interest that the regularities one may identify in the domain of political relationships between the occupiers and the occupied seem to be determined not so much by the moral character of individual actors as by the social space in which the actors happen to be living.

4

BERTRAM M. GORDON

Conclusion: Collaborationist Profiles

Interest in both resistance and collaboration has been strong in English-speaking countries since the early Forties. The reasons for this are instructive. There is plenty of material in the rich panoply of colorful characters on both sides to provide vivid heroes and villains. French fascism and anti-Semitism, unlike its German analogue, attracted leading intellectuals. Their writings were integral to the French literary world in a way unparalleled elsewhere. French fascism, like its counterpart, the French resistance, sold well in fashionable salons as well as in the streets. In addition, American and British intellectuals, especially on the left, have long held the intensely political debate among the French in high regard, even when they have not followed its cues. Furthermore, France, with its armies, navy and empire, its culture and economy, was the most important country in Western Europe to fall into the grips of the German juggernaut. What happened there shaped European history and the world beyond.

Historians are not agreed on the depth of fascism's roots in French society. No fascist movement did very well at electoral politics, but as antiparliamentarians, few French fascists chose to stand as candidates. Throughout the Thirties, and into the occupation, as Gordon's article makes painfully clear, the French fascists were never united. No charismatic leader like Hitler emerged; no disciplined party emerged to squash its opponents even if they were ideologically of the same ilk.

In the following selection, Professor Gordon examines questions relating to determining who the fascists were, their hopes, and their relationship to French political culture and history. In

Reprinted from Bertram M. Gordon: *Collaborationism in France During the Second World War*, pp. 326–346. Copyright © 1980 by Cornell University. Used by permission of the publisher, Cornell University Press.

the end the Germans, as he aptly states, outfoxed both the collaborationists in the Vichy government and those to its oppositional
radical right. Can we conclude that collaborationism was doomed
to fail because of its weaknesses? Or was it due to German guile
and ultimate control over the resources of food, production and
security upon which France's wartime fate hinged?

*We were soldiers. Many [members of the middle classes] were struck
by the fact that only the uniform permitted them to be fully accepted by
and on an equal footing with young workers and young peasants. We
were astonished in exercising the profession of arms to feel vibrating in
us tones we did not suspect existed.*
                    —François Gaucher, Combats, April 15, 1944

By all accounts the collaborationist movements represented a very
small if vocal proportion of the French population during the German
occupation. During the later months of 1943 and into the first half of
1944, however, they constituted one side of what has been called the
"Franco-French" war. Despite a statement made in 1944 by General de
Gaulle to the effect that there was no civil war in France at the time of
the Liberation, the Axis had its supporters to the end. In Paris, Marseilles, Nice, and other cities, collaborationist party memberships ran
into the thousands. By comparison, at the peak of Popular Front
strength in 1937, the Socialist party counted fewer than 3,000 members
in most of its *fédérations*. Memberships in French political parties has
traditionally been small, with the exception of the Communists, but
even here Gounand has pointed out, for example, that the RNP
[Rassemblement National Populaire (National Popular Union) formed
by Marcel Déat in 1941] membership in the Loiret department approximated that of the Communist party of 1935. Add to the RNP figures
those of its rivals, the PPF [Parti Populaire Français, organized in 1936
by the former communist Jacques Doriot], Francistes [an early French
fascist party begun by Marcel Bucard, a World War I veteran, in
1933], and MSR [Mouvement Social Révolutionnaire, established in
1940 as a nationalist and socialist, anti-Jewish organization by Eugène
Deloncle], and the picture of a significant collaborationist faction in
the Loiret emerges.

   Including the figures for Châteaubriant's Groupe Collaboration, a
rough estimate puts the total figure in the range of 150,000 to 200,000

for those involved in the movements of the collaboration over the entire four-year period. Although this figure includes some duplicate memberships, it clearly shows the importance of organized collaborationism in occupied France. Seen in this perspective, the Franco-French war must be viewed as a part of the larger European civil war between fascist and antifascist forces, both with roots deep within the Western cultural tradition. The defeat suffered by the collaborationists in 1944 and their total obliteration as a political force after 1945 constituted but one facet of the massive defeat suffered by fascism in World War II.

Wherever fascism developed it was spawned by crisis: rapid modernization and fears of social revolution, postwar economic and social dislocation after 1918, and real and imagined national grievances and ethnic resentments.

After 1934, France experienced demographic and economic decline, foreign threats, and a progressive discrediting of her parliamentary system which weakened her morale and social cohesion in advance of the 1940 collapse. Many in the aspiring middle classes saw avenues closed to them after 1934 by the depression, which the revolving-door cabinets of the Third Republic appeared unable or unwilling to curb. Younger, more enterprising Frenchmen often criticized a social order stalled by preindustrial economic structures and values with control in the hands of a generation that had come of age before 1914. As the moderate consensus cracked, France like other countries experienced a strengthening of the Left, in the form of the Popular Front, and the Right, in reaction.

By 1936 a new radical Right had formed, a coalition of outsiders who wanted to open wider the avenues to power and wealth in France without undermining the social order or threatening their private holdings. Included were new and dynamic business interests blocked by the petty proprietary economic structure of France, veterans and peasants in protest against deflationary policies, students who saw opportunities being closed to them, and intellectuals in quest of a political order with more panache. Added to these were elements of the white-collar middle and artisan lower-middle classes in fear of Communism and no longer trusting the parliamentary leadership to maintain social order. Some workers, confused and disillusioned by the gyrations of the Communist party which took on the cast of a Soviet tool, were also ready for the radical Right. It is hardly surprising that some began to look for solutions to the models provided by the fascist powers or that others might question the wisdom of and even the motives behind a strong anti-Axis foreign policy.

Fascism is a product of a society in deep crisis, and the shocks of the interwar years were insufficient to produce a movement in France with the strength of German National Socialism. The moderate consensus, although shaken, held when Daladier succeeded the Popular Front with a more conservative government. Many who had been won over to the leagues and parties of the radical Right deserted them in 1938, indicating less intense a disaffection in France than in Weimar Germany after 1929. The potent combination of modernizing business forces and antimodernist lower-middle classes which historically gave fascist movements their strength was mitigated by the relative economic backwardness of interwar France. In addition, the social conservatism of the radical Right offered little new to majority French opinion, which preferred the less turbulent and more traditional parties that comprised the centrist consensus. Their scope of effective activity circumscribed, the new radical Right movements of the interwar years dissipated much of their energy in fruitless internecine quarrels. A similar process was repeated during the occupation.

When the collapse of 1940 further discredited the parliamentary regime and the German occupation gave new life to the radical Right, the tendency toward political fragmentation inherited from the Third Republic was used by Vichy and the Germans to kill any potential chances for effective collaborationist action. By a political education that induced ideological rigidity and by their own interwar experience, the collaborationists were prepared only for oppositional dissidence. Unable to overcome their sectarian origins, Doriot and his rivals showed how weak a common ideology could be in the face of their own national traditions of political behavior.

The components of a strong fascist movement were all present within the collaborationist camp under the occupation. Big business, technocracy, and social engineering were represented prominently in Deloncle's MRS and were present in the other movements, particularly the Groupe Collaboration. Déat's RNP attracted white-collar and professional support, as did the Groupe Collaboration, and some workers. All the parties had lower-middle-class backing. The organizational skills of Doriot and his men combined with the social and academic respectability of the Groupe Collaboration and the doctrinal and propagandistic skills of Déat and Henriot would have produced a powerful force. Add the terrorists of Deloncle and PPF, Milice [literally, militia; an unofficial paramilitary force and collaborationist party; led by Joseph Darnand], and Franciste paramilitary forces and the result would have been potent. Speculation that all who actually joined the various factions would have also joined a unified movement is a luxury afforded the historian but it shows how French factionalism facilitated the work of the Germans in exploiting occupied France.

The inability of the collaborationist groups to unite was assured by Doriot's sectarian strategies. Doriot was the only Ultra leader with the political skill and personal charisma to play the role of fascist leader in the style of Mussolini or Hitler, and the PPF alone among its rivals possessed the will to power and the seasoned political cadres of a powerful fascist movement. Yet Doriot was unable to unify the radical Right, let alone the rest of France during the occupation. A source of political strength, the Communist origins of Doriot and his immediate entourage were also responsible for their political undoing. Their most natural clientele after 1940 consisted of anti-Communists but too many of these were unable to forget Doriot's past and a large number of his potential constituents perceived the PPF, whether correctly or not, as a turncoat opportunist movement. Anti-Communism, after all, was the hallmark of the French radical Right in general and the collaboration in particular. In his recent study of the collaboration, Pascal Ory points out that the French formed no anti-English legion as a parallel to the Anti-Bolshevik Legion, despite the direct attack by English ships upon the French fleet at Mers-el-Kébir in 1940. Radical Right anti-Communism was of a different order than were their other passions.

Career military men and others whose experiences in the trenches of the First World War oriented them toward the far Right could not forgive Doriot his leadership of the Communist campaign against the French military effort in the 1925 war against Abd-el Krim in Morocco. They preferred movements led by military heroes such as Darnand, Bucard, Constantini, and Jean Boissel. The military element was a vital component of fascist movements which Doriot was in general unable to attract. Another weakness of the PPF leader in terms of appeal to the Right was his well-known anticlericalism. Although Doriot attempted with some success a rapprochement with the church during the occupation, many of those who viewed the struggle against Communism as a latter-day Christian crusade opted for the more openly Christian warrior image of Darnand's Milice and to a lesser extent Bucard's Francistes. Paradoxically, while Doriot maintained a firm control over the policies of the PPF, refusing to cooperate with Ultra rivals except on his own terms, he was unable or perhaps unwilling to exert a similar control over his own more extreme and violent followers. The result drove some potential recruits to the milder and more respectable RNP and Groupe Collaboration. The RNP attraction for teachers is a case in point. The ability of Doriot's rivals to attract followings, however small, was a reflection of the PPF leader's inability to unite the radical Right into a single unified movement.

The failure of Doriot to unify the collaborationist camp gave free rein to the fractious tendencies at work in the French radical Right and facilitated the growth of rival movements. Several distinct although related profiles of collaborationism were allowed to emerge. Déat's RNP, especially after the departure of Deloncle, was a combination of professional, academic, and trade-union groups seeking to preserve at least some of the working-class gains made under the Popular Front and the secular French educational system against big business and clericalist interests in Vichy.

The temperamental affinity of the RNP for the more sedate Groupe Collaboration was manifested in the frequent sharing of public podiums by Déat and Châteaubriant at jointly sponsored cultural events. The Déatist activist was less likely to engage in political violence than was his PPF or Milice counterpart, a tendency borne out by the relatively lower proportion of RNP militants volunteering for service in the German armed forces. There were no RNP equivalents of the Milice campaigns against the maquis, campaigns that were sometimes joined by units of the PPF. RNP members who wished to fight against the Resistance had to join the Milice after 1943. Unlike its rivals, the RNP under Déat was not organized for combat. It did not pressure the Germans for arms with the kind of urgency put forward by the Milice, the PPF, and even some elements of the Groupe Collaboration after 1943.

The PPF scored more success among elements of the lower-middle classes, traditionally anti–big business, and prone to associate industrialization and finance capitalism with the Jews. The more dynamic personality of Doriot was reflected in the higher level of aggressiveness in PPF ranks as compared with the RNP. PPF militants, especially among the leadership corps, were more likely to be ex-Communists, although veterans of the Communist party were also found among the Francistes and the RNP. Nonetheless, the higher proportion of former Communists in PPF ranks gave the party a political militancy and sophistication together with the cynicism of the disillusioned and the fervor of the newly converted unmatched in any of its rivals. Doriotist and also Franciste street brawlers were reminiscent of incipient fascism in other countries and the German observer Grimm compared them to early Nazi fighters in Germany.

RNP leaders, in contrast, paid greater attention to organization of subsidiary affiliates and matters of party doctrine, called "national socialist" by Déat. Repeatedly during the occupation Déat pointed to his national socialism as a logical development of his interwar Neo-Socialism. Affected by his experience in the trenches, Déat shared with Doriot a pacifism which in the interwar years was directed primarily toward Franco-German relations. Interwar pacifists who later joined the collaborationist movements, more the leaders than the rank-and-file, might be called militarized pacifists. Pacifist by doctrine, at least with regard to Germany, they had become militarized in temperament by their experiences in the First World War. The phenomenon of the militarized pacifist was described aptly by the British psychologist Peter Nathan, who wrote in 1943:

> Who has not noticed the ferocity of our pacifists, who clench their teeth and fists when one argues with them? . . . Pacifism is the preoccupation with war and its horrors. It is true to say that the horrors of war are more ever-present to the pacifist than they are to the average soldier. May I tell you how to enrage a pacifist? Just tell him what I have been telling you, dig a little hole in his repressive armour. Then you will see with your own eyes the truth in what I have been saying, then you will see the fury, hate and temper which lie behind the total denial of oppression. It is almost the same thing: whether we make war on aggression or whether we indulge in it.

The ambiguities within the RNP closely paralleled those within its leader. Radical in rhetoric yet moderate in practice, Déat was a timid man, a model of ascetic behavior both as platoon leader in World War I and party leader during the occupation. His unwillingness to place the RNP in direct opposition to Laval until almost the end of the occupation marked Déat's timidity in action and his own personal motivation, largely the securing of a cabinet post. Similarly, intellectual timidity on the part of Darnand placed his Milice in the ambiguous position of defending Laval and Vichy while calling for a new fascist order. Unwilling to use the Milice in a real strike for power, Darnand allowed himself and his friends to be exploited in the interest of others. Recruited to preserve order against the Resistance and especially the Communists in the latter stages of the occupation, Milice paratroopers incarnated the contradictory ideals of social order and the incipient fascist spirit of revolt. This contradiction weakened a Milice circumscribed by identification with Vichy, association with the German occupation authorities, and the growing strength of a Resistance associated with the ideal of a renascent independent France. The most discerning Miliciens may have been those who sought to use the organization for their own personal gain. The visceral collaborationism practiced by the Milice lacked the intellectual vision of Déat and his *instituteurs* [instructors] in the RNP.

Opposed in temperament to Déat was Deloncle, who with his MSR supporters was among the most reckless within the collaborationist camp. Recruited in large part, although not exclusively, from the ranks of the conspiratorial *Cagoule* [a secret, conspiratorial fascist organization; Cagoule means "Hood"; founded by Eugene Deloncle] the MSR in the image of its leader comprised the *condottieri* of the collaboration in 1941. During the brief period of Deloncle's association with Deat and the RNP, the more adventurous and violent members looked to the MSR chieftain, whom they followed out of the RNP in November 1941. In its combination of the Saint-Simonian [Claude-Henri Comte de Saint-Simon (1760–1825), a visionary of a technocratically organized society] technocratic tradition, the Blanquist [Louis-Auguste Blanqui, nineteenth century French revolutionary] proclivity toward coups and terrorism, and Renaissance *condottiere* adventurism, the MSR most clearly combined the modernistic and atavistic traits that gave fascist movements much of their appeal to Europe's counterrevolutionaries.

Having acquired a certain allure from his days as head of the *Cagoule,* Deloncle attracted urban brawlers and mad bombers, giving to his movement the quality of technology gone wild. The dynamiting of Parisian synagogues, which alienated many whose support Deloncle would need in a mass movement, was the work of a gang rather than an organized political party such as Déat's RNP or the PPF. No movement headed by Deloncle could seriously hope to govern France, but the existence of his MSR and Bucard's Francistes deprived Doriot of potentially valuable cadres and shock troops. An excellent military tactician, Deloncle would have functioned most effectively heading the paramilitary arm of a party, as he did briefly with the RNP. Egotism and paranoia prevented him from attracting and retaining the men he needed to build a party organization and provide it with even a rudimentary political doctrine.

The virulence and violence of the MSR were matched, although in a different way, by Bucard's Francistes. They were street fighters and marchers, practitioners of minor acts of violence in public view, compared with Deloncle's bombers and conspirators, who practiced major acts of violence in secret. The Francistes developed the cult of personality to its highest degree. Virtually all that kept the small band together was a fierce loyalty to Bucard, the man "who was never wrong" according to their slogan during the occupation years. Resplendent in his uniform with ten medals, Bucard was nonetheless an ineffectual leader, and his followers were limited primarily to peddling copies of the party newspaper on the streets of Paris and the other large cities of France. Selling newspapers gave them ample opportunity for scuffling with Jews, anti-Germans of all kinds, and most frequently the members of rival collaborationist groups.

Organized in 1933 as an openly fascist party, the Francistes felt events had proven their wisdom and resented newer and larger rival groups, whom they called opportunists. More than their rivals, the Francistes retained the violent spirit of the early Italian Fascist slogan "me ne frego" (I don't care), and their combativeness earned for them the grudging respect even of their rivals in the Ultra camp. Bucard, however, did not know what to do with his troops, who even more than the militants of the RNP and PPF came from the ranks of those without prior political experience. To a greater degree than their larger rivals, the Francistes were openly imitative of the Axis parties and lacked roots in French political traditions.

The collaborationist groups whose centers were in Paris shared a clientele there and in the other cities and towns of the northern zone. Although the PPF, Francistes, and some of the smaller Ultra parties extended into the southern zone before 1942, the presence of the German forces favored their development north of the demarcation line. The north was also more industrialized, producing more of the rapid social transformations that were conducive to the growth of the radical Right in Europe. In contrast, Darnand's Milice, a southern zone product, even after many of the original SOL [Service d'Ordre Légionnaire, a forerunner of the Milice] personnel had dropped out in opposition to the move toward collaboration, continued to reflect a more provincial spirit and a more pronounced Catholic traditionalism than its northern rivals. The mission of the Christian crusader was manifested in a more pronounced fashion in *Combats,* the Milicien newspaper, than elsewhere in the Ultra camp. The good soldier Darnand and the anti-Bolshevik crusader Henriot well represented the Milice ideal, although by 1944 Milicien ideas, like those of the Paris-based Ultra groups, had been radically compromised by the actions of many of the members. The political naïveté of Darnand and his lieutenants, which allowed the Milice on occasion to be infiltrated by the PPF, was an indication of the difference in the worldliness of the Milice as contrasted to the PPF. Darnand's men never aroused in German circles the fears expressed concerning Doriot and the PPF.

Despite differences in political origins, doctrinal nuance, and style, the collaborationist movements resembled one another far more than they differed. Generalizations about the composition of camps in civil wars are always difficult in view of the influences of personality, connections, and opportunity in directing the orientation of individuals. Jean Bassompierre, a leader of the Milice who also fought in the Anti-Bolshevik Legion, lost a brother fighting against the Germans. Most members of the collaborationist parties came from the so-called "popular" classes of the cities and towns. These included artisan and merchant lower-middle-class elements who during the interwar years had supported Action Française [an antidemocratic and anti-Semitic newspaper and organization founded in 1908 by Charles Maurras and others] and the Croix de Feu [an anti-Communist veterans' league founded in 1927 by Col. François de la Rocque.] but after 1940 were more willing to follow Germany than were Maurras and de la Rocque. Drawn to collaborationism by anti-Communism and often anti-Semitism, they formed large proportions of all the Ultra groups with the exception of Châteaubriant's Groupe Collaboration. These were the historically moderate centrist elements, which threatened by industrialization turned sharply to the Right in France, as elsewhere in Europe.

The RNP was able to make some limited inroads in its recruitment of workers with its appeals by Georges Dumoulin and others who had opposed the prewar CGT's [Confédération Générale du Travail, France's major trade union organization, dissolved during the occupation] alliance with the Communists under the Popular Front. Those workers who did join the RNP, however, did so as individuals rather than in groups and although Déat's party drew a higher proportion of workers than did its rivals, they remained a minority within the ranks of the movement. Doriot's PPF showed more success in attracting some big names from the Communists after 1939 but relatively few rank-and-file Communists followed them. The social composition of the PPF did not differ markedly from the make-up of its smaller rivals. Indeed, the fact that so many within the collaborationist camp switched parties during the four-year occupation and the numerous instances of cooperation among the Ultra parties on the local level, most prominently in Tunisia but also in metropolitan France reflect the basic similarities in their constituencies. The collaborationist cause attracted the middle-class outsiders of interwar French political life: dissidents of the Right, anti-Communist dissidents of the Left, the young, some businessmen on the make, all those who wished to replace the social and political elites without restructuring the social order.

The collaborationist movements shared certain traits which separated them intellectually and politically from the Resistance and resembled those of other fascist movements in Europe. They all stood for social order and paid at least lip service to conventional moral norms in France even if these were sometimes honored in the breach. Many came from families in which the father had had a military career, leading to a staunch Pétainist paternal political outlook after 1940. Intolerant of ambiguity, some of the sons and daughters of these military men took off from Pétainism to full ideological collaborationism, undoubtedly further than the cautious old marshal wished to go. Nonetheless, Pétain's call for collaboration at the time of the Montoire meeting with Hitler in October 1940 cloaked even the most fanatic of the collaborationists in his mantle. Darnand and many other collaborationists, especially in the Milice and Francistes, believed that they possessed the open approval of the marshal.

Another characteristic of many of the collaborationists was their Catholic fervor, which more often than not was translated into support for the struggle against Communism on the Eastern front and at home. Henriot, Darnand, and many of their Milicien followers from the smaller towns of the southern zone represented a Christian fascism, different in tone from the more secular spirit of Doriot's PPF and Deat's RNP. It is not surprising that in Catholic France, there were many Catholics in the collaborationist movements but there seems to have been a proportionately large number of collaborationists strongly grounded in Catholic education. Darnand and Bucard are examples from among the leaders.

Fascism in general held a special appeal for renegade Catholics searching for a total world view and ritual they could substitute for that of the church. The Milice was particularly oriented toward Catholic ritual and tradition and even pronounced anticlericals such as Doriot and Déat made their peace with the church. (Déat died in exile in the arms of the church ten years after the war ended.) The concept of the Christian warrior or the medieval crusader, evident in the Waffen-SS and movements such as the Rumanian League of the Archangel Michael, was most manifest in the Milice, whose ceremonies and oaths taken on one's knees recalled those of the church. While many members of the Resistance opposed Vichy and the Germans on the grounds of Christian conscience, the image of the crusading Christian knight belonged to the Milice. Milice ideologues called for a rejuvenation of "decadent" France through the appropriation of the Christian crusading tradition and an emulation of the Spartan society they saw in Nazi Germany.

Writers such as Drieu la Rochelle and Brasillach looked toward a new homo fascista to be generated by the Axis conquest of Europe, but they were exceptional and their ideas cannot be said to have been representative of the rank-and-file or even the leaders of the collaborationist parties. Among the volunteers for the Waffen-SS, the number who wanted to become Nietzschean supermen in a Wagnerian New Europe were in the minority. The neopagan Nietzschean warrior fought side by side in the Waffen-SS with the Milicien Christian crusader. The French Ultras reflected as a whole the ambivalence of fascism with respect to the Christian tradition.

Most of those who turned to collaborationism did so in order to improve their situations in France or perhaps gain a measure of revenge against local political enemies. Most were political outsiders, either totally inactive politically or frustrated in their political endeavors during the years between the wars. Examples of the latter include virtually all the collaborationist leaders. Doriot and Déat had failed to convert the Communist and Socialist parties, respectively, to their views and had been expelled. Darnand, denied an officership after World War I, and Bucard, who failed as a political protégé of Tardieu in 1924, both turned against a Republic which had thwarted their ambitions.

Although many in France collaborated with the Germans under the occupation, collaborationism as an ideal was unable to make substantial progress among the public even during the heady days of 1940 and 1941. Large numbers of Frenchmen blamed the Republic for the military defeat and the alleged moral and spiritual decay that had preceded it. They were ready for something new. Pétain and Laval, however, were able to capture the support of most of those who claimed that France required an authoritarian state based on conservative values to repair the damage of 1940. The National Revolution enunciated by Vichy in 1940 incorporated many of the values of the collaborationists and had the appearance of being more French and less under the influence of the occupying power. Indeed, none of the collaborationists attacked the National Revolution as such; rather they argued as late as 1944 that it was yet to be achieved and could be accomplished only under their auspices.

The concepts of the National Revolution themselves were never fully clarified and were subject to a variety of interpretations. There was sufficient identity, however, between the goals of the National Revolution and those of the Ultras—the authoritarian state, a corporate society into which the proletariat was to be "reintegrated" without revolution, a moral renovation of France, and some degree of integration into the New Order—for Vichy and not the Ultras to attract the traditional elites and the majority of French opinion in 1940. Pétain belonged to the men of Vichy and not the Ultras who had nothing to counter his personal prestige. Collaborationism could attract only those who shared many of the goals enunciated in Vichy but were for various reasons dissatisfied with the men or policies of the regime. It was, so to speak, a legal opposition, but when large-scale opposition to Vichy did develop, it took the direction of the Resistance. As German pressure for French wealth and manpower intensified, the prospect of increased collaboration offered little to most Frenchmen. The collaborationists remained a small group of ideologues, adventurers, and bandits.

Those who argued for collaboration in 1940 were strengthened by the "correct" behavior of the Wehrmacht, which came as a relief to many terrified French civilians. The apparent totality of the German victory made even the most ardent collaborationists seem prudent in the summer of 1940. As the war progressed, opportunists of all kinds were attracted to the movements of the collaboration and each undoubtedly had its share. Denunciations and profiteering were commonplace. The many letters secretly denouncing Jews, Freemasons, and other enemies of Vichy and the Axis reflected a society in disarray. The loss in social cohesion during the interwar period had been manifested in a similar wave of epistolary denunciation at the time of the revelations of *Cagoulard* conspiracies in 1937. Hundreds of letters, many written anonymously accusing people of concealing bombs and guns, were received by the Paris Police Prefecture alone.

Members of the Ultra movements informed on the Resistance and, as was pointed out in many postwar trials, facilitated German police action. The most sinister manifestations of collaboration, for example the Bonny-Lafont gang which blackmailed Frenchmen and served the Germans as an auxiliary police in Paris, usually functioned independently of the political parties, although individuals may have been involved in both. The ranks of those who collaborated with the Germans included criminals in it for the money or for personal revenge but also men such as Jean Fontenoy of the MSR, François Sabiani, the son of the PPF mayor of Marseilles Noël de Tissot of the Milice, and other personally disinterested warriors who lost their lives at the Eastern front. For some, especially the leaders who had been excluded from positions of power before the armistice, enhanced opportunities for wealth and careers went hand in hand with political beliefs.

If Vichy has been called the "revenge of the minorities" of the traditional Right against the Republic, the collaborationists represented a new plebeian radical Right, claiming intellectual roots going back to Rousseauist ideas interpreted by the Jacobins of 1793. Déat repeatedly evoked the totalitarian qualities of Jacobin rule while ignoring its message of liberty. Collaborationists often pointed to intellectual roots in the ideas of Proudhon, La Tour du Pin, Sorel, Péguy, Barrès, and Maurras. The Bonapartist tradition was invoked by most collaborationists, who found Napoleon particularly to their liking, seeing in him a precursor to Hitler's attempt to unify Europe and defeat Russia. Concepts of plebeian dictatorship, charismatic leadership, nationalism, militarism, and social welfare without revolution were all present in the Bonapartist tradition to which Barrès and others brought ethnocentric anti-Semitism. Ultra anti-Semitism looked also for inspiration to Drumont and the enemies of Dreyfus. In the words of Robert Soucy, a leading student of French fascism:

If French fascism was influenced by other fascisms, it also had a national past of its own; consequently, in many instances developments abroad merely served to fortify a set of pre-existing attitudes at home. Moreover the fact that fascism failed to achieve mass public backing in France hardly demonstrates that it was an ideology non-indigenous to that country. A political party need not win popular support to be rooted in several of its country's political traditions. Were this not so it might be said that Hitler's Nazi party was "un-German" because it lacked mass public support before the onset of the depression.

The radical Right became the terrain for a group of old Left and old Right dissidents against the elites of the parliamentary system and their own oppositional movements. The ex-Communist Doriot, who opposed the 1925 war against a colonial revolt in Morocco, went off to fight Communism in the Soviet Union and spoke out repeatedly for French imperial interests. Déat could not countenance the spilling of French blood over Danzig in 1939 but four years later his position had changed diametrically. The same Déat who had participated with the Grand Rabbi of Paris in a 1935 rally to protest German harassment of Jews took a very different stand after 1940 when German anti-Semitic policies had been vastly increased in tenor and scope. His progression away from human rights may be read in his journalistic campaign against Château, his former colleague who had remained more true to his earlier ideas. Doriot allowed his anti-Communism after 1934 to consume him to the point where his PPF hardly differed in its goals after 1940 from its rivals of a more rightist pedigree.

The collaborationist movements all described their goals in terms of "socialism," as did most interwar and wartime fascist and national socialist movements. Their socialism was to be moralistic and spiritual rather than structural. All classes were to transcend their differences and work together in harmony for the greater good of the fatherland. Making such socialism attractive was more difficult for the collaborationists in France as their concept of the national good entailed working for or with a hostile occupying power, perceived as a national enemy by the majority of the French. It is one of the ironies of the occupation that the collaborationist movements, seen as treasonous by many of their compatriots, referred to themselves collectively as the "national opposition."

Having inverted the term "national," the collaborationists did the same to the word "socialism." To them it became an emotive word, a call for unity in difficult times. Suffering from a kind of anomie, a feeling of powerlessness and of being cast adrift in a rapidly changing mass society with traditional human ties destroyed, many in the middle classes subconsciously envied what they perceived as proletarian cohesiveness and sense of historical mission. In his statement quoted at the beginning of this chapter, the Milicien François Gaucher articulated a middle-class sense of social dislocation that only a uniform could overcome. As part of a revolutionary political party or a trade union, the worker appeared to have a sense of belonging, knowing his place in the larger unfolding of history. This human solidarity or, more accurately, the perception of it, had a powerful appeal to frightened members of the middle and lower-middle classes, the "losers" in the process of industrialization, to use Wolfgang Sauer's term.

Among the fragmented middle classes of twentieth-century Europe, many hoped to appropriate working-class solidarity without proletarian status. They hoped to emulate the "revolution from above" made when a defeated Prussia under Baron vom Stein had borrowed the mobilizing power without the liberty and equality of the French Revolution. The key word was "socialism," which fascist and national socialist ideologues and propagandists freely used. They transformed the meaning of the word, using it for their own purposes as the Prussians did with the meaning of the French Revolution. In so doing they stripped "socialism" of its revolutionary content and gave it a moralistic meaning acceptable to middle-class outsiders seeking to climb rather than discard the social ladder. Tamed in this way, "socialism" became an acceptable substitute for the far more threatening Communism of Marx and Stalin.

In France after 1940 "socialism" offered the added benefit of providing a point of unity for a society riven by deep political divisions and needing to unite in the face of the German occupation. Each collaborationist faction preached "socialism" to unite the French under trying conditions but the very multiplicity of their organizations and the way in which they were used by the Germans worked in the opposite direction. In France as in Italy, the unity sought vainly by fascism was achieved only in resistance to it.

The PPF evoked the tradition of the Communards of 1871 who had also attempted to strike for power while under German guns. In 1871, however, socialists of many different kinds had fought together and no one ethnic group was targeted for opprobrium. The rights fought for in

1871 were still universal, transcendent, to use the concept of Ernst Nolte. By 1940 the situation had changed drastically. A generation of French who had known the privations of the 1914–1918 war had come of age in a society that offered at best limited prospects for material and social advancement in the interwar years. To the middle-class popular base of the Ultra factions, collaboration offered the right balance between adventure and protection under the occupation. Those who joined the PPF and its rivals were no longer trying to make a revolution but rather trying to stave one off, although employing the means used by "red" revolutionaries. For the collaborationists were France's fascists, far more clearly than the members of Action Française, which Nolte saw exemplifying fascism in France.

To the radical Right in occupied France, those who wished to abort the "red" revolution by means of a dynamic countermovement of their own, Germany provided an example, especially formidable after 1940. France would be given a hierarchical society in which opportunity would be open to talent, like the army. A new toughened generation would take its rightful place at the helm of the French state and in the positions of economic control. The colored shirt or uniform symbolized youthful camaraderie: all would belong to the community.

Those excluded before 1940 would receive their just rewards in the new society; presumably Darnand would receive his previously denied military commission. France's martial tradition, tarnished in 1940, would be restored and enhanced, primarily through the service of volunteers in the German armed formations and also through France's colonial empire. All of this was to be achieved in a New Europe of united and virile peoples, led by the Germans, who, the collaborationists repeated ceaselessly, would "dominate" their victory, that is, use their military victories for the good of all Europeans. In defeat France would find a European if not a world mission which, according to the collaborationists, she had been unable to do in victory in 1918. Solutions to the problems of 1940 were all too easy for the collaborationists. Their plans required gaining for France the respect of the Germans but this could be won only through a cohesiveness and strength which neither the collaborationist parties nor France as a nation possessed after 1940.

Even without the impediments placed in their way by the Germans, the collaborationists could have expected at best a difficult time after 1940. The reasons for the relatively poor showing of fascism in interwar France as compared with Central Europe are well known. France had been spared the worst of the economic ills that had befallen Italy after World War I and Germany in 1923 and again six years thereafter. French society was more stable than her neighbors' in Central Europe and there were fewer *déclassés* in France than in Germany. The French lacked the keen edge of resentment caused after 1918 by Italian "mutilated peace" and German "stab in the back" legends. More basic was the political culture of France, steeped in the revolutionary principles of 1789.

Déat's attempt to tie twentieth-century totalitarianism to Rousseau and the spirit of 1793 and PPF associations with Communard traditions failed to overcome the libertarian and egalitarian ideals so closely associated with France. The precepts of 1789 had been inculcated for generations into French school children in the lay schools of the Republic and had become an integral part of France's national identity. The Axis regimes were perceived increasingly as antipathetic to French political traditions and a threat to her national interests as well. The parliamentary regime had absorbed the impact of the right-wing threat by 1938, and when toppled in 1940 was replaced by the Vichy regime, less fascist-inspired and more deeply rooted in the traditions of the mainstream French Right.

As strident as their calls for national strength might be, it was impossible for collaborationists to avoid the stigma of being perceived as in the service of an enemy with whom France was still legally at war after 1940. They might have been installed as puppet rulers by the Germans but it is difficult to imagine them winning any more popularity in that fashion than Quisling did in Norway. The French collaborationist leaders shared with confrères such as Quisling the quality of being so far beyond the mainstream in their view of Germany as to have been entirely incapable of understanding the anti-German mood of the majority of their compatriots, especially as the war progressed.

From Hitler down, the German leaders outfoxed their would-be allies in France. To win their new world the collaborationists were required to strike a Faustian bargain, selling their souls to the devil. The German Mephistopheles in 1940, however, was far shrewder than his French acolytes. Hitler's offer of an armistice and a measure of sovereignty to the French government went a long way toward compromising much of France's social and political elite, but they at least held real domestic power in the southern zone until 1942. The collaborationists were proportionately more compromised and received far less in return. They got none of the power they had anticipated after the armistice, but the days of reckoning came anyway, after August 1944, with the liberation of France and the explosion of the pent-up wrath of their compatriots. Hitler had played a monstrous hoax on those whose desire had been to bring France into his New Order. He had undermined their very reason for existence, as in his refusal to support Doriot's quest for power in 1942. Small wonder that many of the collaborationists simply refused to believe the reality of German policy, a reality whose existence is still denied today by some survivors of the Ultra camp.

Hitler's policy toward France was consistent in the years before the war and after the armistice. Playing shrewdly upon the fragmentation he knew existed in the French body politic, Hitler exploited divisions within the collaborationist ranks to prevent any one movement from becoming too powerful. He used the entire collaborationist camp as a lever with which to exert pressure when needed upon official Vichy and turned to the collaborationists only when Pétain and Laval refused to cooperate. The significance of the collaborationists lay not in their strength but in the fact of their existence, demonstrating the presence of fascism, even if in a weakened form, in France.

As the war continued and German pressure for French manpower and wealth was intensified, the Resistance grew and collaborationists were targeted for elimination. Some tried to slip quietly back into private life; the more militant and aggressive ones took up arms and fought in the Milice or the PPF formations. Some of the younger ones, especially those who fought in the German armed forces and after August 1944 no longer had a homeland to which to return, took pride in the ostracism they received from their compatriots. In the Milice at home and in the Charlemagne Division fighting in eastern Germany, the younger brothers and associates of the "realists" of 1940 had become the wild-eyed romantic fanatics of 1944, no closer than ever to real political power.

Some one or two hundred thousand French, the manifestation of an evolving radical Right during the occupation, actively identified their own interests and those of France with Hitler's New Order. Anti-Communist, anti-Freemason, anti-Semitic, opposed to the direction taken by modern history in France and Europe, they looked to the National Socialist New Order to open doors previously closed to them. Shaken

less severely than her neighbors by the economic disruptions and social dislocations that followed World War I, France remained more
resistant but hardly immune to the growth of fascism. The 1940 disaster opened up new possibilities promptly squandered by the radical
Right. Half a dozen competing political parties claimed the inheritance
of the radical Right in France. Each asserted its native roots, intellectual and political, in the French soil. The existence of so many of them,
in view of the fractious political tradition of Republican France, justified their claims.

5

Michael R. Marrus

The Final Solution

The civilized world experienced shock in late 1944 and early
1945 as German concentration and death camps were opened by
Allied armies. They revealed the extent to which catastrophe had
fallen upon Europe's Jews and millions of their fellow citizens.
The particular emphasis placed by the Third Reich upon making
Europe Jewish-free through extermination, however, soon re-
ceded from public consciousness. General histories in succeeding
decades often made no mention of the fate of Jews; the word
Holocaust was not a part of the general vocabulary for describing
these years. Since the 1960s that has changed, slowly, but with
increasing force, as studies on many aspects of the destruction of
European Jewry appeared. It is not the place here to review what
has been achieved, nor to outline the main lines of debate. For

that the reader should turn to one of the recent general introductions listed below.

Of special and continuing interest among historians and lay readers alike, however, is the debate between what has been called the *functionalist* and the *intentionalist* approaches to understanding the origins of the decision to impose a Final Solution to the "Jewish Question," that is, mass, industrialized and systematic murder of an entire classification of people. In the following selection Michael Marrus examines the debate in some detail. It relates not only to our understanding of the nature of the Third Reich, Hitler as leader, and the Nazis as followers, but also to issues of how we understand the functioning of any regime. At the same time we must be on guard against obscuring the crimes and the criminals and the suffering of their victims under a mass of analysis. Historical analysis can only go so far; if the Holocaust can ever be represented to those who cannot know it first hand, it will be through the testimonies left behind in diaries, art and literature.

The term *Final Solution (Endlösung)* first appeared as Nazi terminology, used by Germans themselves to designate their policy toward Jews. But what did the Nazis means by these words? And what was the reality behind the phrase they employed? We must take care, in answering, lest we apply our own understanding, invariably associated with European-wide deportations and death camps. For while this undoubtedly *became* the Final Solution, this was not what those who first used these words with respect to Jews intended to convey. As we shall see, the stated objectives of the Third Reich changed over time. A look at how this particular term entered the Nazi lexicon raises the important question of why this occurred and how decisions on the Jews were made in the Third Reich.

... 1938 marked the intensification of persecution of Jews in Germany, with a new round of violence and a drive to expel Jews from the recently expanded Reich. In January 1939, the German Foreign Office told its representatives abroad about the "necessity for a radical solution of the Jewish question," referring also to the long-term goal as "an international solution." At the time, however, to quote the document further, "the ultimate aim of Germany's Jewish policy [was] the emigration of all Jews living on German territory." By "international solution" the Foreign Office meant a negotiated settlement with receiving countries, according to which Jews would leave Germany, possibly taking a pittance of their property with them. Eight months later, just after the German conquest of Poland, Reinhard Heydrich alerted his SS Einsatzgruppen to a forthcoming "final aim" *(Endziel),* which would require extensive periods of time. Heydrich also referred to "planned total measures," which were "to be kept strictly secret." His communication indicates that some sort of vast population movement was contemplated, for one of the purposes of the instructions was to concentrate Jews in large urban areas, at rail junctions, and along railway lines.

As a habitual programmatic short form, *final solution,* or *Endlösung,* may have first appeared in June 1940 in the context of a "territorial final solution" *(territoriale Endlösung),* and clearly linked with evolving schemes for massive forced emigration of Jews to the island of Madagascar, in the Indian Ocean, off the east coast of Africa. At the Jewish desk of the Foreign Office, Franz Rademacher used the phrase in this sense in September of the same year, when he was drafting concrete plans for installing the Jews in Madagascar and planning a visit to the island to map out details. The term appeared increasingly in the first half of 1941 and was mentioned notably by SS bureau chief Walter Schellenberg on 20 May, when discussing Jewish emigration priorities for the SS across Europe. As then understood, the "final solution" had to await the end of the war—the defeat of Great Britain and the definitive settlement of affairs with France through a peace treaty. Early in the Russian campaign, a few months later, the language shifted once more. On 31 July 1941, there was a new, urgent reference in a telegram from Hermann Göring to Reinhard Heydrich, head of the vast SS police apparatus. Göring now instructed Heydrich to begin substantive preparations for a "total solution [*Gesamtlösung*] of the Jewish question in the German sphere of influence in Europe," considering this to be "the intended final solution of the Jewish question." The pace quickened thereafter. In a letter of 28 August Adolf Eichmann referred to an "imminent final solution" as "now in preparation." There was mention once again of a "final solution" at the Wannsee Conference of January 1942, with every indication that it was now underway. Calling the meeting to order, Heydrich told the assembled "Jewish experts" from across Europe that Göring had placed him in charge of preparations for "the final solution of the Jewish question" and that implementation was to be directed through Himmler's office. The time for waiting was over.

Most historians agree that with this meeting, European-wide mass murder emerged as the essence of the Final Solution. I shall now examine how historians have understood the evolution of this particular "solution" to this point, given that the Nazis seemed in earlier times to lean in quite another direction, and given the frequent reference to other kinds of "solutions"—nonmurderous, at least in Pan-European terms—that were apparently taken seriously within the Nazi hierarchy.

The Nazis' own records provide little help. Typically, Hitler and his lieutenants cloaked their most criminal activities in euphemistic language, tried strenuously to keep their murderous plans secret, and were notoriously vague in delimiting lines of authority, especially on the most sensitive issues. Beyond this, Hitler had a positive aversion to orderly procedures and almost never discussed various policy options with his subordinates. As opposed to his British counterpart, Winston Churchill, who left mountains of documents, ruminating endlessly on possible courses of action, the Nazi dictator was reluctant to commit himself to paper with concrete ideas and preferred always to give orders orally, sometimes even then avoiding detailed instructions. As a result, important German officials were used to living with ambiguities and imprecisions on important issues, especially those in which the Führer had shown a special interest. At the top of the Nazi hierarchy, high-ranking Nazis were accustomed to Hitler's procrastination, particularly on the most difficult or dangerous problems. Further down, Nazi underlings avoided asking questions, especially when, as was often the case in the Third Reich, policy lines depended on ideology rather than empirical evidence, and hence could veer off in unexpected directions. On sensitive issues it was unwise to take policy initiatives before the Führer made up his mind.

In the absence of a clear record of Hitlerian decision making on the Final Solution, interpretations have varied considerably. In a book published in 1977, British writer David Irving even suggested that the Führer had nothing to do with the matter. Building his case on the inability of historians to discover written orders from Hitler to kill all the Jews of Europe, Irving contended that the Führer was not responsible for anti-Jewish policy at all, was basically uninterested in Jews, and knew nothing about their terrible fate—at least until 1943. As a chorus of reviewers immediately pointed out, however, this contention not only ignored Hitler's hate-filled rhetoric about Jews, it also disregarded reports on the killings destined for him, plus the repeated state-

ments of his underlings, including Himmler, that policy was determined at the highest level, by the Führer himself.

What was particularly mischievous about Irving's argument was the
notion that without explicit, written orders, it was impossible to assign
responsibility for the Final Solution. Numerous critics have made clear
that such orders were probably not necessary at all to begin the killing
process. Authority in the Third Reich flowed not from laws and orders,
issued by carefully delimited agencies, but rather from expressions of
Hitler's will. Channels of government were frequently circumvented in
favor of proclamations that such or so was "the Führer's wish." This is
what Raul Hilberg, the dean of Holocaust historians, has called "government by announcement." In Hilberg's view, it is quite possible that
a signed order to kill the Jews may never have been issued. What
counted was a "mandate" from Hitler to proceed. Hitler frequently
issued such mandates, and there is plenty of evidence that others understood just what the Nazi leader meant. Those in charge did not
trouble with documentary niceties when the Führer expressed himself.
"What he actually meant, or whether he really meant it, might have
been a matter of tone as well as of language. When he spoke 'coldly'
and in a 'low voice' about 'horrifying' decisions 'also at the dinner
table,' then his audience knew that he was 'serious.' " From one to
another, Nazi leaders transmitted the latest impulse. The problem historians have is reconstructing what these signals were, and when and
under what circumstances they were given.

Intentionalists: The Straight Path

For an important body of historical opinion, the questions asked about
the emergence of the Final Solution can be answered easily with reference to Hitler's anti-Jewish rhetoric, drawn from various points in his
career but seen to reflect a consistent murderous objective. In this
view, Hitler is seen as the driving force of Nazi antisemitic policy,
whose views indicate a coherent line of thought from a very early
point. Hitler is also seen as the sole strategist with the authority and the
determination to begin the implementation of the Final Solution. In
what is probably the most widely read work on this subject, Lucy
Dawidowicz argues that the Führer set the stage for mass murder in
September 1939, with the attack on Poland. "War and the annihilation
of the Jews were interdependent," she writes. "The disorder of war

would provide Hitler with the cover for the unchecked commission of murder. He needed an arena for his operations where the restraints of common codes of morality and accepted rules of warfare would not extend." September 1939, therefore, saw the beginning of "a twofold war": on the one hand there was the war of conquest for traditional goals such as raw materials and empire; on the other there was the "war against the Jews," the decisive confrontation with the greatest enemy of the Third Reich. Orders to begin Europe-wide mass murder, issued in the late spring or summer of 1941, are seen as flowing directly from Hitler's idea on Jews, expressed as early as 1919. On various occasions his "program of annihilation" may have been camouflaged or downplayed. But Dawidowicz insists that it was always his intention: "Once Hitler adopted an ideological position, even a strategic one, he adhered to it with limpetlike fixity, fearful lest he be accused, if he changed his mind, of incertitude, of capriciousness on 'essential questions.' He had long-range plans to realize his ideological goals, and the destruction of the Jews was at their center."

Borrowing from the British historian Tim Mason, Christopher Browning was the first to dub this interpretation "intentionalist," linking it to other historiographical themes in the history of the Third Reich. This line of thought accents the role of Hitler in initiating the murder of European Jewry, seeing a high degree of persistence, consistency, and orderly sequence in Nazi anti-Jewish policy, directed from a very early point to the goal of mass murder. Like much of the interpretative literature on Nazism, this explanation of the Final Solution rests on quotations and depends, in the final analysis, on the notion of a Hitlerian "blueprint" for future policies, set forth in *Mein Kampf* and other writings and speeches. Critics of this approach, referred to as "functionalists," are rather impressed with the evolution of Nazi goals, with the sometimes haphazard course of German policies, and with the way that these are related to the internal mechanisms of the Third Reich.

Intentionalism, it may be supposed, was born at Nuremberg in 1945, when American prosecutors first presented Nazi crimes as a carefully orchestrated conspiracy, launched together with the war itself. At that time American legal experts hoped to prove that there had been a deliberate plan to commit horrendous atrocities as well as other breaches of international law; in this way they expected to designate certain German organizations and institutions as part of a criminal conspiracy, vastly simplifying the work of future prosecutions. Years later, after much historical analysis, many historians still accept the notion of an unfolding Hitlerian plan. In his detailed critique of David Irving, for example, Gerald Fleming sees an "unbroken continuity of specific utterances" leading from Hitler's first manifestations of anti-semitism "to the liquidation orders that Hitler personally issued during the war." A major task of Fleming's work is the collection of such utterances, which the author hopes will tear away the camouflage covering Hitler's primary responsibility.

One can sympathize with an effort to remind a sometimes negligent audience of Hitler's incessant, raving hatred of Jews. And it is similarly valuable to expose the Nazis' linguistic perversions—distortions intended to conceal the killing process from the victims, from the Allies, and from the German public as well. Nevertheless, the problem of interpreting Hitlerian rhetoric still remains. For the fact is that Hitler was forever calling for the most ruthless action; for sudden, crushing blows; for the complete annihilation of his foes; or evoking his irrevocable, ironlike determination to do this or that. We cannot ignore Hitler's amply demonstrated blood lust, and there is no doubt that the contemplation of mass killing inspired him on more than one occasion. In retrospect, historians have little difficulty in tracing "direct lines," but it is much more problematic to ascertain what Hitler actually intended and how he acted on such expressions at specific moments. In May 1938, for example, Hitler told his generals of his "unalterable decision to destroy Czechoslovakia by military action in the foreseeable future." According to Gerhard Weinberg, the Nazi leader indeed wanted military action, but believed he could avoid a general war. When he learned in September, on the eve of his attack, that a general war threatened, that neither Mussolini nor the German public were likely to follow him, and that he could achieve a stunning success peacefully, he changed his mind. So "unalterable decisions" could be altered. The implication is that Hitler's words should indeed be taken seriously, but that they must also be seen in the context of his actions and the concrete situations he faced.

This is a reasonable reply to the use made of Hitler's famous speech of 30 January 1939 by intentionalist historians such as Dawidowicz and Fleming. Adopting a characteristically "prophetic" tone in his address to the Reichstag, Hitler issued a terrible warning: "One thing I should like to say on this day which may be memorable for others as well as for us Germans: In the course of my life I have very often been a prophet, and I have usually been ridiculed for it. During the time of my struggle for power it was in the first instance the Jewish race which only received my prophecies with laughter when I said that I would one day take over the leadership of the State, and with it that of the whole nation, and that I would then among many other things settle the Jewish problem. Their laughter was uproarious, but I think that for some time now they have been laughing on the other side of their face. Today I will once more be a prophet. If the international Jewish financiers outside Europe should succeed in plunging the nations once more into a world war, then the result will not be the bolshevization of the earth, and thus the victory of Jewry, but the annihilation of the Jewish race in Europe."

Fleming is certainly right to stress the importance of Hitler's self-portrayal as a "fighting prophet," and Hitler's subsequent references to this speech in the middle of the war indicate a conscious desire, once the Final Solution was underway, to assert a continuity of actions against the Jews. This is but one of many pieces of evidence that suggest Hitler insisted on a definitive solution to the Jewish question, and in this sense the speech is an important measure of his priorities. Less clear, however, is what the January speech tells us about Hitler's objectives at the time. A look at his words in context shows that Hitler spoke for several hours, but devoted only a few minutes to the Jews. Speaking in the wake of the Munich conference, Hitler focused mainly on economic matters, in an address judged by the British ambassador to be relatively conciliatory. One of the purposes of Hitler's address was likely to sow confusion and division among the Western powers. He probably did envisage war in Europe as his "prophecy" suggested; but this was likely not a world war, but rather a fight over Poland, which would be over quickly. As Uwe Dietrich Adam points out, Hitler and other Nazi leaders looked to an even more ruthless crack-down on Jews in the event of war. We shall never know for certain precisely what plans lurked in Hitler's consciousness and whether his reference to "annihilation" at that particular time should be taken literally. But it is not at all plain that he had fixed upon mass murder, which presumably would have to begin once the short Polish campaign was over. And it is even less likely that Hitler thought concretely about European-wide killings, which he was not in a position to undertake until his stunning military successes in 1940–41.

In utterances such as Hitler's 30 January address, Eberhard Jäckel identifies the "universalist-missionary touch" in the Führer's anti-semitism, which became an integral part of Nazi war aims. Hitler's anti-semitism in *Mein Kampf,* according to Jäckel, "presupposes war, it demands the methods of warfare, and it is therefore not surprising that it should have reached its bloody climax during the next war, which was a part of Hitler's program from the start." Once the fighting continued into 1941 and 1942, "the extermination of the Jews became increasingly the most important aim of the war as such; as the fortunes of war turned against Germany, the destruction of the Jews became National Socialism's gift to the world." Finally, in the eery atmosphere of Hitler's bunker beneath the ruins of Berlin, antisemitism assumed supreme importance. The extermination of the Jews "now appeared to him as his central historical mission." A key suggestion, I think, is that antisemitism *became* ever more salient. But was there a "blueprint" from a very early point, as Jäckel implies? Was extermination an inevitable outgrowth of this antisemitism? These questions remain open.

Some intentionalists link Hitler's determination to murder the Jews with other aspects of his thought and strategy. In his book *The Three Faces of Fascism,* first published in German in 1963, intellectual historian Ernst Nolte presented National Socialism as part of a European-wide opposition to modern ideas and development, of which the Jews were a principal symbol in the eyes of antisemites. In Hitler's thinking, said Nolte, the Jew came to stand for "the historical process itself." Unlike some of his followers, Hitler and Himmler were "logically consistent" in their thought and practice. Assuming that everything they detested in the world derived ultimately from this mainspring of modernity, annihilation made sense. "In Hitler's extermination of the Jews it was not a case of criminals committing criminal deeds, but of a uniquely monstrous action in which principles ran riot in a frenzy of self-destruction." For Andreas Hillgruber, on the other hand, the key lies in the Barbarossa campaign and the struggle against the Soviet regime. The Final Solution, he argues, derived from the ideological fixation with Bolshevism and the east, seen as inseparable in Hitler's mind from "international Judaism." Killing on a mass scale emerged from the ideological mobilization for the onslaught on the Soviet Union that began on 22 June 1941.

In the absence of reliable guides to Hitler's plans for the Jews, apart from his murky "prophecies," intentionalists differ among themselves as to when precisely Hitler's intentions became fixed. In his most recent book, Jäckel rules out the idea that there was "a single killing order." Rather, "extermination was divided into several phases and covered a wide variety of methods and victims." The weight of opinion about a turning point falls on the war against the Soviet Union. According to Helmut Krausnick, there was a wartime decision of the Führer, but its timing remains obscure. "What is certain is that the nearer Hitler's plan to overthrow Russia as the last possible enemy on the continent of Europe approached maturity, the more he became obsessed with an idea—with which he had been toying as a 'final solution' for a long time—of wiping out the Jews in the territories under his control. It cannot have been later than March 1941, when he openly declared his intention of having the political commissars of the Red Army shot that he issued his secret decree—which never appeared in writing though it was mentioned verbally on several occasions—that the Jews should be eliminated." Together with a colleague, Hans-Heinrich Wilhelm, Krausnick has pored over the activity of the murderous Einsatzgruppen, the killing teams of motorized SS troops who followed in the van of the Wehrmacht when they swept into the Soviet Union in the summer of 1941. Ultimately these and related units are responsible for more than 2 million deaths, one of the greatest orgies of mass killing in the history of mankind. Krausnick and Wilhelm have documented the genocidal character of the campaign, which Hitler referred to as a *Vernichtungskrieg,* a war of destruction, and they have incidentally demonstrated the extensive support and assistance given to their slaughters by the regular army. In their view the extermination of the Jews was included in the Barbarossa planning process. This assessment has been contested, however, with other authorities arguing rather that the killing evolved into genocidal proportions during the early course of the fighting. But of genocide itself there is no doubt. Christian Streit and others have documented the active participation of the Wehrmacht in a whole complex of killing orders and massacres— including Jews, Communists, and prisoners of war.

Functionalists: The Twisted Road

Against this interpretation, so-called functionalist historians present a picture of the Third Reich as a maze of competing power groups, rival bureaucracies, forceful personalities, and diametrically opposed interests engaged in ceaseless clashes with each other. They see Hitler as a brooding and sometimes distant leader, who intervened only spasmodically, sending orders crashing through the system like bolts of lightning. While in theory the power of the Führer was without limit, in practice he preferred the role of arbiter, according legitimacy to one or another favorite or line of conduct. Add to this Hitler's curious leadership style—his inability to mount a sustained effort, his procrastination, his frequent hesitation—and one can understand the reluctance of many to accept the idea of a far-reaching scheme or ideological imperative necessitating the Final Solution. Few historians of this school doubt that Hitler was murderously obsessed with Jews; they question, however, whether he was capable of long-term planning on this or any other matter, and they tend to look within the chaotic system itself for at least some of the explanation for the killing of European Jews.

Reflecting this perspective, Martin Broszat's 1977 critique of David Irving's *Hitler's War* presented to a wide public a serious interpretation of the origins of the Final Solution in which Hitler did not have full operational responsibility. Broszat's approach was hardly an exculpation of the Nazi leader. On the contrary, he took Irving to task for his "normalization" of Hitler and pointed to dangerous forces within the German Federal Republic that utilized the apologetic drift in the British historian's work. Broszat reasserted Hitler's "fanatical, destructive will to annihilate" that traditional historiography has always seen at the core of the Führer's personality. He stressed Hitler's "totally irresponsible, self-deceiving, destructive and evilly misanthropic egocentricity and his lunatic fanaticism." As the author of a 1969 work, *Der Staat Hitlers,* Broszat had no doubt about who was in charge and what kind of a person he was.

Nevertheless, the heart of Broszat's argument was that the Final Solution was not begun after a single Hitlerian decision, but arose "bit by bit." He suggested that deportations and systematic killings outside the sphere of the Einsatzgruppen in Russia started through local Nazi initiatives, rather than a directive from the Führer. According to this view, Hitler set the objective of Nazism: "to get rid of the Jews, and above all to make the territory of the Reich *judenfrei,* i.e., clear of Jews"—but without specifying how this was to be achieved. In a vague way, the top Nazi leadership hoped to see the Jews pushed off to the east, and uprooted large masses of people with this in mind. Top Nazi officials had "no clear aims . . . with respect to the subsequent fate of the deportees," however. Their policy was "governed by the concept that the enormous spaces to be occupied in the Soviet Union would . . . offer a possibility for getting rid of the Jews of Germany and of the allied and occupied countries," but they also toyed with other schemes, such as the Madagascar Plan, to achieve their objectives. Expectations of an early resolution heightened during the Russian campaign, which was supposed to finish in a matter of weeks. Deportation trains carrying Jews from the Reich began to roll eastward. Yet by the autumn these plans were upset. Military operations slowed, and then came to a standstill. Transportation facilities were overloaded. Nazi officers in the occupied east, receiving shipments of Jews from the Reich, now complained that they had no more room in the teeming, disease-ridden ghettos. It was then, in Broszat's view, that Nazi officials on the spot started sporadically to murder the Jews who arrived from the west. Killing, therefore, "began not solely as the result of an ostensible will for extermination but also as a 'way out' of a blind alley into which the Nazis had manoeuvered themselves." In its early stages, annihilation was improvised, and its execution was marked by confusion and misunderstanding. Only gradually, in early 1942 did Himmler and the SS establish the coherent structures of the Final Solution, coordinated on a European-wide basis.

Among functionalists, Hans Mommsen has presented the most forceful case for a Führer uninvolved in and perhaps incapable of administration, concerned rather with his personal standing and striking propaganda postures. Mommsen goes even further than Broszat in suggesting that Hitler had little directly to do with anti-Jewish policy. While not denying his intense hatred of Jews, Mommsen sees the Nazi leader as thinking about the Jews mainly in propagandistic terms, without bothering to chart a course of action. The Final Solution, he observes, resulted from the interaction of this fanatical but distant leader with the chaotic structure of the Nazi regime. In the Third Reich, office was piled upon office, and underlings were left to find their way in a bureaucratic and administrative jungle. The only guide to success, and a compelling one, was fidelity to the Hitlerian vision. Underlings competed for the favor of this ideologically obsessed, but essentially lazy leader. Given the Führer's mad compulsions, this competition programmed the regime for "cumulative radicalization," a process that ended ultimately, of course, in its self-destruction. Hitler's heightened rhetoric prompted others to realize his "utopian" ravings about Jews and undoubtedly stimulated murderous excesses. But he issued no order for the Final Solution and had nothing to do with its implementation.

"Hitler's precise role remains hidden in the shadows," says Ian Kershaw, reviewing this literature recently. Given the paucity of documentation, this issue may forever remain obscure, without disputing either the importance of the Führer in the process or the demonic potency of his antisemitism. Whatever their view of Hitler, however, functionalist historians agree that the Final Solution emerged through improvisation, rather than deliberate planning. In his survey of Nazi policy toward the Jews, Karl Schleunes suggested that there was a "twisted road to Auschwitz." The paths that led to the extermination camps, he elaborates, "were by no means direct or, for that matter, charted far in advance." Unlike Broszat, Uwe Adam posits a distinct Hitlerian decision to murder the Jews as occurring sometime "between September and November 1941" and assumes there was an order from the Führer to this effect. But he too considers that there was no course set from a very early point for European-wide mass murder. Instead, one decision led to another piecemeal, with mass murder emerging as a way to resolve a hopeless contradiction. Having set in motion deportations from the west, the Nazis had to do something with the Jews accumulating in Poland. When the "territorial" option in Russia was foreclosed, the Führer decided on the Final Solution. Hitler and his relentless anti-Jewish ideology were the dynamic element, pressing for a solution to the "Jewish Question"; policy evolved, however, in the chaotic institutional environment of the Third Reich, where planlessness and internal contradictions were the norm.

In the most recent scholarly analysis of this issue, Browning settles upon a position that he terms "moderate functionalist." He finds it implausible that Hitler was merely "awaiting the opportune moment" to realize his murderous intentions, since the Nazi leader allowed nearly three years to pass between the conquest of Poland and the onset of European-wide mass murder. If the outbreak of war simply provided Hitler with a "cover" for mass murder, "why were the millions of Polish Jews in his hands since the fall of 1939 granted a thirty-month 'stay of execution'? They were subjected to sporadic massacre and murderous living conditions but not to systematic extermination until 1942." During this time there was no "blueprint" for mass destruction, but rather an ideological imperative that called for some sort of ultimate reckoning with the Jews in a manner that would satisfy Nazi racial preoccupations. Competing Nazi agencies put forward one proposal after the next, schemes that continually shattered against practical obstacles. Nazi activists appealed to a Führer whose mind was sometimes elsewhere, who was worried about tactical issues of many sorts, and who often delayed making up his mind about important matters.

The crisis came with Barbarossa, not only because of the apocalyptic character of the campaign, but also because it promised to bring hundreds of thousands more Jews within the hegemony of the Reich. What were the Germans to do with them? During the early course of the campaign Hitler tipped the scales for mass murder. The decision to massacre the Soviet Jews was probably taken in March, as part of the Barbarossa planning process. Before the end of July, Hitler, buoyed up by the spectacular successes of the Wehrmacht in the early part of the Russian campaign, probably issued his order for European-wide mass murder. At that point, the Führer likely felt, everything was possible. On 31 July, Göring authorized Heydrich to prepare a "total solution" (*Gesamtlösung*) of the Jewish question in the territories under the Nazis' control. Before long, work began on the first two death camps—at Belzec and Chelmno, where construction started in the autumn. On 23 October, Himmler issued a fateful order that passed along the Nazi chain of command: henceforth there would be no Jewish emigration permitted anywhere from German-held territory. On 29 November, invitations went out to the Wannsee Conference, intended to coordinate deportations from across Europe. The Final Solution was about to begin.

Browning and others have criticized the work of various functionalists on three grounds. First, they challenge Adam's notion that pushing great masses of Jews off "to the east" was still an option for the Nazis in the summer of 1941. No concrete preparations for such a massive deportation have ever been discovered, and it is unlikely that serious planning for it could have been underway without leaving a trace in the historical record. Göring's authorization to Heydrich on 31 July to prepare a "total solution" could hardly have referred to such expulsions, they say, since Heydrich already had such authority and had been expelling Jews on a smaller scale since the beginning of 1939. Seen in the context of the furious killings then underway by the Einsatzgruppen, Göring's communication appears rather like a warrant for genocide. Like many, Klaus Hildebrand finds it difficult to distinguish between the gigantic operations of the killing teams in Russia and the other aspects of the Final Solution. "In qualitative terms the executions by shooting were no different from the technically more efficient accomplishment of the 'physical final solution' by gassing, of which they were a prelude." Second, historians have challenged Broszat's idea of locally initiated mass murders. Not only does it seem unlikely that the systematic killing of Jews from the Reich, for example, could have been undertaken without the Führer's agreement, there is also too little evidence of local initiatives with which to sustain this theory. As Eberhard Jäckel noted recently, there is rather "a great deal of evidence that some [local officials] were shocked or even appalled when the final solution came into effect. To be sure, they did not disagree with it. But they agreed only reluctantly, referring again to an order given by Hitler. This is a strong indication that the idea did not originate with them."

Third, Browning contends that the decision for European-wide mass murder was taken in the summer of 1941, in the euphoria of the first victories in the Barbarossa campaign, and not a few months later. He draws upon postwar evidence from Rudolf Höss, the commandant of Auschwitz, and Adolf Eichmann, from the start a key official in the bureaucracy of the Final Solution, to the effect that the Führer's mind was made up during the summer. This sense of timing differs notably from functionalists who conclude that the Final Solution arose from disappointment with the outcome of the fighting in Russia. Adam, for example, sees the Nazis depressed by the prospect of having to spend another winter with the Jews; the journalist Sebastian Haffner imagines, much less plausibly, that Hitler saw as early as the end of 1941 that the European war could not be won and that the other contest, "the war against the Jews," could at least be pursued to its final conclusion.

Outsiders to these disputes may well suspect that some of the sharp edges of the controversy are wearing off and that there is more agreement among these historians than meets the eye. Opinion is widespread that there was some Hitlerian decision to initiate Europe--wide killing. The range of difference over timing extends across only a few months, with intentionalists positing a Führer order sometime in March 1941, with Browning and others opting for the summer, and with a few, such as Adam, looking toward the early autumn. What finally precipitated this decision, however, is likely to remain a mystery. Military historians tell us that, despite the extraordinary successes of the Wehrmacht in the first weeks of the Barbarossa campaign, the Germans found the going difficult as early as mid-July 1941. Although their forces advanced great distances and destroyed much of their opposition, they were surprised at the extent and efficacy of Soviet resistance and were greatly slowed by faulty intelligence, poor roads and bridges, and marshes. Chief of the army general staff Franz Halder portrayed an exasperated Führer after only six weeks of fighting, and it seems likely that by late August Hitler already knew that the war would continue well into 1942. This was a major setback, even though the Germans did not taste real defeat until December. Whether euphoria or disappointment prompted the decision is therefore difficult to say. On the other hand, the idea of Hitler breaking the logjam caused by an ill-defined policy rings true, given what we know of his leadership style. Students of Hitler's behavior in other areas have been struck by his preference for sudden, unexpected, spectacular coups. His was the method of the supreme gambler, "forever looking for short cuts." For someone as ruthless and fanatical as Hitler, a decision for the Final Solution can well be imagined in the apocalyptic atmosphere of Barbarossa, the war to settle once and for all the fate of the thousand-year Reich.

"La guerre révolutionna la Révolution," French historian Marcel Reinhard once wrote about the revolutionary impact of the war of 1792 on the revolutionaries in Paris. So it has been observed that the war against the Soviet Union revolutionized the Third Reich, and it is not surprising that this campaign transformed Nazi Jewish policy as well. It is difficult to follow the process of political and ideological radicalization in detail, for this was a period of extensive fluidity—even for a regime that, as Karl Dietrich Bracher has said, "remained in a state of permanent improvisation." Ian Kershaw observes that "the summer and autumn of 1941 were characterized by a high degree of confusion and contradictory interpretations of the aims of anti-Jewish policy by the Nazi authorities." It seems useful, however, to understand Jewish policy in this period as evolving within a genocidal framework—extending beyond Jews to include the incurably ill, Soviet intelligentsia, prisoners of war, and others as well. In this fevered atmosphere, incredible as it may seem, an "order" to send millions of people to their deaths may have been no more than a "nod" from Hitler to one of his lieutenants.

Functionaries of the Final Solution

For historians of the Holocaust, the greatest challenge has not been
making sense of Hitler, but rather understanding why so many followed him down his murderous path. Given the state of the evidence,
this difficulty may seem curious. For while documentation of Hitler's
acts is relatively scarce, material on the rest of the regime is available
in great abundance, including much of what happened during the Holocaust. Nevertheless, the mystery remains. And in seeking their answer,
students of the Final Solution simply join with other historians of the
Third Reich and the Second World War who confront similar issues.
Why did so many politicians and statesmen fail to get the full measure
of Adolf Hitler? Why did the cream of German generals, renowned for
their professionalism, permit themselves to be led to ruin by a criminal
maniac? Why did the structures of the Reich remain under his spell for
so long in 1944–45, when by all objective standards the adventure of
Nazism was finished? All of these questions are related.

Having depreciated the operational importance of the Führer, functionalist historians tend to broaden the range of culpability associated
with the Final Solution. To them, blame extends across the German
elite, especially in the military and the civil service, for having performed the manifold tasks of mass murder and having done so without
complaint. Martin Broszat describes the evolution of a huge apparatus
represented by the security police and the SS, operating entirely outside the framework of law and state administration. By 1942 this Nazi
elite could direct various branches of the bureaucracy to carry out
portions of the murderous operation, designated in euphemistic administrative language as "removals," "evacuations," "cleansing actions,"
and so on. With regard to the Wehrmacht, several historians' demonstration of the complicity of high-ranking officers with the annihilation
policy of the Barbarossa campaign shows conclusively that direct involvement in genocide was not limited to the SS. Omer Bartov has
come to similar conclusions about junior Wehrmacht officers as well.
Hans Mommsen poses the issue of what accounts for the widespread
elimination of inhibitions to mass murder. Antisemitic indoctrination is
plainly an insufficient answer, for we know that many of the officials
involved in the administration of mass murder did not come to their
tasks displaying intense antisemitism. In some cases, indeed, they appear to have had no history of anti-Jewish hatred and to have been

coldly uninvolved with their victims. Motivation seems to have varied considerably. As students of the Holocaust have long understood, the extensive division of labor associated with the killing process helped perpetrators diffuse their own responsibility. In Mommsen's view, a "technocratic-hierarchical mentality" accounts for a great deal, and he suggests that the political-psychological structure of this process is the real problem for the historical explanation of the Holocaust.

It is on this issue, posed as the how rather than the why of Nazi genocide, that Raul Hilberg has made a signal contribution to the study of the Final Solution. The product of painstaking and wide-ranging research, Hilberg's book offers a magisterial synthesis, on a scale that no one has matched before or since. First published in 1961, and now reissued in a "revised and definitive edition," Hilberg's *Destruction of the European Jews* remains the most important work that has ever been written on the subject. Of breathtaking scope, with a description of the destruction process extending across the entire European continent, his book provided the first detailed and systematic combing of German materials on the Holocaust.

Interestingly, Hilberg does not address the debate on the origins of the Final Solution. In his new edition, he remains on another level, faithful to the objective he outlined more than a quarter of a century ago. "I wanted to explore the sheer mechanism of destruction, and as I delved into the problem I saw that I was studying an administrative process carried out by bureaucrats in a network of offices spanning a continent. Understanding the components of this apparatus, with all the facets of its activities, became the principal task of my life." A political scientist, heavily influenced by his Columbia University mentor Franz Neumann, Hilberg developed the notion of "the machinery of destruction," the description of which is the core of his analysis. This machinery, with awesome power, grinds on ineluctably—not only to destroy its victims, but also to engage an ever-wider circle of perpetrators in the murderous task.

How was the Nazis' project realized? In Hilberg's view the destruction of the Jews proceeded by stages—"sequential steps that were taken at the initiative of countless decision makers in a far-flung bureaucratic machine." First came the definition of the Jews, then their expropriation, concentration, deportation, and finally their murder. The machine remains his controlling image, and his leitmotif is the gigantic scale of its work. Nazi genocide was a truly monumental task, requiring great exertion throughout the whole of the German empire, bureaucratic ingenuity, countless administrative decisions, the continuous cooperation of widely diverse agencies, and many thousands of officials. In hundreds of pages, Hilberg recounts an officialdom across Europe working together in mechanized fashion. Significantly, the perpetrators themselves had no special characteristics; the essential element was the structure into which they fit. "To grasp the full significance of what these men did we have to understand that we are not dealing with individuals who had their own separate moral standards. The bureaucrats who were drawn into the destruction process were not different in their moral makeup from the rest of the population." Faced with its enormous task, to do away with the Jews, the Nazis discovered a remarkable new administrative process that set the machinery of destruction "on its track of self-assertion." At a certain point, the machine needed no operator. It required no master plan or blueprint. "In the final analysis the destruction of the Jews was not so much a product of laws and commands as it was a matter of spirit, of shared comprehension, of consonance and synchronization." This human machine generated its own momentum, "operating with accelerating speed and an ever-widening destructive effect." Efficiency was its hallmark. "With an unfailing sense of direction and with an uncanny pathfinding ability, the German bureaucracy found the shortest path to the final goal."

As with most historians, Hilberg sees Hitler's role in the Final Solution as "salient," but he does little beyond implying that the Führer activated the machinery already programmed for murder in 1941. "For years, the administrative machine had taken its initiatives and engaged in its forays one step at a time. In the course of that evolution, a direction had been charted and a course established. By the middle of 1941 the dividing line had been reached, and beyond it lay a field of unprecedented actions unhindered by the limits of the past." While there can be no doubt about the Nazi leader's inspiration of mass murder, he seems an even more distant figure in the new edition than the first. Passages that considered or speculated about his decisions have been removed, and the role of the machine and its destructive logic and thereby enhanced. At the bottom of a footnote reference to the evidence of Adolf Eichmann and Rudolf Höss, we find Hilberg's sole comment on an issue that has been so widely disputed: "Chronology and circumstances point to a Hitler decision before the summer [of 1941] ended."

Detailed study of particular components of the "machinery of destruction" is likely to help us understand how it worked and how it acted on the impulses of its demented Führer. In his 1978 book on the Jewish section of the German Foreign Office, for example, Christopher Browning portrayed a group of Nazi bureaucrats eagerly pursuing the directions that came from their superiors, but also capable of their own initiatives when opportunities arose. Martin Luther, chief of this section, was an archcareerist with a talent for organization, but no pressing anti-Jewish vocation. Luther "was not a doctrinaire racist like Heinrich Himmler, dreaming of fantasies of a future Aryan heaven-on-earth. Nor was he an *Altkämpfer* like Goebbels, wallowing in nostalgia and ready to stick by Hitler to the end. . . . Primarily, Luther was an amoral technician of power." Strikingly, with the shift toward the Final Solution in the latter part of 1941, these officials sensed a new direction and acted upon it. Browning notes: "when zealous administrators like Luther were desperately trying to anticipate the will of the Führer in the Jewish question . . . a chain of command requiring obedience to the Führer's orders was superfluous. Initiative from below obviated the necessity for orders from above."

It was similar with the development and production of the gas van, a Nazi invention for killing, first utilized in the so-called euthanasia program against mental patients. By early 1942 these machines were in use at Chelmno, in German-incorporated Poland, and with the Einsatzgruppen in captured Soviet territory. There was no Führer order for the gas vans, and it is not clear if Hitler was ever informed about them. According to Browning, the impetus for development came with the problems encountered by killing teams in Russia. Complaints flowed from the field, where murder squads were being demoralized by the inefficient and gruesome process of mass shooting. Ideas flowed from Berlin, where scientists attached to the Führer's Chancellery received directives from Heydrich to design a vehicle using exhaust gas for killing people. All along the line individuals made their contributions. During 1942, with the Final Solution having been deemed an urgent priority, and for want of any better way to do the job, the gas vans were pressed into service to speed the killing process. Who was responsible for the gas van? Hitler set the killing priority but left the details to others. Among the high-ranking dignitaries of the Third Reich, Himmler and Heydrich both had their role. But we are now able to glimpse more humble contributors to the Final Solution—in the machine shops where the vans were assembled and repaired, in the procurement offices and dispatching agencies that sent them on their lethal missions. Officials there loathed bottlenecks and set about to make their work more effective. "Kept fully abreast of the problems arising in the field, they strove for ingenious technical adjustments to make their product more efficient and acceptable to its operators. What could not be remedied had to be blamed on someone else. . . . Their greatest concern seemed to be that they might be deemed inadequate to their assigned task."

According to George Mosse, the heavy reliance upon technology in the Final Solution—the use of gas, railways, controls, and movement of vast numbers of people—"interacted with the dehumanization of the victims." Those involved in the process could take refuge in their professional specialty, banishing all humane considerations. These perpetrators hardly thought of themselves as anything other than skilled technicians, and often seemed genuinely surprised when, years later, they were branded accomplices to mass murder.

Aspects of Nazi Population Policy

Just as the examination of particular aspects of the Final Solution assists historians in understanding the process as a whole, so the study of related themes casts light on the destruction of European Jews. A good example is the Nazis' so-called euthanasia campaign, which reflects, as one student of the matter has recently argued, a much wider involvement by doctors in the racial engineering of the Third Reich. According to psychiatrist Robert Jay Lifton, there was a special affinity between Nazism and a perverted medical outlook, yielding what he calls the "Nazi biomedical vision." Drawing heavily upon eugenic ideas common in much of the Western world in the 1920s, this was a view of the entire German nation as a biological organism, which was threatened by a kind of collective illness—a potentially fatal threat to a formerly healthy society. The task of Nazism was to cure the German *Volk* by eliminating all sources of corruption—carried mainly by the Jews, but evident also in the feebleminded, the incurably ill, and the insane. The goal, Lifton says, was "biocracy," built on the model of theocracy—a state committed to purification and revitalization, applied as if through divine commandment.

These ideas did not remain the province of theory. Beginning with little children, the Nazis encouraged and directed a program of systematic killing of the physically and mentally impaired, eventually using gas chambers, to rid the Reich of those deemed "unworthy of life." It is difficult to establish the death toll in this campaign, partly because many doctors and institutions were allowed to proceed on their own after the campaign was officially stopped; it is generally believed, however, that the total killed was between 80,000 and 100,000 people. All who have examined this killing have noted a link with the Final Solution—in the particular propensity to murder Jews as part of its operation, but also in the development of killing methods and the training of personnel who would eventually find their place within the death camps of eastern Europe.

Another example is the Nazi population policy for eastern Europe, which has been addressed recently in the work of several scholars. Seen from this angle, Nazi Jewish policy was part of a vast German project for the demographic reordering of eastern Europe, to be undertaken in a manner consistent with Nazi principles. In a word, the Nazis encouraged vast population movements throughout the region: non-Germans had to be ruthlessly excluded from the territory of the Reich; at the same time, pure Germans or *Volksdeutsche* were to be taken into the fold, particularly in the new eastern marches. In the autumn of 1939, Heinrich Himmler, head of the SS and master of the gargantuan police apparatus known as the Central Office for Reich Security (Reichsicherheitshauptamt, or RSHA), brought under his control a series of agencies devoted to racial and settlement matters. In October, as soon as the Polish campaign was successfully completed, Hitler authorized Himmler to institute a Reich Commission for the Consolidation of Germandom (Reichskommissariat für die Festigung des deutschen Volkstums, or RKFDV), a powerful bureaucracy to coordinate the Nazis' vast population schemes. Under Himmler's direction, vast numbers of people, Jews and non-Jews, began to move in Nazi-held eastern Europe.

Nazi population policy in the east, it becomes clear, was governed by the same lack of planning and well-ordered priorities as Jewish policy in the period before the Final Solution. Gigantic projects were set in motion, often with the slimmest preparation or appreciation of the constraints of wartime conditions. According to Robert Koehl, "the chaos created by the lack of conformity between theory and reality, and especially by top-level decisions out of touch with reality, led to violent and brutal measures, to fantasy and more false logic, and to cynicism." Gangsterism took command. Officials fought bitterly with each other; Nazi agencies staked out grandiose claims for jurisdiction; and the entire program, deemed of the highest ideological significance, suffered from Hitler's failure to make decisive choices. As with the Final Solution, the climax came with Barbarossa. With his ambitions apparently fed by conquest, Himmler stirred the imagination of his underlings to build a vast SS empire in European Russia. The possibilities seemed limitless. A *Generalplan Ost*, a draft of which emerged from Himmler's bureaucracy at the end of 1941, envisaged the deportation of no fewer than 31 million non-Germans from eastern areas, which would eventually be settled by *Volksdeutsche*. German colonists would hold thirty-six "strong points" in former Soviet territory, and settlement areas would extend to Lithuania, the Leningrad area, and the Crimea.

Killing was an important tool for the achievement of this Nazi utopia. In the end the slaughter was awesome, as we know, with the murder of many millions of Poles, Russians, Ukrainians, Belorussians, and others. In terms of the numbers murdered the bloodbath may have surpassed even the Final Solution, although the grim distinction of *Holocaust* is usually reserved for the massacre of Jews alone. Unlike the Final Solution, the extravagant schemes for the conquered east did not involve murder on a universal scale, as was being simultaneously decreed for the Jews. National entities among such people were to be eradicated, it is true, but some individuals would live. Notably "Nordic" elements among the newly occupied Slavic peoples were to be identified by a complicated racial survey, and there was to be extensive Germanization of the most valued elements among them. Himmler's experts acknowledged that it was impossible to kill the entire Russian population in any event, and Nazi plans referred to a large proportion that were to be enslaved.

Closer examination of Nazi population policy in the east helps put the Final Solution into perspective and may suggest new connections. An East German historian, for example, considers that expansion into the Soviet Union brought home to the Nazi leadership that they now had a limitless reservoir of labor and could finally dispose of the Jews without serious cost. A look at Nazi settlement policy, requiring vast energy and transport for the movement of *Volksdeutsche,* makes more understandable the priorities set for Jews in Poland, the rhythms of ghettoization, and the procrastination regarding the Final Solution. One comes away from this material with the sense that the destruction of European Jewry should not be studied in isolation from other aspects of Nazi policy. Though different in kind from other massacres, it nevertheless fits into patterns we can find elsewhere. Identifying such patterns is likely to enlighten us even further.

Further Reading for Part II

On occupation, collaboration and resistance in Europe

Dallin, Alexander. *German Rule in Russia, 1941–1945: A Study in Occupation Policies.* London, 1957; Boulder, CO, 2nd ed. 1981.

Foot, Michael R.D. *Resistance: European Resistance to Nazism 1940–1945.* London, 1976.

Gordon, B. M. *Collaborationism in France.* Ithaca, 1980.

Gross, Jan Thomasz. *Polish Society under German Occupation: The General-gouvernement, 1939–1944.* Princeton, 1979.

Haestrup, Jorgen. *Europe Ablaze: Analysis of the History of European Resistance Movements, 1939–1945.* Odense, Denmark, 1978.

Hirschfeld, Gerhard. *Nazi Rule and Dutch Collaboration: The Netherlands under German Occupation, 1940–1945.* Oxford, New York and Hamburg, 1988.

Hoffman, Stanley. "Collaborationism in France during World War II." *Journal of Modern History* 40(1968):375–395.

Judt, Tony, ed. *Resistance and Revolution in Mediterranean Europe 1939–1945.* London, 1989.

Kedward, Harry Roderick. *Occupied France. Collaboration and Resistance 1940–1944.* London, 1984.

Lukas, Richard C. *The Poles under German Occupation, 1939–1944.* Lexington, KY, 1986.

Marrus, Michael R. *Vichy France and the Jews.* New York, 1981.

Michel, Henri. *The Shadow War: Resistance in Europe 1939–1945.* London, 1972.

Paxton, Robert O. *Vichy France: Old Guard and New Order, 1940–1944.* New York, 1972.

Sweets, John F. *Choices in Vichy France: The French under Nazi Occupation.* New York, 1986.

On collaboration in Asia

Lebra, Joyce. *Japan's Greater East Asia Co-Prosperity Sphere in World War II.* New York, 1975.

Thorne, Christopher. *The Issue of War: States, Societies, and the Far Eastern Conflict of 1941–1945.* New York 1985.

On the Holocaust

Ainsztein, Reuben. *Jewish Resistance in Nazi–Occupied Eastern Europe. With a Historical Survey of the Jew as Fighter and Soldier in the Diaspora.* New York, 1974.

Bauer, Yehuda. *A History of the Holocaust.* New York, 1982.

Browning, Christopher R. *Fateful Months. Essays on the Emergence of the Final Solution.* New York, 1985.

Dawidowicz, Lucy. *The War against the Jews.* New York, 1975.

Feingold, Henry. *The Politics of Rescue.* New Brunswick, 1978.

Fleming, Gerald. *Hitler and the Final Solution.* Berkeley, 1984.

Gilbert, Martin. *Auschwitz and the Allies, a Devastating Account of How the Allies Responded to the News of Hitler's Mass Murder.* New York, 1981.

———. *The Holocaust: A History of the Jews of Europe during the Second World War.* New York, 1986.

Gordon, Sarah. *Hitler, Germans, and the Jewish Question.* Princeton, 1984.

Hilberg, Raul. *The Destruction of the European Jews.* Chicago, 1961; revised ed. 1985.

Marrus, Michael R. "The History of the Holocaust: A Survey of Recent Literature." *Journal of Modern History* 59(1987):114–60.

———. *The Holocaust in History.* New York, 1987.

Mayer, Arno J. *Why did the Heavens not Darken. The Final Solution in History.* New York, 1988.

Wyman, David S. *The Abandonment of the Jews: America and the Holocaust 1941–1945.* New York, 1984.

Part III

Race, the End of European Empire, and Third World Revolution

To say that the Second World War was not a war against colonialism is as obvious as the observation that postwar decolonialization must somehow be counted among the direct consequences of the conflict. What is more true, though seldom realized, is that the Second World War was a race war whose impact on race relations worldwide has left its mark on relations between whites and the peoples of color throughout the so-called Third World. This is not how the Allies saw it. The Atlantic Charter, announced by Britain and the United States in August 1941, denounced territorial aggrandizement and affirmed self-determination, self-government (but not for the Empire, said Churchill), and a program of economic liberalism. But it made no mention of racial discrimination. The United Nations Declaration of January 1, 1942, also made no reference to racial injustice or repression; it did mention but did not define "human rights." Though the Allies never made race an issue of the war, there are direct connections between European and western racism, the war, and the dissolution of European hegemony over Africa and Asia.

The source of the white man's domination had its roots in Europe's overseas expansion and the domestic social and political transformations attending the growth of the modern European-centered world capitalist economy. By the nineteenth century the scientific and industrial revolutions bequeathed on the west technologies in transportation, communication, and warfare that enabled it to insinuate influence into previously impenetrable empires and societies. Resistance was as sharp and determined as it was futile. The British East India Company began its rise to control over the Indian subcontinent in the mid-eighteenth century, while the Manchu Qing (Ching) empire in China lost the first opium war to Britain in the late 1830s. The first British assault on the Ashanti state in West Africa and against Burma in 1824, the French expedition into Algeria in 1830, the occupation of Australia and massacres of aborigines, British wars against the Maoris in New Zealand, the extension of Dutch domination into present-day Indonesia, and the French seizure in mid-century of Indo-China (present-day Cambodia, Laos and Vietnam) are only a few of the landmarks along the bloody path toward white ruled empires. The United States and Russia carved out great territorial empires as well, as they conquered, decimated, and annexed their way west or, in the case of Russia, east. By the eve of World War I, only Liberia and Ethiopia in Africa and Thailand and Japan in Asia remained free of direct or indirect western supremacy.

Following the explorer, the trader, and the soldier came the administrator, the missionary, and the anthropologist, all too ready to explain and justify European preeminence. Among the results was a "science" of racism pointing to Darwinian evolutionary theory and Western military and productive superiority as evidence that Caucasians, Aryans, Nordics, Anglo-Saxons, or whatever label whites gave themselves, deserved their lordship over other races. Not unexpectedly, some even claimed that in time the demography would shift and that the whites would replace the lower breeds throughout the world as they were already doing in Australia and the Americas.

Within Europe, such racial fantasies served to renew and to fire ethnic conflicts in a continent teeming with all sorts and conditions of peoples. A short list, and only a tiny sample, of these conflicts could include the English and the Irish, the Spanish and the Catalans, the Germans and the Poles, and on to the Hungarians and the Romanians, and the Serbs and the Croats. Perhaps topping the list of feared and despised minorities were the Jews, because they bore the burden of centuries of Christian anti-Judaism and could be found in every nation.

On whatever points they might differ in interpreting the Holocaust, historians are generally agreed that for Hitler the war's goal was *Lebensraum* and a solution to the "Jewish problem" (see Part II above). Realizing *Lebensraum* necessitated the removal and eventual genocide of Slavic peoples in Eastern Europe. Jews posed a different kind of threat, the Nazis thought, and anti-Jewish actions accelerated simultaneously with the invasion of Poland.

In Asia, the war was also a race war. Japanese attitudes toward the Chinese may not exactly parallel the ideas of western racists, and neither genocide nor physical extermination of an entire category of people was a goal, but the Empire of the Rising Sun proclaimed a leading role for the Japanese in Asia. Japanese colonists were settled in Manchuria, and Japan's war against the United States and the European colonial powers was touted as a war against white rule. Raised in a culture where racism pervaded society from the White House and the universities to the churches and town halls, Americans reciprocated, as has been amply documented by John Dower in his study.

That Japan's Co-Prosperity Sphere cannot be considered racist in the same way that Germany's Third Reich was, is evident in the significant response among Asian nationalists to its claim to leadership of Asians. Japan had avoided the European yoke of imperialism through reform and regeneration. Its defeat of Russia in 1905 sent cheers throughout Asia. Japan's attempt to write racial equality into the charter of the League of Nations was only further evidence that the white racists were wrong and that Asians could free themselves under Japan's guidance. Young men and women flocked to Japan to educate themselves and learn first hand about national pride and achievement.

In spite of Japan's aggression in Korea and China, the appeal spread. Jiang Jieshi (Chiang Kai-shek's) leftist critic Wang Jingwei (Wang Ching-wei) bolted the Nationalist government in 1938 to set up a government in Nanjing under Japanese tutelage. In Burma, Ba Maw, disappointed when Britain rejected demands for dominion status in 1941, headed a Burmese government under Japan's occupation. Other examples could lengthen the list. In time, each of these leaders found Japan no less intent on domination than the Europeans. The Japanese advocates of a new deal for Asians under their auspices lost out to the militarists' schemes for exploiting Asian labor and resources to feed the war effort.

Race, however central to the war, does not exhaust the war's impact on imperialism. The strains of fighting one another led the European powers to speed the mobilization of the resources and peoples of their colonies. This had been true in the First World War, when Africans fought in the French armies, and Indians, Arabs, and others fought for the British. Colonial economies were called on to export food, mineral ores, and manufactured goods to replace output lost at home as men were called up for military service and factories turned to war production. Such mobilization fed the growth of colonial middle classes, heightened national awareness, and strengthened indigenous demands for a greater role in government. Though the difficulty of defending the Colonies and maintaining internal control posed new political and military problems, after the war, the British, French, and Dutch empires seemed stronger than ever. Nonetheless, in the 1930s few could see that within a generation direct colonial administration would be swept away. But what role did the Second World War play in all of this?

The answer—or perhaps better put, the question—is more complex than it appears at first. It is well established that war is not simply an interlude in social evolution, though historians, as seems to be their bent, do not agree on what the impact was or to what extent it was beneficial (see Part V below). In addition, there will always remain the question of whether modern war alters the direction of social development or whether it only modifies or accelerates it. Nonetheless, war itself, especially modern war, in some way shapes nations that go through its fiery blasts. Though some may have been peripheral to the military conflict, as in sub-Saharan Africa, colonial societies were not remote from the economic impact of war, nor were they simply bystanders in the changes in the global balance of power.

What is not in doubt is that the shape of world affairs and of global relationships entered a new age during this period of global war. The Soviet Union, though devastated demographically and economically, basked in unprecedented power after 1945. New communist states emerged in Eastern Europe and in China. Among some third world countries, communism's anti-imperialism, antifascism and presumed antiracism appealed to nationalists as an alternative to Western capitalism. Within one short generation, the Soviets appeared to have transformed a peasant society into an industrial giant, able to withstand the German onslaught. And all this without importing foreign capital or yielding national sovereignty.

After the war the United States, even more than the Soviet Union, occupied center stage in global affairs. New York's financial and cultural prominence and its dominance in communications and global transportation, coupled with Washington with its Pentagon and a worldwide network of political influence, replaced London and other European cities as the focus of world capitalism. Furthermore, the United States, especially in the Thirties and during the early years of the war, had opposed European colonialism and supported nationalist aspirations, at least outside of Latin America. While the United States and the Soviet Union emerged as the champions of each side in a bipolar world, Western Europe lay exhausted and bankrupt.

Internationally, the war created an elegant simplicity. Domestically within African and Asian societies, the story is rife with intricacies and puzzles. Though all societies are transformed by and react to the conditions engendered by war, they do not all respond the same way. This is because their social systems vary, political structures are dissimilar, and their economies are keyed to different capabilities. Global diversity means that war presented each society with unique problems; the solutions cannot be easily generalized.

In China, for example, war came after the collapse of an ancient empire and before a new government had firmly established itself. In India, Britain attempted to manage increasingly vocal demands for independence. In the British colonies of Kenya, Southern and Northern Rhodesia, London tried to appease the white settlers while guarding against the complete appropriation of black African lands and rights. In Southeast Asia, France and the Netherlands both employed a mix of divide and rule and brutal repression to squash opposition to their rule. And so forth. What these societies have in common is the crucible of the war years.

6

Hugh Tinker

The Melting Pot of War

In the long march of empire building and the drawn out struggle of colonial peoples for independence, war played a critical role. Certainly, there are examples of powers abandoning colonies and relinquishing control without the decision being forced on the battlefield. The white dominions of the British Empire, the British and French colonies in West Africa, Burma, Iran, perhaps India and others come to mind. But even in these cases, the experience of war suggested the wisdom of yielding to the inevitable. The prospect of costly conflict made self-interest an imperial virtue. The American Revolution against Britain paved the way for Canadian self-rule and independence.

Decades of alternating between artful wooing and harsh repression of the nationalist Indian Congress under the nonviolent leadership of Mohandas Gandhi and Jawaharlal Nehru led to a dead end. With the knowledge of conflict brewing between

Reprinted from Hugh Tinker, *Race, Conflict and the International Order, From Empire to United Nations,* pp. 39–60, with the permission of St. Martin's Press. © Hugh Tinker 1977.

France, the Netherlands and their Southeast Asian subjects in Indo-China and Indonesia, and faced with American and Soviet approval of independence, the British quickly settled with Congress and its opponent, the Muslim League under Mohammad Jinnah, to partition the subcontinent between India and Pakistan. The Dutch got out quickly after two years of fighting. The French fought on in expensive, protracted conflicts before quitting. They persisted in Indo-China until trounced by the Viet-Minh (later Vietcong) in the battle of Dienbienphu in the spring of 1954. In the same year they then went on to pursue a nasty, brutal campaign against Arab nationalist insurgents in Algeria, leaving a decade later.

In the following selection Hugh Tinker, a British historian of Burma and Southeast Asia, sets the issues of Western colonialism, domination, and racial conflict within a broad historical and geographical framework. Writing soon after the 1973 U.S. withdrawal from the Vietnam war and the Vietnam communist victory of 1975, Tinker sees the Second World War and its successors, especially the thirty-year conflict in Indo-China, as the culmination of destruction and of resistance to white global hegemony. Writers such as John Dower and Christopher Thorne later elaborated on this once-submerged theme of race in Asia during the Second World War and have brought it more openly into debates on the significance of those years.

There have been few years during the twentieth century in which a major war was not being waged, but the machinery of destruction reached its zenith in the Second World War and in the war in Vietnam. These were the cauldrons in which the structure of white dominance was melted and broken. The wars which came before were a prelude, though themselves contributing to the transformation.

For Alfred Zimmern, as a young lecturer at Oxford, the defeat of Russia by Japan in 1905 was the watershed. He told his class that he was putting aside Greek history that morning: "Because, I said, I feel I must speak to you about the most important historical event which has happened, or is likely to happen, in our lifetime; the victory of a non-white people over a white people." Many others, especially in the colonised lands of Asia, saw in the victories of Tsushima and Mukden an equal significance. Yet Japan was really imitating the West in its path of conquest and dominance. Japan's victories led to the further subjugation of Asian peoples in Taiwan, Korea and Manchuria.

The First World War involved hundreds of thousands of men from Asia and Africa in the fighting and in support of the armies as workers behind the battle-lines. Indian soldiers fought alongside British troops in France, and beside men from Australia in Gallipoli. French African troops fought in all the great battles, and contributed to the shambles of Verdun. A Labour Corps was recruited in China to work behind the trenches, and among the clerks who accompanied them was an observant young Chinese, Chou En-lai. Even more casually, a Vietnamese cook on a merchant ship found himself in wartime Britain and France: the future Ho Chi Minh. Yet although so many from Asia and Africa were sucked into the jaws of war, the first impact was limited to that of personal experience: black and brown men discovered that on the battlefield they were equal with white men in misery and death, and in survival. The experience produced no immediately discernible political consequences. They did not realise that the First World War had drained the life-force out of the European empires.

The revolution in Russia made a greater impact, for it was Lenin's thesis that Asia and Africa formed the "reserves" of the world revolution." Lenin emphasised that by forming "armies composed of subject peoples" the imperial powers were exposing themselves to possible resistance by their subjects. The (Third) Communist International was founded in 1919 to create the conditions for international communism. The Comintern declared: "Imperialism is therefore capitalism moribund and decaying. It is the final stage of development of the capitalist system. It is the threshold of world social revolution."

However, the immediate effects were limited. Communist attempts to organise revolution in India were largely in the hands of M. N. Roy, an important ideologue but not a successful organiser. The British authorities remorselessly suppressed the Indian Communists in the 1920s, and the party was a spent force for twenty years. The second great offensive was in China, and the efforts of the Kuomintang (K.M.T.) to oppose foreign imperialism (especially the creeping Japanese aggression) were reinforced by the supply of Russian military experts to the Whampoa Military Academy where most of the new Chinese leaders were trained. But the main beneficiary was Chiang Kai-shek who used his Russian-trained generals to wipe out Mao Tsetung's rural guerrillas. In both China and India the Russians guessed wrong. (Concerning Gandhi, the Comintern pronounced: "Gandhism is more and more becoming an ideology directed against mass revolution.

It must be strongly combated by Communism." Not until ten years after independence was Gandhi "rehabilitated" in Soviet ideology.)

The effects of the rise of the Soviet Union were indirect. The Comintern pronounced in 1928 that their task was to ensure "The recognition of the rights of all nations, irrespective of race, to complete self-determination. . . . Wide and determined struggle against the imposition of any kind of limitation and restriction upon any nationality, nation or race. Complete equality for all nations and races." This was a clear call to rising leaders such as Jawaharlal Nehru or Johnson [Jomo] Kenyatta.

As wars continued in the era "between the wars," 1918–39, the dissembling attitude of Britain, France and the United States in the face of aggression seemed to confirm the Leninist thesis that imperialism represented the last, degenerate stage of the capitalist order. Chinese resistance to Japanese invasion seemed to evoke no response from the West; it was left to the U.S.S.R. to furnish aid, and to Indian and other colonised peoples to offer symbolic support. The invasion of Ethiopia by Italy aroused even greater fury. The repulse of the Italian forces at Adowa in 1896 was reckoned as one of the few victories of black or brown men over white invaders. (The repulse of the French by the Chinese at Langson on the northern frontier of Vietnam in 1884 was another symbolic defeat of whites by non-whites which provided an ominous foretaste of things to come.) The conquest of Ethiopia by Mussolini's armies in 1935—while the world found excuses for doing nothing—appeared to be a complete demonstration of how much stronger white solidarity was than Western protestations of democratic belief in freedom and justice. An upswell of black solidarity arose in reply, and black men in the United States, the Caribbean and in British colonies in Africa, who had no effective means of communicating with each other, made their spontaneous gestures of protest in a manner which almost anticipated the mobilising of Black Power movements.

Ethiopia was soon forgotten by the Western world. Haile Selassie was booed by Italian onlookers at Geneva, and the white world turned to other problems nearer at hand: for Britain and France the real issue dominating the later 1930s was the goal of Adolf Hitler.

The racist element in Nazism was less important to the Western democracies than the threat of territorial expansion, for they too accepted many of Adolf Hitler's assumptions about racial difference. Denis Brogan writes: "It would be highly unrealistic not to note the fact that in the years between the wars the United States was only outdistanced by Germany as a market for race theories, some of them crude enough to have suited Hitler." From the start, Hitler made it quite clear that his was a mission to establish a domain of racial difference. The Nazis preached the "leadership principle" which laid down that all Germans must follow Hitler in enforcing the supremacy of the Nordic race over "lower races" like the Latin and Slav and over "subhuman races" like the Jews and Negroes. It was paradoxical that Hitler should draw Mussolini's Italy into his orbit, for the doctrine of Nordic, Aryan supremacy overrode the Fascist pronunciamento that it was Italy's destiny to rule the Mediterranean as heir to Rome. It was part of the Nazi view of world history that decadent Rome had fallen to the "pure" Aryan invaders from the north. Italian fascism was racist in its treatment of non-Europeans, but not in regard to Jews.

Methodically, the Nazis eliminated all Jewish elements from the national life. The books of Jewish writers were burned, and all Jews were removed from positions in public life and education. The shock to the German Jews was traumatic, for they were amongst the most "assimilated" of all their communities; their life-style was indistinguishable from that of other Germans. When Hitler decided to hunt out all the Jews, it was necessary to identify them by pinning the Star of David to their shops and business premises and also to their persons, for they could not be distinguished by appearance, speech or name. The movement of Jewish refugees from Germany to Britain, the United States and other countries was one of the few Jewish emigrations which have aroused no anti-Semitic protests. In part the reason was the sympathetic attitude of all those opposed to Nazism, but perhaps more important the emigrants were almost all middle class, professional people, including a number of distinguished intellectuals.

When the war began in September 1939 it was to be very much a war about race; though this was disguised from almost all the opponents of Hitler, who regarded the struggle as a war for freedom. The two main statements upon the ideals for which the Anglo-American alliance (later called the United Nations) were fighting to defeat Germany—together with Japan—were those issued in 1941 by Roosevelt and Churchill. In January 1941, President Roosevelt in his address to Congress identified "four essential human freedoms": freedom of speech, freedom of worship, freedom from want, and freedom from fear. The "Four Freedoms" clearly did not envisage freedom from racial discrimination or persecution as a basic necessity: probably because for Roosevelt race and racism was only a tiresome feature of domestic southern politics. Eight months later the "Atlantic Charter" was issued, following a meeting between Roosevelt and Churchill aboard a British battleship. The eight points therein promulgated were more concrete than the Four Freedoms, but they also failed to identify race as a salient factor, for the statement that "all the men in all the lands may live out their lives in freedom from fear and want" was merely a recapitulation of Roosevelt's message to Congress: and that was the nearest approach the Allies made to the question of racial equality. Churchill took an early opportunity to make it clear that the third point promising "the right of all peoples to choose the form of government under which they will live" did not mean that the British intended to withdraw from India.

For Hitler, the war on the eastern front gave the opportunity to apply the principles of a superior race ruling over lesser races. His aim was to clear out most of the indigenous peoples and plant German colonies in the eastern lands. The Poles and Ukrainians were treated as *Untermenschen,* lower races, and were mobilised as slave labour on farms and in factories managed by Germans. The Jews and the gypsies were not even *Untermenschen;* for them, the Ultimate Solution, death— genocide—in the gas chamber. The Nazi ideology was transmitted to their allies: the Romanian Iron Guard and the Croatian Fascists applied the Ultimate Solution to their own Jewish communities, and also to the Serbs who were classified as sub-humans. Nazi ideology ran into difficulties in occupied Denmark and Norway, for here the Nordic race was found in its purest form. When Danes and Norwegians resisted the German occupation by non-violent but often effective protest (as when the King of Denmark threatened to cut down the swastika if it were hoisted over the royal palace: so that it wasn't) the Nazis felt unable to apply the methods of repression which were imposed without hesitation upon Poles or Serbs.

Similarly, the Germans waged war upon their enemies according to two completely different codes. In fighting the British, and later the Americans, the Germans stayed fairly closely to the Geneva Convention: indeed, the battle of the *Luftwaffe* against the Royal Air Force was conducted almost in terms of medieval chivalry, especially to the fallen foe. The war against the Russians, and against the different resistance movements, was devoid of any feeling for the enemy, who must be exterminated. Perhaps not surprisingly, the Russians retaliated in the same terms.

If, in the West, the Second World War was a kind of civil war between peoples who had become estranged but who must eventually be reunited (and Allied propaganda emphasised that the war was against the Nazis, not against Germany), the war in Asia was much more openly a race war. The Japanese betrayal—the decision to resign from the Anglo-American club in East Asia and lead a war of brown men against white men—opened up a gulf between Japan and the West which, it seemed, nothing could ever bridge again. Japan announced that the day of the white man in Asia was finished; the Greater East Asia Co-Prosperity Sphere was to be the first international community in which brown men, together, would demonstrate their superiority over the whites. The British—and very much more, the Americans—retaliated with an outburst of hatred which consigned the Japanese to the category of sub-humans.

The Japanese victory in South-east Asia in the early months of 1942 was beyond their wildest hopes. The British were pushed back to the borders of India; the Americans were forced back across the Pacific almost to their naval base at Pearl Harbour, and in their retreat unprecedented numbers of Allied troops became prisoners. The capitulation of the British forces in Malaya at Singapore, in February 1942, was the most disastrous event in British military history; 100,000 British, Australian and Indian soldiers surrendered to a Japanese commander whose own forces were numerically much smaller. Not surprisingly, the Japanese treated these prisoners—and also the Dutch in Indonesia who put up even less of a struggle—as men who had failed to uphold their military honour. The European prisoners were put to humiliating menial labour; the most notorious being the construction of the Death Railway which was built to link Burma and Thailand. The Indian prisoners were wooed as potential recruits for the Japanese.

The build-up of a Japanese-sponsored "Indian National Army" (I.N.A.) was given an enormous boost by the leadership of Subhas Chandra Bose, *Netaji,* or Great General, to his followers. Bose had been under arrest in India in the early months of the war, but he escaped to Afghanistan and from there made his way to Germany. He embraced the whole Nazi philosophy, including the concept of Aryan supremacy which he applied to India to prove that the Indo-Aryans were superior to the *Mlecchas,* the unclean invaders from England.

Bose raised an Indian legion in Germany, but after Japan's triumphant conquest of South-east Asia he made an adventurous journey by German submarine to Indonesia. He became the head of the *Azad Hind* (Free India) government and urged the Japanese to commit the I.N.A. to fight against the British defending the Borderland between Burma and India.

News of the Japanese conquest filtered back to Britain and America. Americans were infuriated by the "betrayal" with which Japan had started the war: the surprise attack upon Pearl Harbour. When news arrived of the hardships endured by American prisoners taken at Bataan in the Philippines and subjected to a "death march" American fury boiled over. They were able to exact revenge upon those Japanese within their grasp: the 112,000 people of Japanese origin—over 71,000 of whom were American citizens—living mainly in the coastal-land of California and Washington State. Immediately after Pearl Harbour the cry arose that this was a fifth column, planted to spy and sabotage the American war effort. Earl Warren, a leading Republican politician (elected Governor of California in November 1942, and later appointed Chief Justice of the United States Supreme Court) called for the expulsion and internment of all persons of Japanese origin. The military commander on the West Coast, General De Witt, underlined the demand with the observation "It makes no difference whether the Jap is a citizen or not. He's still a Jap." Despite his concern for the Four Freedoms, President Roosevelt signed the order for their deportation on 19 February 1942. The order was directed against all persons of enemy origin, but immediately the military command announced that the 80,000 residents on the west coast who had come from Germany and Italy would be exempted. Every Japanese-American was rounded up and removed into the interior to be imprisoned in concentration camps, behind barbed wire and under military guard. Ironically, many of the camps were located in the Indian reservations because of the outcry from citizens of other areas who feared they might have to accept the Japanese.

Many of those who called for repressive measures against the Japanese internees were from the South: they had no personal experience of Asians but were bitterly racist because of their attitude to blacks and Jews. Representative John Rankin of Mississippi called for all blood donated to hospitals by blacks and Japanese to be separately labelled so as not to "contaminate" the veins of Caucasians. The few Americans who opposed internment of the Japanese belonged to radical or left-wing groups. Norman Thomas, who stood several times as Socialist candidate for the American presidency, was virtually the only national leader to speak out. The National Association for the Advancement of Colored People (N.A.A.C.P.) did not miss the overall racist significance of internment. The N.A.A.C.P. announced: "If Asiatic-Americans can be reduced to bondage, deprived of citizenship and of property, the same thing can be done to Afro-Americans and Jews."

Neighbouring Canada adopted a similar policy. Canadian troops had helped defend Hong Kong, and stories of Japanese atrocities followed its capitulation. The Canadian-Japanese community in British Columbia, about 22,000 in number, were also deported from the coastal region and interned. The British Columbia politician, Ian Mackenzie, demanded that after the war they be expelled from Canada to Japan.

In wartime propaganda, emanating from Hollywood and other film studios, the Japanese were invariably portrayed as sub-human monsters. A wartime "Japanese type" was evolved, more ape than man, with huge, hideous teeth, low forehead and shambling gait. In the scenes of brutality in such films as *Betrayal from the East* and *Black Dragon,* the Japanese-Americans, the *Nisei,* were depicted as traitors and spies. When wartime propaganda films handled German themes these almost always emphasised that it was the Nazis who were the enemy; such films took care to include at least one "good German" to indicate that the war in the West was not directed against a whole nation. There were no "good Japanese" in the films about the Pacific war.

President Roosevelt spent quite a lot of his time thinking about the kind of world which would arise out of the Second World War. He was determined that European colonialism should be ended: the nations of Asia (though not of Africa) must be free to embrace the democratic ideal. And so he planned with his advisers how to get the British out of Hong Kong and the French out of Indo-China. In addition, he and his advisers were planning for the democratisation of militarist Japan when the war ended. The process could not be left to the Japanese themselves, and so an American superstructure would be erected to carry out democratisation. Maybe it would be necessary to introduce a new breed of man to replace the stubborn Japanese? The British Minister in Washington spent a weekend with the President and reported that (as one account puts it) Roosevelt had been "burbling away . . . on the possibility of bringing about a cross-breeding of European and various Asian races in the Far East in order to produce a stock less delinquent than the Japanese."

The same solution to the inadequacy of the brown peoples—cross-breeding with those of the superior race—occurred independently to Leopold Amery, the British Cabinet Minister in charge of India. Ruminating over the possibility of independence for India in future, he suggested to the Viceroy:

> If India is to be really capable of holding its own in future without direct British control from outside I am not sure that it will not need an increasing infusion of stronger Nordic blood, whether by settlement or intermarriage or otherwise. Possibly it has been a real mistake of ours in the past not to encourage Indian princes to marry English wives . . . and so breed a more virile type of native ruler. Perhaps all that may yet come about.

It is not easy to discover how these racial ideas, enunciated by Roosevelt and Amery, differed essentially from Hitler's ideology of a master race in Europe.

As America mobilised for war, military conscription was introduced on a massive scale. When black Americans were called to arms they were drafted to separate black units, as had been the invariable custom since the Civil War of the 1860s. Most Negroes were drafted into the army and were put into the transport, the stores and other "rear echelon" units. There were Negro combatant units, and these were organised into all-black brigades and divisions. Although after the United States found itself at war with Japan, all the *Nisei* who were in the armed forces were discharged, a few of them were permitted to get out of their camps by volunteering for an all-*Nisei* fighting unit. In the Pacific war American intelligence needed personnel knowing Japanese, and *Nisei* were recruited for intelligence work. No *Nisei* combatants were sent to the Pacific theatre of war. Similarly, there were no black and brown fighting men in Normandy and the invasion from the West: they were sent to Italy, where it was assumed by the American general staff that conditions were not so tough.

Some black non-combatant units spent a period of time in Britain before D-Day, and this posed a delicate problem in Anglo-American relations. The British attitude to race was still based upon the theory that in Britain everyone was treated equally, regardless of colour. The American approach (strongly influenced by the high proportion of southerners who graduated from West Point) was that black troops must be segregated from white. If black and white American soldiers collided in British pubs or dance halls there was trouble. The American army tried to persuade the British authorities to designate certain places of entertainment exclusively for the Negroes and to exclude them from other places; the British somewhat sanctimoniously declined to cooperate. However, the white and black American soldiers made their own arrangements for going their separate ways.

Questions of race and colour were salient in other countries of the United Nations, fighting for democracy and the rights of free peoples. South Africa joined Britain in the war against Germany by a very narrow margin of choice; a substantial proportion of the Afrikaners were strongly sympathetic to Hitler, and had their own quasi-Nazi organisation, the *Ossewa Brandwag*. Under the leadership of Smuts, British South Africans—and a proportion of the Afrikaners, especially of the Cape—participated actively in the war effort. South African forces served in the North African campaigns, and later in Italy. The fighting men were all white; black Africans, and also Indians, were recruited, but only for transport, engineer, and other services in which the soldiers did not carry arms. When these black and brown South Africans found themselves in the Western Desert alongside soldiers from India operating infantry weapons, artillery and armour they were humiliated. For South Africa, the comradeship of arms was confined to the white race. When ships carrying Indian troops docked at South African ports, the Indian officers stayed on board; to disembark was to invite exclusion from hotels and clubs.

The war progressed with scarcely any recognition by American or British leaders that these things existed. Nor did they realise that among the civilian population the war was having a massive effect upon non-white people. In the United States, the major war industries were located in the North and the Midwest and on the Pacific coast. It was in these areas that the mass production of tanks and planes and ships was concentrated. Industry needed labour, and was ready to pay good wages. Under these conditions, skin-colour was not the main consideration. Out of the rural South, Negro workers in thousands moved to Detroit, to Los Angeles, and to all the other centres where the weapons of war were being built. They migrated never to return.

On a much smaller scale, the British war industry—mainly reliant upon a massive mobilisation of British women—turned to sources overseas. From the Caribbean and from India there arrived technicians to work in British factories; the "Bevin boys" as they were called. To these black and brown newcomers, Britain—even in wartime—seemed a good place to live in.

There was a reverse process: the exposure of many thousands of British and American service personnel to the experience of Asia and the Middle East. Previously, the small numbers of professional British soldiers and American marines in India and China had lived largely self-contained lives in cantonments, forts, and other restricted areas. They had developed a certain contemptuous familiarity with Asian ways, and the vocabulary of British regular soldiers was much inter-larded with Hindustani terms, while the speech of American marines and sailors had a Chinese flavour. The encounter between East and West, in so far as it took place, reinforced the Western sense of innate superiority.

When British and American conscripts were decanted in the unfa-miliar East they were more vulnerable to the environment. They took over the outlook of racial superiority of the professional soldiers, and their vocabulary was augmented to include such all-embracing terms as *Wog, Gippy, Gook, Sambo* (they actually addressed all Asians as Joe). However, they lacked the panache of the old professionals; they were bewildered, bored, rather pathetic, and far from home. They got drunk disgustingly; they lusted after the local women without discrimi-nation; they drifted about on leave looking woebegone and bedraggled. In the case of the British they had too little pay, and so tried to beat down a shopkeeper or a bartender; in the case of the Americans they had too much pay, and they earned contempt from the bell boys and call girls to whom they handed out dollars when the local price was in cents.

The British conscripts, most of them good Labour voters, were just as imperialistic in their attitude to the "lesser breeds" as any Poona colonel of fiction; the Americans took with them their innate sense of superiority to black and also brown peoples. The effect of this tempo-rary exposure of millions of Anglo-Americans to unknown cultures has been portrayed with cautious sentimentality in *South Pacific* and more crudely in the novel *Virgin Soldiers* by Leslie Thomas. Racist attitudes, previously latent, were now active; and they did not become dormant with the coming of peace. When conscripts went home, the Arabs and Indians and Chinese remembered that they were not supermen after all.

The effects of the Second World War were least obvious in Africa. Apart from the restoration of Haile Selassie to his throne, there were no moves toward African self-government. Indeed, the African territories under British rule now attained their widest extent. It was in Asia, and particularly in South-east Asia, that the decline and fall of Western colonialism was made inevitable by the wartime experience.

From 1942 until 1944, the Japanese Greater East Asia Co-Prosperity Sphere appeared to have established a permanent Pan-Asian order over a region larger than Europe or North America. In their treatment of their Asian vassals the Japanese often did not bother to disguise their dominant status. A Japanese sergeant would administer a face-slapping to a Burmese or Indonesian without hesitation. At higher levels, there was not much effort to disguise the puppet status of those Southeast Asians installed in authority: "One had to recognise the 'Made in Japan' stamp on one's forehead" observed U. Nu who was designated as the Foreign Minister of Burma. And yet South-east Asians who would have risen no higher than schoolmasters or customs inspectors or sergeants under the Europeans now found themselves ministers, generals, judges. Burma, the Philippines, and eventually the former Dutch East Indies—now Indonesia—were declared to be independent nations, allies, not subordinates of the Japanese. The top leaders—Subhas Chandra Bose, Dr. Ba Maw of Burma, José P. Laurel of the Philippines and Sukarno of Indonesia—were invited to participate in spectacular war conferences at Tokyo. More important, young South-east Asians were trained to lead armies. The Burmese Thirty Comrades, led by *Bogyoke* (Great Captain) Aung San, formed the leadership for a Burma National Army; and similar forces were raised in Indonesia and the Philippines. These military forces provided the strongest guarantee that the independence conceded by Japan could not easily be snatched away.

Not all the peoples of South-east Asia shone in the glory of the Rising Sun. In Malaya and Singapore the Chinese community—over one-third of the total population—were treated from the start as the enemies of Japan. Many young Chinese took to the jungle, where they were supplied by the Home Army, the Chinese of the villages and towns. The jungle guerrillas—the Malayan People's Anti-Japanese

Army (M.P.A.J.A.)—were led by Chinese Communists, formerly active in trade unions. Their activities were confined to sabotage and ambush but they established a firm reputation among the Malayan Chinese as resistance heroes.

Similarly, in Indo-China—that is, in the territories which later became Vietnam—an anti-Japanese resistance movement was organised by Ho Chi Minh under the name of Viet Minh. Although receiving sparse military aid from China, and later from American sources, the Viet Minh was essentially a national movement opposed to the domination of all foreigners.

Japan's empire suddenly crumbled under the weight of the Allied attacks from 1944 onwards. On the Burma front, Bose's dream of an I.N.A. victory and a March on Delhi dissolved into the reality of the I.N.A.'s defeat, along with their Japanese overlords, and the re-occupation of Burma by British-Indian forces. Dr. Ba Maw was jailed as a Japanese collaborator, but Aung San and the Thirty Comrades were more skillful in switching sides at the correctly judged moment. Their Burma Army disappeared into the jungle, and re-emerged as the Anti-Fascist People's Freedom League (A.F.P.F.L.). Although some British military administrators found this *bouleversement* hard to take, the Supreme Commander, Admiral Mountbatten, decided to accept Aung San's proffered support. His army was supposed to be disbanded, with some units being enlisted into the British forces while the others were demobilised. However, with great skill, Aung San succeeded in keeping former units together under their old officers, notably the Thirty Comrades, while those demobilised were formed into what was presented as an old comrades' association, the People's Volunteer Organisation (P.V.O.). In reality the P.V.O. remained an organised, uniformed military force, available to Aung San in a national struggle.

The British government had planned to put post-war Burma into a kind of political deep-freeze, but thanks to Aung San's determined leadership independence could not be postponed into the future. Britain had been accustomed to rely upon Indian battalions to keep order in Burma when required; but now India was demanding its own independence, Indian soldiers could no longer be employed as British mercenaries. Under the threat of a general strike and a possible armed rising, Aung San got all he wanted. Independence was won in January 1948; but by then Aung San was dead—shot by an assassin. South-east Asia was to undergo a long and terrible experience of the truth of the prophecy that "they that take the sword shall perish with the sword." And so, though Burma was reoccupied by the former imperial power, this was temporary. The Philippines were reoccupied by American forces, though only after the path had been blasted by bombing, leaving the old city of Manila a smoking ruin. The rest of South-east Asia still remained under over-all Japanese control when, on 6 August 1945, the American atomic bomb was dropped on Hiroshima and 100,000 people died. Three days later a second atomic bomb was dropped, and the Emperor of Japan capitulated.

The technical development of the vast "Manhattan Project" reached the critical point where a bomb could be exploded from the air only after the defeat of Germany in Europe. Nevertheless, Asians have not ceased to speculate whether an American President would have dared to order an atomic attack upon a German city. It remains a grim fact that the only nuclear attack ever made was performed by white men against brown men. The poison from that decision will suppurate until the twentieth century is finished.

Because of the sudden and unexpected capitulation of Japan, most of the countries of South-east Asia went through an interlude in which one master had stood down and no other had arrived. In Malaya, the guerrillas of the M.P.A.J.A. heard of the news of Hiroshima and emerged from the jungle expecting to meet representatives of the Chinese army. They were amazed when British forces under Mountbatten landed at Penang and Singapore and proceeded to take over the administration. In a daze, the jungle guerrillas handed over most of their arms and permitted themselves to be demobilised. It was another three years before they made their bid for power again. However, in the brief moment between the fall of the Japanese and the arrival of the British, the Chinese jungle fighters exacted vengeance upon those who had collaborated with the Rising Sun: most of the collaborators were Malays, and the Malay population did not forget that moment when the Chinese exercised their mastery over Malaya.

The reassertion of the Western presence was much less easy in Indo-China and Indonesia. The task of occupation was suddenly and unexpectedly switched from the American forces under General MacArthur to the British-Indian forces under Admiral Mountbatten. Mountbatten was one of the few Anglo-American commanders sensitive to the reality that the old pre-1939 world had departed forever. He was only prepared to use his forces in the limited role of disarming the

Japanese and rescuing Allied prisoners of war; he was not going to commit them to the attempt to renew Western colonial domination. He had the responsibility of taking over Indo-China and Indonesia. He approached the task cautiously.

Neither France nor the Netherlands wanted the British to settle into the occupation of their territories: perhaps they might decide to stay permanently! These two countries, staggering out of five years of Nazi occupation, tried to rush their own forces to South-east Asia. By the time they arrived, they found that Mountbatten's representatives had gone a long way to recognising the legitimacy of Ho Chi Minh in Vietnam and Sukarno in Indonesia. Hastily taking over from the British, the French and the Dutch tried to reassert the colonial overlordship they had so ignominiously surrendered to the Japanese.

For four years the tenacious Dutch tried to bring Indonesia back into their orbit. Their forces were opposed by the Indonesian army created by the Japanese and, despite limited successes, the Netherlands could not substitute for the Sukarno government a regime of their own which was acceptable. Dutch military operations depended heavily upon a reconstituted colonial army, whose soldiers were drawn largely from the island of Ambon or Amboyna in the South Moluccas. The Ambonese belonged to the Melanesian, not the Malay race. Ambon had been Dutch for over three hundred years, and its inhabitants were all pious Calvinists, strongly responsive to Dutch influence and with no feeling of identity with the Muslims of Java and western Indonesia.

The Dutch campaign led to the first counter-action by Asians, expressing solidarity in the fight against imperialism. Led by India, the new states of Asia, together with some in the Middle East, imposed a ban upon all Dutch ships, the Netherlands government decided to recognise the independence of Indonesia, and in 1949 a formal agreement was signed and the Dutch withdrew from their former empire in the Indies, retaining control of New Guinea for a limited period.

At the same time, the Ambonese proclaimed their own separate independence as the Republic of the South Moluccas. They were unable to resist Indonesian pressure, and the little republic was ruthlessly repressed. Feeling a responsibility to their colonial soldiers, the Dutch government evacuated many Ambonese troops, together with their families, to the Netherlands. The move was expected to be only temporary until a *modus vivendi* could be arranged with Indonesia. Still demanding their own independence, the Ambonese remained in the

Netherlands, and by the 1970s there was no possibility of their return. However, they declined to integrate into Dutch society, formed their own government in exile, and lived apart in their own camps; yet another group of refugees who could not go home. The young Dutch-born Ambonese remain as strongly attached to the island they have never seen as their elders. When a Dutch train was hijacked by the Ambonese in 1975, the urban guerrillas involved were all young men.

The realistic Dutch turned their backs upon their old empire and proceeded to create a new prosperity within the emerging European community. France was less prepared to forget the glories of empire. It was necessary to accept the independence of Syria and the Lebanon, but in north and west Africa, in the Caribbean, and in Indo-China a great French empire remained intact: or so it seemed. Very soon it became clear that the main challenge would come from Vietnam. The rest of Indo-China—Laos and Cambodia—could be restored to the former, traditional order of things, But Ho Chi Minh was not prepared for any compromise which denied the reality of independence. More and more French troops were ordered to Vietnam; almost the whole of the Foreign Legion (a high proportion of whom were former Nazis) and colonial troops from Morocco, Algeria and Senegal. Although all the advantages seemed to be with the French command they were gradually compelled to abandon their frontier posts, and then many of their positions in the rural areas. The forces of Ho Chi Minh, led by General Giap, were transformed from jungle guerrillas into well-trained operational troops. This transformation was observed with growing alarm by the United States.

It will be recalled that the American Office of Strategic Services (O.S.S.: the forerunner of the C.I.A.) had actively assisted Ho Chi Minh in organising his guerrillas. However, American policy towards "liberation movements" was undergoing a total about-turn, in consequence of events in China. China had been a major field for American economic exploitation since the nineteenth century. It had also been *the* major field for American idealism. American Protestant missionaries had gone to China in thousands, and hundreds of young Chinese had been sent to the United States for higher education. There were even American universities, such as "Yale in China" which were transplants of American culture in the Far East.

Americans had been subjected to a remarkable propaganda exercise by the "China Lobby" in the United States Congress which succeeded in convincing Americans that the struggle waged by the forces of Generalissimo Chiang Kai-shek against Japan was much more formidable than the dismal reality of retreats and covert understandings with the Japanese which the K.M.T. leaders conducted while they accumulated their private fortunes. Madame Chiang, a member of a Methodist family, projected a most effective image of "Christian China" standing up to heathen Japan. It was assumed that because China was a republic, with a president, it was really remarkably like America.

When the K.M.T. forces ignominiously collapsed in the face of Mao Tse-tung's Red Army, and the whole of China rapidly became the People's Republic, the shock was traumatic. Nothing like this had ever happened before. The United States myth was that they won all the wars. Yet despite massive American military aid to Chiang Kai-shek, and the attachment of senior American military advisers to his staff, this war was decisively lost and the rump of the K.M.T. forces were evacuated to Taiwan by the American navy. Thus it had to be acknowledged that the United States had "lost" China to communism. No American leader was prepared to ask the question as to exactly how, or in what sense, the United States had a China to lose. Once again, a nation which had been admitted to honorary membership of the white club (at any rate by American humanitarians and idealists) had resigned from the club. American ideas underwent galvanic changes. Defeated Japan, subjected to all kinds of humiliation, suddenly became an important bastion of the United States, and began that return to esteem which, by the 1970s, had re-established that country in American eyes as perhaps the finest example of the Protestant work ethic.

Meanwhile, there was Vietnam, visibly failing to stand up to communism. When the French government approached America for arms, planes and other equipment, they found willing listeners. Along with American military hardware, American observers began to arrive in Saigon. They were not impressed by what they saw. The French colonial regime was paramount, and the attempt to rehabilitate the puppet Emperor, Bao Dai, failed to evoke any Vietnamese response. The implication of any American intervention was that they must take over responsibilities from the French; there could be no handover to Vietnamese leaders, as yet. Almost imperceptibly, the Americans began to ease aside the French.

The process was accelerated by two main factors. In 1953, John Foster Dulles became Secretary of State, and under the easygoing presidency of Eisenhower assumed virtual control of foreign policy. He adopted the policy of "brinkmanship," of escalating military pressure almost but not quite to the point of outright war. He carried the conception of foreign policy as morality to a similar extreme. For him, South-east Asia was a set of dominoes, standing upright in file; if one domino should fall, all would fall. Hence, Vietnam was vital, as the outstanding tottering domino.

The Vietnamese domino almost toppled over when the French high command committed its forces to the defence of a remote outpost, Dien Bien Phu. From March until May 1954, Dien Bien Phu withstood attack after attack. Reinforcements and ammunition were parachuted in, for the French command believed that the Viet Minh would destroy themselves in their attempt to take the place. They had fatally underestimated the determination of their opponents, who enjoyed artillery superiority and pounded the defenders under the ground. At last, a human assault wave roared over the defence, and Dien Bien Phu's 16,000 defenders surrendered.

John Foster Dulles offered to provide the French with two nuclear weapons in order to retaliate, but France had had enough. Premier Mendès-France undertook to secure a settlement, and by July 1954 a truce was negotiated at Geneva whereby France withdrew from all Vietnam north of the 17th parallel of latitude. The Geneva agreement was virtually the end of the French presence in Vietnam. Most of the French military transports bore the dejected legionaries and colonial troops to Algeria. Among those who had fought for the French in Vietnam was the Algerian sergeant, Ahmed Ben Bella. On 1 November 1954, a revolt broke out in the Aures Mountains of Algeria; among the resistance leaders was ex-sergeant Ben Bella.

However, the eyes of the world were more and more fixed upon Vietnam. When the French withdrew, the Americans planned to "Vietnamese" the fight against the Communists and their attention turned to a pious Catholic functionary, Ngo Dinh Diem, then a recluse in the United States with the Maryknoll Fathers. In July 1954 he replaced Bao Dai as head of state—President Diem. He soon gave evidence of all the necessary determination and ruthlessness, but he did not satisfy the American dream of "democratising" South Vietnam. Although he despised and rejected the French, his political philosophy, Personalism, was a form of the French cult of Existentialism. Looking around for a solution, Diem turned for advice to British officers who had helped to end the Communist "Emergency" in Malaya.

The anti-insurgent campaign in Malaya was the one success-story for "the free world" in the 1950s in Asia. The British had succeeded in containing the revolt which was launched in 1948 by former M.P.A.J.A. fighters. They isolated the jungle Communists, first by persuading the Malays that this was a purely Chinese affair, and then by successfully changing the image of the guerrillas into that of *terrorists*, bandits, enemies of the people. And finally they picked off the Communist leaders, one by one. Napoleon said the British were a nation of shopkeepers; he might equally have called the Chinese a nation of shopkeepers. Now, in Malaya, the British went shopping. They put a price on the head of every Communist leader. If it was not enough to buy him, they raised the price. Sooner or later one of his followers brought in the head for identification, and hastily departed to set up a filling station or a hotel on the other side of Malaya. By 1960, the Emergency was officially ended.

So President Diem tried to benefit from British advice. One of his ideas was to found *agrovilles,* strategic hamlets, which had been a part of the success in isolating the Communists in Malaya. The American advisers were not pleased by this adoption of seemingly unaggressive, un-American methods.

Dulles remained Secretary of State until 1959. With his departure, the momentum of American intervention slowed down. It was very worrying that despite a large counter-revolutionary programme to win the "hearts and minds" of the Vietnamese peasants, the countryside remained largely under the grip of the Communist guerrillas, to whom the name of Viet Cong was now attached. What should be done? Many insisted that what was needed was more effective economic aid, so that the Vietnamese could see that democracy brought greater prosperity than communism. The most popular exposition of this point of view was contained in *The Ugly American.*

With John F. Kennedy's installation in the presidency in January 1961 the pace quickened. Kennedy enunciated the doctrine of the "New Frontier" and announced that wherever freedom was threatened the United States would respond. His first unfortunate adventure was the attempted invasion of Cuba by C.I.A. hirelings, quickly overwhelmed by Castro's troops in the Bay of Pigs fiasco. Of more long-lasting consequence was his decision to send the American marines to Thailand in response to violations of the ceasefire in Laos which had followed the Geneva agreement. For the first time, the United States was totally committed; not just by providing advisers or cloak-and-dagger C.I.A. operators but by actually mustering ground combat troops in the Indo-China theatre.

American dissatisfaction with President Diem intensified, and in 1963 Diem was murdered in a military coup allegedly promoted by the C.I.A. with Kennedy's direct approval at a cost of $U.S. 20 million. Kennedy was assassinated a few days after Diem, and the new President, Lyndon Johnson, found the administration committed to Americanising the war. He obtained a blank cheque from Congress through the Gulf of Tonkin resolution (1964) and thereafter the numbers of American troops in South Vietnam rose steadily until they stood at 520,000 in 1968. These were additional to the army of South Vietnam (600,000 men), and foreign troops brought in to fight (50,000 from South Korea, and smaller numbers from Thailand, the Philippines, Australia and New Zealand) like the Hessians hired by George III to fight against Washington's army.

The lesson which Vietnam had for Asia and Africa was that the American people—those who had "fired the shot heard round the world" which began the process of revolution—were now the arch-imperialists, the suppressors of revolution. The Americans, who continued to preach their message of democracy, never understood that to the black and brown nations they were now the symbol of white oppression.

As the countryside became increasingly devastated by American bombing and raiding, more and more Vietnamese moved into Saigon which became a gigantic tourist centre catering for the American troops. Hundreds of American deserters settled in the city, opening bars and gambling-joints and taking Vietnamese wives. A great many American soldiers also acquired temporary Vietnamese mistresses. The orphanages were filled with children whose unknown fathers were Americans—white or black. A feverish atmosphere enveloped the city which had become a vicious parody of the American way of life. To a lesser extent, Bangkok, Singapore and Hong Kong were also corrupted by the frenzied search of the young American servicemen for an escape from the war. A great tide of resentment and hatred welled up against this crude American exploitation of South-east Asian cities and peoples. The Americans did not seem to care.

What Americans did understand was that the massive call-up of conscripts was causing an internal crisis in their country. At first, middle-class youths avoided the draft by going to college, or by getting married. As the regulations were tightened, they endeavoured to get away to universities abroad or to obtain exemption by declaring their opposition to the war. Working-class whites, and almost all blacks, were unable to opt out in these ways, so that a high proportion of the Americans in Vietnam—especially in the fighting units—were blacks, along with poor southern whites. Gradually, the draft began to affect suburban, middle-class, White America. Now came the era of campus protest; sincere, without doubt, but only aroused after the college students became personally exposed to the octopus of conscription. While unprecedented numbers of Americans were getting involved in Vietnam, something like an emotional civil war was tearing America itself apart. When in April 1970 President Nixon sent American forces into Cambodia there was a nationwide student protest of violent dimensions. At Kent State University the National Guard fired upon the students, killing four. By now, it was clear that if the United States was destroying Vietnam by air bombing heavier than throughout the whole of the Second World War, by the defoliation of its forests and the massacre of its people (as at My Lai), then also Vietnam was destroying the United States.

Gradually, the American army in Vietnam began to fall apart. The incidence of drug-taking was higher than among equivalent age groups in the United States, and indeed drugs were treated as a normal part of the combatant soldier's life, in order to counteract tension and fear. The black soldiers separated themselves from their white counterparts, wearing Black Power insignia and giving Black Power salutes instead of the normal salute (though they rarely saluted their white officers). The American army had become "integrated" at the time of the Korean War, abandoning the old segregated units, but once again the army was dividing into black and white; with a new sense that they were on opposing sides, for increasingly black leaders declared that they would not fight a war for the white men against the Vietnamese people.

President Nixon had promised the American voters he would end the war with a victory over communism; instead it was obvious that the war must be ended on any terms possible. Negotiations with the Viet Cong and with North Vietnam opened in Paris in May 1968, but a ceasefire agreement was not concluded until January 1973. By then, many American soldiers had been withdrawn, and after the agreement they all departed. From the American standpoint, the last remaining objective was to secure the release of American prisoners of war.

When they were returned in February, Vietnam ceased to dominate the television screens of America.

A high price had been paid. The Communist forces were holding their own recognised zones in South Vietnam, and within two years the military regime, propped up for so long by mountainous American military aid, abruptly collapsed. The Communists took over, renaming Saigon as Ho Chi Minh city.

At the last moment there was a scramble to get out by those Vietnamese identified as American collaborators: and also by hundreds of others caught up in the mood of panic. About 12,000 were admitted into the United States and a few (mainly orphans) came to Britain and other countries. Then America turned its back upon Vietnam. Unlike the "loss" of China, this much more real loss, costing so much in American lives and American public money and American prestige, brought no witch-hunt in the United States. Too many leading Americans had been involved in the tragic misadventure. And the lesson was too painful: brown men could defeat white men, even when the whites had all the big guns and the big bombs.

Beside the American defeat in Vietnam the French withdrawal from Algeria was less obviously a world disaster, and yet for a time it appeared as though it might destroy both Algeria and France. The crisis came in 1958 when French military leaders, in conjunction with the European population of Algiers and Oran, rebelled endeavouring to overthrow the French government. The crisis was resolved by the return of de Gaulle as President, putting all his immense prestige behind finding a solution. The war in Algeria dragged on, with the same brutality as in Vietnam, and the same mobilisation of brown men to fight other brown men at the orders of white officers. Finally, in 1962 the Algerian nationalists won: at a cost of 1½ million dead in a nation of 11 million. Agreement was reached upon a procedure whereby France withdrew and recognised the F.L.N. *(Front de Libération Nationale)* as the government. The new situation involved the departure of most of the white colonists who had lived in Algeria for generations and were known to the metropolitan French as *pieds noirs*. Uneasily, they tried to make a new life; many settling in Corsica. The thousands of Algerians who had fought in the French army against the F.L.N. could not be abandoned, and like the Ambonese they went into exile into the homeland of their European masters. Algerians had long gone to France as temporary workers, filling an essential role in the construction industry and other sectors demanding cheap manpower.

After Algeria became independent, French sentiment turned against the Algerians and they paid for their country's independence by becoming outcasts in France, liable to be set upon at any time, or even murdered, without the French police feeling any kind of responsibility.

Vietnam and Algeria were the only countries which overthrew Western colonialism by a prolonged armed struggle, but in important ways their struggle was reflected in the attitude of other Third World countries to the West. Algeria and Vietnam demonstrated that the façade of Western imperialism was vulnerable. Between 1945 and 1970, Western imperialism—white dominance—came to an end everywhere, except in the southern extremity of Africa. Brown men absorbed the lesson that the white metropolitan strongholds were vulnerable too, and after the jungle fighter was to come the urban guerrilla.

7

ROY FRASER HOLLAND

Mobilization, Rejuvenation and Liquidation: Colonialism and Global War

Alongside the rise of the United States and the Soviet Union as the globe's superpowers, decolonization stands as a prime characteristic of the post–World War Two era. In the years since the foundation of the United Nations at the San Francisco Conference of 1945, its membership has more than tripled from the original fifty-one members. This increase is no small indication of a

Reprinted from Roy Fraser Holland, *European Decolonization 1918–1981: An Introduction,* copyright © 1985, pp. 37–69, with the permission of St. Martin's Press.

changed world. In hindsight, the decline of European empires has taken on an air of inevitability. The British Empire, spread over every continent except Antarctica, encompassed one-fourth of the globe's surface in 1939. When Britain joined the European Community in 1973, its empire had shriveled to a scattering of miscellaneous islands. Its successor, the Commonwealth, enjoys only a shadowy existence. The Dutch, French, and Portuguese empires have gone the same road. Was this inevitable? If not, who or what was responsible? Did the war play a decisive role? What specific place did it have in the decline of colonial domains in the postwar world?

In the following selection, Roy Fraser Holland rejects simplistic answers. He is surely correct in stating that the wartime period itself saw an extension of British imperial power. Without its global financial connections, and colonial raw materials and manufacturing to draw on, the island kingdom might not have withstood the year in which it fought alone against Germany. Holland eschews unicausal factors, however, and leads the reader into an intricate and condensed, though lucidly presented argument. In approaching the debate, he analyzes five topics: the impact of Japan's conquests in East Asia, the mobilization of colonial societies (especially by Britain, since France and the Netherlands fell too quickly for them to do much), the effect of the Anglo–American alliance on European colonies, the story in the Empire's most opulent colony, India, and finally the impact of the war on Africa.

The Second World War poses some difficult interpretive problems when viewed from the perspective of later European decolonizations. The standard textbook theme on this matter is that the impact of total war on the UK's strategic and, above all, economic capacities was such as to make the loss of empire inevitable, even if the African dénouement was subsequently delayed. In this bald state, however, the argument is facile. The facts were rather to the contrary: the successful orchestration of massive colonial war efforts indicated that Britain still had the leverage to operate an aggressive imperial states-system, if it chose to accept the costs of doing so. In this sense, as John Gallagher has so vividly portrayed, the Second World War was a time of imperial revival, when the traditional collaborative coalitions at the periphery were shocked into a new and powerful, if short-lived, equilibrium. On the other hand, quite clearly the 1939–45 conflict did trigger changes at a variety of levels—diplomatic, strategic and economic—which transformed the contexts of European empire and shifted the odds against, not in favour of, their long-term (and sometimes even their short-term) survival. But there is no contradiction in these superficially contrasting facets: it was the very scope and scale of the colonial war machines which held within them elements likely to react against any return to the pre-war patterns of rule. We shall try to elucidate these processes by looking at five aspects of wartime experience: the effects of Japan's conquests in east Asia after December 1941; the consequences which sprang from the mobilization of colonial societies for Allied purposes; the implications of the Anglo–American alliance for colonial empires; the course of affairs in India; and social change and settler power in Africa.

I. The Japanese Revolution in East Asia

The Japanese presence in Asian diplomacy had constituted a challenge to western domination since the 1890s. Japan's subsequent commercial expansion, culminating in its massive export-led growth after 1931, held out the possibility that the British, French and Dutch empires could be progressively penetrated by Japanese economic mastery. Indeed, in retrospect it is easy to see that such a strategy of informal influence eating its way through the forms of European colonialism would have suited Japanese ambitions best of all; as it was, Japan gambled all on a war and, in defeating the European colonialists, merely opened the door wide for the Americans and a medley of local political operators. It is because the Japanese attack on Pearl Harbour during December 1941 was such a seminal event on the way to Asian decolonization that some brief remarks on its rationale must be made.

The key to Japanese history during the approach to war lay in the astonishing transformation of its economy during the 1930s. In 1929 that economy had remained locked into a textile phase of industrialization, with its prime export commodity, raw silk, as much an agricultural as a manufactured article; by 1939, against all earlier expectations, Japanese industry had developed a capital goods sector and a technological underpinning equal to most of its chief western competitors. Population growth, far from preventing this internal revolution, had hurried it forward by concentrating the mind of the imperial bureaucracy in Tokyo on diversification of employment and incomes. This route to social stabilization, however, required access to markets and raw materials in the surrounding region (in Manchuria, for example) which, under prevailing conditions, could only be secured by force, thus increasing the power of the army and the xenophobes. By the end of the decade Japanese industrialism was driven to seek new economies of scale in an Asian mastery which brought it into inevitable deadlock with western powers.

The Japanese, however, were curiously convinced right up to mid-1941 that their regional objectives were attainable without a big war. This was because they were confident that ultimately the Americans would join them in a re-partition of east Asia; thus China and the western colonies in the area would be reallocated within Japanese and American "spheres" and hitched more securely than ever to external metropoles. This Japanese expectation that the United States could be detached from its European partners (above all, Britain) seemed sensible enough in the Pacific context, but it failed to grasp the fundamental Atlanticism of American commerce and diplomacy. Thus the steady Japanese encroachments throughout 1940 on French Indo-China and the Dutch East Indies failed in their general aim of refashioning American policy. But in the process the militarists came to dominate policymaking in Tokyo. An uneasy "war consensus" finally prevailed in Japan, based on the assumption that one decisive assault upon the Americans would induce them to negotiate a "new order" settlement. In effect, President Roosevelt was to be forced to choose between the British and the Japanese; in subsequently sticking to the former he made inevitable a prolonged Pacific conflict which transformed the history of Asia.

Once the American Pacific fleet had been substantially destroyed in the attack on Pearl Harbour it did not take long for Japanese authority to extend itself throughout much of east Asia. French Indo-China had already been under effective Japanese domination from August 1940 onwards; with the fall of Singapore in mid-February 1942 the whole of the Malayan archipelago was absorbed within the Japanese empire; the Dutch East Indies was similarly digested. These territories remained under occupation until the atomic onslaught on Hiroshima and Nagasaki in early August 1945. Thus for four years these Asian societies had Japanese influences deeply implanted upon them; the ideology of a "Greater East Asia Co-Prosperity Sphere" was rooted into the local environment and this bundle of ideas (with its material emphases implied in the title) played a vital historical role in generating an Asian consciousness which, after 1945, could not be forced back into colonial containers.

It was the fall of Singapore, however, which of all the events of this period, has been taken as the vital moment at which western supremacy in the East was broken. The full weight of this point may be somewhat misjudged, reflecting more the shock which the Singapore debacle administered to the British public than to its effects on Asian populations. Nevertheless, the collapse of the British defence of Singapore, the great imperial bastion in the region, indicated the essential hollowness of colonial power in the face of external pressure. To those observers, such as Mao Tse-tung or Ho Chi Minh, who had already grasped a good deal of the theory and practice of revolutionary guerrilla action, here was convincing evidence that determined campaigns using the cover of the jungle could break a colonial system seated in the towns and cities. Meanwhile in Britain there was a pained surprise that the Malay and Chinese populations of Singapore had not risen in loyal defiance of the Japanese, and assisted the British forces in a courageous last-ditch resistance; instead, the civil populations had passively accepted their fate, and the British military preparations proved to be inadequate. From this point onwards the British public had an alternative image of colonialism in Asia, peopled by a whisky-sodden old-guard of administrators and traders incapable of meeting the needs of modern business and government. Certainly it was during the Second World War, and not least under the impact of the Singapore disaster, that colonial rule began to be viewed with dislike and disdain in many quarters of the British home democracy.

In all Japanese-occupied territories, the events which took place in the war years had vital long-term significances. Thus the origins of the Chinese Communist insurgency in Malaya, which broke out in 1948, lay in the 1942–45 period. The chief victims of Japanese rule in Malaya and Singapore had not been Europeans, however bitter the impositions suffered by the white inmates of Changi jail, but the preponderant Chinese population. The Japanese, here as elsewhere, attempted to cow the one Asian race capable of challenging their regional dominance; thousands of Chinese were executed in Singapore to ensure the liquidation of underground leaderships. The experience of this subjugation, however, bound the hitherto disparate Chinese community into a greater degree of solidarity, and the fact that the Communists were the only segment of the Malayan Chinese to effect any outright resistance to Japanese authority invested them, in particular, with great prestige. In fact the Malayan Peoples' Anti-Japanese Army (MPAJA) largely remained in its isolated jungle hide-outs, and only made very rare contact with Japanese forces, but the continuity of their guerrilla existence had political importance. Their survival was helped by the manner in which the Japanese, to reduce the problem of feeding the towns, forced thousands of Chinese out into the country-side to become rural squatters. This scattered rural migration created pockets from which MPAJA (and, after 1948, anti-British insurgents) could be supplied with food and recruits. Ironically, Lord Louis Mountbatten, as Supreme Allied Commander South-East Asia, reinforced MPAJA's local legitimacy by forging contacts with them in 1944, and establishing a supply-line preparatory to the projected Allied attack on Japanese positions in the archipelago. The suddenness of the Japanese defeat precluded this final drama, and presented MPAJA with a clear opportunity to move into the resulting vacuum before the British had a chance to appear on the scene and take over from the Japanese forces, who had promptly thrown down their arms. In fact MPAJA resisted the temptation to exploit these circumstances, simply paying off a few old scores, in the hope that the returning British would repay them in political kind. It was the sense that their restraint had not been recompensed after 1945 which antagonized much Chinese opinion. Thus in Malaya the war years were crucial in breaking the old balances of colonial politics beyond repair.

Perhaps the dominant fact about Japanese administration in occupied east Asia was that it exercised a looser rein than its British or Dutch predecessors. It was, of course, militarist in nature, and stringently carried out the tasks integral to the war effort, but these terms of reference left much of local society, especially in the countryside, relatively uncontrolled compared to the long-established machines of the old European bureaucracies. Apart from forays by the Japanese secret police, intense but sporadic campaigns of food procurement and some dramatic cases of forced labour (such as the construction of the Burma Road) there was a sense in which the years between 1939 and 1945 were a fresh experience of freedom from external interferences. The organizational vitality of much local Asian politics under Japanese occupation was partly an expression of this situation, although it was, even more, a product of the characteristic style of Japanese supervision. Thus whereas the European colonialists had always sought to break up mass organizations wherever possible, fearing that at some point they were bound to become infected by political or religious assertiveness, the Japanese sought to manipulate opinion through the encouragement of associations and clubs. Above all, the latter tried to diffuse the enthusiasms surrounding the Greater East Asian Co-Prosperity Sphere by allowing Asian youths to participate in mass sport and (under certain controlled conditions) militia training. The classic instance of this was the Pemuda organization in Indonesia, which cultivated the ruthless authoritarian ideals of Japanese militarism. Just how successful this strategy of linking Japanese power with these youthful and malleable cadres might have been is unknowable, since the experiment was cut short by the Anglo–Americans' own brand of technological brutality at Hiroshima. But the organizational initiatives of the period of Japanese occupation galvanized a whole generation into racial consciousness and introduced them to the basic military arts; again, such a massive psychological arousal of these societies created a texture of life radically different from that of the pre-war Asian world.

The relationship which existed between the Japanese authorities and the secular nationalists is particularly worthy of note, since it was the latter who were to rise to prominence, rather than their erstwhile religious allies, after 1945. At first the Japanese had been sensitive to the fact that secularists such as "Engineer" Sukarno in Indonesia would be more difficult to graft into the Co-Prosperity Sphere than the volatile but pliable revivalism of such religious bodies as the Muhammadija. A competitive dynamic set in during which the secular politicians established "reading clubs" as a front for their continued activities while the Japanese syphoned off their potential supporters into sporting associations, youth-militias and coordinated religious gatherings; this multiplication of institutions enhanced that splintering of Indonesian political culture which was to be the prime motif of the republican revolution after 1945. But the Japanese were nonetheless careful not to suppress the political nationalists altogether. Sukarno and his associates were given jobs and periodically used as a means whereby the Japanese could communicate with the population through a local agency other than the Islamic authorities. Between 1942 and 1945 Indonesian politicians were continuously being moved out of, and back into, the spotlight; never allowed to become independent actors, they were retained as people who might, one day, have their uses for the occupiers. Indeed, after late 1944 the Japanese did begin to build up Sukarno as a "man of destiny." In this way they ensured that, regardless of their own likely defeat in the war against the Americans, the returning Europeans would not be able to piece together the fragments of their old mastery. It was during this last phase of Japanese rule, when local populations were exposed to enormous uncertainties as to the future direction of affairs, that nationalism became a majority sentiment amongst the political classes of many areas, since it afforded a point of anchorage in a confused and frightening world.

Of all the Japanese-occupied parts of wartime Asia, the most anomalous position was that prevailing in Indo-China. This merits particular attention since that area was to figure so largely in later regional transformations. In August 1940 the Vichy authorities in France and the Japanese Government negotiated an agreement whereby the French colonial administration remained *in situ* in Indo-China, while a Japanese occupying force ensured that its constituent territories (above all, Tonkin and Cochin) were meshed into the war economy managed from Tokyo. This humiliating and precarious position not surprisingly split local French residents into Vichyites and Gaullists; such internal divisions did not go unnoticed amongst the Vietnamese cadres whose confidence in their old rulers was instantly affected. Nevertheless, the French Governor-General, Admiral Decoux, sought to shore up his administration by experiments designed to rally local opinion. Educational opportunities were expanded, and the curriculum reformed out of its narrow vocational bias; Vietnamese were admitted to the higher branches of the bureaucracy, a concession they had unavailingly sought throughout the 1930s; and police surveillance of all Vietnamese political life was toned down. Under the impact of war, and with the *possibility* of a decisive Japanese coup never more than days away, Decoux had to broaden and deepen the collaborative link between French authority and the middle orders of Vietnamese society; but in doing so the Governor-General risked the catalysis of social and political forces which were incompatible with any effective restoration of the old colonial regime at the war's end.

Just as important as Decoux's frantic signals to Vietnamese elites, however, was the wartime progress made by the Indo-Chinese Communists, or Viet Minh. The Viet Minh organization had been formed in 1941, and was largely the creation of Ho Chi Minh, who eleven years earlier had set up the Indo-Chinese Communist Party (ICP). The latter body, however, had been almost wholly isolated in Indo-Chinese politics, and was constantly harassed by the French security services. The war, in effect, suddenly opened up new opportunities for Ho Chi Minh just when all had seemed lost. It greatly increased the number of dissident factions which, while not adhering to Communist ideology, nevertheless saw the benefits which could flow from the eviction of the French. It was to attract this new constituency that the ICP leader established the Viet Minh as a popular anti-colonial "front," but within which Communist control was absolute from the first. Furthermore, the war, by cutting off the local French authorities from metropolitan reinforcement, and by forcing them to concentrate their troops in positions from which the in-coming Japanese garrisons could be kept in some sort of check, meant that the Viet Minh were given a breathing space to establish strongholds in remote areas, particularly in the isolated, upland regions of the south-west. Here were the ideal conditions for the setting-up of Communist guerrilla bases, since the terrain was matched by a population (the tribal Thos) who had long resisted all outside intruders, be they French or Vietnamese. The Viet Minh themselves were hardly welcome guests to the tribal communities, but at least they initially caused less displacement, and therefore less resentment, than the full panoply of colonial administration. By building up a presence in this milieu, therefore, the Viet Minh were able to enjoy a rare period of security in which they could develop logistical procedures, forge a consensus on military strategy and, above all, accumulate weaponry. On this last point it was a matter of vital significance that the most northerly Viet Minh strongholds lay athwart the Chinese border; the warlords of south China supplied the Viet Minh with guns and ammunition during the war on the grounds of a shared enmity with the Japanese. This supply was later cut off, but by August 1945, when the Viet Minh triumphantly marched into Hanoi, the capital of Tonkin, they had large stocks of weapons at their disposal.

But although the war thus helped the Viet Minh construct baseareas, there always remained the possibility that they would be bottled up in these isolated retreats and finally throttled by whoever (French or Japanese) ended up controlling the cities and delta-routes of IndoChina. So why did this scenario not occur and why, instead, did Viet Minh influence spread through Tonkin and, to a lesser extent, Cochin? At the risk of simplification, it can be said that the war brought together two sensations, the combination of which was to prove politically explosive: hunger and nationalism. In an agricultural economy whose excess population always kept it on the verge of food shortage, the wartime disruption of production (with the Japanese appropriation of much of the surplus crop, the frequent conscription of the workforce and the drying-up of rural credit) pushed it over the edge into a famine which killed millions of people. The scale of this dislocation can only be guessed at; the dramatic contortions of post-war Indo-China arose, in no small part, from this collective trauma. Meanwhile the Viet Minh were careful to play down their Communist identity and adumbrate their own central position in a nationalist spectrum; they struck a cautiously ambivalent note on land reform, so as not to alienate landlord classes; they even liquidated, at least officially, their own institutional forms and merged with a new organization, the Dong Minh Hoi, which was allegedly representative of all nationalist factions. By promoting themselves as the spearhead of an anti-Japanese, anti-French front, the Viet Minh leadership were able to tap into profound political emotions at almost every level of Vietnamese society.

Indeed, nowhere were the convolutions of the last stages of the war in Asia more significant for the future than in Indo-China. In March 1945 the Japanese finally moved against the French administration, disarming its forces and interning its political and civil leaders. In this way the Japanese put themselves in a position to arrange a *de facto* Indo-Chinese succession which would confront the Anglo–American allies when they finally fought their way back into the area. An "independent" government was set up at Hue, with sovereignty over Tonkin and Annam, with Tran Trong Kim as Prime Minister, and Kim, though fearful of taking actions which might offend the western powers on the point of victory, soon found himself besieged by student demonstrators demanding tangible signs of a new autonomy. In northern Indo-China the Japanese had thus unleashed a popular nationalism most likely to embarrass the western "restorationists." Meanwhile, in Cochin, with its endemic factionalism, there could be no pretence of transferring power to a single authority, and therefore the Japanese satisfied themselves with arming those groups (including nationalists and religious sects) most likely to oppose a renewal of European authority. This was the position when the Japanese surrender reduced them to mere spectators of Indo-Chinese affairs. In Tonkin the Viet Minh were able to carry out the "August Revolution," taking Hanoi with barely a shot fired. The puppet government at Hue was disbanded. In so far as there could be any certainties under contemporary conditions, it was clear that Ho

Chi Minh's new republic represented the only viable point of consensus. The position in Cochin now became dramatically different. Here the neutralization of Japanese authority was the signal for internecine warfare to break out between rival groups, with assassination as the favoured *modus operandi*. The British reoccupation of Saigon in early September 1945 did little to restore stability, and when these (mostly Indian Army) troops were withdrawn following pressure from the Government of India, the British command had to yield responsibility to the French earlier than had been anticipated. By the autumn therefore, a Viet Minh regime was firmly installed in the north, while French reinforcements were beginning to pile up in the south; both these groups were committed to the unification of Vietnam under their own sole hegemony. In this way the stage had been set for the most disastrous of all Asian decolonizations: the Franco-Communist war in Indo-China between late 1946 and 1954.

II. The Consequences of Imperial Mobilization

The key to success in modern warfare has been the ability to effect a rapid increase in industrial and agricultural production, and to keep it at that level long enough to effect a military decision. It might, therefore, be wondered why Great Britain was able even to consider going to war with Germany in 1939, since the latter's economy was, in most important respects, already markedly stronger by comparison. British strategic credibility, however, derived from a very special combination of factors: an advanced industrial base, a position at the centre of the world's commodity trades and island-status (the last fact, usually emphasized as the source of British security, is almost devoid of explanatory power on its own). It was the UK's ability to act as an imperial economic state, weaving together the varied resources of many societies well out of the Luftwaffe's range, which meant that her potential opposition had always to be taken seriously. Nevertheless, such a imperial *tour de force,* successfully executed in 1914–18, was subject to many uncertainties, and in 1939 there was no guarantee that the necessary formulae for success, in India, for example, still existed. In this sense, the great continental states—the United States, Russia and Germany—could contemplate war mobilization rather more equably, since the materials and manpower to be employed existed very largely within the metropole's own frontiers. For Britain (and France, and

Holland) it was, in contrast, necessary to push and pull the administrative levers which connected their societies with such distant and fragile entities as colonial India, Indo-China and Indonesia. A prolonged war thus exposed imperial relationships at all levels to pressures which were permanently to affect the future course of affairs.

In fact the defeats of metropolitan France and Holland meant that it was only Britain who had to *sustain* the challenge of colonial mobilization. The pattern this took was, in many instances, a matter of improvisation dictated by events. Once the Japanese had overrun the rubber estates of Malaya, British (and American) needs had to be met by shifting production of that commodity to West Africa, significantly extending the frontiers of the cash-crop economy in the latter region. Similarly, food production in East Africa had to be boosted in order to avert the disastrous shortages in that area which had occurred during the First World War; the result was that many more Africans were brought within the money economy than hitherto. It was the network of industrial trade, however, which underwent the most radical transformation as British factories were forced to concentrate on meeting domestic demand for military and civilian goods, and were thereby less able to cater for export markets. Colonial consumers had to seek new sources of supply; sometimes this meant turning to U.S. manufacturers, but often it was domestic industry which expanded to fill the gap. Thus, as we noted earlier, revenue pressures in the 1930s had pressed some colonial governments towards a modest, tariff-nurtured industrialization; wartime foreign exchange and shipping shortages continued this transformation. Again, the most striking example of this process can be found in India. Before 1939 industrialization in India had largely been limited to consumer articles; between 1939 and 1945 the British bureaucracy actually encouraged local entrepreneurs to enter the capital goods sector, such as the manufacture of chemicals, motor cars and light tanks. By 1945 the consolidation of this industrial master class at the heart of the Indian economy gave it the resources and patronage to do what, in the 1930s, had been unthinkable: to face the *Raj* as a co-equal power. India, of course, is a rare example of such dramatic wartime change; mostly, where the internal availability of skills and raw materials were distinctly limited, industrialization meant little more than the growth of such activities as cement- and brick-making, or food-processing. Nevertheless, it can be seen that the Second World War had entailed a massive rejigging of production structures in many parts of the British empire; for this reason alone the political relations which span from these economic facts were bound to be discontinuous with the pre-1939 world.

A nice example of what war mobilization meant in a particular case can be found in the allied Middle East Supply Centre (MESC). The necessity of building up local production in this region was obvious from the start of the war, since the proximity of the Italian Navy made Anglo–American supply especially difficult; not only did British armies in North Africa need a continuous flow of material, but so did the civilian population of Cairo—after all, the prospect of riots in the rear of the desert campaigns was a potential nightmare for British commanders. In 1939, however, the Middle East had only a very limited capacity for modern economic activity; Egypt, at least, had a relatively developed railway system, but in most other respects lacked the assets for self-transformation, while neighbouring states were characterized by a pervasive rural stagnancy. The task of the MESC was to nullify these disadvantages by building roads, distributing seeds, exploiting existing machinery to the full (sometimes pooling equipment drawn from a variety of localities into a single productive centre) and only where absolutely vital importing capital goods. For the duration of the war economic expansion in the Middle East was much less subject than hitherto to the constraints of market values and the absence of local skills, and instead was driven by the Allies' military and political necessity. Naturally, this expansion of modern productive activity was very localized, and the military situation set up blockages of its own, but the MESC provides one illustration of how Anglo–American mobilization reworked the fabric of those underdeveloped societies which found themselves exposed to its full weight.

Such resource mobilization, however, inevitably involved inflationary consequences. The presence of Allied armies, and the boost to local commodity production, increased money circulation just when the availability of consumer goods was being curtailed, pushing up prices to record levels. This inflation was predictably at its peak in the grain markets, where the large landowners and mercantile cliques made fortunes out of hoarding and speculation. Three chief effects of these processes can be isolated. Firstly, wartime inflation advanced the conjunction of urban and countryside elites, adding strength and coherence to local ruling classes. Thus landed magnates equipped with liquid funds from grain profits invested them in urban assets and so extended their own range of contacts and influence; such tightening links between rural and town cadres were a precondition of modern mass nationalism, since previously the European authorities had alone been able to span the contrasting social worlds in colonial territories. Secondly, rising prices diffused grievances amongst those urban "middle orders" who did not have access to their own food stocks and who were especially vulnerable to grain speculation; those on fixed incomes, which meant (among others) the employees of the colonial bureaucracy, saw their living standards critically eroded during the war years. Thus individuals who, when educational access had expanded during the 1920s and 1930s, rushed to equip themselves with the weapon of literacy and then scrambled their way to a clerical job in some government office, found these slender gains being clipped back by the impact of inflation and shortage in the 1940s; it was among this "petty bureaucracy" that nationalism was to lodge with such explosive power in the post-war era. Thirdly, rising prices also put light consumer goods out of reach of the mass of colonial peasantries. Of course, the effective purchasing power of peasant incomes had been low before the war, but the flow of western goods had represented a marked improvement in living standards for rich and middle peasants; their sense of deprivation when this flow was greatly diminished gave political nationalism a vital means of access to the rural masses. In all these ways the inflationary effects of war government broke the traditional balances of colonialism and quasi-colonialism; new alignments, grievances and leverages were created within local societies which made it much harder for the old mechanisms of European power to operate.

The British dilemma over wartime inflation (whether in India, Egypt or elsewhere in Africa) illustrates the bind in which colonial rule was now caught. To some extent inflationary pressures could be reduced by freezing the sterling credits which the UK came to owe colonial governments for war expenditure; indeed, there was no way to pay these debts under war conditions anyway—and there were many, not least the Americans, who took the view that they were not UK liabilities at all, but legitimate contributions by colonial populations for their own protection. The British Government, looking to its future relations with indigenous bourgeois classes, was not prepared to go this far down the path of appropriation, but it made sure that the funds used to requite the colonial economic effort remained in paper form and securely stashed away in the Bank of England, and so did not add to the "ready" cash flows in the areas concerned. But the line against inflation could not be held so easily as this. There was, for example, the problem of the *working* funds which were necessarily pumped directly into local economies through military procurement and increased civil employment in factories, canteens and transport functions. These extra monies alone, relative to the size of the economies involved, were enough to threaten a ripping inflation, the only hope of controlling which lay in stringent price controls. The attempt to impose such controls, and under extreme circumstances to requisition scarce grain supplies, pitched the British authorities against those elites on whose collaboration the colonial polity had always depended. The emergence of black markets in British-ruled Asia and Africa marked not only the determination of local producers to maximize the market opportunities which the war economy had held out to them, but also a line of political cleavage between ruler and ruled which was bound to have long-term consequences. British wartime propaganda, therefore, was packed full of the statistical successes of colonial mobilization; what went unnoticed, except by a very few, was the manner in which, amidst this flurry of official achievement, the delicate structure of local collaborative understandings had been shattered.

One adjunct of this "collaborative decomposition" lay in a heightened competitiveness between political factions in colonies and quasi-colonies which made the efficacy of imperial intervention more than ever problematical. What, more specifically, this could mean can be deduced from the Egyptian crisis of 1942, when the King, eager to keep open his lines of communication with the growing anti-British sentiment in his country, appointed a new Prime Minister whose credentials anything but pleased the British Ambassador, Sir Miles Lampson. Lampson acted with characteristic decisiveness, surrounding the royal palace with tanks and effecting the rapid appointment of a new premier. However, this action gravely undermined the popular prestige of the monarchy, on which the 1922 Anglo–Egyptian settlement was not least founded, and the events of 1942 can be seen as inaugurating that decline of royalist politics which led to the Army coup of 1952 and so to the anti-British regime of Gamal Abdul Nasser. The British were therefore able during the Second World War to shunt their dependent (and semi-dependent) partners into a massive war effort which helped them to victory in the strategic theatres of a world-wide conflict, but this (perhaps surprising) success created patterns of social and political antagonism inimical to longer term British interests.

III. Colonialism and the Anglo–American Alliance

Recently historians have devoted considerable attention to the course of Anglo–American relations during the Second World War. Shifting away from the old preoccupation with the "Great Alliance," these investigations have focused on the divided perspectives within the London–Washington relationship. In fact Allied objectives in Europe between 1941 and 1945 remained a matter for relatively easy consensus, despite differences over tactical priorities; it was in relation to non-European theatres that the British and US Governments were at loggerheads. Thus, for the Americans, the war was a great opportunity to forge access to regions which hitherto the UK had monopolized. Indeed, US interests had been attempting to penetrate the Middle East since the 1920s, with some success; the historic alliance struck between President Roosevelt and the ambitious Saudi monarch, Ibn Saud, on board USS *Murphy* in February 1945 marked the end of Britain's success in choking off the intrusions of great-power competitors into Middle Eastern politics. If the Saudis provided the Americans with a *point d' appui* in Arab affairs, Washington circles looked to General Chiang Kai-shek to provide them with similar facilities in the crucial case of China. Roosevelt wished to elevate China to the status of a great Asiatic power whose voice, characterized, of course, by a distinctively American accent, would be heard on all the chief regional issues; it was with this end in view that Roosevelt insisted that Chiang Kai-shek and his formidable wife should attend the Cairo Conference in November 1943. The US President, in short, tried to direct the future shape of Asian affairs in ways that shifted power and influence from those states long held within the European orbit (India, Indo-China and Indonesia) to a Nationalist China firmly brought under American patronage. Implicit in this, too, was Roosevelt's consistent desire to foster the congruency of aims between American strategy and anti-colonial nationalism, an axis which seemed to hold out limitless possibilities for the moulding of world affairs when peace came. Only Chiang Kai-shek's crushing defeat at the Communists' hands, and the inexorable manner in which anti-colonialism and anti-Americanism overlapped after 1945, showed these Rooseveltian subtleties to be streaked with illusion.

Roosevelt's critical attitude towards European empires, however, only partly arose from the lust for a world role which gripped the Washington bureaucracy after 1939 (and especially after 1941). It was also a response towards mainstream American opinion. A profound aversion to "British imperialism" had always run deeply (if unevenly) in American society. This was particularly marked between September 1939 and December 1941, because it could be held that US treasure was being poured out through the Lend-Lease Act for the support of a British imperial war. America's entry into the war after Pearl Harbour against Germany as well as Japan did not fully dissipate these sentiments, so that Roosevelt required some solid emblem of the fact that the alliance stood, not for the salvage of old colonial privileges, but for a new world of universal democracy. This was the rationale behind the Atlantic Charter, which the President persuaded a reluctant Churchill to sign at the end of the Argentia Conference in August 1941. In fact, Churchill soon contended that the "freedom" alluded to in the Charter as the touchstone of Allied desiderata referred to that of the European peoples under Nazi subjugation, not colonial populations at all. "I have not become His Majesty's Chief Minister" the Prime Minister portentously declared in his Mansion Hall speech of that year "in order to preside over the liquidation of the British Empire." Nevertheless, the Atlantic Charter could not be unsaid, and although historians have probably exaggerated the significance of this piece of windbaggery, it did play some part in stimulating nationalist ideas in the non-European world by giving them the touch of Anglo–American acceptability.

It was in order to deflect Rooseveltian criticisms of empire that the British Cabinet and Colonial Office set out to articulate a modern variant of colonialism transparently concerned with development and welfare. In 1940 this approach was inaugurated when a Colonial Development and Welfare Act was passed through Parliament, authorizing the expenditure of £5m [the pound sterling in the 1940s was equal to about $4.00; in 1990 dollars £5M is approximately $150M] annually. This legislative action also reflected the burgeoning consensus, which had begun to emerge in the late 1930s, that the gamut of colonial political problems hinged for their solution on the promotion of economic change. This thinking was rooted in an enormous naïvety as to what the implications of, and the constraints upon, such change were. Nevertheless, it was at least recognized that the route to prosperity in the non-advanced world necessarily lay in a closer coordination of resources within "natural" regions, since individual colonies were invariably too small to form effective units of development. The establishment of the Caribbean Advisory Commission (with US participation) and the appointment of a Resident Minister in West Africa expressed this awareness of the regional dimension; after the war it was to blossom into full-blown federation-making, the fragrance of which was not to prove universally popular. Whether this wartime attempt to cull together the rhetorics of liberal-welfarism and a continuing colonialism actually made any impression on American opinion must be doubted; anti-British sentiment in much of small-town America was too strong for such verbal froth to carry weight. But in the process the interior atmosphere of the British Colonial Office was itself metamorphosed. Its professional mystique became entwined with the progressive enhancement of colonial change—under, of course, Whitehall supervision. This was not so much a case of intellectual conversion, as of collective career strategy, since it was clear that the Colonial Office had to find new ways of protecting itself at a time when its position in the ministerial pecking order was slipping fast. Thus the Foreign Office, which had always resented the Colonial Office meddling in matters of high diplomacy, was determined to see the latter relegated to the lowly position it had occupied in the early part of the century, and by the time of the Yalta Conference in early February 1945 this demotion had essentially taken place. This switch in the bureaucratic culture of the Colonial Office, and its reduced leverage within Whitehall, both had significance for the direction of post-war policy.

Ironically, during the latter stages of the war the US Government did come to view British and European colonialism rather more sympathetically than had earlier been the case. Given the degree to which the UK and US publics had been locked together in dramatic common emotions, it would have been surprising if the old edges of their relationship had not been rounded off. The greater, if still very selective and ambivalent, sensitivity evinced by American policy-makers towards colonial dilemmas by 1944, however, evolved more directly out of a continuing revolution within Washington officialdom. Thus the US military establishment (especially the navy) became struck by the future benefits of acquiring its own string of sovereign bases in the Pacific, and in consequence developed a much more circumspect attitude to political "rights" on the part of Asian peoples. More broadly, however, the American foreign policy establishment, while reaching out for the global pre-eminence it had come to covet, became conscious that this glittering prize was extremely fragile. Before 1941 anti-imperialism had come easily to an official America whose responsibility for stability in other continents was minimal; by 1944/45 US prestige and interests had become closely bound up with the wider world, such that in administration circles European empires (for all their faults) began to be seen as a means of keeping the lid on Asian and African volatilities, at least until the post-war order had been decided upon and its construction set in motion. When peace came liberationist perorations still sporadically emitted from American lips on colonial questions, but the tone had become one of wavering anxiety.

It was over the planning of the post-war world, however, which had begun in Allied circles in 1942, that British and American views were in real danger of shearing decisively apart. British policy-makers and interest groups had accepted a subordinate role relative to their American counterparts as a necessity of war. They had acquiesced in the stripping of the UK's gold and monetary reserves, and the surrender of many export markets, as the price that had to be paid if Roosevelt was to carry the measures through Congress which allowed him to put the American economy at the disposal of the war effort. At the same time, however, the British were acutely suspicious of American intentions to "fit them out" for a permanent inferiority along these lines. In particular, there was intense equivocation on the matter of a liberalized international economy under Anglo–American (but mainly American) aegis. This was clearly in the US interest: six million people, including a great mass of women and blacks, had been added to the American labour force after 1941, and this level of employment could only be sustained if export markets remained buoyant. Commercial multilateralism, as free trade was commonly referred to at the time, was not so evidently desirable from the British vantage point, since it was uncertain that UK industry would be strong enough to face the full blast of open world markets after two decades of depression and war. Many British industrialists were adamant that their firms could not survive unless accorded some degree of protection through those tariffs and imperial preferences which had become so inimical—after fifty years of grand tariff-mongering on their own part—to the Americans. British planning of post-war policies revolved around one straightforward but agonizing question: were the prospects of living with American economic hegemony more painful than living apart from it?

The outcome to this debate had profound implications for colonial systems. As the end of the war approached there was no doubt that most informed British opinion accepted that, on balance and given reasonable transitional terms, an expansionist, American-led future was preferable to the sackcloth and ashes of an imperial (but inevitably unstable) commercial alliance. This was the point at which the concept of a British imperial economy finally dissipated, although the Sterling Area [those countries whose currencies are tied to the British pound sterling] was to have tactical significance for years ahead. Furthermore, although the British reluctantly embraced an American-orchestrated free trading order as the lesser evil, they did so with forebodings that led to a new importance being ascribed to the underdeveloped world in general, and especially to those parts of it where the UK still exercised colonial functions. Thus it was argued that the competitive power of the US economy could only be made bearable for other industrial producers if the world market as a whole was rapidly boosted, and that the most immediate scope for such accretions of consumer demand lay in Africa, Asia and Latin America. It was out of this school of thought, essentially concerned with industrial survival in an age of American hegemony, that the theme of "colonial development" was articulated. In 1945 the British Government pushed a new and considerably extended Colonial Development and Welfare Act through Parliament, and commenced an era of grants-in-aid for infrastructural improvements in dependent areas. Britain's African colonies, with which most of this early "aid" history is concerned, had become more relevant to Whitehall's wider economic strategy than they had ever been in the backwater days of indirect rule; it was only in the mid-1950s that these commercial calculations were revised, and then blanket decolonizations were not long in coming.

IV. The Bending of the *Raj*

The colonial dependencies most dramatically affected by the Second World War were those wrested from western rule by Japanese occupation. India was not to be counted among these, although the Japanese offensive through Burma in 1942/43 posed a very real threat to northeastern India and played a part in dissipating British prestige. Nevertheless, the impact of war on Indian politics and society was to have an enormous significance within the wider story of Indian decolonization. In September 1939 the 1935 Government of India Act was in limited operation, with Congress ministries governing seven provinces. One option for Congress at this stage was to exploit the pressures of war to tilt the operation of the status quo in their own favour. This the Gandhian leadership chose not to do; they were much too concerned that *any* cooperation in war administration would crystallize understandings between the imperial centre and provincial politicians, and so break their ability to control the nationalist movement. The Congress leadership were not bent on effecting changes in the 1935 legislation, but on destroying it by forcing their colleagues in the provincial ministries to resign. In this they succeeded, since those ministries could hardly be seen cooperating with a war effort against the injunctions of Gandhi and Nehru. Subsequently the Congress instinct was to sit on the sidelines, leaving the British administration to break itself in the complex task of mobilization, and awaiting the opportunity to assert its status as the only truly popular political force in the country. In retrospect, this Congress gamble can be seen to have both succeeded and failed: it succeeded in so far as the war effort effectively exhausted the capacities of British rule, and lost because that war effort nurtured the Muslim League and thus broke the Congress monopoly of nationalism in India.

In many ways the resignation of the Congress ministries was a blessing for the British authorities. By returning to direct rule in the old Congress-dominated provinces, the Government of India was able to bend local resources to the war effort without constantly having to negotiate with other parties. But the Viceroy, Lord Linlithgow, could not simply revert to pure authoritarianism; the *Raj* had to maintain some progressive credentials if the enormous conflicts of loyalty felt by the literate classes were to be pacified. This was the motive for the August Offer authorized by the British Cabinet in 1940, which defined India's post-war goal as that of Dominion Status and proffered the inclusion of party representatives in the Viceroy's wartime Council. There was little chance of Congress responding to this formula. It was designed, instead, to communicate Britain's good intentions regarding Indian constitutional advance to three main constituencies: the mass of Indian political opinion, President Roosevelt and the British Labour Party. In the ensuing months, however, this particularly hollow sort of posturing became inadequate. The UK's increasing dependence on US economic assistance meant that the American public's sensitivity to Indian "freedom" (however mixed in motive) had to be taken into closer account. The fall of Singapore delivered a dramatic blow to the UK's military stature throughout Asia, and profoundly affected the texture of Indian political life. In March 1942 Churchill was constrained into authorizing a radical attempt to break the constitutional deadlock in India; this took the form of a mission to the country by a leading Cabinet member, Stafford Cripps, with a mandate to use the August 1940 Offer as a basis for further negotiation.

The details of Cripps' visit to Delhi and his labyrinthine dealings with British officials, Indian politicians and American envoys (the latter in the shape of Roosevelt's personal representative in India, Louis Johnson) must be obtained elsewhere. The conclusion of one close study of this affair is that Cripps was "dished" by an alliance of Churchillian conservatism in London and the Viceroy's determination in Delhi to keep Congress out of the administration. By allowing Cripps to hold out the bait of an Indianized and party-dominated Council, but preventing him from giving any reasonably satisfactory promise that the resulting Cabinet would possess the confidence of the Viceroy, Churchill and Linlithgow ensured that the talks would last long enough to have therapeutic effects in certain quarters, not least the White House, while conveniently breaking down in the end. There is no doubt a good deal of veracity to this account, but it seems equally probable that the Congress negotiators themselves had little real interest in Cripps' ramblings. Gandhi and Nehru were both convinced that Congress absorption into war government could be politically fatal to them; the bait of participation in some quasi-Cabinet was never likely to entice them into putting their head inside this lion's mouth. The 1942 mission was a means by which all the participants could posture to their respective constituencies: Churchill to Roosevelt, Cripps to a Labour Party which held him in no great warmth, and Linlithgow and Nehru towards the middle ranks of Indian society over whose loyalties they were in bitter competition.

However, the break-up of the Cripps negotiations left Congress in an intensely vulnerable position. The events of the 1930s had convinced its leaders that British power was slowly crumbling, and when war came they had looked forward, at some point in its duration, to being able to impose terms on the *Raj* rather than vice versa. But after more than two years of war the British position relative to that of Congress seemed remarkably secure. Outside India, the Germans had not been able to strike decisively at the British mainland, the US had entered the war on the UK's side and, however spectacular the Japanese success at Singapore had been, it seemed doubtful that the latter would be able to sustain the logistical feats required for a credible invasion of India. Inside India, and most threatening to the nationalists, the British authorities had managed to construct a war machine which in its scale exceeded that of 1914–18. This *tour de force* was shattering not least because it clashed so starkly with Gandhian expectations. Here was another explanation for Cripps' failure to establish a negotiated solution: the only war administration which Congress could possibly enter was one in which the British were already hanging limply on the ropes, a state of affairs which, at least to the naked eye, was not the case. But if in early 1942 Gandhi, Nehru and their colleagues had never expected talks in Delhi to get very far, they were surprised and appalled at the brazen confidence exhibited by the British Cabinet and Linlithgow. Indeed, Cripps' humiliation at the hands of Churchill directly implied, not only that Congress was being taken less seriously than ever, but that it was in real danger of being thrust to one side as an irrelevance. This was why the Congress high command was soon panicked into unleashing the massive Quit India rebellion of August 1942: it signalled to the British, in the only conceivable way under the circumstances, that their organization remained too large an entity to be bulldozed flat by the processes of war government. It is possible that Gandhi actually believed that the rebellion, the most widespread Indian disturbance since the 1857 Mutiny, would bring the *Raj* staggering to a complete halt; it is much more likely that this subtle tactician was seeking to staunch the momentum of the war effort and thus redress the balance of power between imperialism and nationalism. If so, the judgement of the saintly *Mahatma* can rarely have been so grossly flawed. The Indian Army held firm in British hands when it came to crushing the outbreak. The Congress leadership, including Gandhi, were interned in large numbers. This proved one of the great turning points on the road to partition: for it was the effective disappearance of Congress as a negotiating force in Indian politics during the next two years which allowed the Muslim League to consolidate its claims as legitimate heir to British power in much of north India.

To emphasize the statistical achievements of the Government of

India's mobilization for war (the number of battalions recruited, the volume of tanks and munitions produced) is, however, likely to obscure more profound developments which ran parallel with them. The pressures of war, in fact, were consistently undermining imperial rule in India, especially in the rural areas, but not in ways fully compatible with Congress's own ambitions. In this context events in the Punjab are illustrative. British supremacy in this large and fertile province had for decades been based on an alliance between the imperial administration and the more prosperous agricultural classes. With the spread of "politics" after 1918, this collaboration was expressed through the provincial hegemony of the Punjab Unionist Party, which succeeded in preventing either Congress *or* the Muslim League from making inroads amongst Punjabi opinion. The system, however, only worked so long as British rule benefited the dominant agrarian interests. War industrialization after 1939, however, clearly favoured big-city groups, villages were starved of consumer goods and, most significantly, grain prices were controlled. Thus while the Punjab provided enormous quantities of manpower for the Indian Army, it was denied the prize of inflated grain profits. The climax of this disillusionment came in 1943 when the authorities in Delhi, badly shaken by the rippling effects of the Bengal famine, ordered the partial conscription of the Punjabi grain surplus as a "bank" for the deficit provinces. This decision was, under the circumstances, inevitable; the British could not let Bengal continue to starve without reaping a whirlwind sooner rather than later. But each sack of grain requisitioned for a Bengali stomach meant cash filched from the Punjabi growers, so that the latter increasingly turned away from their old imperial partner and sought a new patron in the Muslim League—a process that climaxed in the 1946 provincial elections. The local administrators had forewarned the Viceroy of the effects of his policies on the Punjab, but from the perspective of Delhi the necessities of war far outweighed the shoring-up of a rotting colonial fabric. This point of breakage between the "centre" decision-makers concerned exclusively with the winning of a war, and the subtly different priorities of administrators in the localities, lay at the heart of the decolonization process in India at this time.

It was the Muslim League advance in provinces such as the Punjab, where previously it had not had much success in "stampeding" Muslim opinion, which confirmed its President, Jinnah, as a political figure who could not be excluded from any constitutional settlement in India, and which thereby put partition on the agenda, however much Congress or the British, in their respective ways, might resist such a solution to Indian problems. In fact during the 1930s Jinnah—a London-trained lawyer, secularist and chain-smoker—had distanced himself from those political and religious extremists within the League who called for a separate Muslim state, or "Pakistan." But at the 1940 Congress of the Muslim League in Lahore the "Pakistan Resolution" was passed which committed the party to the goal of a partitioned independence in the subcontinent. Quite why this new consensus within the League had come about—and, more particularly, why Jinnah's stance had undergone a radical shift—is not clear. There is no doubt that the alleged communal favouritism exhibited by the Hindu-dominated Congress ministries after the 1937 elections had caused a backlash amongst Muslims generally, and Jinnah grasped how this could be turned to League advantage. The origins of the "Pakistan Resolution," however, probably lie in the specific dilemma facing Jinnah and the League in the months after September 1939. Thus to have meekly joined in the Congress boycott of the British war effort would have confirmed the League's purely subordinate role in Indian political life. On the other hand, to have simply cooperated with the government in Delhi would have allowed Congress to lambast Jinnah as a stooge of the imperial power, and probably broken him politically once and for all. But beating the Pakistan drum allowed the League to reach out for the prizes which collaboration with the British put within its grasp, and to maintain a nationalist legitimacy—albeit a nationalism which had sheared completely apart from Congress conceptions.

However, the wartime growth of the Muslim League was crucially linked to the support it received from the Viceroy, Lord Linlithgow. Obsessed with the threat posed by Congress to India's mobilization, Linlithgow latched on to Jinnah as a weapon to stun Congress into immobilism. Indeed, it was at this late stage in the history of the *Raj*, and driven by military necessities, that British rule began a calculated exploration of Hindu–Moslem rivalries, and when peace came the machine of communal politics could not just be slammed into reverse. But quite apart from Linlithgow's private war on Congress, the process of communalization was knit into the social and economic impact which the war had on India. After 1939 imperial mobilization entailed an enlarged bureaucracy, an intensified industrialization and a boost to agricultural production. All of these varied factors provided wider avenues of personal advancement for some, while inflicting the pains of inflation on others. Thus as the scope for economic gains and losses was expanded, individual and group anxieties were raised to a new pitch, so that Indians thrashed around to find methods of protection against the displacements of the period. Under subcontinental conditions, it was logical that this need for social armour more often than not took the form of communal loyalism. It was because Jinnah was able to exploit the British need for a local ally at a point when social divisions were being burnt into the Indian fabric that the Muslim League was able to become a mass party capable of defeating Congress in those provinces which had Muslim-majority populations—although in certain instances, such as that of the North-West Frontier Province, even this still remained problematical in 1945. Overall, the British *Raj* was able to achieve what Congress in 1939 had thought was beyond its power: the bending of Indian resources towards a grand strategy in Asia. Nevertheless, the price of such success was to be the loss of that all-India creation which had always lain at the heart of the British imperial apologia in south Asia.

In October 1943 Linlithgow had been succeeded as Viceroy by Lord Wavell, and as the Japanese threat to India eased, the essential problem became that of a "re-entry" into civilian politics. The gradual return of normality also meant the recrudescence of nationalist sentiment amongst the middle orders of society which had been unwilling to involve themselves in outright opposition to the war. The British Government acted at various points in ways that served only to assist this revival of nationalist fortunes. The use of Indian Army troops to reoccupy Cochin China and Indonesia at the end of the war, while triggering old resentments about the use of Indian revenues for purely imperial purposes, was probably unavoidable at the time; Wavell's decision, however, to put on trial those Indian soldiers who had defected to the Japanese and fought in the Indian National Army *against* the British, and to hold that trial in the Red Fort in Delhi (symbolic seat of the old Moghul power), was an error of immense proportions. The intention was to draw a very visible line beyond which anti-British sentiment was to be severely disciplined; the effect was to catalyse nationalist consciousness after four years of repression. Wavell's instincts in Indian politics, however, fitted into a mould of liberal, if distinctly old-fashioned, paternalism. Towards the end of the war he had become convinced that British interests lay in pushing through a solution to India's future status while the political situation remained fluid and Congress's leaders were locked in a weak bargaining position. Throughout 1944 and early 1945 the Viceroy therefore pressed the British Cabinet to authorize him to convene a conference of Indian party leaders at which the various factions might be levered into a coalition government; amidst this process the moderates (inside and outside Congress) might force an all-India compromise. Gandhi was released from prison in May 1945 in the hope that this would help open the way to negotiation. In the end, Churchill, who was not a little sad to terminate a period of Indian affairs in which Congress had sustained considerable damage, did agree to Wavell's promptings, and the Viceroy subsequently hosted the Simla Conference of June 1945, during which he sought tirelessly to weave together some patchwork of League–Congress understanding to form the basis of a joint interim administration. But when Jinnah insisted on his right to nominate *all* the Muslim representatives in such a government, the proceedings inevitably broke up. Two weeks after the failure in Simla, Clement Attlee became British Prime Minister in a Labour Government. Clearly some new slant on British policy towards India was imminent. But by this point, too, the great imperial war effort was coming home to roost in the form of disintegrating administration and communal tensions far more intense than anything which had been experienced within the living memory of the *Raj*.

V. Social Change and Settler Power in Africa

In terms of the great "theatres" of Second World War strategy, most of Africa was a backwater between 1939 and 1945. Recently the wider military significance of the North African campaigns has been questioned; certainly their rippling effects on sub-Saharan Africa were relatively minor. In West Africa the only fighting was a short, sharp fracas between the Vichyites and Gaullists for control of the French colonies; and although the Italian forces put up some resistance to the British in Abyssinia, there was no East African front on the scale of 1914–18. Politics and society in Africa were therefore not exposed to the same physical and psychological shocks characteristic of much of Asia during wartime. Hence in 1945 western opinion could be under no illusion that a return to pre-war routines in Asia was at all possible, but in European-ruled Africa such an expectation was deeply rooted, whatever the official rhetoric of welfare and development for indigenous populations.

However, no intelligent observer of African affairs could fail to note the important ways in which the massive conflicts elsewhere were reverberating (albeit indirectly) within the sub-Saharan region. The great expansions of output in the Northern Rhodesian and Katangese Copperbelts to meet Anglo–American demands, boosting their turn-over of migrant labour, were extreme examples of how the war intensi-fied the rhythms of the modern economy in African life, but few localities were left outside the penumbra thrown by the interaction of war and money. It was between 1939 and 1945 that cities such as Nairobi, Leopoldville and Salisbury "took off" from the modest scale they had attained in the 1920s, and which had remained relatively stable through the 1930s; shortages, inflation and war-employment boosted wage-labour opportunities and accelerated the drift from vil-lage to town, with growing numbers of young, single males drawn to the ill-equipped townships fringing the cities. As important as urban-ization in this structural shift to cash-based norms, however, were the administrators' "grow more food" campaigns in the countryside. Dur-ing the depression there had been some modest encouragement given to African farmers by the state but these bureaucratic pressures were considerably extended after 1939, such that indigenous producers were permitted to cultivate cash-crops which they had previously been banned from growing. Furthermore, although the colonial authorities tried to stifle inflationary profits by stringent marketing regulations, there is good reason to believe that African growers were able to obtain considerable cash returns from the endemic black markets. Dur-ing these years the opportunities for Africans in commercial agricul-ture, urban jobs and administration were considerably expanded, although not sufficiently quickly to prevent the townships becoming pockmarked by un- and underemployment; for most people standards of living were raised markedly above those prevailing in the preceding decade (although the drift to the towns often had gravely deleterious effects on many villages, not least by depleting them of manpower at harvest times). Inflationary and demographic trends snipped at the margins of these gains, but the massive boost to economic activity which the war entailed outweighed these factors, at least for the dura-tion. In this way the balance was critically affected between what was popularly labelled the "old" and the "new" Africa, and a diffused sense of material expectation became characteristic of millions of rural, as well as urban, Africans. The growth of post-war political consciousness amongst indigenous masses was an outcrop of this war-induced transformation.

This African metamorphosis was too striking for European colonial administrations to ignore its implications altogether until the war ended. If only to ensure the cooperation of Africans in war measures, both British and French administrations had to provide some evidence of sensitivity to changing times. They met this necessity in characteristically different style. Thus the "Free French" Gaullists, with their love of the grand gesture, and conscious of their own tenuous position, convened a conference at Brazzaville in January–February 1944 at which African representatives were feted with talk of self-government; it was, however, stressed that this self-government would not affect the continuance of French sovereign authority. What this actually meant was not clear, and no attempts were made at definition. The British approach to change in wartime Africa was much less vivid; it began with the commissioning of Lord Hailey, perhaps the most noted colonial expert of his day, to produce a revised version of his *African Survey* (first published in 1938). Hailey's conclusions were shot through with evasive caution. In particular the growing disjunctures within African colonial life led him to be very circumspect about any further undermining of the institution of chieftaincy, since it represented, he argued, one of the few reliable anchorages for colonial society in the modern world. This nervous (if responsible) conservatism on colonial issues was characteristic of much of Whitehall thinking and restrained British officialdom from striking extravagant gestures which, though they would have been useful in propaganda terms, might have generated uncontrollable aspirations amongst African cadres—cadres which, in the case of British Africa, were much more mature than in their French-ruled counterparts.

Within the British Colonial Office, however, there was a younger generation of policy-makers who came to the fore during the Second World War, and who were prepared to move considerably in advance of Hailey's hesitant gradualism. These were middle-ranking officers touched by the interventionist culture of the war bureaucracy; they were, in consequence, all for "doing things," and the only thing which could, under the likely circumstance of the future, be done with the colonial empire—the goal which could provide a career full of drama, with a peerage and a ribbon at the end of it—was to plan and execute its demise. The representative man of this strand in the Office ethos was Andrew Cohen, who later, as Head of the Africa Division in the Colonial Office, was to be the most powerful advocate of rapid constitutional change. According to his biographer, Cohen became convinced during the war that the business of British colonialism was no longer viable and should be put into the receiver's hands. In fact this brand of hardheaded anti-colonialism within British Government did not harden into a consensus until the later 1950s, but it is important to note that such a species of bureaucratic radicalism was first nurtured under wartime conditions.

The balance of Colonial Office thinking between 1939 and 1945 was naturally less adventurous than that taking shape in Cohen's original mind. At bottom, it boiled down to little more than that the educated, detribalized African had now to be recognized as the archetype of progress in his society, and given a role in government to match his social significance; this was the critical assumption which permeated the wide-ranging memoranda surfacing in the Office from 1943 onwards, with their emphasis on municipal elections and broadened rural African representation in provincial councils. In effect, this was an acceptance of "African politics" within the colonial setting which marked an end to that "anti-politics" embedded in indirect rule, but the implications of such a departure remained obscure while officials remained above all preoccupied with the main task of keeping the African war effort on the road.

It is all too easy, indeed, to ascribe an undue importance to wartime "planning" as it affected Africa. Of all Whitehall's myriad planning exercises at this time, those concentrating on colonial areas were most ephemeral and, within this colonial category, those focusing on Africa had a particularly fake portentousness. Thus, whenever the Colonial Office indulged in earnest talk of African "progress," it really did so (implicitly if not explicitly) with reference to West Africa, where there was no substantive white-settler presence to complicate calculations. On the contemporary dilemmas of white-settled Africa, however, metropolitan officials largely maintained a discreet but pregnant silence. They were (from their own standpoint) wise to do so, since the impact of war was to make these dilemmas sharper and more brittle than they had been in the 1930s. In east and central Africa, while, as elsewhere, the war economy had boosted African material aspirations, it had also entrenched settler supremacy more deeply than ever. The depletion of British administrators through the military call-up had led to their being replaced by local white farmers, so that the latter as a group obtained a purchase on the administration which they had failed to achieve in the inter-war years. Most importantly, the settlers effectively dominated the network of marketing and agricultural agencies put in place after 1939. If this was true in Kenya, it was even more true of Southern and Northern Rhodesia where the stimulus to extractive and secondary industries fed directly into the existing channels of white-settler power. Both "on the ground" and in London British officials became conscious that, whereas they had succeeded in maintaining a racial equilibrium in these areas between 1918 and 1939, during the war years the local whites had stolen a march on their metropolitan keepers. There were even those, such as Lord Cranborne, the Colonial Secretary in 1942, who allowed themselves to think aloud that the war might provide a convenient cover under which full authority could be handed over to the European settler communities, thus disentangling the UK from a set of conflicts which had gone beyond the realm of the manipulable. This was not a majority view; it would have alienated much of British as well as American opinion, and handed hegemony in Africa to the regime in Pretoria—a defeat which would horrify right-wing, as well as left-wing, elements in the UK. Instead, the British authorities muddled through, saying as little on East African matters as possible. At the end of hostilities the officials turned their minds privately to the rolling back of those positions of power occupied by settler minorities, and the nurturing of African agriculture as a countervailing force. This was implicit in the discussions which Sir Philip Mitchell, about to return to Kenya as Governor, had in the Colonial Office in late 1944 on the subject of East African reconstruction. Even in Kenya, however, such a reversal of wartime developments was to prove exceedingly difficult; in the two Rhodesias it was to prove impossible.

There was one other wartime fact which overhung British possessions south of the Sahara: the growing economic and political power of the Union of South Africa. During the Second, as in the First, World War the British found that organizing African resources on anything like a continental basis required a close partnership with Pretoria;

through this collaboration South African influence seemed set to break the regional limits within which the UK had always striven to keep it. Thus South African industry became a chief source of supply for many African territories, and much, too, of the Middle East; between 1939 and 1945 the gravitational weight in the sub-Sahara came to lie decisively within the Union. The British Government feared, quite correctly, that this was likely to generate tensions between blacks and whites on a novel scale, and make European communities in British colonies more insensitive than ever to invocations based on liberal notions of "trusteeship." Above all, they feared that the pro-British Prime Minister in South Africa, Jan Smuts, who had regained that office in 1939, might be swept out of power after the crisis had passed (just as he had been in 1924), leaving the Afrikaner Nationalists in control. In the later 1920s and 1930s the British had proved strong enough in regional terms to force Hertzog into a working accommodation; whether they could hope to perform the same feat with any Nationalist successor under the different conditions of the 1940s seemed problematical. By 1945 suspicion of South Africa's expansionist aims was endemic in Whitehall; post-war perspectives in London were to be crucially influenced by this fact.

But although the war had created external opportunities for South African expansion, it had also intensified the internal dilemmas of that country. Rapid economic growth, by increasing the flow of blacks into the industrial areas, meant that the old Hertzogite compromises were breaking down: for whites the limited urban segregation enshrined in the legislation of the inter-war years seemed now to offer insufficient protection against the mounting African presence in European residential districts, while for blacks the more stringent application of influx controls began to impose restraints and humiliations on a new scale. The wartime dissatisfactions of urban Africans expressed themselves in the growth of trade unions and radical political organizations, while the Afrikaner intelligentsia moved towards more thoroughgoing concepts of segregationism; Smuts' attempt to limit these polarities by setting up the Fagan Commission in 1944 to investigate "reform" could, at the very best, only buy him, and South Africa, a small breathing-space. By 1945 therefore it was in the Union, the economic fly-wheel of much of the African continent, that the critical struggle for the racial balance of power was taking place. This was not because South African comes could, in any direct sense, determine events elsewhere in the continent, but they were bound—given the Union's commercial pre-dominance—to dictate many of the assumptions on which Africa's future turned. Against this background, Colonial Office discussions about local government initiatives in Nigeria or the Gold Coast were small beer indeed.

8

LLOYD E. EASTMAN

Conclusion:
Of Storms and Revolutions

Among the casualties of the postwar world was the Nationalist Guomindang (Kuomintang) government of Jiang Jieshi (Chiang Kai-shek). Educated in a Japanese military staff college, Jiang supported Sun Yatsen (Sun Yat-sen) and the new Chinese Repub-lic after 1911, when it emerged from the ruins of the Qing (Ch'ing) empire. Jiang quickly consolidated his hold on the Na-tional party when Sun died, leading it until his death in Taiwan in 1975. In the Thirties he was hailed in the United States as a Christian leader of a struggling democratic republic faced with the twin challenges of modernizing a traditional economy and meeting Japanese invasion.

The Anti-Japan War devastated much of China. The Japanese occupied northern China by 1939 as well as the coastal areas and

Reprinted from *Seeds of Destruction*, pp. 216–26, by Lloyd E. Eastman with the permission of Stanford University Press © 1984 by the Board of Trustees of the Leland Stanford Junior University.

major ports, including Guangzhou (Canton). This forced Jiang's government inland to Qonqing (Chungking), away from its political base. Though fighting eased in 1942 after Tokyo opened war on the United States and invaded Southeast Asia, Japan always had far more troops in Manchuria and China than in its other theaters. The Japanese army launched its greatest and final offensive of the war, Ichi Go, against China in April 1944. The Chinese, with American assistance, only regained the initiative in the spring of 1945. Soon Japan was defeated, not in China, but in Hiroshima and Nagasaki.

After the war, Americans concluded Jiang and the nationalists were directing a corrupt, authoritarian military dictatorship. Dependence on military factions and right-wing land owners hindered Nationalist efforts to bring significant reform to China. The Chinese Communist Party, originally a part of the Guomindang, was periodically hounded by Jiang, but never crushed. When the Sino–Japanese War opened in 1937, Nationalists and Communists occasionally cooperated, but after Japan surrendered in 1945 a civil war broke out. After five years the communists won and Mao Zedong (Mao Tse-tung) proclaimed the People's Republic of China from Beijing's Tian'anmen Square in October 1949.

Opinions about Jiang (Chiang), the Nationalists, Mao and the Communists have ranged to all extremes, but as passions have calmed and more sources have been opened to scholars, the debate has become less polemical and based more firmly on evidence. In the following conclusion to his book *Seeds of Destruction: Nationalist China in War and Revolution 1937–1949* Lloyd E. Eastman searches out the causes of the Nationalist defeat. Since the conflict between the nationalists and the Communists over the country's future originated before the war, the impact of the war on China is not easy to discern.

Nonetheless, the Communist victory has had great significance for China and its world role as well as for Third World nationalists and revolutionaries attempting to transform and free their peasant societies from oppressive agrarian regimes and the influence of foreign interests. Did war make this outcome more likely? Was it only another factor which could have had a different consequence? Did the Communists, unlike the Nationalists, have a form of organization and a program which enabled them to capture the peasantry and portray themselves as the true patriots? Are Nationalist movements similar to Jiang's (Chiang) likely to fail? Professor Eastman's views are relevant not only to evaluating the interaction of war and society, but also to understanding China.

If a building collapses in a windstorm, what is the cause of the collapse? A scientific answer would require careful consideration of, first, the structural characteristics of the building and, second, the velocities of the winds. If it were discovered that the building had already deteriorated structurally, one would have to weigh whether, in the absence of a storm, it would have remained erect. But the storm did blow, and the building did collapse. Was, then, the storm the cause of the building's collapse? This question is not without philosophical subtleties. Neither is the question of why the National Government succumbed to the Communist revolution in 1949.

Never did the Nationalists succeed in creating a sound, sturdy political structure. Coming to power in 1927, they were heirs to a political system that had been disintegrating for over a century, and that during the warlord era (1916–27) all but ceased to function. That the Nationalists were able to reverse this process of national disintegration is indisputably to their credit, but nonetheless the authority of the National Government was still limited by the continued existence of warlords in the provinces and by the resistance of local elites in the villages.

The Nationalists' structure was further weakened by the failure to create an effective political administration that would be sensitive to popular needs and capable of carrying out its proclaimed programs of political and economic reform. Shortly after the establishment of the regime, the left wing of the Kuomintang, headed by Wang Ching-wei and Ch'en Kung-po, had proposed institutional and policy alternatives that might have enabled the Nationalists to shore up their political structure. Denouncing Chiang Kai-shek for instituting a one-man dictatorship, the leftists demanded that the Kuomintang revive the policies and spirit that had energized the Nationalist movement during the period of Sun Yat-sen's revolutionary leadership in 1924. They advocated land reforms, punishment of counterrevolutionaries, and greater democracy within the Kuomintang. They also believed that the Kuomintang must strengthen its relations with the common people by promoting autonomous peasant, worker, and other mass organizations. Only with such a mass base, they insisted, could the revolution be prevented from becoming a plaything of bureaucrats and militarists— as indeed it did. Chiang correctly viewed these leftists as a threat to his leadership, and in 1928 he launched an intensive, albeit generally bloodless, suppression of them. Youths, who made up a large part of the rank and file of the left wing, were unequivocally ordered to get out of politics and return to their studies. Other leftists were effectively stripped of power; Wang Ching-wei was reprimanded and Ch'en Kung-po was "expelled forever" from the party. From 1929 on, therefore, Chiang Kai-shek was able to impose his own conception of the revolution upon the party and the government.

During Sun Yat-sen's lifetime, the military had been a relatively disparaged element in the nationalist movement. Under Chiang, however, Sun's relative ranking—first the party, then the government, and last the army—was turned upside down. During the Nanking Decade the army, led by Chiang Kai-shek, became the dominant branch of the movement, and Chiang himself became the overshadowing presence in the regime. As Franklin Ho, a onetime adviser to Chiang, recalled: "The real authority of the government went wherever the Generalissimo went. In terms of authority, he was the head of everything." Or as Chiang himself told Edgar Snow in 1940, "Wherever I go there is the Government, the Cabinet, and the center of resistance [to the Japanese]."

Because Chiang so dominated the regime, his political outlook was of central importance in determining the character of Nationalist rule. He was, in his view of the political process, profoundly traditional. Like an emperor of the Ch'ing Dynasty, politics for him was a matter of competition among elites. To maximize his power, therefore, he manipulated and combined the support of one group of elites against rival elites. He seemingly never realized that the strong states in the world at the time were those that had successfully mobilized significant segments of the populations, and not just of the elites, in support of their goals. He never comprehended—as Mao Tse-tung did—that it was possible to generate new sources of power by mobilizing support from outside the elite structure. Chiang, of course, talked a great deal about democracy, and he undoubtedly desired popular support. But his concept of democracy and popular support was that the masses should follow their leader unquestioningly, as soldiers obey officers. That concept revealed how poorly he understood the psychology of mass politics, and it prevented him from developing the kind of political participation and economic programs that might have given his regime a firm foundation in society. Thus he never transcended elitist politics and trapped himself in the practice of ruling through the balance of weakness.

Nothing in the preceding paragraphs is meant to imply that if Wang Ching-wei and the left wing of the Kuomintang in 1928–29 had succeeded in the power struggle instead of Chiang, the path to national power and prosperity would assuredly have been smooth. Indeed, there is reason to suspect that they, too, might have been afflicted with the same bureaucratism, corruption, factionalism, and jealousy of power that proved so destructive to the regime under Chiang. What is clear, however, is that Chiang, in silencing the leftists' advocacy of autonomous mass organizations, land reform, democratic procedures within the Kuomintang, and Kuomintang control of the government and army, rejected measures that might possibly have created a sound basis for a popular and efficient government.

Of the winds that assailed the Nationalist structure during its twenty-odd years of rule in China, none was so violent, none imposed such brutal strains, as the war with Japan. The most direct and palpable damage inflicted by the war upon the regime was the weakening of Chiang's army. The wholesale losses sustained by the central forces during the first year of fighting erased, in large measure, the improvements in personnel and equipment, however modest, that had been achieved during the preceding decade. Subsequent combat, diminished sources of supply, and the prolonged stalemate also exacted a heavy toll of Chiang's army. The political effects of the army's enfeeblement were momentous. As Theda Skocpol has observed: "Even after great loss of legitimacy has occurred, a state can remain quite stable—and certainly invulnerable to internal mass-based revolts—especially if its coercive organizations remain coherent and effective." During the war, however, the Nationalists' chief coercive organization, the army, ceased to be "coherent and effective."

The regime had also been weakened by its enforced retreat to West China. On the coast and in the cities of the east, it had possessed secure sources of revenue, an established administrative apparatus that (although never strong at the local level) provided a measure of stability, and ready access to both domestic and foreign sources of supply. In the provinces of West China, by contrast, the Nationalists discovered a strange, almost alien, world. Modernization had barely touched even the major cities there. All of West China, some three-fourths of the nation's territory, had only 4 percent of the nation's electrical capacity and 6 percent of its factories. The economy was overwhelmingly agrarian, and the population felt little identification with the citified officials from "downriver." Local society was dominated by secret societies and rural elites, which were jealous of their long-standing political, military, and economic dominance, and resented the intervention of and competition from the Nationalist regime. The National Government consequently could mobilize resources in West China only with difficulty, and its revenues quickly fell by 63 percent.

The Nationalists committed a serious error in failing to adapt their methods of ruling and fighting to the constraints of the new environment in West China. Prior to the war, the government could ignore the problems of the countryside, because the economic resources of the urban centers were sufficient to sustain it. Its army could also emphasize the orthodox tactics and technologies derived from the West, because it could easily draw weapons and matériel from factories in East China and abroad.

Even though the situation in West China was radically different from that on the coast, the regime made minimal efforts to adjust its political, economic, and military policies to the primitive resource base there. Instead, for example, it attempted to create virtually overnight a modern industrial base in Szechwan and Yunnan. It therefore pumped enormous sums of money into the economy to remove factories from the coast, to import expensive equipment and raw materials from the West, and to construct new highways and railroads. Because it lacked the tax base to support these expenditures, the inflationary spiral began. An alternative would have been for the government to encourage a simpler and cheaper form of industrial production, drawing upon the rich tradition of handicrafts indigenous to West China. The Chinese Industrial Cooperative Association, launched in July 1938, was in fact a privately inspired attempt to provide such an alternative source of industrial goods. The full potential of the industrial cooperatives was never realized, however, because government leaders suspected that this mass-based movement, so different from their own highly bureaucratized system, was manipulated by Communists.

Because the countryside, and not the cities, was the primary wartime source of grain, money, and men, the Nationalists needed to develop a system that would enable them to derive the maximum resources from the rural areas and yet maintain the good will and cooperation of the producing masses. Rather than adjusting their policies to achieve those ends, however, they continued to employ a top-heavy and expensive bureaucracy that ruled in uneasy conjunction with the corrupt and inefficient rural elites. The Nationalists might also have adopted the tactics of guerrilla warfare against the Japanese. But guerrilla warfare requires intimate cooperation between the army and the civilian population, and such cooperation could have been achieved only by improving the discipline of the troops and by revamping the government's social and economic policies so that the people had incentives to contribute to the success of the army.

The Communists in their base areas demonstrated that the primitive and impoverished interior of the nation could indeed sustain a vital political and military movement. Relying on guerrilla tactics, nurturing mass mobilization, and developing small-scale industrial production, the Communists became stronger as the war progressed. The Nationalists, by contrast, retaining their prewar conceptions of ruling and fighting, weakened economically, politically, and militarily.

The most serious result of the failure to adapt to the changed conditions in the interior, and the most pervasively destructive influence of the war upon the Nationalists, was the inflation. By retreating from the eastern seaboard, the Nationalist government largely lost its main sources of revenue, most notably the customs duties, salt taxes, and manufacturing taxes. Because its political controls in the interior—horizontally over the provinces, and vertically down to the rural elites and the urban moneyed classes—remained weak, it never adequately developed alternative sources of revenue, and consequently had to rely inordinately upon deficit financing. Inflation was the result. Initially, prices rose moderately enough, increasing only about 40 percent during the first year of the war. By the latter half of 1941 and through 1944, however, prices were more than doubling each year. Thereafter the rate of increase again spurted sharply upward, prices rising 251 percent in just the seven months from January to August 1945. The results were devastating and enfeebled the entire body politics—the army, the government, the economy, and society generally. The inflation was a major reason why corruption reached unprecedented levels, why the mass of the population suffered grinding poverty, and why the army became dispirited and ineffective.

The war also hurt the Nationalists because it enabled the Communists to grow and become strong. During the decade prior to the war, the Nationalists had hounded the Communists the length and breadth of the country, inflicting substantial losses upon them and preventing them from securing a large, stable base of operations. Nationalist pressure abated after 1937, however, and guerrilla operations in the nominally Japanese-occupied areas permitted the Communists to spread their revolutionary networks to an extent that had been unimaginable prior to the war. During the war, too, the Communists developed organizational skills and acquired military experience that benefited them in the civil war period.

Thus did the war buffet the Nationalist regime. Yet the regime did not collapse in 1944 or 1945, and survived for four years beyond the end of the war with Japan. What were the sources of its staying power? How could it remain standing as long as it did, despite the pervasive infirmities? Some of the answers may lie in the low political consciousness of most Chinese, and in the regime's extensive reliance upon political repression to silence those few who did have the temerity to engage in antigovernment actions within the areas controlled by the Nationalists. Both these subjects deserve further study. Systemic features that actually made the regime weak may also have contributed, paradoxically, to its durability. For example, the lack of a social base and institutionalized means of incorporating the population into the political process left the regime not directly accountable for its sins of omission and commission. If it had been a parliamentary democracy, its term in office would have been short indeed; but because it was a regime supported by the army, public opinion had little direct effect on its political longevity. Military force at this time was the primary source of political power, and if the regime were to fall, it would probably be the result of armed opposition. That might have happened when the provincial militarists formed an alliance against Chungking in 1944. Chiang was, however, a master at manipulating his rivals, and as he had done innumerable times in the 1920s and 1930s, he successfully prevented his rivals during the war from forming a firm alliance against him . . . for instance, he several times mollified Lung Yün and the Yunnanese by granting them financial compensation for provincial concessions. During the Ichigo campaign, too, he supplied them with weapons in return for their abandoning the planned revolt.

The regime also survived because it generally accommodated, rather than challenged, the status quo. If the Nationalists had attempted to carry out their proclaimed programs of land reform, or if they had tried during the war to take control of the tax-in-kind and conscription systems out of the hands of the local elites, or again if they had ordered the provincial militarists to demobilize their armies, they would surely have faced large-scale revolts. Because the regime tolerated the elites of the old society, however, those elites tolerated the regime. This was not a formula that produced progressive reforms or strong government, but in the short run, at least, it helped keep the Nationalists in power.

The Nationalist government might have remained in power longer than it did, however, had it not been for the Russian intervention in Manchuria following the war with Japan. On the basis of the Yalta Agreement of February 1945, the Soviet Union declared war against Japan on August 8—two days after the first atomic bomb burst over Hiroshima—and quickly occupied the whole of Manchuria. Once in control there, the Russians facilitated the Chinese Communists' entry into the northeastern provinces and turned over to them large stores of surrendered Japanese war matériel. They also delayed Nationalist efforts to reestablish a military and administrative presence there and carried away much of Manchuria's industrial plant. Much has been written about these events—many of which blatantly violated Chinese sovereignty and which the United States opposed—but their effect upon the fate of the Nationalist regime has seldom been brought into sharp focus.

If, for example, the Russians had not entered Manchuria, thereby providing the Chinese Communists with a springboard for the conquest of China proper, the Nationalists could arguably have devoted their attention and resources to postwar reconstruction, rather than being forced to conduct a full-scale civil war. The Chinese Communists would still have posed a threat within China proper, of course, but the scale of the hostilities would presumably have been smaller, and the insurgent forces would not have been strengthened by the supply of Japanese arms and equipment.

The consequences for the Nationalist regime of such a scenario might have been profound. Economically, the rich resources of Manchuria could have been reintegrated into the economy of China proper. Rather than having to send large stores of food and grain to the Nationalist troops in the Northeast, thereby contributing to the impoverishment and anger of farmers in China proper, the Nationalists could have used the large food surpluses of Manchuria to relieve the chronic shortages of North China. The sizable industrial base created by the

Japanese could have provided the products of heavy industry to facili-
tate the industrial recovery of China proper, and of light industry to
ease the enormous postwar need for consumer goods. Manchuria's
potential to contribute to the nation's economic recovery is suggested
by the fact that, for example, during 1944–45 it produced 8.5 times
more pig iron than had ever been produced in a single year in China
proper, 2.5 times more electric power, and 8.5 times more cement.
Manchuria in 1944 also harvested 3,549,000 tons of soybeans; if that
amount had been available to Nationalist China in the postwar period,
it would have generated annually through exports some U.S. $60 mil-
lion to $90 million in foreign exchange. And Manchuria's 144 lumber
mills would largely have eliminated the need for imports of foreign
lumber.

Moreover, because the industrial sector of China proper was
plagued after the war by a multitude of problems, including shortages
of raw materials and fuel (much of which might have been obtained
from Manchuria), it could not produce the consumer goods so desperately needed after eight years of war. To ease this demand and thereby
to lessen the inflationary pressures, the National Government felt constrained to encourage imports from abroad, which then flooded into the
country. As a direct consequence of this policy, the country's reserves
of foreign currency had by February 1947 been virtually depleted.
Imports also injured China's native industries, and foreign shipments
of cotton, rice, and other agricultural products pushed down farm
prices hurting the farmers and delaying recovery of the rural areas.

The most damaging effect of the events in Manchuria, however, was
the increased inflation they brought about. During the period 1945–49,
fully 65–70 percent of government spending was devoted to the military, and much of it was used to fight the war in Manchuria. To finance
the civil war, the government resorted, as it had done during the war
against Japan, to printing paper money. Significantly, the amount of
deficit spending during the post-1945 period—65 percent—was approximately equal to the figure for military expenditures. Without the
large military budget, therefore, the National Government could nearly
have covered its total expenditures by means of taxation and other
noninflationary measures, and would then have avoided the hyperinfla-
tion that proved to be so costly to the regime and to the people.

These are only some suggestions of how the course of events in
China might have been altered if the nationalists had been able to

reassert sovereign control over Manchuria after the war. The National Government's passage through the shoals of the postwar period would still have been fraught with difficulties, yet it is at least arguable that the difficulties would have been of lesser magnitude, and that the National Government would have been able to cope with them, had it not been for the train of events set in motion by the Russian occupation of Manchuria.

Yet the Russian occupation of Manchuria was at most one of the immediate causes of the regime's collapse. The basic causes lay deeper, in the inherent structural infirmities of a military-authoritarian regime lacking a base in society and in the enervating effects of the war with Japan. As a result of these two factors, the Nationalist movement was by 1945 utterly debilitated, its weaknesses evidenced in the limited reach of its political sway, the corruption and ineffectiveness of its administration, the self-destructive fighting of its several factions, and the pervasive incompetence and demoralization of its army. In view of this thoroughgoing disintegration, it appears highly unlikely that the Nationalist regime would have been able to consolidate effective rule over the nation even with full control of the Northeast. The Russian intervention, therefore, was but a gust of wind that helped topple the rotting structure. Without that wind, the building might have stood a little longer, but that it would come down—and sooner rather than later—seems certain, because no government exists without problems, any more than the building in our original metaphor was likely to exist in a vacuum, untouched by the elements.

Further Reading for Part III

Albertini, Rudolph von. "The Impact of Two World Wars on the Decline of Colonialism," *Journal of Contemporary History* 4 (1969):17–35.

Dower, John. *War without Mercy: Race and Power in the Pacific War.* New York, 1986.

Gifford, Prosser. *The Transfer of Power in Africa: Decolonization 1940–1960.* New Haven, 1983.

Hargreaves, A. D. *Decolonization in Africa.* London, 1988.

Holland, Roy Fraser. *European Decolonization 1918–1981: An Introduction.* New York, 1985.

Kiernan, V. G. *The Lords of Human Kind: Black Man, Yellow Man, and White Man in an Age of Empire*. New York, 1984.

Killingray, David. *Africa and the Second World War*. New York, 1986.

Lebra, Joyce C. *Japan's Greater East Asia Co-Prosperity Sphere in World War II*. Kuala Lumpur, 1975.

————. *Jungle Alliance: Japan and the Indian National Army*. Singapore, 1971.

Louis, William R. *Imperialism at Bay: The United States and the Decolonialization of the British Empire*. New York, 1978.

McCoy, Alfred W. *Southeast Asia under Japanese Occupation*. New Haven, 1980, reprinted 1985.

Newell, William H. *Japan in Asia, 1942–1945*. Singapore, 1981.

Pluvier, Jan. *South-East Asia from Colonialism to Independence*. New York, 1974.

Polenberg, Richard. *War and Society. The United States. 1941–1945*. Philadelphia, PA, 1972.

Thorne, Christopher. *Border Crossings: Studies in International History*. Oxford, 1988.

————. *The Issue of War: States, Societies, and the Far Eastern Conflict of 1941–1945*. New York, 1985.

Tinker, Hugh. *Race, Conflict, and the International Order*. New York, 1977.

Wilson, Henry S. *The Imperial Experience in Sub-Saharan Africa since 1870*. Minneapolis, 1977.

Wynn, Neil. *The Afro-American and the Second World War*. New York, 1976.

Part IV

Intelligence at War

Spies, secret messages, sabotage, and undercover operations—these are the stock-in-trade of imaginative as well as factual literature on the Second World War. Almost by definition, clandestine activities retain their distance from the sleuthhounds in academic history, leaving, as they do, too few documents to permit reliable retelling of their accomplishments and failures. Numerous examples from World War II dot the histories. Cicero, alias for Elias Basna, sold British secrets to the Germans in Turkey. Richard Sorge, a Soviet spy in Tokyo, in 1941 tipped off Stalin about the pending Operation Barbarossa and reported that Japan intended to attack southward into the southwest Pacific and not renew the war against the Soviet Union in Siberia. The Germans broke one of the war's most successful spy rings, the Soviet Red Orchestra network, but only after it had passed much valuable military information to the Red Army. The evidence, however, points not toward the exploits of spies and saboteurs as the prime contributors to the achievements of wartime intelligence, but to more prosaic labors such as deciphering enemy messages and analyzing newspapers, the reports of military attachés, businessmen, journalists, and other sources of information that might yield clues about the enemy, his capabilities, and intentions. The most vital information source of the Second World War, however, was that derived from communications used in the performance of diplomatic and military duties. That information was transmitted by wire, but more often than not by radio broadcast.

Already in the First World War, radio had sped military communications and had eased the coordination of armies over greater distances than had the telegraph and telephone in the generation before. That the enemy could also listen in was a disadvantage which was quickly corrected, but only by launching a race between devising techniques to encrypt messages and methods to decipher them. The mechanization and automation of cryptology soon followed, first in Germany, then elsewhere. Whereas before World War I coding and decoding messages played a minor role in military operations, by the 1930s it assumed ever greater importance as new enciphering devices replaced the tedium of manual cryptography. The Germans, who were clearly ahead in the field, manufactured some hundred thousand of their Enigma machines for use throughout their armed services. Simultaneously, IBM tabulators and Hollerith cards automated much of the work of codebreakers.

Though the Germans, and later the Japanese, used encrypting machines whose messages they considered unbreakable, in fact by late summer 1940 the British were able to decipher German Enigma messages and the Americans could read top-level diplomatic traffic enciphered on Japanese Purple machines. The British achievement, generally referred to as Ultra, is the topic of the article by Williamson Murray reprinted below. The American operation, known by its codename, Magic, was revealed soon after the war during the height of the controversy over the surprise attack at Pearl Harbor. Ultra, however, remained concealed from the public and all but official historians until 1974.

Since the British and Americans had access to top Axis communications, they also knew during the war that neither Germany nor Japan could consistently read Allied encrypted messages. The defeat of the Axis and the subsequent Allied capture of their records during the occupation confirmed that fact. In the case of the Soviet Union, matters are less clear. There is little evidence that Britain or the United States made any special effort to break Russian cryptography, though it might be the case that Moscow had access to German Enigma signals. As historians have greater access to Soviet records and are more free to publish them under *glasnost,* revisions of the interpretations of many phases of the war in which intelligence played a role may result.

Acquiring information is only the first of many steps in its transformation into useful intelligence. The sheer quantity of signals to be analyzed requires mammoth organizations. Those who worked on Ultra during the war continually warn that it is easy to overrate intelligence and the role it can play. Ralph Bennett, one of many professional British historians involved in Ultra, writes of the "laborious piecing together of maddeningly irreconcilable fragments."[1] Added to the difficulties in finding patterns amid disparate data, which is often contaminated with misinformation, is the need to draw conclusions quickly. Speedy analysis is essential; once orders and plans are implemented, intelligence becomes worthless. Then, the intelligence has to enter into the decision making process, always complicated in any bureaucracy and perhaps more so in hastily developed wartime military organizations. All of this has to be done so that the fewest possible persons know what is going on and that the security of the intelligence,

---

[1]Ralph Bennett,"Intelligence and Strategy in World War II," in K. B. Robertson, ed., *British and American Approaches to Intelligence* (New York, 1987), p. 130.

and especially its sources, are not revealed. Karl von Clausewitz wrote about the friction of war, the myriad ways in which things that can go wrong or not happen clog movement toward success. Nowhere is friction more present than in intelligence services.

Spies and cryptographers have provided the bulk of World War Two intelligence history. There were other groups that complemented the achievements of Ultra and Magic. In many cases they performed valuable tasks. The British Secret Intelligence Service (SIS) lost its network of spies inside occupied Europe to the Gestapo in 1940. Like the spies of the American Office of Strategic Services (OSS), they played minor roles compared to other accomplishments. SIS's Y-Service, on the other hand, kept a twenty-four hour global watch on all Axis radio traffic. Aside from providing Ultra with its raw material, the service also analyzed radio traffic for clues about the location of specific personnel and military units. The volume of traffic, the length of broadcasts, and the frequencies used often revealed vital information about enemy intentions even when the content of the messages could not be read.

Elaborate deception schemes enabled the Allies to lead the Germans to draw wrong conclusions about future operations. The case of "double cross" is unique (see John Masterman's book, noted below). Beginning in 1940 MI5, a branch of SIS, turned the first of 120 German spies in Britain. For the rest of the war, they reported insignificant and misleading information to their German masters, who continued to trust this source until the very end of the war.

Other important sources of intelligence included aerial photography and the interviewing of prisoners of war. Special Operations Executive (SOE), a new branch established by Churchill in 1940, had as its task the fomenting of resistance and sabotage inside Europe. Not a part of the regular intelligence community in Britain, it sometimes rivaled SIS for influence.

Unlike Britain, the United States entered the war with weak intelligence services, largely as a result of civilian American suspicion of such activities. In an oft-quoted comment made in 1929, Henry L. Stimson, Secretary of War during the war, noted that "gentlemen do not read each other's mail." Breaking the Purple machine did not come as a result of concerted government effort, but through dedicated men within naval intelligence. The United States Army Signal Intelligence Service had a mere seven members in 1939, though that rose to over three hundred in 1941, and to more than ten thousand before 1945. Naval intelligence grew in similar proportions. After the spring of 1942, embarrassed by the failure at Pearl Harbor and strongly supported by Admiral Chester Nimitz, naval intelligence began breaking Japan's top level codes as well as the operational ones. By 1943 it knew the location and movement of almost every Japanese ship and vessel in the world.

The accomplishments of the Americans and the British in the field of intelligence have been, of course, a source of pride. But they have also raised questions, many going back to the wartime period itself, about the use of intelligence. The two main questions seem to be, if intelligence was so successful, then how did the enemy achieve surprise to do the damage that was done? Secondly, if the Allies had such an advantage, why did the war last so long? The following two essays may not resolve those questions, but they will introduce the reader to the kinds of problems involved in reaching an answer.

9

Roberta Wohlstetter

Surprise

After fifty years, the surprise attack by the Japanese Navy on the United States naval base at Pearl Harbor remains one of the most persistant traumas in the American psyche. Gordon E. Prange devoted his life to unraveling the mystery, leaving behind on his

Reprinted from *Pearl Harbor: Warning and Decision,* pp. 382–401, by Roberta Wohlstetter with permission of Stanford University Press © 1962 by the Board of Trustees of the Leland Stanford Junior University.

death in 1980 a mammoth, inconclusive manuscript, including *At Dawn We Slept* and three other books. That the Japanese could accomplish such a feat, that they could remain undetected, even when approaching Hawaii, struck many in 1941 and since as impossible. From the beginning, theories of complicity involving the White House and down the line circulated along with a desire to find those responsible and find them guilty of treason or negligence. There were no fewer than eight major official Pearl Harbor investigations which left behind a hoard of evidence and testimony. Prange was undoubtedly the most thorough historian to go over the evidence. He familiarized himself with Japanese sources and interviewed as many participants on both sides as possible. While unused material may exist, and will be eagerly seized upon when it appears, it is doubtful that it will alter scholarly consensus significantly.

Roberta Wohlstetter examined the available evidence from the American side and wrote a detailed study explaining her findings in 1962, near the beginning of the nuclear missile age and in the same year as the Cuban missile crisis. Though not all readers will be persuaded about the issues of responsibility and culpability, her conclusions well outline the difficulties and complexities in transforming information, messages and signals into usable intelligence. Although in September 1940 the poorly financed Office of Naval Intelligence broke the Japanese Purple machine, so that its Magic operation read top diplomatic traffic between Tokyo and its worldwide embassies and also managed to provide other signals, as Wohlstetter makes clear, that was not enough. She points out that in 1941 the absence of a central agency for coordinating intelligence, a gap only partly filled by the creation of the OSS, rendered the efforts of collecting intelligence of limited value. As she states at the onset, the failure was not one of having enough information. It lay elsewhere.

Surprise

If our intelligence system and all our other channels of information failed to produce an accurate image of Japanese intentions and capabilities, it was not for want of the relevant materials. Never before have we had so complete an intelligence picture of the enemy. And perhaps never again will we have such a magnificent collection of sources at our disposal.

Retrospect

To review these sources briefly, an American cryptanalyst, Col. William F. Friedman, had broken the top-priority Japanese diplomatic code, which enabled us to listen to a large proportion of the privileged communications between Tokyo and the major Japanese embassies throughout the world. Not only did we know in advance how the Japanese ambassadors in Washington were advised, and how much they were instructed to say, but we also were listening to top-secret messages on the Tokyo-Berlin and Tokyo-Rome circuits, which gave us information vital for conduct of the war in the Atlantic and Europe. In the Far East this source provided minute details on movements connected with the Japanese program of expansion into Southeast Asia.

Besides the strictly diplomatic codes, our cryptanalysts also had some success in reading codes used by Japanese agents in major American and foreign ports. Those who were on the distribution list for MAGIC had access to much of what these agents were reporting to Tokyo and what Tokyo was demanding of them in the Panama Canal Zone, in cities along the east and west coasts of the Americas from northern Canada as far south as Brazil, and in ports throughout the Far East, including the Philippines and the Hawaiian Islands. They could determine what installations, what troop and ship movements, and what alert and defense measures were of interest to Tokyo at these points on the globe, as well as approximately how much correct information her agents were sending her.

Our naval leaders also had at their disposal the results of radio traffic analysis. While before the war our naval radio experts could not read the content of any Japanese naval or military coded messages, they were able to deduce from a study of intercepted ship call signs the composition and location of the Japanese Fleet units. After a change in call signs, they might lose sight of some units, and units that went into port in home waters were also lost because the ships in port used frequencies that our radios were unable to intercept. Most of the time, however, our traffic analysts had the various Japanese Fleet units accurately pinpointed on our naval maps.

Extremely competent on-the-spot economic and political analysis was furnished by Ambassador Grew and his staff in Tokyo. Ambassador Grew was himself a most sensitive and accurate observer, as evidenced by his dispatches to the State Department. His observations were supported and supplemented with military detail by frequent reports from American naval attachés and observers in key Far Eastern ports. Navy Intelligence had men with radio equipment located along the coast of China, for example, who reported the convoy movements toward Indochina. There were also naval observers stationed in various high-tension areas in Thailand and Indochina who would fill in the local outlines of Japanese political intrigue and military planning. In Tokyo and other Japanese cities, it is true, Japanese censorship grew more and more rigid during 1941, until Ambassador Grew felt it necessary to disclaim any responsibility for noting or reporting overt military evidence of an imminent outbreak of war. This careful Japanese censorship naturally cut down visual confirmation of the decoded information but very probably never achieved the opaqueness of Russia's Iron Curtain.

During this period the data and interpretations of British intelligence were also available to American officers in Washington and the Far East, though the British and Americans tended to distrust each other's privileged information.

In addition to secret sources, there were some excellent public ones. Foreign correspondents for *The New York Times, The Herald Tribune,* and *The Washington Post* were stationed in Tokyo and Shanghai and in Canberra, Australia. Their reporting as well as their predictions on the Japanese political scene were on a very high level. Frequently their access to news was more rapid and their judgment of its significance as reliable as that of our Intelligence officers. This was certainly the case for 1940 and most of 1941. For the last few weeks before the Pearl Harbor strike, however, the public newspaper accounts were not very useful. It was necessary to have secret information in order to know what was happening. Both Tokyo and Washington exercised very tight control over leaks during this crucial period, and the newsmen accordingly had to limit their accounts to speculation and notices of diplomatic meetings with no exact indication of the content of the diplomatic exchanges.

The Japanese press was another important public source. During 1941 it proclaimed with increasing shrillness the Japanese government's determination to pursue its program of expansion into Southeast Asia and the desire of the military to clear the Far East of British and American colonial exploitation. This particular source was rife with explicit signals of aggressive intent.

Finally, an essential part of the intelligence picture for 1941 was both public and privileged information on American policy and activities in the Far East. During the year the pattern of action and interaction between the Japanese and American governments grew more and more complex. At the last, it became especially important for anyone charged with the responsibility of ordering an alert to know what moves the American government was going to make with respect to Japan, as well as to try to guess what Japan's next move would be, since Japan's next move would respond in part to ours. Unfortunately our military leaders, and especially our Intelligence officers, were sometimes as surprised as the Japanese at the moves of the White House and the State Department. They usually had more orderly anticipations about Japanese policy and conduct than they had about America's. On the other hand, it was also true that State Department and White House officials were handicapped in judging Japanese intentions and estimates of risk by an inadequate picture of our own military vulnerability.

All of the public and private sources of information mentioned were available to America's political and military leaders in 1941. It is only fair to remark, however, that no single person or agency ever had at any given moment all the signals existing in this vast information network. The signals lay scattered in a number of different agencies; some were decoded, some were not; some traveled through rapid channels of communication, some were blocked by technical or procedural delays; some never reached a center of decision. But it is legitimate to review again the general sort of picture that emerged during the first week of December from the signals readily at hand. Anyone close to President Roosevelt was likely to have before him the following significant fragments.

There was first of all a picture of gathering troop and ship movements down the China coast and into Indochina. The large dimensions of this movement to the south were established publicly and visually as well as by analysis of ship call signs. Two changes in Japanese naval call signs—one on November 1 and another on December 1—had also been evaluated by Naval Intelligence as extremely unusual and as signs of major preparations for some sort of Japanese offensive. The two changes had interfered with the speed of American radio traffic analysis. Thousands of interceptions after December 1 were necessary before the new call signs could be read. Partly for this reason American radio analysts disagreed about the locations of the Japanese carriers. One group held that all the carriers were near Japan because they had not been able to identify a carrier call sign since the middle of November. Another group believed that they had located one carrier division in the Marshalls. The probability seemed to be that the carriers, wherever they were, had gone into radio silence; and past experience led the analysts to believe that they were therefore in waters near the Japanese homeland, where they could communicate with each other on wavelengths that we could not intercept. However, our inability to locate the carriers exactly, combined with the two changes in call signs, was itself a danger signal.

Our best secret source, MAGIC, was confirming the aggressive intention of the new military cabinet in Tokyo, which had replaced the last moderate cabinet on October 17. In particular, MAGIC provided details of some of the preparations for the move into Southeast Asia. Running counter to this were increased troop shipments to the Manchurian border in October. (The intelligence picture is never clear-cut.) But withdrawals had begun toward the end of that month. MAGIC also carried explicit instructions to the Japanese ambassadors in Washington to pursue diplomatic negotiations with the United States with increasing energy, but at the same time it announced a deadline for the favorable conclusion of the negotiations, first for November 25, later postponed until November 29. In case of diplomatic failure by that date, the Japanese ambassadors were told, Japanese patience would be exhausted, Japan was determined to pursue her Greater East Asia policy, and on November 29 "things" would automatically begin to happen.

On November 26 Secretary Hull rejected Japan's latest bid for American approval of her policies in China and Indochina. MAGIC had repeatedly characterized this Japanese overture as the "last," and it now revealed the ambassadors' reaction of consternation and despair over the American refusal and also their country's characterization of the American Ten Point Note as an "ultimatum."

On the basis of this collection of signals, Army and Navy Intelligence experts in Washington tentatively placed D-day *for the Japanese Southeastern campaign* during the week end of November 30, and when this failed to materialize, during the week end of December 7. They also compiled an accurate list of probable British and Dutch targets and included the Philippines and Guam as possible American targets.

Also available in this mass of information, but long forgotten, was a rumor reported by Ambassador Grew in January, 1941. It came from what was regarded as a not-very-reliable source, the Peruvian embassy, and stated that the Japanese were preparing a surprise air attack on Pearl Harbor. Curiously the date of the report is coincident roughly with what we now know to have been the date of inception of Yamamoto's plan; but the rumor was labeled by everyone, including Ambassador Grew, as quite fantastic and the plan as absurdly impossible. American judgment was consistent with Japanese judgment at this time, since Yamamoto's plan was in direct contradiction to Japanese naval tactical doctrine.

Perspective

On the basis of this rapid recapitulation of the highlights in the signal picture, it is apparent that our decisionmakers had at hand an impressive amount of information on the enemy. They did not have the complete list of targets, since none of the last-minute estimates included Pearl Harbor. They did not know the exact hour and date for opening the attack. They did not have an accurate knowledge of Japanese capabilities or of Japanese ability to accept very high risks. The crucial question then, we repeat, is, If we could enumerate accurately the British and Dutch targets and give credence to a Japanese attack against them either on November 30 or December 7, why were we not expecting a specific danger to *ourselves?* And by the word "expecting," we mean expecting in the sense of taking specific alert actions to meet the contingencies of attack by land, sea, or air.

There are several answers to this question that have become apparent in the course of this study. First of all, it is much easier *after* the event to sort the relevant from the irrelevant signals. After the event, of course, a signal is always crystal clear; we can now see what disaster it was signaling, since the disaster has occurred. But before the event it is obscure and pregnant with conflicting meanings. It comes to the observer embedded in an atmosphere of "noise," i.e., in the company of all sorts of information that is useless and irrelevant for predicting the particular disaster. For example, in Washington, Pearl Harbor signals were competing with a vast number of signals from the European theater. These European signals announced danger more frequently and more specifically than any coming from the Far East. The Far

Eastern signals were also arriving at a center of decision where they had to compete with the prevailing belief that an unprotected offensive force acts as a deterrent rather than a target. In Honolulu they were competing *not* with signals from the European theater, but rather with a large number of signals announcing Japanese intentions and preparations to attack Soviet Russia rather than to move southward; here they were also competing with expectations of local sabotage prepared by previous alert situations.

In short, we failed to anticipate Pearl Harbor not for want of the relevant materials, but because of a plethora of irrelevant ones. Much of the appearance of wanton neglect that emerged in various investigations of the disaster resulted from the unconscious suppression of vast congeries of signs pointing in every direction except Pearl Harbor. It was difficult later to recall these signs since they had led nowhere. Signals that are characterized today as absolutely unequivocal warnings of surprise air attack on Pearl Harbor become, on analysis in the context of December, 1941, not merely ambiguous but occasionally inconsistent with such an attack. To recall one of the most controversial and publicized examples, the winds code, both General Short and Admiral Kimmel testified that if they had had this information, they would have been prepared on the morning of December 7 for an air attack from without. The messages establishing the winds code are often described in the Pearl Harbor literature as Tokyo's declaration of war against America. If they indeed amounted to such a declaration, obviously the failure to inform Honolulu of this vital news would have been criminal negligence. On examination, however, the messages proved to be instructions for code communication after normal commercial channels had been cut. In one message the recipient was instructed on receipt of an execute to destroy all remaining codes in his possession. In another version the recipient was warned that the execute would be sent out "when relations are becoming dangerous" between Japan and three other countries. There was a different code term for each country: England, America, and the Soviet Union.

There is no evidence that an authentic execute of either message was ever intercepted by the United States before December 7. The message ordering code destruction was in any case superseded by a much more explicit code-destruction order from Tokyo that was intercepted on December 2 and translated on December 3. After December 2, the receipt of a winds-code execute for code destruction would therefore have added nothing new to our information, and code destruction in itself cannot be taken as an unambiguous substitute for a formal declaration of war. During the first week of December the United States ordered all American consulates in the Far East to destroy all American codes, yet no one has attempted to prove that this order was equivalent to an American declaration of war against Japan. As for the other winds-code message, provided an execute had been received warning that relations were dangerous between Japan and the United States, there would still have been no way on the basis of this signal alone to determine whether Tokyo was signaling Japanese intent to attack the United States or Japanese fear of an American surprise attack (in reprisal for Japanese aggressive moves against American allies in the Far East). It was only after the event that "dangerous relations" could be interpreted as "surprise air attack on Pearl Harbor."

There is a difference, then, between having a signal available somewhere in the heap of irrelevancies, and perceiving it as a warning; and there is also a difference between perceiving it as a warning, and acting or getting action on it. These distinctions, simple as they are, illuminate the obscurity shrouding this moment in history.

Many instances of these distinctions have been examined in the course of this study. We shall recall a few of the most dramatic now. To illustrate the difference between having and perceiving a signal, let us [consider] Colonel Fielder. . . . Though he was an untrained and inexperienced Intelligence officer, he headed Army Intelligence at Pearl Harbor at the time of the attack. He had been on the job for only four months, and he regarded as quite satisfactory his sources of information and his contacts with the Navy locally and with Army Intelligence in Washington. Evidently he was unaware that Army Intelligence in Washington was not allowed to send him any "action" or policy information, and he was therefore not especially concerned about trying to read beyond the obvious meaning of any given communication that came under his eyes. Colonel Bratton, head of Army Far Eastern Intelligence in Washington, however, had a somewhat more realistic view of the extent of Colonel Fielder's knowledge. At the end of November, Colonel Bratton had learned about the winds-code setup and was also apprised that the naval traffic analysis unit under Commander Rochefort in Honolulu was monitoring 24 hours a day for an execute. He was understandably worried about the lack of communication between this unit and Colonel Fielder's office, and by December 5 he finally felt that the matter was urgent enough to warrant sending a message directly to Colonel Fielder about the winds code. Now any information on the winds code, since it belonged to the highest classification of secret information, and since it was therefore automatically evaluated as "action" information, could not be sent through normal G-2 channels. Colonel Bratton had to figure out another way to get the information to Colonel Fielder. He sent this message: "Contact Commander Rochefort immediately thru Commandant Fourteenth Naval District regarding broadcasts from Tokyo reference weather." Signal Corps records establish that Colonel Fielder received this message. How did he react to it? He filed it. According to his testimony in 1945, it made no impression on him and he did not attempt to see Rochefort. He could not sense any urgency behind the lines because he was not expecting immediate trouble, and his expectations determined what he read. A warning signal was available to him, but he did not perceive it.

Colonel Fielder's lack of experience may make this example seem to be an exception. So let us recall the performance of Captain Wilkinson, the naval officer who headed the Office of Naval Intelligence in Washington in the fall of 1941 and who is unanimously acclaimed for a distinguished and brilliant career. His treatment of a now-famous Pearl Harbor signal does not sound much different in the telling. After the event, the signal in question was labeled "the bomb-plot message." It originated in Tokyo on September 24 and was sent to an agent in Honolulu. It requested the agent to divide Pearl Harbor into five areas and to make his future reports on ships in harbor with reference to those areas. Tokyo was especially interested in the locations of battleships, destroyers, and carriers, and also in any information on the anchoring of more than one ship at a single dock.

This message was decoded and translated on October 9 and shortly thereafter distributed to Army, Navy, and State Department recipients of MAGIC. Commander Kramer, a naval expert on MAGIC, had marked the message with an asterisk, signifying that he thought it to be of particular interest. But what was its interest? Both he and Wilkinson agreed that it illustrated the "nicety" of Japanese intelligence, the incredible zeal and efficiency with which they collected detail. The division into areas was interpreted as a device for shortening the reports. Admiral Stark was similarly impressed with Japanese efficiency, and no one felt it necessary to forward the message to Admiral Kimmel.

No one read into it a specific danger to ships anchored in Pearl Harbor. At the time, this was a reasonable estimate, since somewhat similar requests for information were going to Japanese agents in Panama, Vancouver, Portland, San Diego, San Francisco, and other places. It should be observed, however, that the estimate was reasonable only on the basis of a very rough check on the quantity of espionage messages passing between Tokyo and these American ports. No one in Far Eastern Intelligence had subjected the messages to any more refined analysis. An observer assigned to such a job would have been able to record an increase in the frequency and specificity of Tokyo's requests concerning Manila and Pearl Harbor in the last weeks before the outbreak of war, and he would have noted that Tokyo was not displaying the same interest in other American ports. These observations, while not significant in isolation, might have been useful in the general signal picture.

There is no need, however, to confine our examples to Intelligence personnel. Indeed, the crucial areas where the signals failed to communicate a warning were in the operational branches of the armed services. Let us take Admiral Kimmel and his reaction to the information that the Japanese were destroying most of their codes in major Far Eastern consulates and also in London and Washington. Since the Pearl Harbor attack, this information has frequently been characterized by military experts who were not stationed in Honolulu as an "unmistakable tip-off." As Admiral Ingersoll explained at the congressional hearings, with the lucidity characteristic of statements after the event:

> If you rupture diplomatic negotiations you do not necessarily have to burn your codes. The diplomats go home and they can pack up their codes with their dolls and take them home. Also, when you rupture diplomatic negotiations, you do not rupture consular relations. The consuls stay on.
>
> Now, in this particular set of dispatches that did not mean a rupture of diplomatic negotiations, it meant war, and that information was sent out to the fleets as soon as we got it . . . .

The phrase "it meant war" was, of course, pretty vague; war in Manila, Hong Kong, Singapore, and Batavia is not war 5000 miles away in Pearl Harbor. Before the event, for Admiral Kimmel, code burning in major Japanese consulates in the Far East may have "meant war," but it did not signal danger of an air attack on Pearl Harbor. In the first place, the information that he received was not the original

MAGIC. He learned from Washington that Japanese consulates were burning "almost all" of their codes, not all of them, and Honolulu was not included on the list. He knew from a local source that the Japanese consulate in Honolulu was burning secret papers (not necessarily codes), and this back yard burning had happened three or four times during the year. In July, 1941, Kimmel had been informed that the Japanese consulates in lands neighboring Indochina had destroyed codes, and he interpreted the code burning in December as a similar attempt to protect codes in case the Americans or their British and Dutch allies tried to seize the consulates in reprisal for the southern advance. This also was a reasonable interpretation at the time, though not an especially keen one.

Indeed, at the time there was a good deal of evidence available to support all the wrong interpretations of last-minute signals, and the interpretations appeared wrong only *after* the event. There was, for example, a good deal of evidence to support the hypothesis that Japan would attack the Soviet Union from the east while the Russian Army was heavily engaged in the west. Admiral Turner, head of Navy War Plans in Washington, was an enthusiastic adherent of this view and argued the high probability of a Japanese attack on Russia up until the last week in November, when he had to concede that most of Japan's men and supplies were moving south. Richard Sorge, the expert Soviet spy who had direct access to the Japanese Cabinet, had correctly predicted the southern move as early as July, 1941, but even he was deeply alarmed during September and early October by the large number of troop movements to the Manchurian border. He feared that his July advice to the Soviet Union had been in error, and his alarm ultimately led to his capture on October 14. For at this time he increased his radio messages to Moscow to the point where it was possible for the Japanese police to pinpoint the source of the broadcasts.

It is important to emphasize here that most of the men that we have cited in our examples, such as Captain Wilkinson and Admirals Turner and Kimmel—these men and their colleagues who were involved in the Pearl Harbor disaster—were as efficient and loyal a group of men as one could find. Some of them were exceptionally able and dedicated. The fact of surprise at Pearl Harbor has never been persuasively explained by accusing the participants, individually or in groups, of conspiracy or negligence or stupidity. What these examples illustrate is rather the very human tendency to pay attention to the signals that support current expectations about enemy behavior. If no one is listening for signals of an attack against a highly improbable target, then it is very difficult for the signals to be heard.

For every signal that came into the information net in 1941 there were usually several plausible alternative explanations, and it is not surprising that our observers and analysts were inclined to select the explanations that fitted the popular hypotheses. They sometimes set down new contradictory evidence side by side with existing hypotheses, and they also sometimes held two contradictory beliefs at the same time. We have seen this happen in G-2 estimates for the fall of 1941. Apparently human beings have a stubborn attachment to old beliefs and an equally stubborn resistance to new material that will upset them.

Besides the tendency to select whatever was in accord with one's expectations, there were many other blocks to perception that prevented our analysts from making the correct interpretation. We have just mentioned the masses of conflicting evidence that supported alternative and equally reasonable hypotheses. This is the phenomenon of noise in which a signal is embedded. Even at its normal level, noise presents problems in distraction; but in addition to the natural clatter of useless information and competing signals, in 1941 a number of factors combined to raise the usual noise level. First of all, it had been raised, especially in Honolulu, by the background of previous alert situations and false alarms. Earlier alerts, as we have seen, had centered attention on local sabotage and on signals supporting the hypothesis of a probable Japanese attack on Russia. Second, in both Honolulu and Washington, individual reactions to danger had been numbed, or at least dulled, by the continuous international tension.

A third factor that served to increase the natural noise level was the positive effort made by the enemy to keep the relevant signals quiet. The Japanese security system was an important and successful block to perception. It was able to keep the strictest cloak of secrecy around the Pearl Harbor attack and to limit knowledge only to those closely associated with the details of military and naval planning. In the Japanese Cabinet only the Navy Minister and the Army Minister (who was also Prime Minister) knew of the plan before the task force left its final port of departure.

In addition to keeping certain signals quiet, the enemy tried to create noise, and sent false signals into our information system by carrying on elaborate "spoofs." False radio traffic made us believe that certain ships were maneuvering near the mainland of Japan. The Japanese also sent to individual commanders false war plans for Chinese targets, which were changed only at the last moment to bring them into line with the Southeastern movement.

A fifth barrier to accurate perception was the fact that the relevant signals were subject to change, often very sudden change. This was true even of the so-called static intelligence, which included data on capabilities and the composition of military forces. In the case of our 1941 estimates of the infeasibility of torpedo attacks in the shallow waters of Pearl Harbor, or the underestimation of the range and performance of the Japanese Zero, the changes happened too quickly to appear in an intelligence estimate.

Sixth, our own security system sometimes prevented the communication of signals. It confronted our officers with the problem of trying to keep information from the enemy without keeping it from each other, and, as in the case of MAGIC, they were not always successful. As we have seen, only a very few key individuals saw these secret messages, and they saw them only briefly. They had no opportunity or time to make a critical review of the material, and each one assumed that others who had seen it would arrive at identical interpretations. Exactly who those "others" were was not quite clear to any recipient. Admiral Stark, for example, thought Admiral Kimmel was reading all of MAGIC. Those who were not on the list of recipients, but who had learned somehow of the existence of the decodes, were sure that they contained military as well as diplomatic information and believed that the contents were much fuller and more precise than they actually were. The effect of carefully limiting the reading and discussion of MAGIC, which was certainly necessary to safeguard the secret of our knowledge of the code, was thus to reduce this group of signals to the point where they were scarcely heard.

To these barriers of noise and security we must add the fact that the necessarily precarious character of intelligence information and predictions was reflected in the wording of instructions to take action. The warning messages were somewhat vague and ambiguous. Enemy moves are often subject to reversal on short notice, and this was true for the Japanese. They had plans for canceling their attacks on American possessions in the Pacific up to 24 hours before the time set for attack. A full alert in the Hawaiian Islands, for example, was one condition that might have caused the Pearl Harbor task force to return to Japan on December 5 or 6. The fact that intelligence predictions must be based on moves that are almost always reversible makes understandable the reluctance of the intelligence analyst to make bold assertions. Even if he is willing to risk his reputation on a firm prediction of attack at a definite time and place, no commander will in turn lightly risk the penalties and costs of a full alert. In December, 1941, a full alert required shooting down any unidentified aircraft sighted over the Hawaiian Islands. Yet this might have been interpreted by Japan as the first overt act. At least that was one consideration that influenced General Short to order his lowest degree of alert. While the cautious phrasing in the messages to the theater is certainly understandable, it nevertheless constituted another block on the road to perception. The sentences in the final theater warnings—"A surprise aggressive move in any direction is a possibility" and "Japanese future action unpredictable but hostile action possible at any moment"—could scarcely have been expected to inform the theater commanders of any change in their strategic situation.

Last but not least we must also mention the blocks to perception and communication inherent in any large bureaucratic organization, and those that stemmed from intraservice and interservice rivalries. The most glaring example of rivalry in the Pearl Harbor case was that between Naval War Plans and Naval Intelligence. A general prejudice against intellectuals and specialists, not confined to the military but unfortunately widely held in America, also made it difficult for intelligence experts to be heard. McCollum, Bratton, Sadtler, and a few others who felt that the signal picture was ominous enough to warrant more urgent warnings had no power to influence decision. The Far Eastern code analysts, for example, were believed to be too immersed in the "Oriental point of view." Low budgets for American Intelligence departments reflected the low prestige of this activity, whereas in England, Germany, and Japan, 1941 budgets reached a height that was regarded by the American Congress as quite beyond reason.

In view of all these limitations to perception and communication, is the fact of surprise at Pearl Harbor, then, really so surprising? Even with these limitations explicitly recognized, there remains the step between perception and action. Let us assume that the first hurdle has been crossed: An available signal has been perceived as an indication of imminent danger. Then how do we resolve the next questions: What specific danger is the signal trying to communicate, and what specific action or preparation should follow?

On November 27, General MacArthur had received a war warning very similar to the one received by General Short in Honolulu. MacArthur's response had been promptly translated into orders designed to protect his bombers from possible air attack from Formosan land bases. But the orders were carried out very slowly. By December 8, Philippine time, only half of the bombers ordered to the south had left the Manila area, and reconnaissance over Formosa had not been undertaken. There was no sense of urgency in preparing for a Japanese air attack, partly because our intelligence estimates had calculated that the Japanese aircraft did not have sufficient range to bomb Manila from Formosa.

The information that Pearl Harbor had been attacked arrived at Manila early in the morning of December 8, giving the Philippine forces some 9 or 10 hours to prepare for an attack. But did an air attack on Pearl Harbor necessarily mean that the Japanese would strike from the air at the Philippines? Did they have enough equipment to mount both air attacks successfully? Would they come from Formosa or from carriers? Intelligence had indicated that they would have to come from carriers, yet the carriers were evidently off Hawaii. MacArthur's headquarters also pointed out that there had been no formal declaration of war against Japan by the United States. Therefore approval could not be granted for a counterattack on Formosan bases. Furthermore there were technical disagreements among airmen as to whether a counterattack should be mounted without advance photographic reconnaissance. While Brereton was arranging permission to undertake photographic reconnaissance, there was further disagreement about what to do with the aircraft in the meantime. Should they be sent aloft or should they be dispersed to avoid destruction in case the Japanese reached the airfields? When the Japanese bombers arrived shortly after noon, they found all the American aircraft wingtip to wingtip on the ground. Even the signal of an actual attack on Pearl Harbor was not an unambiguous signal of an attack on the Philippines, and it did not make clear what response was best.

Prospect

The history of Pearl Harbor has an interest exceeding by far any tale of an isolated catastrophe that might have been the result of negligence or stupidity or treachery, however lurid. For we have found the roots of this surprise in circumstances that affected honest, dedicated, and intelligent men. The possibility of such surprise at any time lies in the conditions of human perception and stems from uncertainties so basic that they are not likely to be eliminated, though they might be reduced.

It is only to be expected that the relevant signals, so clearly audible after an event, will be partially obscured before the event by surrounding noise. Even past diligence constructs its own background of noise, in the form of false alarms, which make less likely an alarm when the real thing arrives: the old story of "cry wolf" has a permanent relevance. A totalitarian aggressor can draw a tight curtain of secrecy about his actions and thus muffle the signals of attack. The Western democracies must interpret such signals responsibly and cautiously, for the process of commitment to war, except *in extremis,* is hedged about by the requirements of consultation. The precautions of secrecy, which are necessary even in a democracy to keep open privileged sources of information, may hamper the use of that information or may slow its transmission to those who have the power of decision. Moreover, human attention is directed by beliefs as to what is likely to occur, and one cannot always listen for the right sounds. An all-out thermonuclear attack on a Western power would be an unprecedented event, and some little time (which might be vital) would surely have to pass before that power's allies could understand the nature of the event and take appropriate action.

There is a good deal of evidence, some of it quantitative, that in conditions of great uncertainty people tend to predict that events that they want to happen actually will happen. Wishfulness in conditions of uncertainty is natural and is hard to banish simply by exhortation—or by wishing. Further, the uncertainty of strategic warning is intrinsic, since an enemy decision to attack might be reversed or the direction of the attack changed; and a defensive action can be taken only at some cost. (For example, at Pearl Harbor, flying a 360-degree reconnaissance would have meant sacrificing training, would have interrupted the high-priority shipment program to the Philippines, and would have exhausted crews and worn out equipment within a few weeks.) In general, an extraordinary state of alert that brings about a peak in readiness must be followed by a trough at a later date. In some cases the cost of the defensive actions is hard to estimate and their relevance is uncertain. Therefore the choice of action in response to strategic warning must also be uncertain. Finally, the balance of technical and military factors that might make an attack infeasible at one time can change swiftly and without notice to make it feasible at another. In our day such balances are changing with unprecedented speed. Pearl Harbor is not an isolated catastrophe. It can be matched by many examples of effective surprise attack. The German attack on Russia in the summer of 1941 was preceded by a flood of signals, the massing of troops, and even direct warnings to Russia by the governments of the United States and the United Kingdom, both of whom had been correctly informed about the imminence of the onslaught. Yet it achieved total surprise. Soviet arguments current today that Stalin and Marshal Zhukov, his Chief of the General Staff, knew and failed to act have obvious parallels with the accusations about President Roosevelt's conspiracy of silence. These Soviet reinterpretations of history aim not only to downgrade Stalin, but also to establish that Soviet leaders were not *really* surprised in 1941, and the Soviet Union can therefore count on adequate warning in any future conflict. But the difficulties of discerning a surprise attack on oneself apply equally to totalitarian and democratic states.

The stunning tactical success of the Japanese attack on the British at Singapore was made possible by the deeply held British faith in the impregnability of that fortress. As Captain Grenfell put it, newspapers and statesmen like their fortresses to be impregnable. "Every fortress," he wrote, "that has come into the news in my lifetime—Port Arthur, Tsing Tao, the great French defensive system of the Maginot Line— has been popularly described as impregnable before it has been attacked. . . . One way or another it became a virtually accepted fact in Britain and the Dominions that Singapore was an impregnable bastion of Imperial security." Yet the defenses of Singapore were rendered useless by military surprise in the form of an attack from an unexpected, northerly direction.

More recently, the Korean War provided some striking examples of surprise. The original North Korean attack was preceded by almost weekly maneuvers probing the border. These regular week end penetrations built up so high a level of noise that on June 25, 1950, the actual initiation of hostilities was not distinguished from the preceding tests and false alarms. The intervention of the Chinese, at a later stage of the Korean War, was preceded by mass movements of Chinese troops and explicit warnings by the Chinese government to our own, by way of India, that this was precisely what they would do if we crossed the 38th parallel. Nonetheless, in important respects, we were surprised by the Chinese Communist forces in November, 1950.

How do matters stand with reference to a future thermonuclear aggression by a totalitarian power? Would such an attack be harder or easier to conceal than the Japanese aggression against Pearl Harbor? There have been many attempts in recent years to cheer us with the thought that the H-bomb has so outmoded general war that this question may appear unimportant. However, such attempts to comfort ourselves really beg the question. The question is, Will it be possible in the future for a totalitarian power so to conceal an impending attack on the forces that we have disposed for retaliation as to have a high probability of virtually eliminating them before they receive warning or have time to respond to it? In this connection it is important to observe that there is no cause for complacency. In spite of the vast increase in expenditures for collecting and analyzing intelligence data and in spite of advances in the art of machine decoding and machine translation, the balance of advantage seems clearly to have shifted since Pearl Harbor in favor of a surprise attacker. The benefits to be expected from achieving surprise have increased enormously and the penalties for losing the initiative in an all-out war have grown correspondingly. In fact, since only by an all-out surprise attack could an attacker hope to prevent retaliation, anything less would be suicidal, assuming that some form of attack is contemplated by one major power against another.

In such a surprise attack a major power today would have advantages exceeding those enjoyed by the Japanese in 1941. It is a familiar fact that with the ever-increasing readiness of bomber and missile forces, strategic warning becomes harder and harder to obtain; and with the decrease in the flight time for delivery of massive weapons of destruction, tactical warning times have contracted from weeks to minutes. It is no longer necessary for the aggressor to undertake huge movements of troops and ships in the weeks immediately preceding in all-out war, such as we described in our account of the Japanese war plan. Manned bombers capable of delivering a blow many times more devastating than anything dreamed of by the Japanese might be on their way from bases deep inside their homeland without yielding any substantial intelligence warning; they might conceivably follow routes that, by avoiding detection or at least identification among the friendly and unknown traffic appearing on radars, would be unlikely to give even any considerable tactical warning. Submarines might be kept on station several hundred miles off our coast during years of peace and might launch ballistic missiles on the receipt of a prearranged signal. Finally, intercontinental ballistic missiles might be kept for years at a high degree of readiness, and, if there were enough of them, they might be launched after simply being "counted down," with no further visible preparation. Total flight time for such rockets between continents might be less than fifteen minutes and radar warning less than that. Most important, such blows, unlike those leveled by the Japanese at Pearl Harbor, might determine the outcome not merely of a battle, but of the war itself. In short, the subject of surprise attack continues to be of vital concern. This fact has been suggested by the great debate among the powers on arms control and on the possibilities of using limitation and inspection arrangements to guard against surprise attack. The very little we have said suggests that such arrangements present formidable difficulties.

This study has not been intended as a "how-to-do-it" manual on intelligence, but perhaps one major practical lesson emerges from it. We cannot *count* on strategic warning. We *might* get it, and we might be able to take useful preparatory actions that would be impossible without it. We certainly ought to plan to exploit such a possibility should it occur. However, since we cannot rely on strategic warning, our defenses, if we are to have confidence in them, must be designed to function without it. If we accept the fact that the signal picture for impending attacks is almost sure to be ambiguous, we shall prearrange actions that are right and feasible in response to ambiguous signals, including signs of an attack that might be false. We must be capable of reacting repeatedly to false alarms without committing ourselves or the enemy to wage thermonuclear war.

It is only human to want some unique and univocal signal, to want a guarantee from intelligence, an unambiguous substitute for a formal declaration of war. This is surely the unconscious motivation of all the rewriting of Pearl Harbor history, which sees in such wavering and uncertain sources of information as the winds code and all of the various and much-argued MAGIC texts a clear statement of Japanese intent. But we have seen how drastically such an interpretation oversimplifies the task of the analyst and decisionmaker. If the study of Pearl Harbor has anything to offer for the future, it is this: We have to accept the fact of uncertainty and learn to live with it. No magic, in code or otherwise, will provide certainty. Our plans must work without it.

10

WILLIAMSON MURRAY

Ultra: Some Thoughts on Its Impact on the Second World War

The publication of F. W. Winterbotham's memoirs of his wartime intelligence work *The Ultra Secret* was the first public indication of the existence of this powerful source. A short time later the British archives were opened and researchers rushed to find new details and to rewrite the history of the Second World War. Many of the early books were sensationalist and often inaccurate. The mass of information to be sorted through is mind-boggling. In order to determine its significance, it is not only necessary to discover what Ultra knew, but also to know when its findings were reached, and what happened to the intelligence afterwards. Could the intelligence be used and how was it used? That requires linking the intelligence to decision making and operational history on a variety of levels. In the years since, much reliable material has been published and more will continue to become available.

The German Enigma machine was a typewriter-like contraption with keys electrically connected to a set of cylinders, each containing the letters of the alphabet. As a letter is struck on the keyboard, the cylinders print a string of characters to represent that letter. At the same time, the cylinders change their configuration so that the second time the same letter is hit the character string changes. In this way, the code for a particular letter is not repeated during the message. In breaking codes and encipherments before Enigma, the key to decipherment lay in establishing the frequency with which certain letters or codes appeared. With Enigma, however, the same string of characters for a particular letter recurs only once in the number of letters used raised to the

Reprinted from *Air University Review* 25:5 (July-August, 1984).

power of the number of cylinders used; in practice this meant that the same coded string for any letter never reappeared twice in a text. Thus the Germans considered their messages unbreakable.

The receiver of Enigma signals would have to know the initial settings in order to recover the message. Since the possible combinations were much too large, that could not be done manually by trial and error. By the invention of a digital computer that could rapidly test and reject wrong combinations, the problem was solved mathematically. Solutions, however, were not long-lasting because initial settings varied among German users and were frequently changed. Then, the usual problems (discussed in the introduction) of turning information into intelligence had to be faced.

It is not possible to survey all aspects of Ultra in one article, but in the following essay, Professor Williamson Murray examines several instances where Ultra was misused or not used, where it made a difference, and where it could have made no contribution. It is doubtful that the history of the war will have to be completely rewritten, but there is still much to ponder in the new perspectives the discovery of Ultra has opened up. As for why Ultra did not bring the war to an earlier conclusion, readers will have to make up their own minds. One answer may be that indeed it did.

Only now, nearly forty years after the end of the Second World War, has the essential role and contribution of intelligence to the winning of that conflict become clear. Central to the new evaluation of that importance has been the discovery of the fact that throughout the war the intelligence services of the Western powers (particularly the British) were able to intercept, break, and read a significant portion of the top secret message traffic of the German military. The dissemination of that cryptographic intelligence to Allied commanders under the code name Ultra played a substantial and critical role in fighting the Germans and achieving an Allied victory.

The breaking of the German high-level codes began with the efforts of the Polish secret service in the interwar period. By creating a copy of the basic German enciphering machine, the Poles were able to read German signal traffic through the 1930s with varying degrees of success. However, shortly before the Munich Conference in September 1938, the Germans introduced additional rotors into their enciphering machine—the so-called enigma machine—and in approximately mid-

September, darkness closed over the German message traffic. The Poles continued their work nevertheless, and after the British guarantee in March 1939 to Poland, they passed along to Great Britain what they had thus far achieved. (Earlier, there had also been considerable cooperation between the Poles and the French.) Building on what they had learned from their continental allies, the British finally managed to break into some of the German codes in April 1940, just before the great German offensive against France and the Low Countries.

This first success would soon be followed by others that would give Allied intelligence and commanders valuable insights into German intentions and capabilities. Nevertheless, these cryptographic successes covered only a small proportion of the specific codes that the Germans used. The German navy at the end of 1943, for example, used up to forty different ciphers, all requiring different settings on the enigma machines. Given the priorities in the Battle of the Atlantic, the transmissions from U-boat to shore and from the commander of submarines to his boats received the highest priorities from British code breakers at Bletchley Park (the location of the major Allied code-breaking effort in Europe). Even with the exceptional resources available at that location and at that time, it would take the experts several days and in some cases up to a week to find the solution for a particular day's settings to the enigma machine.

The task of getting invaluable intelligence information out to the field where it could be of direct help to Allied commanders was, of course, immensely difficult, especially given the fear that should the Germans find out that their codes were being compromised on a daily basis, the entire source of Ultra would dry up. In 1940 during the Battle of Britain, this need for concealment was not a great difficulty; but as the war spread throughout Europe and the Mediterranean, it became an increasing problem. Basically, the British and their American allies evolved a carefully segregated intelligence system that kept the flow of Ultra information down to a limited number of senior commanders. The entire Ultra dissemination process lay outside of normal intelligence channels. For example, the intelligence officers at Eighth Air Force would not even know of the existence of Ultra and would not know what the Ultra officer's duties were. He, in turn, would talk only to General Carl Spaatz, General James H. Doolittle, and the Ninth Air Force commander. The system worked, for the Germans never caught on to how extensively their ciphers were being compromised.

Unfortunately, there were drawbacks. Intelligence can be of use only if it is placed in the hands of those who understand its significance. Three specific incidents underline this point with great clarity. The first occurred in early September 1944 as Allied armies were pursuing the beaten Wehrmacht back to the frontiers of the Reich. On 5 September, Bletchley Park made the following information available to Allied commanders in Western Europe:

> For rest and refit of panzer formations, Heeresgruppe [army group] Baker ordered afternoon fourth [4 September] to remain in operation with battleworthy elements: two panzer, one arc six panzer, nine SS and one nought [ten] SS panzer divisions, elements not operating to be transferred by AOK five for rest and refit in area Venloo—Arnhem—Hertogenbosch.

This intelligence (along with a second Ultra confirmation on 6 September) indicated that at the very time when British plans for Operation Market Garden were to move forward, some of the best panzer divisions in the German armed forces would be refitting in the town selected as the goal of the British 1st Airborne Division and the final objective on the Rhine for the operation [in Operation Market Garden, General Bernard Montgomery's British Second Army led an armored thrust intended to join airborne troops that had landed north of the Rhine River in the Netherlands. This attempt to outflank the Germans failed]. Putting this message together with intelligence that soon began coming out of Holland from the Dutch underground that SS panzer units were refitting in the neighborhood of Arnhem, Allied commanders should have recognized that Operation Market Garden had little prospect of success. Unfortunately, they did not put these pieces together, and those at the highest level in Field Marshal Sir Bernard L. Montgomery's headquarters with access to Ultra refused to draw the correct conclusions.

A second example comes from a period three months after Operation Market Garden: December 1944. One of the unfortunate results of the rush to print after the Ultra secret was out has been the appearance of a number of legends with little basis in fact. One of the most persistent is the legend that Ultra gave no advance warning to Allied commanders in December 1944 that the Germans were preparing to launch a major counterthrust through the Ardennes. It is true that Hitler's sixth sense that German security measures had been compromised led him to undertake a series of unprecedented measures to veil the Ardennes attack. Thus, there were no overt, operational indications as to what the Germans intended. However, a number of other indicators were uncovered by the decoding of enigma messages. These indicated that the Germans were moving supplies as well as large numbers of troops into the region behind the Ardennes. Since the Germans were desperately low of supplies and troops, such allocations of resources could only portend major operations in the Ardennes. The Germans had no reason to expect that the Allies were planning to launch a major offensive in this area—especially since the Allies were so obviously trying to kick in the door to the Reich at so many other points. Unfortunately, the mood in higher Allied headquarters and in intelligence circles was close to a feeling that the war was virtually over and the Germans could not possibly launch an offensive.

The third case in which Ultra information was available but remained unused was in one instance during the Battle of the Atlantic. The Allies moved their convoys through the North Atlantic very much on the basis of Ultra information, when available, so that these great formations of merchant shipping could avoid the patrol lines of German submarines established to pick up their movement and course. In this particular case, decoding of enigma transmissions had picked up a heavy concentration of German submarines to the north of the Azores. Thus, a major convoy of aviation gasoline tankers from the refineries at Trinidad to the Mediterranean was rerouted to the south of the Azores. Unfortunately, because his escorts needed refueling and the weather was better to the north of the islands, the convoy commander disregarded his instructions, sailed to the north of the Azores, and ran smack into the U-boats. Only two of the tankers reached port. What made the episode even more surprising was the fact that the convoy commander had just come from a term of duty in the Admiralty's convoy and routing section, where he surely must have had some awareness as to the Admiralty's reasons for rerouting convoys.

If Ultra information was misused at times, it is clear that such instances were the exception rather than the rule. However, it is difficult to assess Ultra's full impact on the war. At times (particularly early in the war), no matter how much Ultra tipped the British off to German intentions, the overwhelming superiority of the Wehrmacht made any successful use of the information virtually impossible. For example, enigma decodes in the spring of 1941 forewarned the British about German intentions against the Balkan states, first against Greece and then, after the anti-German coup in Yugoslavia, against that country as well. Such intelligence was, of course, practically useless, due to the overwhelming power that the Reich was able to deploy in the region at that time. On the other hand, from the intercepts and decodes during the summers of 1941 and 1942, the British government (particularly Churchill) was able to obtain an accurate picture of Rommel's tank strength and to determine that the British army had considerable superiority in numbers against the Afrika Korps in the North African theater. What quantitative returns could not indicate were such factors as the technological superiority of some German tanks and particularly the qualitative superiority of German doctrine and training. The intercepts do help in explaining why Churchill kept such considerable pressure on Eighth Army commanders to attack Rommel.

In war, so many factors besides good intelligence impinge on the conduct of operations that it is difficult to single out any single battle or period in which Ultra was of decisive importance by itself. Yet there is one instance where one can say that the intelligence achieved through the breaking of the German codes by itself played a decisive role in mitigating enemy capabilities. By the first half of 1941, as more and more submarines were coming on line, the German U-boat force was beginning to have a shattering impact on the trade routes on which the survival of Great Britain depended. The curve of sinkings of British, Allied, and neutral shipping was climbing upward ominously.

	Number of ships sunk	Tonnage sunk
November 1940	12	146,613
December 1940	37	212,590
January 1941	21	126,782
February 1941	39	196,783
March 1941	41	243,020
April 1941	43	249,375
May 1941	58	325,492

Through the spring of 1941, the British had had virtually no luck in solving the German navy's codes. In mid-May 1941, however, the British captured not only a German weather trawler with considerable material detailing the settings for the naval codes but also a German submarine, the U-110, with its cipher machine and *all* accompanying material. With these two captures, the British held the settings for the next two months for the German navy's enigma machines. Thus, the British were able to break into the U-boat traffic by the end of May. Also, because German U-boats were controlled closely from shore and a massive amount of signaling went back and forth to coordinate the movement of the wolf packs, the British gained invaluable information, ranging from the number of U-boats available to tactical dispositions and patrol lines. Moreover, once they had a full two months' experience inside the German U-boat traffic, British cryptologists were able to continue breaking the submarine message traffic for the next five months. The impact that this intelligence had on the Battle of the Atlantic was almost immediate.

	Number of ships sunk	Tonnage sunk
June 1941	61	310,143
July 1941	22	94,209
August 1941	23	80,310
September 1941	53	202,820
October 1941	32	156,534
November 1941	13	62,196

The dramatic decline in sinkings (compared with those that had occurred during the first five months of the year) has no explanation other than that Ultra information enabled the British to gain a decisive edge over their undersea opponent. There was no introduction of new technology, no significant increase in the number of escorts available, and no extension of air coverage. Ultra alone made the difference.

Unfortunately for the Anglo-American powers, within two months of U.S. entrance into the war, the Germans introduced an entirely new cipher, Triton, which closed off the flow of Ultra decrypts for the remainder of 1942. Thus, at the very time that the vulnerable eastern and southern coasts of the United States opened up to German submarine operations, Ultra information on German intentions and operations ceased. Direction-finding intelligence was available, of course, but it remained of limited assistance.

When the Germans turned their full attention back to the Atlantic in early 1943, enormous convoy battles occurred with increasing frequency. German Admiral Karl Dönitz had available to him in the North Atlantic nearly one hundred submarines. In opposition, the Allies possessed far greater numbers of escort vessels, including escort carriers whose aircraft made U-boat shadowing of convoys almost impossible. Moreover, long-range aircraft from Newfoundland, Iceland, and Northern Ireland were reaching farther and farther into the Atlantic.

At the beginning of 1943, the Allied naval commanders enjoyed one further great advantage. Bletchley Park had succeeded once again in breaking the German naval ciphers. That intelligence proved somewhat less useful than the Ultra intelligence in 1941 that had allowed the British to steer convoys around U-boat threats. The Allies were able to carry out similar evasive operations at times, but the large numbers of German submarines at sea at any given time made such maneuvers increasingly difficult and oftentimes impossible. Initially during the great three-month battle from March to May 1943, the Allies were badly battered. In May, however, the Allies smashed the U-boat threat so decisively that Dönitz was forced to end the battle. Ultra intelligence played a major role in the turnaround. However, because of additions to Allied escort strength and increases in long-range aircraft patrols, one must hesitate in identifying the Ultra contribution as decisive by itself. Yet, the leading German expert on the Battle of the Atlantic does note:

> I am sure that without the work of many unknown experts at Bletchley Park ... the turning point of the Battle of the Atlantic would not have come as it did in May 1943, but months, perhaps many months, later. In that case the Allied invasion of Normandy would not have been possible in June 1944, and there would have ensued a chain of developments very different from the one which we have experienced.

Meanwhile, Ultra affected the air war on both the tactical and on the strategic levels. British decoding capabilities were not sufficient during the Battle of Britain to provide major help to Fighter Command to defeat the German air threat. Similarly, for the first three years of Bomber Command's war over the continent, Ultra could provide little useful intelligence. On the other hand, throughout 1942 and 1943, Ultra information provided valuable insights into what the Germans and Italians were doing in the Mediterranean and supplied Allied naval and air commanders with detailed, specific knowledge of the movement of Axis convoys from the Italian mainland to the North African shores. By March 1943, Anglo–American air forces operating in the Mediterranean had virtually shut down seaborne convoys to the Tunisian bridgehead. Allied information was so good, in fact, that the German air corps located in Tunisia reported to its higher headquarters (in a message ironically intercepted and decoded):

> . . . the enemy activity today in the air and on the sea must in [the] view of Fliegerkorps Tunis, lead to the conclusion that the course envisaged for convoy D and C was betrayed to the enemy. At 0845 hours a comparatively strong four-engine aircraft formation was north of Bizerte. Also a warship formation consisting of light cruisers and destroyers lay north of Bizerte, although no enemy warships had been sighted in the sea area for weeks.

As was to be the case throughout the war, the Germans drew the conclusion that traitors either in their High Command or elsewhere (in this case, in the *Commando Supremo,* the Italian High Command) had betrayed the course of the convoys.

In the battles with German fighters for control of the air over Sicily, Ultra proved equally beneficial to Allied air commanders. It enabled them to take advantage of German fuel and ammunition shortages and to spot Axis dispositions on the airfields of Sicily and southern Italy. However, in regard to U.S. strategic bombing, Ultra may well have exerted a counterproductive influence in 1943. Intercepts from the Luftwaffe's message traffic indicated quite correctly how seriously Allied attacks in the air were affecting German air units, but these intercepts may have persuaded General Ira Eaker, Commander, Eighth Air Force in 1943, and his subordinate commanders to go to the well once too often. The second great attack on Schweinfurt in October 1943, as well as the other great raids of that month, proved to be disastrous for the Eighth Air Force crews who flew the missions. (Sixty bombers were lost in the Schweinfurt run.)

Moreover, U.S.A.A.F. theories about the vulnerability of the German economy to precision bombing proved somewhat unrealistic. While bomber attacks did inflict heavy damage on the German aircraft industry, the industry was in no sense destroyed. Likewise, the attacks on ball-bearing plants failed to have a decisive impact. True, damage to Schweinfurt caused the Germans some difficulties, but the batterings that Eighth's bombers took in the August and October attacks were such that despite intelligence information that the Germans would be back in business quickly, the Eighth could not repeat the mission again.

In 1944, however, the nature of Eighth's capabilities and target selection changed. Most important, the Eighth Air Force received the long-range fighter support to make deep penetration raids possible. The initial emphasis in the strategic bombing attacks in late winter and early spring of 1944 was in hitting the German aircraft industry and then in preparing the way for the invasion of the European continent. In May 1944, however, General Carl Spaatz persuaded Eisenhower that he possessed sufficient bomber strength to support both the invasion and a major new offensive aimed at taking out Germany's oil industry. In attacking that industry, Spaatz, in fact, would hit the Germans at their most vulnerable economic point. Not only would attacks on the oil industry have an immediate impact on the mobility of the Wehrmacht's ground forces, but increasing fuel shortages would prevent the Germans from training a new generation of pilots to replace those lost in the terrible attrition battles of the spring.

On 12 May 1944, 935 B-17s and B-24s attacked synthetic oil plants throughout Germany. Almost immediately, Eighth's commanders received confirmation through Ultra that these attacks threatened Germany's strategic position severely. On 16 May, Bletchley Park forwarded a message to Eighth canceling a general staff order that *Luftflotten* 1 and 6 (Air Fleets 1 and 6) surrender five heavy and four light or medium flak batteries each to *Luftflotte* 3 (assigned the task of defending France). Those flak batteries were to move instead to protect the hydrogenation plant at Troglitz, a crucial facility in Germany's synthetic fuel industry. In addition, four heavy flak batteries from Oschersleben, four from Wiener Neustadt, and two from Leipzig-Erla (defending aircraft factories) were ordered to move to defend other synthetic fuel plants. This major reallocation of air defense resources were clear indications of German worries about Allied attacks on their oil industry. On 21 May, another Ultra decrypt (originating headquarters not identified) noted:

> Consumption of mineral oil in every form . . . [must] be substantially reduced . . . in view of effects of Allied action in Rumania and on German hydrogenation plants; extensive failures in mineral oil production and a considerable reduction in the June allocation of fuel, oil, etc., were to be expected.

On 28 and 29 May 1944, Eighth returned to the skies over Germany to attack the oil industry again. These two attacks, combined with the raids that Fifteenth Air Force (in Italy) had launched against Ploesti, reduced German fuel production by 50 percent. On 6 June, Bletchley Park passed along the following decrypt:

> Following according to *OKL* [German Air Force High Command] on Fifth. As a result of renewed interferences with production of aircraft fuel by Allied actions, most essential requirements for training and carrying out production plans can scarcely be covered by quantities of aircraft fuel available. Baker four allocations only possible to air officers for bombers, fighters and ground attack, and director general of supply. No other quota holders can be considered in June. To assure defense of *Reich* and to prevent gradual collapse of German air force in east, it has been necessary to break into *OKW* [German Armed Forces High Command] reserves. Extending, therefore, existing regulations ordered that all units to arrange operations so as to manage at least until the beginning of July with present stocks or small allocation which may be possible. Date of arrival and quantities of July quota still undecided. Only very small quantities available for adjustments, provided Allied situation remains unchanged. In no circumstances can greater allocations be made. Attention again drawn to existing orders for most extreme economy measures and strict supervision of consumption, especially for transport, personal and communications flights.

Throughout the summer, Albert Speer's engineers and construction gangs scrambled to put Germany's oil plants back together. As fast as they succeeded, however, Allied bombers returned to undo their reconstruction efforts. Throughout the remainder of the year, Allied eyes, particularly of American bomber commanders, remained fixed on Germany's oil industry. The punishing, sustained bombing attacks prevented the Germans from ever making a lasting recovery in their production of synthetic fuel.

Clearly, Ultra played a major role in keeping the focus of the bombing effort on those fuel plants. Speer had warned Hitler after the first attack in May 1944:

> The enemy has struck us at one of our weakest points. If they persist at it this time, we will no longer have any fuel production worth mentioning. Our one hope is that the other side has an air force general staff as scatterbrained as ours!

Speer's hopes were not realized, largely because Ultra intelligence relayed to Allied air commanders both the size and successes of German reconstruction efforts, as well as the enormous damage and dislocations to Germany's military forces that the bombing of the plants was causing. The intelligence officer who handled Ultra messages at Eighth Air Force headquarters reported after the war that the intercepts and decrypts of enigma transmissions had indicated that shortages were general and not local. This fact, he indicated, convinced "all concerned that the air offensive had uncovered a weak spot in the German economy and led to [the] exploitation of this weakness to the fullest extent."

On the level of tactical intelligence during the preparation and execution of Overlord, Ultra also was able to provide immensely useful information. Intercepts revealed a clear picture of German efforts and successes in attempting to repair damage that the Allied air campaign was causing to the railroad system of northern France. A mid-May staff appreciation by Field Marshal Gerd von Rundstedt (Commander in Chief, Panzer Group West) warned that the Allies were aiming at the systematic destruction of the railway system and that the attacks had already hampered supply and troop movements. Ultra intelligence made clear to Allied "tactical" air commanders how effective the attacks on the bridge network throughout the invasion area were and the difficulties that German motorized and mechanized units were having in picking their way past broken bridges at night.

Ultra intercepts also gave Western intelligence a glimpse of the location and strength of German fighter units, as well as the effectiveness of attacks carried out by Allied tactical air on German air bases. Furthermore, these intercepts indicated when the Germans had completed repairs on damaged fields or whether they had decided to abandon operations permanently at particular locations. Armed with this information, the Allies pursued an intensive, well-orchestrated campaign that destroyed the Germans' base structure near the English Channel and invasion beaches. These attacks forced the Germans to abandon efforts to prepare bases close to the Channel and to select airfields far to the southeast, thereby disrupting German plans to reinforce *Luftflotte* 3 in response to the cross-channel invasion.

When the Germans did begin a post-invasion buildup of *Luftflotte* 3, the destruction of forward operating bases forced them to select new and inadequately prepared sites for reinforcements arriving from the

Reich. Ultra intercepts picked up information on a substantial portion of the move and indicated bases and arrival times for many of the reinforcing aircraft.

Another substantial contribution of Ultra to Allied success was its use in conjunction with air-to-ground attacks. Ultra intercepts on 9 and 10 June gave Allied intelligence the exact location of Geyr von Schweppenburg's Panzer Group West headquarters. Obligingly, the Germans left their vehicles and radio equipment in the open. The attack not only destroyed most of Panzer Group West's communications equipment but also killed seventeen officers, including the chief of staff. The strike effectively removed Panzer Group West as an operating headquarters and robbed the Germans of the only army organization in the west capable of handling large numbers of mobile divisions.

It is worth examining the reasons why the British were able to break some of the most important German codes with such great regularity and with such an important impact on the course of the war. The Germans seem to have realized midway through the war that the Allies were receiving highly accurate intelligence about their intentions and moves. Nevertheless, like postwar German historians, the German military looked everywhere but at their own signals. Enthralled with the technological expertise that had gone into the construction of the enigma machine, the Germans excluded the possibility that the British could decrypt their signals.

After the sinking of the *Bismarck* and the rapid clearance from the high seas of the supply ships that the Germans had sent out ahead of her, the German navy did order an inquiry. Headed by a signal man (obviously with a vested interest in the results), the board of inquiry determined that the British could not possibly have compromised the enigma system. Rather, the board chose to blame the disaster on the machinations of the fiendishly clever British Secret Services. By 1943, the success of British antisubmarine measures in the Battle of the Atlantic again aroused German suspicions that their ciphers had been compromised. In fact, the commander of U-boats suggested to German naval intelligence that the British Admiralty had broken the codes.

> B.d.U. [the commander of U-boats] was invariably informed [in reply] that the ciphers were absolutely secure. Decrypting, if possible at all, could only be achieved with such an expenditure of effort and after so long a period of time that the results would be valueless.

One British officer serving at Bletchley Park records that German "cryptographic experts were asked to take a fresh look at the impregnability of the Enigma. I heard that the result of this 'fresh look' appeared in our decodes, and that it was an emphatic reassertion of impregnability."

The Germans made a bad situation worse by failing to take even the most basic security measures to protect their ciphers. Indeed, a significant portion of Bletchley Park's success was due to silly, procedural mistakes that the Germans made in governing their message traffic. Among other basic errors, the Germans in midwar started to reuse the discriminate and key sheets from previous months rather than generate new random selection tables. If that carelessness were not enough, the Germans (particularly the Luftwaffe) provided a constant source of cribs to enable the British to determine the enigma settings for codes that had been broken. These cribs turned up in numerous, lengthy, and stereotyped official headings, usually in routine reports and orders all sent at a regular time of day. Gordon Welchman, who served at Bletchley Park for most of the war, reports that "we developed a very friendly feeling for a German officer who sat in the Qattara Depression in North Africa for quite a long time reporting every day with the utmost regularity that he had nothing to report."

The German navy proved no less susceptible to critical mistakes. Dönitz's close control of the U-boat war in the Atlantic rested on an enormous volume of radio traffic. The volume itself was of inestimable help to the cryptanalysts at Bletchley Park. Although the Germans introduced a fourth rotor into the enigma machine in March 1943, thereby threatening once again to impose a blackout on their North Atlantic operations, the new machines employed only a small fraction of their technical possibilities. Unfortunately for the U-boats also, there was considerable overlapping between old and new machines. As a result of these and other technical errors, the British were back into the North Atlantic U-boat radio transmissions within ten days of the changeover. Furthermore, at about the same time, Bletchley Park decrypted a signal to U-boat headquarters indicating that the Germans were breaking the Allied merchant code.

One final incident should serve to underline the costliness of German carelessness where security discipline was concerned. The great German battleship *Bismarck* had broken out into the central Atlantic in May 1941 on a raiding expedition. After sinking the battle cruiser

Hood, the *Bismarck* managed to slip away from shadowing British cruisers. The pursuing British admiral decided at 1810 hours on 25 May that the German battle ship was making for Brest. Within an hour, the Admiralty had confirmation through air force signals. Luftwaffe authorities had used their wireless transmissions to inform their chief of staff (then visiting Athens during the Crete operation) that the *Bismarck* was heading for Brest.

Obviously, there are important lessons that we in the West can learn from these German errors. To begin with, Patrick Beesly, who worked closely with the naval Ultra throughout the war, notes that "while each nation accepted the fact that its own cryptanalysts could read at least some of their enemy's ciphers, they were curiously blind to the fact that they themselves were being subjected to exactly the same form of eavesdropping." Above all, the Germans seem to have been overly impressed with their presumed superiority in technology. Thus, not only did they make elemental mistakes in their communications discipline, but they arrogantly refused to believe that their enemies might have technological and intelligence capabilities comparable to their own.

In recent years, there has been considerable interest in German operational and tactical competence on the field of battle. There is an important subheading to that competence: while the historians and military analysts tell us that the Germans were extraordinarily good in the operational and tactical spheres, we should also recognize that the Germans were sloppy and careless in the fields of intelligence, communications, and logistics, consistently (and ironically) holding their opponents in contempt in those fields. Thus, we would be wise to examine the German example closely in all aspects of World War II. We can learn from the Germans' high level of competence in the tactical and operational fields; equally, we have much to learn from their failures in other areas. Above all, the German defeat in World War II suggests that to underestimate the capabilities and intelligence of one's opponents can have only very dangerous and damaging consequences for one's own forces.

Further Reading for Part IV

Andrew, Christopher. *Codebreaking and Signals Intelligence.* London, 1986.

———. *Her Majesty's Secret Service: The Making of the British Intelligence Community.* New York, 1986.

Andrew, Christopher, and David Dilks. *The Missing Dimension: Governments and Intelligence Communities in the Twentieth Century.* Urbana and Chicago, 1984.

Beesly, Patrick. *Very Special Intelligence.* London, 1977.

Bennett, Ralph. *Ultra in the West: The Normandy Campaign of 1944–45.* New York, 1979.

———. "World War II Intelligence: The Last 10 Years' Work Reviewed." *Defense Analysis* 3(1987):103–17.

Calvocoressi, Peter. *Top Secret Ultra.* New York, 1980.

Cookridge, E. H. *Inside SOE: The Story of Special Operations in Western Europe, 1940–1945.* London, 1965.

Garlinski, Jozef. *The Enigma War.* New York, 1980.

Hinsley, Francis H. *British Intelligence in the Second World War.* Cambridge, 1979–1990.

Jones, Reginald Victor. *Most Secret War: British Scientific Intelligence, 1939–1945.* London, 1978.

Kahn, David. *Hitler's Spies.* New York, 1978.

Kozaczuk, Wladyslaw. *Enigma: How the German Machine Cipher was Broken and How It Was Read by the Allies in World War II.* Frederick, MD, 1983.

Langhorne, Richard, ed. *Diplomacy and Intelligence During the Second World War.* Cambridge, 1985.

Lewin, Ronald. *The American Magic: Codes, Ciphers and the Defeat of Japan.* New York, 1982.

———. *Ultra Goes to War.* New York, 1978.

Masterman, John. *Double Cross System.* London, 1972.

May, Ernest R. *Knowing One's Enemies: Intelligence Assessment before the Two World Wars.* Princeton, 1984.

Prange, Gordon. *At Dawn We Slept: The Untold Story of Pearl Harbor.* New York, 1981.

———. *December 7, 1941: The Day the Japanese Attacked Pearl Harbor.* New York, 1988.

———. *Pearl Harbor, the Verdict of History.* New York, 1986.

Smith, R. H. *OSS: The Secret History of America's First Central Intelligence Agency.* Berkeley, CA, 1972.

Welchman, Gordon. *The Hut Six Story: Breaking the Enigma Codes.* New York, 1982.

Winterbotham, F. W. *The Ultra Secret.* New York, 1974.

Wohlstetter, Roberta. *Pearl Harbor, Warning and Decision.* Palo Alto, CA, 1962.

Part V

The Social Impact of War

Historians have been of several minds about the relationship between war and society. Some, following a Social Darwinist tradition, have maintained that war is the arena of competition in which the fittest society survives. As the character Harry Lime in *The Third Man,* put it: "In Italy for thirty years under the Borgias they had warfare, terror, murder, bloodshed—they produced Michelangelo, Leonardo da Vinci and the Renaissance. In Switzerland they had brotherly love, five hundred years of democracy and peace, and what did that produce ... ? The cuckoo clock."[1] Other historians have seen war as a catastrophic accident, an interruption in the normal flow of historical developments. Its effects are negative, setting human development back. Though few today would disagree that the direct human impact of war is baneful in an age of total war, while some have denied significant influence, most have affirmed it. For them, the debate has been over how to evaluate the impact of war

Before 1914, war usually affected only a small portion of the population, the fighting soldiers and the populations unfortunate enough to live along their routes of march. The French revolutionary era and the American Civil War were exceptions to this rule. As we can now see, they were harbingers of the future, though contemporaries viewed them as aberrations. Even Napoleonic and American Civil War battles, however, lasted only a day or so. Combat was costly for those involved, but still limited in scope and impact on society.

World War I changed all that. As the contesting armies came to grips with each other across northern France, a front spread from Switzerland eastward to the English Channel. Instead of one decisive battle lasting a few days, an extensive network of trenches, barbed wire, and machine-gun nests sprawled along the horizon. The soldiers settled down, as it were, to a daily ration of excruciating drudgery, boredom, and horror: Endless combat with no relief, no advances, no defeat, with nothing but an interminable struggle against mud, rats, and death.

Previous wars had been fought on the stores of arms, ammunition,

---

[1]Cited in Arthur Marwick, *War and Social Change in the Twentieth Century* (New York, 1974), p. 7. For the classic statement on war as an instrument of progress see Werner Sombart, *Krieg und Sozialismus* (Berlin, 1915), reprinted in translation as *War and Socialism* (Salem, NH, 1975). John U. Nef, *War and Human Progress; an Essay on the Rise of Industrial Civilization* (Cambridge, MA, 1950), is the classic argument against Sombart's viewpoint.

and food accumulated during the years of peace. This time, those stocks were soon exhausted and governments called upon civilians to grow and manufacture the sinews of war during the conflict itself. Quickly, war economies of the belligerents mushroomed. First in Germany, the hardest hit by the new warfare because it was the most dependent on foreign imports of food and raw materials, then in other countries, total war turned its all-devouring jaws on civilians, men, women and children alike. The home front, the battle of production, rivaled the military front for primacy. Labor unions, the bane of pre-war free wheeling entrepreneurs and industrialists, now joined the ranks of flag-waving patriots. They supported the war effort, but in return gained an improved lot for their working class members.

Women, before then encouraged to the domestic virtues of child rearing and caring for their husbands (paid work was a man's prerogative) were wooed from the home into war production. European states which had espoused a *laissez-faire* disinterest in the workings of their national economies, especially as they affected the rights of labor, now strained to shape and to discipline capitalists and workers alike into instruments of victory. The greater the demands of war, the greater the impact of the warfare state on society. Thus emerged the notion of a military participation ratio, a term coined by Stanislav Andreski to suggest that the greater the demands of war and the greater the degree of social mobilization, the greater the degree of equality resulting from the war.[2] The cooperation of the masses in war flattens the pyramid of social stratification. At the conclusion of the Great War, the extension of the power of labor unions in Europe and of the right of women to vote seem to confirm his hypothesis.

The experience of the First World War weighed heavily on Europe's elite during the 1930s. Hitler, for example, wanted to avoid making strenuous demands on German workers. They might strike or revolt. To keep them satisfied, he avoided ordering a total war economy until late 1941, when Blitzkrieg failed to achieve quick victory on the eastern front and required a shift away from guns and butter to guns and more guns. The British Conservative government also worried whether the Labour Party and its working class voters would support the war, and that if they did, the cost would be a postwar

---

[2]Stanislav Andreski, *Military Organization and Society* (Berkeley and Los Angeles, 1968).

Labour victory. Their worst fears may have been exaggerated, but many wartime measures to redress the great social inequality in British society became permanent. Labour won an overwhelming victory at the polls in 1945, as did other left wing, mass parties throughout Europe. Of the major belligerents, only the United States remained immune from this leftward, populist drift; but it experienced the impact of total war in a different way. Uniquely among the major powers, the Americans had both guns and butter.

Society in the United States went through an unparalleled experience during the war. In 1939 it was the least prepared for war of all the major participants. The U.S. Army had only 176,000 men and the government military spending was only 1.5 percent of the gross national product or 1.5 billion dollars, compared with 8 percent for Great Britain, 16 percent for Germany and 25 percent for Japan. By 1945 12 million men had been recruited into the services and the defense budget soared to over 100 billion dollars. Even more remarkably, private consumption continued to grow. War exchanged the depression for affluence. Government, as everywhere, assumed a greater role in the economy, a place it never relinquished. Wages went up; unions increased their influence. Women entered factories as never before. Blacks migrated to the North and West to work in war production. Roosevelt, pressured by A. Philip Randolph's plan for a black-led March on Washington, set up a Fair Employment Practices Committee in 1941. Though ineffective, this was the first time the federal government acted to end racial discrimination in hiring. Though blacks faced continued discrimination and segregation throughout society, Japanese-Americans had their civil liberties suspended as they were concentrated into relocation centers, and Jews faced suspicion and hostility, the war otherwise reduced ethnic tensions, especially between German-Americans and Italian-Americans on the one hand and their fellow citizens on the other.

The United Kingdom's experience differed in significant ways. Under the strain of squeezing every ounce of production from a limited labor force and scarce material resources, Britain underwent a minor social revolution after 1940. Rationing limited access to food, but it guaranteed that the lower classes were better fed than before the war. Since they now had jobs, they had the income to pay for food and housing. Medical care was in effect socialized, a change confirmed by the National Health Service Act of 1946. As in the United States, but not as in Germany and Japan, both of which tried to limit female employment, British women entered the labor force in large numbers—in fact, they were forced in when the government required unmarried women to take jobs. The state-directed total war economy produced a degree of social equality never attained before and not reached in any other democratic society. Though the social repercussions of mobilization penetrated deeply, they did not eliminate class distinctions. Moreover, male predominance survived and patriarchy reasserted itself after the war. Thus the lingering question remains, how should the social impact of war be measured?

As we saw in Part III, the Second World War had greatly varying consequences on different west European colonies in Africa and Asia. The same is true for the major belligerents at home. With few exceptions, most historians interested in the relationship between war and domestic, social history, have focused on one country, and often on one social group (studies published by Arthur Marwick are a notable exception). Their efforts, which are particularly noteworthy in the case of Britain and the United States, are building the necessary basis for cross-cultural comparisons. Perhaps in time research will enable us to develop a truly global perspective of the social impact of the war.

Finally, a word of caution. The Second World War was the crucible through which international relations, military institutions, imperialism, and national societies passed. Its social impact was not limited, however, to the social consequence of greater mobilization. As a formative experience in Jewish history, the Holocaust has been compared with God's covenant with Abraham, the escape to freedom and nationhood from Egyptian slavery, and the Babylonian captivity. The twenty million Soviet dead will long remain a trauma in its peoples' national consciousness. The mushroom clouds over Hiroshima and Nagasaki will haunt the Japanese and all humanity far into the future. Populations may have replenished themselves; cities may have been rebuilt; the socially and psychologically destructive forces of war may have run their course; and, the progressive advances in science, technology, and social experimentation engendered by war may persist. For both better and worse, the world's greatest man-made catastrophe, the Second World War, will remain a turning point in the history of our species.

11

SHEILA FITZPATRICK

Postwar Soviet Society: The "Return to Normalcy," 1945–1953

Beyond doubt, Soviet society bore the brunt of fighting during the Second World War. Three-fourths or more of all wartime casualties occurred on the Russo-German front; the fighting continued unabated from June 1941 until May 1945. Axis armies occupied the western portions of the country where about 40 percent of the population lived. Though these were the most urbanized and industrialized areas, they also produced most of Russia's foodstuffs. Nearly ten million soldiers died at the front and another 3.5 million in captivity, most deliberately starved or killed. Neither the Germans nor the Soviets adhered to the Geneva Convention. The Germans fought the war as a racial conflict, killing some seven million civilians (700,000 of whom were Jews) through deportation, occupation, or the siege of Leningrad.

Although many United States citizens recall the Second World War as "the good war," there is no question that for citizens of the Soviet Union the war was cataclysmic and that death and destruction far outweighed any benefits. Susan Linz estimates that the war cost the Soviet Union 18 to 25 years of earnings. She also notes that "there is, however, no a priori reason to believe that the net effect of World War II was negative when taking into account political and social factors."[1] She points to the gain in territory, new technologies and greater social cohesion. Even so, the con-

---

Reprinted from *The Impact of World War II on the Soviet Union*, pp. 129–156, by permission of Rowman and Littlefield, Totowa, NJ, 1985.

[1]Susan J. Linz, "World War II and Soviet Economic Growth," in Susan J. Linz, ed., *The Impact of World War II on the Soviet Union* (Totowa, NJ, 1985), pp. 25 and 34.

trast with American society could hardly be greater. As Professor Fitzpatrick notes in the following selection, Soviet society had its own particular restraints and a "return to normalcy" may not be the best way to characterize the impact of war.

The two great wars of the twentieth century were fought by societies, not simply by their armies. In the belligerent countries, civilians as well as military conscripts found their way of life, occupation, and often place of residence changed for the duration of the war. The disruption was greatest when there was enemy occupation of territory (as in much of the Soviet Union in World War II), mass evacuation, and flight of population. But even in the direst wartime circumstances, as long as hope of victory remained, civilians and soldiers thought of this disruption as temporary. They expected that when the war ended normal life would be resumed.

For the Soviet population, however, normalcy and stability remained elusive goals in the postwar years from 1945 until Stalin's death in 1953. In the first place, the process of ending the war produced social dislocations almost comparable with those associated with fighting it since tens of millions of people had to be demobilized, repatriated, returned from evacuation, and released from wartime jobs that their holders regarded as temporary or to which they had been drafted. Many chose not to return to their prewar homes and occupations. Many others found themselves unable to do so.

In the second place, the regime's coercive policies precluded the kind of relaxation and peacetime readjustment that the Soviet population hoped for after the war. Some types of postwar Soviet repression had prewar analogues, others were modeled on wartime experience. Some coercive policies were particularly associated with the incorporation of new territories into the Soviet Union and others with the perceived imperatives of postwar economic reconstruction, but it would be difficult to find a sphere of postwar Soviet life in which coercive policies were entirely absent. In the aftermath of war, the regime wanted to tighten controls on the society, not loosen them.

After the Second World War, as after the First World War and Civil War in Russia, millions of people were in movement from one geographical or social location to another, and a substantial part of the movement was spontaneous and uncontrolled. But in the second half of the 1940s, unlike the early twenties, there existed a strongly entrenched regime with coercive capacities and intentions; and the regime's own policies (resettlement, deportation, and labor conscription) added significantly to the demographic and social upheaval. The regime quickly demobilized much of the Red Army after the Second World War, but it was not ready to demobilize society in 1945. For the long-suffering Soviet population, more years of privation, storm, and stress lay ahead.

The War and Its Immediate Impact on the Soviet Population

During the Second World War, German and Axis troops occupied the Ukraine, Belorussia, the Baltic Republics, the Crimea, the Northern Caucasus and large areas of European Russia—in all, territory with a prewar population of 85 million, or 45 percent of the total Soviet population. Some 12 to 15 million Soviet citizens were evacuated or fled eastward away from the Germans. Moscow almost fell in October 1941, and German troops penetrated as far east as the Volga before being turned back at the Battle of Stalingrad. According to official Soviet claims, the occupying forces destroyed and plundered 1710 towns and more than 70,000 villages. In addition 32,000 industrial enterprises and 65,000 kilometers of railroad track were completely or partially destroyed. As they retreated, the Germans drove off livestock, seized or destroyed agricultural machinery, set fire to buildings, and blew up bridges. In addition to this devastation, banditry and anti-Soviet resistance movements were rife at the end of the war in reclaimed areas like the Ukraine and the newly acquired Western territories.

In the course of the war, over 5 million Soviet soldiers and officers were captured by the Germans, although only one million of these were alive in prisoner-of-war (POW) camps at the end of the war. To provide labor for the Reich, several million Soviet citizens were transported to Germany and, like the surviving prisoners of war, required repatriation at the end of the war. Out of 3 million Jews in the Soviet population of 1939, it is estimated that 800,000 were captured in German-occupied territories and perished in Nazi concentration camps, and an additional 909,000 Jews were captured in eastern Poland—the area occupied by the Soviet Union in 1939, taken by the Germans in 1941, and reoccupied and incorporated into the Soviet Union in 1944–1945—and met the same fate. For the Soviet population as a whole, the official Soviet estimate of wartime population losses—usually expressed as casualties, but probably also covering Soviet citizens who remained in or fled to the West at the end of the war—is a staggering 20 million, out of a total population of something over 190 million at the outbreak of war. Of the 20 million, about half are attributed to military casualties and half to civilian losses. The male population suffered much heavier losses, particularly in the fighting age-groups, than the female.

On the home front, war brought drastic changes in the composition of the work force. Perhaps 20 million men were conscripted into the armed forces during the war, and this meant that agriculture and industry—particularly agriculture—were drained of male workers. On the collective farms, the number of working-age men (16–59 years old) dropped by 12.4 million between 1940 and 1944, leaving a sexual imbalance of four women of working age for every man. In Belorussian kolkhozy in 1945, there were almost six women of working age for every man. Among civilian wage earners in industry, agriculture, and other sectors of the national economy, the number of men dropped by 8 million between 1940 and 1945, and the proportional share from 61 to 44 percent. Previously unemployed women, adolescents, invalids, and the elderly were drawn into employment to replace the men.

Strict labor discipline was characteristic of the wartime period, as was labor conscription (*trudovaia mobilizatsiia*). By a law of 26 June 1940, all workers were prohibited from leaving their jobs without the permission of their employers, violations being punishable by imprisonment of two to four months. After the outbreak of war, the defense industry and transport workers were put under military discipline, with punishment of five to eight *years* imprisonment for unauthorized departure from the job. Boys and girls in the 14–17 age group were liable to compulsory draft into labor reserve schools, after which they were supposed to work at assigned jobs for a period of four years. Urban adults became liable for labor conscription to industry and construction projects in 1942, and a decree of the same year authorized temporary conscription of urban adults and schoolchildren to help with agricultural work. But the rural population was also subject to labor conscription: in the years 1942–1944, 1.4 million rural dwellers were drafted, mainly for industrial work in the same region. Altogether, 7.6 million persons were conscripted for work in industry, construction, forestry, and agriculture in 1943.

Just before the war, as a result of the Nazi-Soviet pact of 1939, the Soviet Union acquired new territory in the west by occupying and incorporating eastern Poland (divided between the Ukrainian and Belorussian Republics); part of Romania (Moldavia); and the three Baltic states, Lithuania, Latvia and Estonia. About 20 million people were thereby added to the Soviet population; and in the short period before German occupation of the whole area in 1941, the Soviet authorities took the first steps toward Sovietization—land reform, nationalization of industry and trade, and the arrest and deportation to distant parts of the Soviet Union of many local bourgeois nationalists. Poland suffered most from the repression: an estimated 880,000 of its former citizens were deported to special settlements and labor camps in 1940–1941 (though it was also more fortunate than the other countries in that, by special agreement with the Polish government in exile, half the Poles were released before the end of the war).

Population Transfers, Resettlement and Sovietization Policies

Transfers of large ethnic populations, by decision of the Soviet government or as a result of agreements between the Soviet Union and foreign states, were characteristic of the 1940s (before, during and after the war). They deserve particular attention in any study of the impact of the Second World War on Soviet society and the Soviet regime because this was a form of social engineering that the regime had not practiced on any significant scale before 1939. Its introduction was associated with broader changes in Soviet policy toward the non-Russian Soviet population in the late Stalin period the significance of which has yet to be adequately assessed by historians. This was a period of unprecedented suspicion, repression, and arbitrary handling of non-Russian nationalities by the Soviet regime.

The first ethnic population transfers took place in the period from 1939 to 1941, probably not on Soviet initiative. By the terms of the Nazi-Soviet pact, tens of thousands of Baltic Germans were repatriated to Germany, and more than 100,000 Germans living in Soviet-controlled Polish territory were moved into the areas of Poland occupied by the Germans. In return, the Soviet Union acquired about 50,000 Ukrainians, Russians, Belorussians, and Lithuanians who were transferred from German-controlled territory in 1940–1941. By a similar population exchange with Finland in 1940, after the Winter War, 415,000 inhabitants of the Karelian provinces captured by the Soviet Union were transferred to Finnish territory.

Although these transactions were not Soviet-inspired, and in the case of the German exchange were clearly related to the Nazi drive to reunite the German *Volk,* they provided the Soviet regime with a precedent for uprooting whole ethnic groups. The idea evidently took hold since after the outbreak of war the Soviet regime carried out operations of a similar kind involving Soviet ethnic minorities. The first such operation, formally prophylactic but actually punitive in nature, was the removal of the entire German population of the Volga region (about 400,000 people, according to the 1939 census) and its resettlement in Siberia and Central Asia in the fall of 1941. This was followed in 1943–1944 by the forcible deportation of the Crimean Tatars and five small nationalities from the Northern Caucasus (Chechens, Ingushi, Karachai, Balkars and Kalmyks), a total of about a million people who were resettled in Kazakhstan and Central Asia. These peoples had lived in the areas that came under German occupation, and the stated reason for their deportation was that they were collectively guilty of collaboration with the Germans.

The postwar settlement in Europe involved large-scale population transfers in which the Soviet Union participated. These were necessitated by the existence of millions of displaced persons and by the reconstitution of nations with new borders. In this settlement, the Allies were guided by the principle that ethnic homogeneity within a given area was desirable, because heterogeneity had been the cause of so much recent conflict. As in the immediate prewar period, the Soviet Union was a participant rather than an initiator of the postwar policies of population transfer. But its participation cannot be dissociated from the emergence of coercive russification tendencies, especially in the western territories of the Soviet Union in the late Stalin period.

The major postwar population exchange involving the Soviet Union was with Poland, a country that was newly reconstituted under Soviet auspices, with the loss of its former eastern provinces to the Soviet Union and compensatory gains in the west at the expense of Germany. By Soviet-Polish agreements of 1944 and 1945, ethnic Poles and Jews (but not other nationalities) who had been Polish citizens before 17 September 1939 and who resided in the eastern provinces that were now incorporated into the Soviet Union, had the option of moving from the Soviet Union to Poland. Conversely, Ukrainians, Russians, Belorussians and Lithuanians (but not Jews) living in Poland had the option of moving to the Soviet Union. More than half a million Ukrainians, Russians, Belorussians, and Lithuanians actually moved from Poland to the Soviet Union under this agreement—probably involuntarily in many cases, since they evidently constituted the great majority of the population eligible for transfer. Two million Poles, or about half those eligible for transfer, made the journey in the opposite direction. In addition, a substantial group of Jews got out of the Soviet Union via the Polish-Soviet exchange though a high proportion of them subsequently left Poland for Palestine and other destinations.

In resettling the transferees, Soviet authorities showed more anxiety about the security of border areas than about ethnic homogeneity. The incoming Ukrainians and Belorussians were not settled in the border districts of the western Ukraine and western Belorussia from which the Poles had been repatriated. Instead, most of them were settled in the southern Ukraine while Russians and Ukrainians who had formerly resided in Siberia and Kazakhstan were brought in to rebuild the population of the border districts. Western Ukrainian towns like Borisov, denuded of skilled workers and specialists by war and population exchanges, were sent cadres from Russia and Azerbaidzhan, and this kind of organized mixing and reshuffling of nationalities seemed to be typical of postwar policy. Despite Belorussia's heavy wartime population losses and labor shortage, many Belorussian peasants were sent to work in industry and construction in Karelia, Altai, Siberia, and the Far East. According to Harrison Salisbury, Jews deported from central and western regions of the Soviet Union during the "anticosmopolitan" campaign of the late 1940s were not sent to Birobidzhan, the Jewish autonomous region in the Far East, but to Yakutia. But when Salisbury visited Birobidzhan in 1945, he found a large contingent of Crimean Tatars who had been resettled there after their wartime deportation and who were still not permitted to return to their homeland.

The Baltic states and other newly acquired territories were subjected to heavy Russification in the postwar period. Estonia, with a prewar population of not much over a million, lost many of her own nationals through deportation and received in return an influx of 180,000 non-Estonians, mainly Russians, in the years from 1945 to 1949. The same happened in Latvia, where Russians rose from 12 percent of the population in 1935 to 27 percent in 1959. In an allegedly voluntary program of "organized resettlement," half a million peasants from over-crowded regions of European Russia were moved to the border areas of Kaliningrad (formerly Königsberg and recently acquired from Germany), Sakhalin (the southern half of which had just been acquired from Japan), Eastern Siberia, the Far East, and elsewhere. The Russification element in the program was sometimes overt: "Slavs are again settling on this ancestral Slavic soil," wrote *Izvestiia* in December 1946, describing the trek of Russian and Belorussian kolkhozniks with "their livestock, poultry, farm implements, and seeds" to Kaliningrad.

The newly acquired territories—the Baltic states, western Ukraine, western Belorussia, and part of Moldavia—had to be "Sovietized" as well as "Russified" after the war, continuing the process begun in 1940–1941 and interrupted by German occupation. "Sovietization" meant nationalizing industry and trade, expropriating the old bourgeoisie, intimidating the local intelligentsia, creating new administrative cadres and, finally, collectivizing peasant agriculture. Reaching back to the experience of the Soviet Russian past, the authorities deported large numbers of "class enemies" and created temporary "Sovietizing" institutions like *rabfaks,* whose purpose was to bring workers and peasants into higher education and thus transform the old elites who were no longer to be found in the old territories of the Soviet Union. In the spring of 1949, an all-out collectivization drive was launched in the newly acquired territories. This closely followed the model of its Russian precursor (the collectivization drive of the winter of 1929–1930) and included expropriation of kulaks and their deportation to Siberia and other distant parts. As in the earlier Russian case, collectivization was a major social upheaval, accompanied by large-scale migration of peasants from countryside to town. In Estonia, the rural share of total population dropped from 53 percent at the beginning of 1950 to 46 percent only four years later, representing an out-migration from the countryside of over 50,000 peasants.

Repatriation and Demobilization

By January 1953, 5.5 million Soviet citizens were repatriated to the Soviet Union, the majority of them returning within a year of the end of the war. Most of the repatriates were former Soviet POWs and civilians from occupied Soviet territories who had been transported to the Reich as foreign laborers during the war although some had probably left the Soviet Union voluntarily during the German army's retreat.

Repatriation was a tricky question from everybody's point of view. As far as the Soviet authorities were concerned, Soviet soldiers and officers who had allowed themselves to be captured were a suspect group: on the one hand, they should have preferred death to the dishonor of falling into enemy hands, on the other hand, there was the possibility that they had been collaborators (like the million or more Soviet POWs who had served with the Wehrmacht's *Osttruppen* or joined the Vlasov Army) or been recruited as spies during their period of internment. The same suspicion attached to the *Ostarbeiter* group (some of whom had volunteered to go to work in Germany), and indeed to all Soviet citizens other than those on active service with the Red Army who found themselves in Europe at the end of the war.

At Yalta the Allies had obliged themselves to repatriate all Soviet soldiers and civilians from Europe, and between May and September 1945 they did so conscientiously, despite growing uneasiness as it became clear to the Allied personnel directly involved that many of their charges did not want to be repatriated. The effort slackened after September, and, in the end, an estimated half million Soviet displaced persons remained in the West. However, over 2 million Soviet citizens were repatriated from Western occupation zones to the Soviet Union in 1945.

There were many accounts of the strange reception the repatriates received as they crossed the border into the Soviet Union—"first welcomed at the dock with a brass band," as an American diplomat reported in Murmansk, "and then marched off under heavy armed guard to an unknown destination." The repatriates were interrogated on arrival by the NKGB's Vetting and Screening Commissions, which sought to establish who were the collaborators and who might have been recruited for espionage. Part of the group—how large a proportion is not clear—received labor camp sentences, thus passing from one form of confinement to another; and the rest either returned home, were drafted back into the Army, or drafted for civilian labor.

Demobilization of Red Army servicemen was a similarly massive operation, though less fraught with political and internal security tensions. There were 11.4 million men in the army in May 1945. Large-scale demobilization began in July of that year, and by September almost 3.5 million soldiers and officers were returning to civilian life. By 1948, the total number of demobilized Soviet soldiers had reached 8.5 million—an enormous influx for the civilian economy to absorb. In contrast to the repatriation operation, demobilization was a fairly loosely organized process. Initially, those discharged were given their papers on the spot and allowed to go where they pleased. The practice was reportedly changed later so that soldiers had to pick up their papers—necessary documents for reentry into civilian life—at the place where they had been inducted into the service. The purpose of this policy was to ensure that peasant soldiers returned to the kolkhoz after demobilization.

But there were still many ways of evading this requirement. Since labor shortages were endemic immediately after the war, local authorities and enterprises did everything possible to encourage soldiers stationed in the area to remain after demobilization, regardless of their place of induction. In Azerbaidzhan, for example, soldiers stationed there at the end of the war were wooed with concerts, movies, and meetings with workers from local plants and oilfields, and lectures "on the economy of the republic and its prospects for development"; and as a result, 50,000 settled in Baku after demobilization. Soviet historians estimate—there are not exact statistics, underlining the spontaneous aspect of the process—that about half of all demobilized soldiers found work in the towns after the war, while half went to the countryside. But this indicates a significant demographic shift: before the war, not half but two-thirds of the Soviet population was rural, and presumably the same applied to the cohort conscripted for military service. Clearly, large numbers of peasant soldiers chose not to return to their former homes and occupations after the war, and the controls were not strict enough to force them back.

While it is clear that veterans had many informal privileges in the poverty-stricken society of the immediate postwar period, their treatment in the Soviet Union was not generous by comparison with other Allied countries. On demobilization, veterans were entitled to the cost of their transport home; food for the journey; a set of clothes; a pair of shoes; and a lump sum calculated on the basis of army pay and length of service (not, however, a significant amount except for officers). There was no Soviet equivalent of the G.I. Bill in the United States, encouraging ex-soldiers to continue their education. Soviet admissions boards did favor veterans in practice, but those who went to college after the war had to live on the same low stipends as other students. Employment was supposed to be arranged by the veterans' local soviets, "taking into consideration their experience and specialties acquired in the Red Army, but not in positions lower than those they held before they joined the Army."

For many soldiers, however, army service in World War II turned out to be a channel of upward mobility. This was true of peasants who entered the urban labor force after demobilization. It was also true of soldiers who rose to be noncommissioned officers (NCOs) and officers during the war, joined the Communist party, and moved into administrative and managerial positions after the war. It should be remembered that at the end of the war half the Communist party was in the armed forces. A quarter of all soldiers (more than 3 million) belonged to the Party, most having joined during the war. The dominant prewar pattern of elite requirement—large-scale admission of workers in the Party and systematic promotion of lower-class Communists into administrative jobs—had begun to lose favor with the political leadership before the war and was dropped altogether in the 1940s. What took its place in the immediate postwar period was the appointment of veterans who had joined the Party during the war to positions of civilian leadership.

Aggregate figures on this process are not available, but a good deal of fragmentary data is provided by Soviet historians. By the end of 1946, almost 30,000 demobilized Communists had been appointed to leading work in the Ukrainian oblasts of Kharkov, Odessa, Stalino, and Poltava. Of 22,000 demobilized soldiers starting work in enterprises of the Ministry of Ferrous Metallurgy in 1946, almost 7,000 went into managerial-technical jobs, where they constituted 15 percent of the whole managerial-technical cohort. Very large numbers of veterans from peasant backgrounds became kolkhoz chairmen after the war. In the Krasnodar oblast alone, 1720 demobilized soldiers were elected chairpersons of kolkhozy in 1946.

Urban Life and Labor Recruitment after the War

Life in the towns was even harder in the postwar years than it had been in the 1930s. The overwhelming problem was the shortage and low quality of housing. Overcrowding, including multiple-family occupancy of communal apartments not designed for the purpose, had been characteristic of Russian urban housing since the great peasant migration to the towns in the First Five-Year Plan. But during the war, more than 50 percent of urban living space in the territory occupied by the Germans was damaged or destroyed; and housing in other parts of the Soviet Union deteriorated because of lack of upkeep and pressures of accommodating large numbers of evacuees. In Moscow at the end of the war, for example, 90 percent of central heating and 48 percent of water and sewage systems were out of commission, and urgent repairs were needed on 80 percent of roofs, 60 percent of electrical equipment, and 54 percent of gas equipment.

Urban population grew rapidly after the war (by 1950 the number of urban dwellers was more than 6 million above the 1940 level), and housing construction and repair did not keep pace with it. Per capita urban living space dropped from 4.09 square meters in 1940—already below any acceptable minimum—to 3.98 square meters in 1950. In Kemerovo (Siberia), the *obkom* reported in 1946 that a substantial proportion of workers "still lived in hostels with two tiers of bunks, and the real average norm of living space for one inhabitant does not exceed two square meters." In Moscow, too, hundreds of thousands of workers lived in hostels, the great majority of which were actually barracks or improvised accommodations in basements, factory premises, and unfinished buildings. Ministries and enterprises in Belorussia, where wartime damage to towns had been particularly severe, built barrack-type housing for their workers in the first postwar years, and it was not until 1949 that this form of housing construction became less common.

Rationing of food and manufactured goods was introduced in the summer of 1941 and remained in force until 1947. Of course it was no novelty for the Soviet urban population since the rationing imposed during the First Five-Year Plan had been lifted only in 1935. In 1942–1943, bread was often the only rationed commodity distributed, and the bread ration in Moscow at the end of 1943 was 300–650 grams per day according to the rationing category. However, as in earlier periods of stringency, most wage earners could get a hot meal, albeit of low quality, at their place of work. In 1944, "commercial stores," selling food and other goods at very high prices, were revived, but those were far beyond the means of the average wage earner.

Real wages were at a very low level in the first postwar years. Because of the drought and harvest failure of 1946, rationing was not lifted on schedule and food shortages became more severe. Prices on rationed goods were approximately tripled in September 1946. Consequently, the fact that commercial prices were simultaneously lowered did not benefit the average wage earner. The lifting of rationing in 1947 was accompanied by a currency reform designed to take excess cash out of circulation. This was primarily aimed at urban speculators and peasants who had amassed savings during the war by selling produce at high prices on the free market, but it was also intended to encourage the largest possible number of urban dwellers to remain or become wage earners. Only in 1949, with the first of three successive rounds of price cuts, did the economic situation of the urban population begin to improve.

During the war, the work force was boosted by the presence of "temporary" workers—women who had not previously worked, pensioners, invalids, and adolescents. It was feared that when the war ended, large numbers of these workers would withdraw from the labor force despite the continued critical need for labor. Although adolescents did, in fact, withdraw, primarily to continue their education, it seems that many of the other temporary workers remained in the work force after the war. This was probably because food prices were so high that families could not afford nonworking members. There may have been some withdrawal from the work force by urban women in 1945–1946, but as Table 8.1 suggests, this was not significant over the longer term (even allowing for the increase associated with peasant women coming into the labor force). In Moscow, for example, the proportion of women among blue- and white-collar workers dropped between January 1945 and March 1947, but the actual number increased slightly. The number of pensioners employed in the national economy also increased—from 400,000 in 1945 to 484,000 in 1946—reflecting not only the high price of food but also the inadequacy of pensions.

The twelve-million person increase in the size of the employed labor force between 1945 and 1959 (Table 8.1) was unmatched in Soviet history except in the First Five-Year Plan period. Demobilized veterans must have provided the largest single recruitment source, but the contingent of new workers included repatriates, peasants coming from the kolkhozy, graduates of the labor reserve schools, young urban dwellers entering employment, and labor conscripts. Quite a large proportion of the new workers, including all the veterans and most of the urban entrants to the labor force, were hired individually by the given enterprises from the labor market. But there were also mechanisms of

Table 8.1

Wage and Salary Earners in the Soviet National Economy in Millions, with Breakdown by Sex

	Average No. for Year	No. of Men	as percent	No. of Women	as percent
1940	33.9	20.7	61	13.2	39
1945	28.6	12.7	44	15.9	56
1950	40.4	21.2	53	19.2	47

Source: Narodnoe khoziaistvo SSSR 1922–1972 g. Iubileinyi statisticheskii ezhegodnik, 345, 348.

organized recruitment—*orgnabor,* the labor reserve system, and labor conscription—all of which took recruits from the kolkhozy (for the most part) and transported them to assigned employment, often in distant regions of the country.

Orgnabor (organized recruitment) was a term from the 1930s that was usually (that is, in the usage that was prevalent during the 1930s and the postwar Stalin period) applied to recruitment of labor from the kolkhozy for work under contract with specific enterprises. The organizing agent in the postwar period was the Ministry of Labor Reserves (created in 1947); and *orgnabor* was used mainly to provide unskilled labor for high priority sectors of heavy industry in areas of the country where labor was scarce. Thus, as Tables 8.2 and 8.3 suggest, *orgnabor* recruits were much more likely to be sent to Siberian coal mines than to the more sophisticated and accessibly located enterprises of the heavy machine-building industry. In 1948, 73.6 percent of *orgnabor* recruits went to the north, the Urals, and Siberia. Kolkhozniki signed 71 percent of *orgnabor* contracts in 1950.

The *orgnabor* share in total labor recruitment during the Fourth Five-Year Plan (1946–1950) cannot be determined with precision. One set of figures puts the number of *orgnabor* recruits for this period at 3.8 million, another at 2.4 million. This would mean that *orgnabor* provided a fifth to a third of all labor recruited during the Fourth Five-Year plan (a total of 11.6 million), but the upper estimate—and perhaps even the lower one—is too high, judging from the breakdowns for particular industries and regions of which Tables 8.2 and 8.3 provide a sample. If in the late 1940s, as in the 1950s, it was not uncom-

Table 8.2

Labor Recruitment Sources for Heavy Machine-Building Enterprises of the USSR, 1946–1949

	1946	1947	1949
Number of new workers	22,344	26,631	27,803
Percentage recruited from			
Individual hiring	66.1	49.5	55.5
Labor Reserve Schools	3.5	27.4	23.3
Orgnabor	—	0.6	1.6
Transfer from other enterprises	1.8	1.2	7.8
Other sources	28.4	21.3	7.8

Source: A.V. Smirnov, "Changes in the Number and Composition of Workers of the Heavy Machine-Building Industry in the USSR in the Years of the Fourth Five-Year Plan (1946–1950)," in *Izmeneniia v chislennosti i sostave sovetskogo rabochego klassa. Sbornik statei,* 235.

Table 8.3

Composition of Labor Force of Kuzbass Coal Combine (Siberia), with Breakdown by Sources of Recruitment (percentage)

	1 Dec. 1945	1 May 1946	1 Oct. 1947
Cadre (prewar) workers	21.4	19.0	17.2
Hired by enterprises	6.1	9.0	23.1
Labor reserve schools	5.3	5.5	7.8
Orgnabor	—	9.7	11.9
Evacuees	2.8	2.3	1.1
Conscripts *(mobilizovannye)*	23.2	18.3	7.8
Other	41.2	36.2	31.1

Source: G. A. Dokuchaev, *Rabochii klass Sibiri i Dal' nego Vostoka v poslevoennye gody (1946–1950),* 66.

mon for one individual to sign a succession of *orgnabor* contracts, this would explain why the figures are exaggerated.

The system of labor reserve schools, created in 1940 . . . and generally regarded as a wartime expedient, remained in active operation after the war. 1948 was the peak year, but while the schools' output dropped rapidly in the early 1950s, it was not until 1959 that the system was abolished and the schools became ordinary technical schools. In the postwar period students were still being drafted into labor reserve schools rather than volunteering. In contrast to the *org-*

nabor draft, which one memoir of the period describes as often welcomed by the kolkhozniki (though not by the kolkhoz administration),
the labor reserve draft was evidently unpopular; "The boys disliked the
schools because living conditions there were bad and because they had
to do very hard work; to avoid being drafted into the schools, boys
would run away from the villages to hide in the cities, where they
frequently became delinquents. But the labor reserve schools were
conduits to more skilled employment than *orgnabor,* as well as supplying different branches of industry (see Table 8.2 and 8.3). During the
Fourth Five-Year Plan period, 3.6 million students are said to have
passed through the schools, thereby amounting to over 30 percent of
all labor recruitment.

The share of free hiring in labor recruitment obviously varied enormously according to circumstances. Looking at Table 8.2, for example,
we can see that the heavy machine-building industry was doing a lot of
individual hiring in 1946 as the veterans returned from the war, but
less in 1947 and 1949 when there were fewer veterans and more labor
reserve graduates. However, Kuzbass Coal, with its remote location
and heavy dependence on conscript and other involuntary labor, did
relatively little individual hiring. All in all, assuming that 5 or 6 million
new workers came into the work force via *orgnabor* and the labor
reserve schools during the Fourth Five-Year Plan and that there was
not a high rate of renewal within the conscript labor contingent, it
seems likely that a bit less than half of the total labor recruitment in
this period was done by individual hiring on the labor market. The
"other" category in Table 8.2 is likely to cover the labor of convicts or
deportees.

However, a much higher figure, 79 percent, is quoted for the proportion of all job openings in 1950 that were filled by individual hiring. This reflected an increase in individual hiring at the end of the
Fourth Five-Year Plan period. But it was also a product of that old
Soviet *bête noire,* high labor turnover, for we must assume that among
the almost 3 million people who found themselves new jobs in 1950, a
proportion had earlier been assigned other jobs (that they had subsequently quit) as labor reserve school graduates or *orgnabor* recruits.
Despite the law of 26 June 1940, binding workers to their jobs—which
stayed on the books, along with other disciplinary measures of the
immediate prewar and early wartime period, until 1956 (although the
penal stipulations were quietly dropped in 1951)—people who took

new jobs were not necessarily new workers. In 1951, it was estimated that more than 40 percent of newly recruited workers were either transferring from other jobs or returning to their original work place after an absence.

The main causes of labor turnover in the postwar period were poor living and housing conditions. From January to May 1946, according to data of the Ministry of Ferrous Metallurgy, 32,000–33,000 workers were taken on and 62,700 left, 10,000 of them without permission from the authorities. In the year from September 1947 to September 1948, 289,300 workers left the mines of the Donetsk and Moscow basins, a quarter of them without permission. At the Glukhovo Cotton Combine in Noginsk almost half the workers hired in 1946 left in the same year. Out of 13,650 graduates of labor reserve schools sent to Belorussian industrial enterprises in 1947 only 7459 were still at their jobs on 1 January 1948, and 6191 had departed for unknown destinations because of bad housing and problems of food supply.

Convict and Conscript Labor

At the end of the war the Soviet Union had two different types of convict labor at its disposal: its own indigenous convicts (together with foreigners arrested in the Soviet Union and sent to labor camps) and German, Japanese, and other prisoners of war captured during World War II. In both cases the question of numbers seems intractable. Estimates of the population of Soviet labor camps in the postwar period range from 3–5 million to 12–15 million (the higher estimates evidently including Axis POWs, the lower ones not), but they are all quite speculative. The estimates depend heavily on extrapolations from data on the immediate prewar period, almost ignoring the specific postwar situation.

Information on the number of enemy POWs in Soviet hands after the war is also highly unsatisfactory. Soviet wartime communiqués claimed that 3.7 million German military prisoners had been taken, but Molotov stated in 1947 that after the return of a million German POWs only 890,532 remained in Soviet hands. The first figure is probably exaggerated, whereas the second is likely to be an underestimate since Molotov was responding to criticism of the Soviet Union for not releasing its prisoners of war. In addition to the Germans, some hundreds of thousands of Japanese, Hungarian, Romanian, and other POWs were in Soviet hands after the war.

Although the order of magnitude may be disputed, some statements about the convict population in the postwar Soviet Union can be made with reasonable confidence. First, the number of Soviet convicts (excluding enemy POWs) must surely have been greater in 1945–1946 than it had been in 1939. It had been swollen by waves of arrests associated particularly with territorial changes and war: the occupation and initial Sovietization of eastern Poland and the Baltic states in 1939–1941, the liberation of Soviet territories from German occupation and the punishment of collaborators, anti-Soviet partisans, and bandits in the Ukraine, Belorussia, and elsewhere; renewed Sovietization in the Baltic states, Moldavia, western Belorussia and the western Ukraine; and the return of millions of Soviet POWs and repatriates whose loyalty was regarded as suspect.

Second, convict and POW labor in the immediate postwar period was useful to the Soviet Union—much more useful and central to the economy than it had been in the prewar period. It was the most extreme form of drafting labor to areas of acute need as for example, in the rebuilding of cities and the repair of roads, bridges, and railroads in territories heavily damaged under the German occupation, not to mention the "traditional" forced-labor sphere of mining and lumbering in remote parts of the Soviet Union. The political leaders may have perceived forced labor as essential to postwar economic reconstruction—whatever the merits of this judgment—in view of wartime population losses and the difficulties of mobilizing free labor and keeping it on the job when living conditions were bad.

By the beginning of the 1950s, however, the economic argument in favor of maintaining such a large convict population had become much less plausible. The daunting economic situation of the early postwar years had improved, and the most urgent and basic tasks of postwar economic reconstruction were done. In the sphere of nonconvict labor, conscription of various kinds was giving way to unorganized recruitment. Nevertheless, the prisoners and POWs were not released, and some of the projects on which they were used in the early 1950s—the Volga-Don Canal and the construction of the new Moscow University building on Lenin Hills—had a grandiose rather than strictly practical quality.

From the swift dismantling of the convict labor empire following Stalin's death, it must be surmised that Stalin himself was the roadblock, either because he was generally blocking policy change or because he had developed an attachment to the idea of forced labor. Release of political prisoners—those arrested in the prewar purges, as well as wartime and postwar internees—began on a small scale in 1953. Soviet citizens accused of collaboration with German occupation forces were amnestied in 1955, and the Soviet POWs and repatriates who had been arrested on their return to the Soviet Union were released not long afterwards. An unofficial Soviet estimate, which unfortunately cannot be confirmed or documented in any way, puts the number of prisoners released in 1956–1957 at 7–8 million out of an estimated total labor-camp population of 12–13 million.

German POWs, whom the Soviet authorities had refused to repatriate earlier on the grounds they were war criminals, were also released after Stalin's death: about 10,000 returned to West and East Germany in 1953–1954 and another 10,000 were repatriated following the Bulganin-Adenauer talks in 1955. This, of course, was only a small fraction of the number of German soldiers believed to have been taken prisoner by the Soviet Union. If, as seems to be generally thought, the Soviets really did return almost all of the surviving German POWs in 1955, the implied mortality rate is staggering.

Conscript labor in the postwar period is a less familiar and less dramatic topic than convict labor. But the two are linked—functionally, if not institutionally—and the more accessible data on conscript labor should throw light on the broader phenomenon. Labor conscription (*trudovaia mobilizatsiia*) of the civilian population was introduced during the war, and in 1943–1944, 2.4 million labor conscripts were working in industry and construction. Labor conscription was not a punishment but an obligation comparable to military service, and historians have generally treated it as purely a wartime expedient. It continued into the postwar period, however; and, although many conscripts were probably just serving out terms begun during the war, others must actually have been conscripted for labor after the war ended. Conscript labor was used all over the Soviet Union in the period between 1945 and 1948, but its share *vis-à-vis* nondrafted labor was highest in eastern Siberia and the Far East, remote but developing areas; in the Northern Caucasus and Crimea, presumably because of the deportations of nationalities; and also in Moldavia (much of which was newly acquired territory) where over half of all workers in 1945 were labor conscripts. Between 1945 and 1948 quite large numbers of

Table 8.4

Breakdown of the Industrial Work Force of the USSR, 1945 and 1948

	1 April 1945		1 April 1948	
	Number	Percentage	Number	Percentage
Total	9,505,300	100	11,607,600	100
Workers	6,525,900	69	8,251,200	71
Employees	487,500	5	559,800	5
ITR[a]	746,200	8	926,700	8
Others	1,745,700	18	1,869,900	16

[a]Engineers and technical personnel
Source: B.I. Gvozdev, "Size of the Working Class," 114–16.

Table 8.5

Livestock and Sown Area of Kolkhozy, 1941–1950

	Cattle (millions)	Horses (millions)	Sown area (million hectares)
1941	20.1	14.5	117.7[a]
1945	15.4	6.2	83.9
1946	15.9	6.5	84.0
1947	15.8	6.6	89.2
1948	17.0	6.9	101.8
1949	20.9	7.9	111.1
1950	25.4	9.7	121.0

[a]1940 figure.
Source: Sovetskaia derevnia v pervye poslevoennye gody 1946–1950, 212, 255.

labor conscripts were sent to the Western Borderland regions: Belorussia, the Ukraine, the Karelo-Finnish Republic, Latvia, and Estonia.

According to the Soviet historian B. I. Gvozdev, postwar labor shortages made it necessary to use conscript labor on a surprisingly large scale throughout the Soviet Union. In his breakdown of the industrial work force (see Table 8.4), conscript labor evidently accounts for most of the category "others," which is notable not only for its size but also for the fact that it actually grows in absolute terms between 1945 and 1948. (Other fragmentary data, such as those cited in Table 8.3, do not confirm this, but Gvozdev's figures are certainly the most comprehensive available.) It may be inferred from Gvozdev's data that

Table 8.6

Size and Breakdown of the Kolkhoz Population of the USSR (boundaries of 1939), in Millions

	1940	1944	1945	1946
Working-age[a]	35.4	22.0	23.9	25.0
Men	16.9	4.5	6.5	8.2
Women	18.6	17.6	17.4	16.8
Adolescents	7.1	6.4	6.1	5.4
Outside working-age				
not fit to work, etc.	33.3	34.0	34.5	33.1
Total number	75.8	62.4	64.5	63.5

[a]Excluding invalids
Source: Iu. V. Arutiunian, Sovetskoe krest'ianstvo, 318.

labor conscription had been completely phased out by the spring of 1950. But this is only an inference, and the actual terminal date of labor conscription (not counting short-term drafting of kolkhozniki for lumbering, road building, etc.) has still to be established.

Rural Life and Migration from the Kolkhoz

The war greatly weakened the material base of the kolkhozy (see Table 8.5). Horses and manpower were taken for military purposes, and the sown area contracted. As they retreated from the occupied territories, the Germans plundered the kolkhozy of animals and machinery and destroyed buildings. Moreover, a good deal of kolkhoz property found its way into private hands during the war as external supervision slackened. In occupied Belorussia and the Ukraine, expropriated kulaks came back and repossessed their old houses, blacksmith shops, and mills. Elsewhere, peasants expanded their private plots at the expense of the kolkhoz, and there were concealed sales and leasing of land.

Procurement levels were high throughout the war, and the average daily payment to the individual kolkhoznik for his workdays dropped from 350 grams of cereal and 330 grams of potatoes in 1940 to 190 grams of cereal and 70 grams of potatoes in 1945. On the other hand, prices on the kolkhoz market were very high, and many peasants acquired large savings in cash by selling produce from their private plots. The most vexing problem for the kolkhozy was the shortage of manpower resulting from wartime military conscription. The working-age men were gone, and even some of the working-age women had been conscripted to work in industry (see Table 8.6). The old and the young had to become full-time workers on the kolkhoz, and women who had normally spent most of their time on the private plots had to take the men's place cultivating the kolkhoz fields.

The war's end brought men back to the countryside, but in far smaller numbers than had departed. This was not only because of casualties but also because many of the surviving peasant soldiers chose not to go home after demobilization, or at least chose not to stay. Of those that did return, many were invalids and unable to work. A year after the war ended, the ratio of working-age women to men in all Soviet kolkhozy was two to one (Table 8.6) whereas on Russian kolkhozy it was three to one. This must surely have been the cause of much bitterness and disappointment. In territory that had been occupied by the Germans, war damage was still visible on every side, and agriculture was often reduced to a primitive level. Many kolkhozy in Russia, the Ukraine, and Belorussia were still using cows as draft animals in 1946, and others were digging with spades instead of ploughing and sowing by hand. There were no horses at all in 120 kolkhozy in the Novgorod oblast.

But 1946 was also a year of natural disaster. A severe drought hit large parts of the Soviet Union—Moldavia, most of the Ukraine, parts of the central black-earth region, the lower Volga, and the Maritime Province in the Far East—causing harvest failures in these regions. Despite this, procurements quotas remained high; and by dint of enormous pressure on the peasants, grain deliveries were actually not much lower in 1946 than they had been in 1945 (17.5 million tons as against 20 million). But this reduced much of the rural population to a desperate condition because so little was left for the peasants' own consumption. As Table 8.6 shows, departures of working-age peasant women and adolescents went up—probably a combined result of drafting for industry and hunger—and the total number of very old and very young persons in the kolkhoz population fell, suggesting increased mortality associated with famine.

In the postwar years, Alec Nove has written, it was "as if Stalin was determined to make the peasants pay for the necessary postwar reconstruction." Compulsory state deliveries and payments to the Machine-Tractor Stations (MTS) amounted to half of all kolkhoz grain

Table 8.7

Money Income of Kolkhoz Households by Region, 1945–1950 (in rubles of the given year)

	1945	1946	1947	1948	1949	1950
USSR	1,144	1,112	1,319	1,196	1,387	1,684
Uzbekistan	4,627	4,260	4,405	4,345	7,165	11,861
Caucasus	2,308	2,212	2,584	2,264	2,777	3,323
Central black-earth region	1,237	1,056	1,267	1,000	1,070	986
Ukraine	619	618	830	834	925	1,103
Belorussia	236	335	503	458	485	463

Source: Sovetskaia derevnia, 288.

production in 1947 and 1948 and to more than half the kolkhoz production of milk and meat. Moreover, prices paid by the state for deliveries were not only far below market prices, they were also way below production costs, leading some Soviet scholars to refer to postwar procurements as a tax-in-kind rather than an equivalent exchange. Prices for grain had scarcely been raised since the beginning of the 1930s; in 1950 they covered about one-seventh of production costs. Moreover, prices varied by region, to the disadvantage of some of the regions most severely affected by the war. In Belorussia, for example, the state bought pigs at one-twentieth the cost of raising them.

However, there were exceptions to the general pattern of low procurements prices. Cotton, citrus products, and tea were the main items for which the state was paying high prices after the war, and the result was a great disparity of income between kolkhozy in favored areas like Uzbekistan and the Caucasus on the one hand, and Belorussia on the other (see Table 8.7).

Payment for work on the kolkhoz was in kind (mainly grain and potatoes) as well as in money, but the payments were well below the prewar level, and kolkhozniki were very much dependent on their private plots for subsistence and money income. However, the private plots were a source of revenue to the state as well as the individual households in the postwar years. First, individual households had to make compulsory deliveries of vegetables, eggs, milk, and so on at below-market prices. If a household could not make deliveries out of its private plot—for example, if it had no cow to produce milk—the

Table 8.8a

Kolkhoz Population of the USSR (excluding newly acquired territories), in Millions, 1945–1950

	1945	1948	1949	1950
Total	64.4	65.4[a]	63.8	62.3
Working-age	23.9	no data	26.7	25.9

[a]I. M. Volkov, "The Kolkhoz Peasantry in the First Postwar Years (1946–1950)," *Voprosy istorii,* 1970, no. 6: 7.
Source: Sovetskaia derevnia, 109.

Table 8.8b

Kolkhoz Population of the RSFSR in Millions, 1940–1950

	1940	1944	1945	1946	1947	1948	1949	1950
Total	44.8	35.7	36.6	36.1	37.6	37.1	35.7	34.5
Working-age	20.8	12.5	13.5	14.2	15.7	15.9	15.4	14.7

Source: Verbitskaia, "Changes in the Size and Composition of the Kolkhoz Peasantry," 126, 131.

specified amount of milk had to be borrowed or bought on the market and delivered to the state regardless. Second, individual households had to pay the agricultural tax in addition to taxes levied on the kolkhoz as a whole. The agricultural tax was calculated by assigning a ruble value for each private-plot asset—animals, vegetable garden, fruit trees—and taking a percentage.

Add to this the fact that the December 1947 currency reform wiped out peasant savings and that *corvée* obligations laid on the kolkhoz were a constant source of resentment, and it is not hard to find explanations for peasant dissatisfaction, expressed in the high rate of out-migration from the kolkhozy (only temporarily balanced in 1945–1947 by the return of the demobilized soldiers) in the postwar years. Kolkhoz population in Russia had far from reached the prewar level when the tide turned in 1947–1948 and numbers started to drop again (see Table 8.8b). In 1948 and 1949, more than a million working-age peasants left Russian kolkhozy. Many of those departing, though by no means all, were *orgnabor* recruits. But the migration cannot be satisfactorily explained as a government-sponsored effort to attract peasant workers to industry. There was actually an excess of workers in industry after the 1947 currency reform encouraged nonworking urban residents to find jobs: in 1948, industry had 147,000 workers more than its planned contingent, and the situation had not changed by 1951. From the government point of view, the utility of peasants staying in the countryside was greater than the utility of their migrating to towns and becoming urban wage earners at this time.

Yet the agricultural policies of the latter part of the Stalin period were not calculated to enhance the quality of rural peasant life. In many parts of the Soviet Union, notably in Russia, the old Ukraine, and Belorussia, fiscal and economic pressure on the kolkhozy became almost intolerably severe at the end of the 1940s. The tax on kolkhoz income was raised in August 1948, and the burden of this was felt most in areas like the Central black-earth region and Belorussia where kolkhoz incomes were low and falling (see Table 8.7). Quotas for kolkhoz delivery of meat and milk also went up at the end of the 1940s, meaning that less was available for consumption and sale on the market.

As for the individual households and their private plots, an average of 16.6 percent of eggs, 12.9 percent of grain and 5–6 percent of potatoes and milk products produced on private plots went to the state in the form of compulsory deliveries in 1950. The agricultural tax became a very heavy burden since the value assigned to peasant assets did not reflect falling free-market prices and since the percentage taken for tax was increased: according to a Soviet calculation, the average agricultural tax on a kolkhoz household in 1950 was 93.6 rubles, as against 59.5 rubles in 1945. In fact, the burden was so great that in 1949–1950 peasants started to dispose of their assets—chopping down orchards (in the example made famous by Khrushchev), selling off animals, and reducing the acreage under cultivation in their private plots. The percentage of peasant households owning a cow, which in the first postwar years had held fairly steady at a level comparable with that of 1940, fell from 74 in 1948 to 64 in 1950. In the period from 1950 to 1953, the area under cultivation in private plots declined from 7.5 million hectares to 6.9 million.

It was in these years, 1950–1953, that migration from countryside to town became a flood. In the period of 1950–1954, 9 million persons are said to have migrated permanently to the towns, out of a total

Table 8.8c

**Population of the USSR, Rural and Urban, 1940–1954
(in millions, data for the beginning of each year)**

	Population Total	Of Which		As Percentage of Total Population	
		Urban	Rural	Urban	Rural
1940	194.1	63.1	131.0	33	67
1950	178.5	69.4	109.1	39	61
1954	191.0	83.6	107.4	44	56

Source: *Narodnoe khoziaistvo SSSR 1922–1972*, 9.

rural-urban migration of 24.6 million over the twenty-year period 1939–1959, and the rural share of total population dropped from 61 percent to 56 percent (see Table 8.8c). The rate of departure was greatest in areas where the economic plight of the kolkhozy was most acute, which in Russia meant the Moscow, Smolensk, Ryazan, Kaluga, Penza, Tambov, and Orlov oblasts, where in 1950 from 60 to 90 percent of kolkhozy were paying out no more than one kilogram of grain per workday. In a raion of Moscow oblast said to be fairly typical, the number of working-age kolkhozniki, expressed as a percentage of the number in 1946, went up to 108.5 percent in 1949 only to drop to 80 percent in 1952.

In response to this crisis, the basis of *orgnabor* recruitment was changed to draw proportionately more heavily on the urban population than on the rural, and one would suppose that rural soviets were instructed to place strict limitations on the number of passports issued to kolkhozniki. But these measures were obviously not effective in stemming the flow. After Stalin's death, the leadership decided that "mistakes" in policy toward the kolkhoz peasantry were to blame, and later Soviet historians have held to this opinion. The outflow from the countryside slowed down in the mid-1950s only after a series of policy changes had made the economic situation of the peasantry more viable.

The concept of a "return to normalcy" is often applied to postwar societies. It implies release from wartime obligations and constraints, relaxation of tension, going home, and settling down. But these qualities, however desired by Soviet citizens, were not characteristic of the Soviet Union in the immediate postwar period. Obligations and constraints were scarcely diminished. Many survivors uprooted by the war could not or did not return home. The kolkhoz had to cope with abnormally great government demands despite its depleted population and predominance of women. Peace brought *un*settlement to all those who were involved in population exchanges and resettlement programs, as well as the population of the newly acquired territories subject to Sovietization measures.

If the anticipated return to normalcy did not occur in the immediate postwar years, how is this to be explained? The first point to bear in mind is that the prewar Soviet Union did not provide a very satisfactory or complete model of normalcy to which the society could return after the war. Though the turmoil of social revolution had subsided by the mid-1930s, the spirit of struggle and conflict—kept alive by the growing threat of war in the latter part of the decade—was deeply rooted in the Party's political culture. The kolkhoz still seemed an alien institution to most peasants, whose idea of a return to normalcy was a return to the old precollectivization village. The New Economic Policy of the twenties, with its private businesses, small traders, and generally more relaxed and *gemütlich* atmosphere, was probably still the model of normal life for most town dwellers. Within the elite, the purges of the late 1930s had left a traumatic legacy of fear and insecurity. As a result of collectivization, the liquidation of NEP, and the purges, the Soviet Union had acquired a large convict population in prisons and labor camps. Although forced labor was to some extent integrated into the national economy, the camps were treated as a shameful secret, and it is very doubtful that the Soviet leadership—let alone the population—saw them as normal or systemic in the prewar decade.

After the war, the perpetuation of an essentially wartime atmosphere can partially be explained in terms of the urgent problems of economic reconstruction and manpower shortages. However, this rationale faded as the economy became stronger at the end of the 1940s. A contrast must surely be drawn, for example, between the pressures on the kolkhoz in the first postwar years, and the even greater pressures imposed at the beginning of the 1950s. The former were harsh, but acceptable within a context of war-associated sacrifice. The latter seemed almost gratuitous, reviving old suspicions that the regime was basically antagonistic to the peasantry, and leading millions of peasants to abandon the kolkhoz and seek a new life in the towns.

The regime itself was a major barrier to a return to normalcy in the immediate postwar years. In the first place, it was taking a stance of repressive vigilance in all areas, indicating to the population that the time of crisis, emergency, extraordinary measures, and sacrifice was not yet past. Soviet leaders were undoubtedly aware of differences between their own definition of normalcy and that of the population, or large segments of it: they knew that during the war peasants had talked of a postwar abolition of the kolkhoz, intellectuals of a postwar easing of cultural controls, and so on. Before any return to normalcy occurred, from the regime's standpoint, it was necessary to establish that the relevant norms were "Soviet," not "counterrevolutionary."

In the second place, the regime's policies toward non-Russians were an impediment to normalization. It was trying to Sovietize the newly acquired territories in the west with extremely disruptive social consequences, while at the same time promoting Russification of the population of these and other border regions. The antisemitic aspects of the "anticosmopolitan" campaign reinforced the impression that non-Russians were in deep disfavor as a group and further destabilizing innovations in official nationalities policy might be expected. If the regime had not quite replaced the old "class enemies" with ethnic enemies in Stalin's last years, it certainly seemed to be moving in that direction.

However, in talking of regime attitudes in Stalin's last years, we should possibly make a distinction between the attitudes of Stalin himself, and those of his colleagues and potential successors. To judge by the speed and thoroughness of change after Stalin's death, there must have been something like a silent consensus of dissatisfaction, or at least uneasiness, with Stalin's position on many questions emerging within the Party leadership at the end of his life. Part of the consensus might be expressed as a desire to lift wartime obligations and constraints that had survived into the postwar period, lower the level of repression and social tension, and put the society on a more normal peacetime footing.

Within a few years of Stalin's death, there were to be basic changes of policy toward the kolkhoz peasantry, relaxation of labor discipline measures, abandonment of the labor reserves system, and a partial dismantling of the whole empire of convict labor. Overt Russification policies were dropped, and some ethnic groups deported during the war (though not the Crimean Tatars or Volga Germans) were allowed to return to their homelands. Soviet "collaborators," together with the Soviet POWs and *Ostarbeiter* imprisoned on their return from Europe after the war were released. German POWs were finally—ten years after the war's end—repatriated.

This was essentially the long-awaited postwar relaxation, the return to normalcy that had never really occurred in the years 1945 to 1953. That harsh and stringent period, seen by many contemporary Western observers as the quintessence of Stalinism, perhaps deserves a less grandiose label like Jerry Hough's "petrification." The system, clumsily attempting a transition from war to peace, seemed to have stuck halfway and be floundering. It was only when Stalin died that the balance eventually tipped, allowing Soviet society to lurch forward into the postwar era.

12

D'ANN CAMPBELL

The War and Beyond: Women's Place in American Life

American society at war has been closely examined by many historians. Some accounts have been fascinating narratives, detailing what life was like during the war. Others have sought to analyze how the nation was organized to produce war material and to fight; they have wanted to know whether such mobilization transformed American life. Though not the most catastrophic war in terms of number of people killed (the Civil War claimed more American dead and left widespread destruction in the South), the war left few American homes untouched. Some have argued that basic American institutions changed little, while others have seen in the war years a watershed.

From the 1970s on, the upsurge of women's rights advocacy and the broad challenge to women's "traditional" roles combined with a renewed interest in women's history to find, in the Second World War, the source of the new woman. The number of women in the work force climbed from 10.8 million in March 1941 to over 18 million in mid-1944 (compared with 1.5 million in World War I). William Chafe found the beginnings of the later transformation in paid employment outside the home for married women.[1] Other, less optimistic historians have identified "Rosie the Riveter" as a temporary phenomenon. By war's end, government and businesses were pushing women out of the workplace. The domestic housewife as mother of her children and homemaker for her husband crowded the career woman from the movies and magazines.

In the following selection, Professor Campbell drew conclusions from a comprehensive study which goes beyond the liberating effect of receiving a paycheck. Campbell examined many kinds of American women—their wartime experiences and the obstacles they faced—and defines their goals and accomplishments within the context of values of the 1940s. She looked at women who served in the armed forces, including nurses, those who did volunteer work, those who took outside employment, women in labor unions, and women who chose neither employment nor volunteering. By setting her discussion within the broad context of American society for the period, she built a basis for understanding the impact of war that goes beyond simplistic, one-dimensional concepts of wartime mobilization as a catalyst for greater equality.

From 1941 to 1945, American women were at war with America in a double sense. In households, the labor market, and the services, women cooperated with—sacrificed for—national goals; in the same arenas, women also waged their own wars against those goals, which they frequently viewed as subversive of their own most deeply held values. Throughout the period, private goals remained overwhelmingly important for many women. Yet women's experience of and attitudes toward the war cannot be explained simply as a struggle between the claims of patriotism and those of private interest. Both patriotism and

---

[1] William Chafe, *American Woman: Her Changing Social, Economic, and Political Roles, 1920–1970* (New York, 1972).

private interest informed women's cooperation as well as their conflict with national priorities. The two sets of categories do not mesh neatly, but rather cut across each other like a grid. In their evaluation of national goals, women responded from their own deeply rooted moral evaluations of good and evil, which they associated intimately with what they considered proper or improper behavior for women in society. American women responded to the demands of the war as women.

Women, like other Americans, answered the call of patriotism, and felt themselves to be patriotic. Yet women, also like other Americans, reinterpreted the public definitions of patriotism in relation to their own values, experiences, and goals. At best, patriotism is an elusive concept, and especially hard to identify during the war years. Women's patriotism, understood as their support for the war against the Axis, resulted both from a willingness to offer unquestioning support to national policies and, perhaps more important, from a sense of moral outrage at the perfidy of the attack on Pearl Harbor, the atrocities of the Japanese, and the immoral conduct of the Nazi government. These contemporaneous justifications for the war were captured in the media's depiction of Tojo and Hitler as personalized enemies. The emphasis fell on the personal and the concrete. In recent years, it has become common to judge the barbarity of the war by more general criteria, such as genocide—the Holocaust or total war on civilian populations—but it was not at the time. And women expressed their patriotism in concrete personal ways also. Women felt patriotic when they volunteered for USO work, took a war job, saved fats, bought war bonds, or sent a loved one to the Army. Other women felt patriotic when they resisted the intense propaganda for women to take war jobs. "I have plenty of defense work myself taking care of the nine-month-old baby and the five-year-old boy," explained the wife of a welder in Pittsburgh. In May 1943, 58 percent of all women thought they could best help the war effort by staying home. The government was concerned by the proliferation of individual interpretations of patriotism that assumed the virtues of loyalty while resisting specific directives. Business shrugged; to coax more women into the labor force it raised pay scales and improved working conditions.

In effect, for most women, universal moral values probably carried more weight than patriotism, which they most readily assumed out of moral concern and the dictates of which they persisted in defining for themselves. Women's concern with conforming to their own understanding of moral imperatives helps to explain the confusion between the categories of patriotism and private interest and cooperation and conflict. The private decisions of women and their families normally reflected a balance between particular self-interest—both economic and psychic—and universal moral beliefs. But women's understanding of morality itself requires careful investigation.

By 1940 (and probably earlier) the special link between morality and gender roles had largely dissolved. Americans of the late nineteenth century had, by and large, accepted the notion that women inherently possessed a superior sense of morality to that of men. This ideology associated moral purity with the home, in which female values should dominate; less spiritual male values held corresponding sway in the public realm of work and politics. Women leaders of the Progressive era had relied upon this view to argue that women should have the right to vote in order to protect the home and to purify politics. By the third decade of the twentieth century, however, the special association of women with morality had largely dissipated, a casualty perhaps of the fiasco of prohibition, perhaps of woman suffrage, perhaps of the steady increase in women's labor force participation, perhaps only of the more relaxed social mores of the 1920s, perhaps of the blow of the depression. Whatever the causes, by the 1940s, with the exception of the literature of the Women's Christian Temperance Union, few references to the notion of inherently superior female morality could be found. Claire Boothe Luce's smash Broadway hit *The Women* (1937) openly proclaimed that the fair sex could be inherently nasty, if not actually evil. The polls of the war years still showed that women displayed greater pacifism than men, but the national commitment to fighting, hating, and unconditional surrender submerged the possible impact of this tendency. No women peace leaders of the stature of Jane Addams or Emily Balch emerged, nor did anything resembling the large peace movement of the 1920s. When, after the war, Eleanor Roosevelt earned a place as an influential peace leader, she did so on new grounds.

The central moral issues of the war were not specifically linked to gender. Equality, in particular, assumed the proportions of a central moral value, but equality of sacrifice appealed to both liberals and conservatives, and to both men and women. Both the Roosevelt administration and labor unions strongly promoted economic equality. Rationing, taxes, and selective service appeared far more tolerable to those who believed that the rules were being applied uniformly to everyone regardless of status. Indeed, in practice the rules were seen as equitably administered. Americans' main moral complaint concerned labor strikes, which appeared as illegitimate efforts to profiteer from the emergency. Union spokesmen emphasized their "no-strike" pledge, pointing out how small a proportion of work time was lost through strikes. But not even the most militant unionists tried to explain away the massive coal strikes that threatened the fuel supply of homes and factories. The public mood of hostility toward unions, especially on the part of housewives, grew.

The claims of racial equality for blacks aroused little support outside the black community, the CIO leadership, and leftist groups. The reason seems to have been a remarkable misperception on the part of white America that blacks actually did enjoy equality in terms of jobs, housing, schooling, police protection, and welfare services. The white, segregated South was more aware of the reality of inequality, but vigorously defended it, arguing that blacks, being morally and intellectually inferior and lacking ambition, were getting all they deserved. The contradictions of southern racism were already beginning to unravel, although black women had little reason to discern signs of change, except perhaps for the improvement in salary scales for black teachers.

For the American population as a whole, inequality of actual living conditions lessened during the war. The share of family income going to the top 5 percent declined from 30 percent in 1929 to 21 percent in 1944. During the war boom, working-class families with two or three wage earners frequently reached the $100-a-week level that placed them in the top fifth of income distribution. The diminishing inequality of standards of living proved even more dramatic: rationing, price and rent controls, the relative rise of blue-collar versus white-collar incomes, selective service, EMIC, and the rapid spread of hospitalization insurance all combined to narrow the gap in consumption between the richest and the poorest thirds of the population. The evidence on narrowing gaps in food consumption and nutritional standards underscored the implications of the changes for housewives. Other forces also tended to lessen inequality. The exodus out of rural America transferred millions of families from areas with poor prospects for men and few jobs for women into a more promising urban or small town environment.

Minority families made especially dramatic gains during the war. The labor force participation rates for the major ethnic and racial groups of women living in cities and small towns had begun to con-

Table 20

Employment of Urban Women Aged 24–44, by Race and Ethnicity, 1950

Census group	In labor force (%)	White collar (%)
Native white, native parents	36	65
Japanese	51	50
Chinese	33	45
Indian	32	31
Black	53	14
Filipina	29	10
Native white, immigrant parents:	36	58
Irish	41	78
Scandinavian	37	73
British	36	70
German	36	65
From Russia	29	62
Czech	37	50
Italian	36	43
Polish	38	42
Puerto Rican (mainland)	37	41
French Canadian	43	35
Mexican	28	31
Foreign-born white	35	46
All urban women	36	55

Source: Donald J. Bogue, *The Population of the United States* (New York, 1959), pp. 367–369, 437, 506; U.S. Bureau of the Census, *U.S. Census of Population: 1950,* vol. IV, *Special Reports,* part 3, chap. A, *Nativity and Parentage* (Washington, D.C., 1954), pp. 58–59, 136–161.

verge by 1950, though black women stood out as especially committed to paid employment. The rate at which the groups held white-collar jobs reflects the strong impact made by differential access to education and by the lingering effects of discrimination (see table 20).

The income of black families more than doubled between 1939 and 1945, though their incomes and opportunities still fell far below whites. The wretched poverty on Indian reservations had worsened during the 1930s; of the New Deal welfare programs only the Civilian Conservation Corps had reached the reservations. During the war, military service rates were high among Native Americans, and several hundred women enlisted. Their family allowance and dependency checks poured welcome cash into the community, as did the earnings of men and women who found jobs at nearby military installations or who trekked to industrial centers. Extensive military activities in Alaska also provided job opportunities for Eskimo, Indian, and Aleut families, although many of the latter were forced to resettle in camps when the Japanese threatened the Aleutian Islands. On the whole, blacks were able to hold their wartime income gains, though fierce discrimination blocked them from further advances. The reservation Indians, however, relapsed into poverty after the war boom ended. The only permanent gain they made was the acquisition of skills that would permit them to survive in the cities when they eventually decided to abandon the reservations. Incomes doubled in overcrowded Puerto Rico, thanks to higher sugar prices and new military installations. Continued rural poverty, combined with rapid population growth rates, set the stage for large-scale postwar migration to New York.

In the southern Appalachians, 700,000 moved north to industrial centers such as Dayton, Detroit, and Muncie. In the face of considerable hostility toward "hillbillies," they clung to strong extended kin networks, often driving back and forth to the mountains after a week's work in the city. The remittances from war workers and soldiers helped ease the poverty in the mountains. The Appalachians responded to their new contact with cities by a dramatic change in fertility. In 1940, mountain women had a birth rate 50 percent higher than the national average; by 1950 they were only 20 percent higher, and by 1960 were slightly below the national rate. The women also sharply increased their labor force participation rates, and, to some degree, helped nudge their families away from patriarchy.

To the extent that an economic leveling took place during the war, the sense of injustice regarding structural inequality seems to have dimmed. Certainly the moral fervor of liberalism faded, and the postwar political mood became distinctly more conservative, a trend reinforced by the grudging acceptance of the income tax that was now routinely withheld from the paychecks of all classes. During the war, little attention was paid to economic inequality. In any case, far more attention centered on the equality of personal sacrifice. With every neighborhood in the land displaying blue stars and gold stars, the immediacy of the sacrifice was clear even to those who did not have a loved one in uniform. Women shared a bondage of grief, a point constantly reiterated by media images of servicemen saying farewell to their mothers, wives, and sweethearts, which further strengthened the sense of sisterhood in their sphere of suffering. But a deep spirit of equality and community in general resulted from the hardships imposed upon everyone and the complex adjustments needed to meet the challenge, especially on the part of housewives. Long after the war, the generations who had lived through it would wax nostalgic about their equality of sacrifice and of suffering, and about the resurgence of a sense of civic duty and community participation.

The big loser in the wake of equality of sacrifice was the Red Cross. Its elitist social pretensions offended average Americans, while its disdain for its own volunteers relegated society women to make-work tasks. Blacks were outraged at its segregated blood policy. The Red Cross lost its important role in controlling nursing to the military nurse corps on the one hand, and the newly invigorated civilian American Nurses' Association on the other. Most damaging of all, the Red Cross had alienated its most important clients, the soldiers. They returned home with a highly negative view of the bureaucratic aloofness (and alleged promiscuity) of the agency's staff, producing a sharp decline in public support. Although the Red Cross desperately reorganized itself after the war, allowing more of a voice to local chapters and concentrating on blood supply and disaster services, it never regained its status as the nation's premier social service agency. Its place was taken by more representative local organizations, especially the Community Chest, which built on the more open, more democratic wartime experience of volunteers.

But what of equality between the sexes? While the labor force participation of women increased sharply, and remained permanently well above previous levels, the breakdown of historic sex roles in the workplace was marginal at best. Only in obviously temporary sectors, such as munitions, airplanes and shipbuilding, were large numbers of women holding jobs traditionally held by men. Even there, gender segregation was high, as the men held the skilled and supervisory positions. In the blue-collar realm the men, and their unions, reluctantly accepted women as temporary co-workers, but they effectively blocked them from permanent entry into their shops and assembly lines. In the white-collar realm, however, women did make permanent gains, especially in retail sales jobs and middle management. The status of so many women as part-time or part-year workers gave them a weak bargaining position for factory jobs, but made them ideal workers in the retail, office, and service sectors of the economy.

The labor unions, cresting in size and political power, yet fearful that postwar reaction would sweep away their astounding new gains, distrusted and even feared women. No one who switched into and out of the labor force, and who proclaimed primary loyalty to the family, could fit the intensely masculine image of the brotherhood banded together. The willingness of wives and single women to work for less pay than men demanded was even more disturbing. The equal-pay clause CIO leaders sought was only partially a reflection of equalitarianism; the men who ran the unions were so certain that women were inferior workers that they figured companies would not displace men if they had to pay women the same wage. Blinded by a historic shop-floor sense of male supremacy, and fearful for their sudden gains, most unions refused to take advantage of the opportunity to embrace a major element of the labor force. Conversely, the weakness of unions in the increasingly feminine white-collar sector raised a barrier to union expansion for decades to come.

Management, long accustomed to the luxury of picking from a surfeit of qualified male job applicants, discovered by 1942 that women would have to be hired in large numbers, trained, and supervised if war contracts were to be filled on time. The federal government offered some generalized advice and lavish publicity, and provided some vocational training, but had little direct influence on how women should be handled. The chief state contribution was suspension of "protective" legislation for the duration. The unions, abjuring any direct involvement, divided in their response to these ninety-day wonders. The unions failed even to educate their men on such elemental matters as sexual harassment and the common courtesies of the workplace.

The engineers who ran industry soon appreciated the need for suitable sanitary, rest, and eating facilities and for the installation of devices to increase safety and reduce heavy muscle work. They also tailored job tasks so that unskilled women could learn them quickly. The importance of human relationships had become more apparent to management in the 1930s. During the war the newer, more technologically sophisticated industries making aircraft, ships, and electrical equipment hired matrons to patrol the shop floor, used interviewers to assist in personnel offices, and occasionally—as in the Kaiser shipyards in Oregon—provided day-care centers and grocery shops. While women were added in staff roles, they were rarely given line responsibilities. The women workers themselves preferred male supervisors, provided they avoided the crudities that had historically marked the way foremen dealt with workers.

The wages in war industry were high. Women marveled at their take-home pay, even if men in comparable jobs were paid more. Women knew about the wage disparity (which lessened during the war), but blocked from having a voice in union affairs, did little more than grumble. A feminist consciousness was scarcely visible in the factories. Women participated in official strikes, and occasionally led walkouts against the hiring of black women co-workers, but few agitated for equal pay or equal rights. Numerous factors were involved. The turnover of women was so high that a leadership cadre seldom formed; men who totally controlled the unions rarely listened to women; and the lack of specialized skills meant women had weak bargaining advantages. Women, furthermore, were typically more dissatisfied with unequal burdens caused by home duties. They responded to bad conditions not by voice but by exit—switching jobs or returning to the home. Black women, who had vastly fewer job options and who needed to work, were more likely than whites to protest, even to the post of organizing strikes in Atlanta laundries.

Paid employment was not a new experience for women. Their opportunities shifted during the war, however, with more jobs available at much higher pay, and women responded accordingly. When asked if they planned to continue work after the war, the unmarried women said "yes"—and they did continue. The married women were more ambivalent. About half needed to work to help support their families; the permanent lowering of barriers against employment of wives was a significant gain for them. But other wives worked because their husbands were away, and they eagerly looked forward to the day when they could become housewives again. After the war, most of them did quit readily, although a large fraction were responding to their husbands' demands that they stay home. In a relatively small number of cases, notably in the automobile industry, women were forced out of good jobs by a combination of hostile unions, indifferent management, and the favoritism shown to male veterans. Some became housewives; others scrambled for poorly paid, traditionally female jobs. The unemployment compensation system, biased against women workers who had taken up housekeeping, or who had non-traditional skills, provided little protection to women.

The feminist dream of equal opportunity seemed for a brief while to hold most promise in the military. The systematic planners in the high command, especially the more daring aerial services, readily overcame the traditional prejudices against women in uniform when their calculations showed how significant the manpower advantages would be. However, the WAAC/WAC, WAVES, Spars, and women Marines were so hurriedly organized that an experienced leadership cadre never matured. The dispersal of women into small groups inhibited the emergence of support networks, mentors, and role models upon which leadership skills must be based. Perhaps that would have come in time, but no time was allowed because the men resisted the challenge to their masculinity (or, more often, their status and their very lives) by a vicious slander campaign. As successful as it was false, the slander campaign kept women from enlisting. Those who did serve were largely assigned low-level stereotypical female jobs, despite their superior education, skills, and versatility. While the pay was good, the oppressive atmosphere and absence of training programs, together with the favoritism shown civilian women, undercut and finally destroyed the women's morale. The generals and admirals after the war, on looking over the same manpower calculations, decided they wanted women permanently in uniform. However, the women veterans and the feminists had become uncertain about the wisdom of the experiment, and the rank-and-file men remained so obdurate that full utilization of women by the military remained a distant goal even after the feminist revolution of the 1970s.

The nurses, by contrast, made striking feminist gains. Slanders there were aplenty, especially by corpsmen relegated to a traditionally female role under the control of women. Yet the structure of the situation was favorable. The nurses were virtually drafted, so they could not avoid the challenge. Military service was congruent with their technical skills, their careers as nurses, and their humanitarian motivations. Most soldiers and sailors were not corpsmen threatened by loss of status but potential casualties who welcomed the availability of expert treatment. Most important, the Army and Navy Nurse Corps were distinctive, semiautonomous, all-female units, with a female chain of command, clear-cut career stages, unique traditions, and a structure that facilitated the development of support networks, administrative skills, de facto command over men, and pride in accomplishing a highly valued, difficult job. After the war, the civilian nurses, encouraged and eventually led by their veterans, seized control of their own profession and emerged as the only major institution in American society controlled by women.

To understand American women in the 1940s, it is essential to concentrate, not on the formerly male roles that some women occupied, but on the family roles that the vast majority of women at the time defined as central to their lives. The housewife, not the Wac or the riveter, was the model woman. As purchaser and consumer, women had never been as important. With the purchase of automobiles at a low ebb, husbands had a drastically reduced role in deciding family expenditures. With strict rationing, severe shortages, overcrowded stores, jammed transportation facilities, and hidden cost increases, the task of shopping became far more complex, though the abundance of money meant that the privations of depression could at last be left behind. The government's policy of diverting all of the increase in GNP to the military necessitated an elaborate structure of taxes, bond sales, price fixing, and allocations of scarce goods. Housewives accepted the system realistically, and soon were able to decipher the mysteries of coupons and controls. Despite shortages, the nation's nutritional practices and standards of health care improved sharply during the war, as a result of government and media information campaigns, Red Cross programs, the spread of health insurance (Blue Cross especially), EMIC, and above all, the awareness by housewives that their patriotic and family interests were identical. Had the war lasted another five years, the impact on morale generally might have been adverse, but the housewives would have maintained a highly supportive consumer sector.

Housekeeping and purchasing duties, while important, do not reach the core of what married life was like in the 1940s. To interpret the meaning of marriage for women we must inquire what it implied in terms of a woman's self-image and her relationship to husband, children, and community.

Why did women marry? The question may seem superficial—sociologists in the 1940s did not even bother asking. But we must ask, because women clearly changed their behavior in the decade: more of them married, they married at younger ages, and they had more children. Three types of explanatory factors can be considered: changes in external factors, notably the economy and the draft; new social pressures, as expressed through the media and informal interpersonal contacts; and the emergence of different values among young couples. Statistical techniques that could weigh the importance of each factor require detailed data that does not now exist (though possibly it could be created by very ingenious oral histories), so our conclusions must be tentative.

The improved economy certainly provided the jobs and income that made marriage feasible for millions of couples, including many who had been forced to delay their plans by the depression. The psychology of war seems to have encouraged quick marriages, until the sheer physical segregation of young men by 1943 or 1944, together with the severe problems faced by camp followers, had their impact. The good jobs available for civilian husbands, furthermore, encouraged working women to leave the labor force and become housewives. The sense that newlywed women, and especially new mothers, should quit their jobs, at least temporarily, remained strong. In making their ideal life choices, young women in 1943 preferred the housewife role (75 percent) over being single with successful career (6.5 percent) or combining marriage and career (19 percent). If forced to choose, only one woman in five in the last group spoke of career over marriage. Evidence from cohorts of college alumnae, as well as from the census reports, shows that marriage and motherhood were more favored by the younger women than the older; the increases in both marriage and fertility in the 1940s were greatest among the best-educated, urban women—the ones with the most privileges and the most opportunities in life. The chief critique younger alumnae made about Barnard College was that it had not given enough preparatory training for family life. The greater opportunity to combine marriage with a career doubtless played a role in their planning, but something more profound was also involved.

Young women were discovering marriage to be not just a social obligation or a mechanism to provide children and financial security. It was increasingly seen as a vehicle for independence and self-fulfillment. The daughters of these women, who today seek similar goals through careers or companionate relationships rather than marriage, might find the 1940s quaint, or even systematically oppressive. For young women emerging from the high school and college campuses in the 1940s, marriage represented a declaration of independence from the traditional family economy in which parental control was strong over the behavior and the wages of unmarried daughters. Marriage provided release from these constraints and marked full entry into the adult world. Of course, marriage had long provided a measure of independence, but we can hypothesize that the growing gap between the generations quickened the desire for freedom.

The war hastened a major transformation in a significant aspect of American family life, the relationship of parents and adolescents. A growing proportion, probably a majority, of the nation's teenagers were part of an emerging "youth culture." Older observers at the time noted the new phenomenon with alarm; much of the concern over "ungovernable" youth and "juvenile delinquency" reflected, not young hoodlums, but large numbers of young people struggling to break free of family and social controls. The military had siphoned off a majority of men aged eighteen to thirty, so teenagers now constituted a larger percentage of the home front population and their activities were more conspicuous to law enforcement. "It's odd," complained one bobby-soxer, "how grown-ups stress the wrong things. They're blind to the dangers of race discrimination, but they get terribly excited about the effects of boogie woogie."

Even more important was the rapid increase in length of stay in school, including the colleges, of course, but especially the high schools. Unlike their parents, the great majority of the World War II adolescents started, and many finished, high school. While there, they were subjected to peer group pressure that molded their behavior in a far different fashion than would have been the case had they entered the work force. Instead, in high school, adolescents were among their peers for at least one-third of each day. Cliques and small informal support groups provided both support and pressure to conform. As one student observed, "This school is full of cliques. You go into the hall or the common room and you will find the same kids together day after day." High school cliques controlled the personal grooming, dating patterns, and general behavior of their members. The students acknowledged that peer group pressure determined what they wore at parties and how they acted when out with the gang or on a date. "You buy loafer moccasins because your friends do . . . You go to Joe's grill . . . or Doc's for cokes not because those places are charming, or the food good—but because the crowd goes. Most of your surface habits are picked up from people your own age."

Farm boys and girls reacted differently to high school than did city students. The girls reported being "too nervous" and worrying excessively about their possible social inferiority. They reported more difficulty in expressing themselves well. As a result, farm teenagers did not enjoy classes as much as city students, nor were they as likely to make plans to continue their education by attending college. Farm girls also complained about too few social activities and more trouble than other girls with their parents about outside activities. Farm boys, however, seemed to have less trouble than other boys in getting the family car or resisting parental interference with their private lives. Rural black teenagers had a different set of priorities than whites; they sought to escape the oppressive environment of the rural South. The young women wanted to marry any man except a farmer. They had begun working in earnest in the cotton patches and tobacco fields as five- and six-year-old children. Few finished grammar school; even fewer considered high school. Rural and black youth, therefore, were less likely than their urban white counterparts to have participated fully in the emerging youth culture, but their yearnings for independence were also quite strong.

Besides more education, young adults had more money. During the depression, any income they generated went into the family till. Now money was plentiful and youth who had jobs could spend far more than ever before. At seventeen or eighteen, they could earn as much as many adults. Since high school students were at school much of the day and worked in the evenings, they were not supervised very closely by their parents, nor did they obey automatically any longer. Teenage girls continued to date older boys, but now these boys were in uniform and from out of town. The girl's usual form of community protection no longer worked. If she got pregnant, the soldier did not "have" to marry her. He might be transferred at any time and never be heard from again.

The development of a youth culture speeded the transformation of the family structure from authoritarian to equalitarian. More and more parents consulted with children, advised and suggested rather than commanded. Parents still tried to guide their children, especially in the choice of friends. The older youth, aware that the draft was imminent, turned increasingly to their peers for standards of behavior, fashion, entertainment, and morality. The youth culture did not peak until later decades, but by the end of the 1940s it had already made its mark on the American family. Young adults found more freedom, more responsibility, and more autonomy than their parents had known.

The popular image of marriage and the family involves a timeless, unchanging institution. Historians of the family, however, have discovered dramatic changes, particularly in the psychological interactions among husbands, wives, children, and other kinfolk. Did the 1940s mark a watershed, ushering in a new American family? Changes do not come so quickly. The working out of roles and responsibilities takes years for every family, and it seems likely that little change took place in the majority of established marriages in the 1940s. Younger couples were much more likely to adopt new relationships. The combination of the emergent youth culture and the unprecedented stresses faced by service families doubtless hastened the transformations that shaped the main family forms of the 1950s and 1960s.

A permanent equalitarian shift in the war generation could still be detected three decades later. Asked in 1977 whether male and female employees should be treated the same during cutbacks, or whether wives whose husbands have jobs should be laid off first, the men and women who came of age before 1940 were much less equalitarian than the war generation. Of the older women, 36 percent were equalitarian, compared to a much higher 56 percent among those who became twenty-one during the war. The men showed the same difference (47 percent and 69 percent). The youthful experiences of each generation thus tend to fix their values permanently.

The most valuable aspect of marriage for half of all American wives at mid-century was "companionship in doing things together with my husband." The chance to have children was most important for a fourth of the wives, with considerations like love, understanding, and standard of living trailing in importance. The severe loneliness of the separated service wives, and the difficulties children caused during reunions, suggests the women correctly understood their needs. But the historian must raise another issue—one seldom openly discussed at the time—the distribution of power within the family. Interviews during the 1940s and 1950s consistently indicated that women were acknowledged to have the major responsibility for raising children and maintaining the family budget. In practice, however, the power within the family could be hoarded by the husband (or, less often, the wife), or parceled out with little communication, or used in democratic fashion after full mutual consultation. The experiences of service wives suggested an increased equalitarianism owing to their experiences. What of labor force participation? Did it enhance the power of wives? Did it help liberate women?

In blue-collar households in the 1950s, employed wives exercised a bit more power over decisions than full-time housewives. In some cases the pattern was a statistical artifact: very dominant husbands disproportionately prevented their wives from working in the first place and, conversely, more dominant wives could successfully insist on taking a job. But in other cases, outside employment itself increased the power of the wife inside the family. In 25 percent of Detroit families in the early 1950s, the husband dominated decisionmaking: the rate was 37 percent when the wife had never been employed, 24 percent when she once worked but was now a housewife, and 13 percent when she was employed. Equalitarian decisionmaking characterized 31 percent of the families (28 percent when the wife never worked, 29 percent when she previously worked, 39 percent when she currently was employed). A few families (3 percent) were largely dominated by the wife, while in 42 percent the husband and wife were each dominant in their separate spheres. In terms of money decisions, the wife was dominant in 40 percent of the families, had equal say in 34 percent, and was subordinate in 26 percent. The war generation (wife aged thirty to thirty-nine in 1954) was more equalitarian overall (40 percent) than either older (27 percent) or younger (24 percent) couples. The wives in equalitarian marriages were more likely to report high marital satisfaction (61 percent) than others (45 percent).

The paycheck itself increased the value of the woman's contribution to family finances but did not necessarily give her a stronger voice. In the first place, the great majority of wives rejected the notion that if a man brings in all the income he has more right to be boss. Her paid hours involved costs—to her leisure or that of the husband and children, or to the level of services she performed inside the house. Furthermore, the fact of employment frequently gave rise to new quarrels and new tensions between husband and wife; most husbands wanted their wives to quit war jobs when the war was over. Working daughters had long been accustomed to turning over their paychecks to their fathers and remaining under paternal control. More likely, the enhanced power of working women derived from their broader contacts with the larger world, which increased their intellectual input during conversations regarding spending decisions. Power was not a fixed quantity, to be divided one way or another. It could be expanded so that everyone had more of it, and the increased exposure of women to a wider world beyond the home did increase the total power. However, the learning experience that was most valuable came *before* marriage, in school, jobs, and voluntary activity. Less-educated women could gain useful new experiences through paid employment, but the better-educated, with a limited range of jobs open, typically preferred to learn through voluntary work and informal social contacts. It seems unlikely, therefore, that higher labor force participation during the war—or lower rates after the war—significantly affected the distribution of power inside the family.

Jobs had other implications for women besides power. Most important was the money itself, most of it saved, which enhanced the family's financial security and fueled dreams of postwar comfort. Before she took a job a housewife might entertain thoughts of gaining independence, escaping troublesome children, exercising rusty talents, and relieving boredom by meeting new people and seeing more of the world. The quest for independence was especially keen on the part of women in unhappy marriages, particularly if divorce loomed as a possibility. For most, however, the reality of war jobs was tedium, compounded by transportation and shopping difficulties. The dream of escaping housework was simply unrealistic. Working women held two jobs and were forced to curtail their recreation, visiting, and passive leisure. As for the high pay, the women who decided not to take jobs had predicted correctly that it would prove only temporary.

Some feminists at the time believed that deep down housewives wanted to escape their confines and that paid employment would be a panacea for liberation. "If we free women now from the care of children, it is like letting the stopper out of a bottle of carbonated water. Women will come pouring out of the home—permanently—and will never be satisfied to go back home once they get accustomed to a paycheck, to the satisfaction that comes from productive work, and above all if they know their children can be better cared for by professionals than by amateurs."

The misperception about children was striking. The vast majority of mothers enjoyed their children immensely and were highly dubious about "professional" day-care center employees, especially in comparison with their own "amateur" skills. Their standards of right behavior made them feel guilty if they could not be confident of the supervision their children received, or if their own activities made them inaccessible in time of emergency. Those women who had trouble with their small children often did enroll them in day-care centers, which in turn made the centers less attractive to other mothers. The government propaganda encouraging use of the centers was as systematically ignored as the massive media campaigns to coax women into war jobs or the Army. Feeling that motherhood was not only patriotic but typified the right to a private life for which the war was being fought, mothers could in good conscience devote themselves to the needs of their families.

Asked whether running a home or a full-time job was more interesting for women, 50 percent of the entire population said the home, 30 percent picked the job, the rest were unsure or thought them equally interesting. A half dozen reasons typified the responses of the first group: more activity, rearing children, extra leisure time, more independence, sheer enjoyment, and the basic duty of women. Those who thought a full-time job might be more interesting usually cited the opportunity to meet more people and do more things, only occasionally mentioning independence or becoming better informed.

The broad consensus after the war was that women with children should not work unless circumstances were severe. What if there were no children under sixteen? Of a cross-section of the entire adult population, 39 percent said she should work, 44 percent said no, and it depended on circumstances for the rest. Why should she work? One in eight pointed to a more interesting life (13 percent), one in six cited equal rights (9 percent) or freedom of choice (6 percent), while the extra income was only occasionally noted (5 percent). Why she should not work prompted one American in five to warn that it would cost someone else a job (22 percent) or that it was just not the way things ought to be (15 percent). To make a hypothetical situation more realistic, interviewers asked about Mrs. Jones: "The Jones family lives in a small modern home. Mr. Jones earns a good but not a high salary. There are two children, both in school. Mrs. Jones would enjoy doing something besides running her home if she could arrange it. [What] do you think Mrs. Jones should do?" Only a handful thought Mrs. Jones should take a full-time job (4 percent); most recommended a part-time job (32 percent) or suggested volunteer work (30 percent). But one in three (35 percent) would tell her to stay home.

The hypothetical nature of questions about wives working was underscored by the strong consensus that homemaking was (or ought to be) a full-time job. Seven out of eight adults thought so in 1946. With regard to their own situation, two out of three wives said that housekeeping was indeed a full-time task. One-third of all wives (33 percent) said they had enough spare time to do other things, and one in seven did have paid employment. In truth, housewifery, in contrast to gainful employment, offered a peculiar opportunity for autonomy. The housewife could set her own standards of performance and her own schedule, subject not to time clocks and deadlines but to her perception of the needs and demands of family (and, perhaps, the neighbors). If women themselves insisted that women's work was never done, women themselves also defined that work. Just as farmers valued their autonomy, despite the hard work, so too did housewives. With marriages more companionate, and family life so psychologically rewarding to the vast majority of women, it required no mysterious packet of social or economic forces to keep women at home.

The historian of the 1940s who accepts the primacy of family and agrees that paid employment produced little liberation might still ask about freedom of choice. What about the minority of women who did have a taste for male jobs, or aspired to a rewarding career? Did not society systematically discriminate against them? Yes, it certainly did. The dominance of men in all sectors of employment gave them a decisive advantage, for they were protecting historic patterns and could laugh off women's efforts or, if necessary, assault them with sexual innuendoes. Not many men had read Freud, but they did feel that anatomy was destiny. Women were too small, too weak to handle the inner core of a "man's job." They could and did point out that few women had the technical training requisite for a crafts or managerial position, and they immediately concluded that women had no aptitude for such matters. The constant movement in and out of the labor market could be cited as evidence that women lacked the drive and ambition to stick to careers. Counselors, employment bureaus, and personnel officers who steered men one way and women another did not create the culture, they merely reflected it, and they often had elaborate evidence to show women that they would be unhappy in certain lines of work. As the labor market changed, so did the advisers. Early in the war, they had to convince women that domestic skills could be put to good use in industry, that anyone who could run a sewing machine could operate a drill press. As clerical jobs became feminized, the advisers began to steer men away from them, even veterans who had been trained as clerks in the Army.

"Social forces" are sometimes assumed to have generated the socializing mechanisms that steered girls away from aspiring to male jobs. But what are "social forces"? The media could be examined, but it would not explain very much, for images of women were often ambiguous and could be interpreted in many ways. As the failure of the propaganda drives proves, even intensive media campaigns had little effect in changing deeply held values. The ways in which girls were raised by their families to become feminine clearly counted more. Here the socialization intended to replicate in the child the values of the parents. Girls who deviated could be gently rebuffed. One Chicago mother explained in 1944 that Santa gave her five-year-old daughter a doll house so she could learn "feminine interests." The mother recalled that she had grown up a tomboy, and did not want her daughter to do so. The little girl had asked Santa for a Wac uniform. Churches, schools, and clubs further facilitated the transmission of parental values, especially middle-class values. The peer pressure of other girls, especially during adolescence, could operate as a countervailing influence. However, in this instance peer pressure strongly reinforced notions of femininity and effectively prevented the vast majority of girls from developing "masculine" tastes. With all, the prevailing mood was neatly captured in a hit 1946 movie, *It's a Wonderful Life*. When the despondent hero (James Stewart) contemplates suicide, a heavenly angel reveals to him what would have happened had he never lived. The idyllic small town would be in the grasp of an evil moneylender; it would be ruined by poverty, violence, hatred, and alcoholism. To climax the horrible image, the fate of Donna Reed, Stewart's faithful wife and marvelous mother of his children, is shown: she would have become a spinster career woman, the town librarian. Stewart decides not to jump off the bridge, the movie ends happily.

Freedom of choice was highly regarded as a democratic value worth fighting for. But in the 1940s it meant freedom to choose within strictly defined guidelines that emerged from the people, particularly from the women who were charged with responsibility for guiding children to do the right and proper thing.

Suppose the wartime government had been more successful in inducing women to join the Army, or to take jobs, or to keep them when they married, or to place their children in day-care centers. What might have been the results? Possibly the GNP would have been a bit higher and more desk-bound servicemen could have been shipped to Europe or the Pacific. It appears highly unlikely that the war would have ended any sooner, or that the necessary massive intrusion into private lives would have had no deleterious impact on American morale. What of the postwar era, assuming that the government relaxed its direct controls over people's lives but instituted effective equal-pay rules? The closing of the munitions plants still would have thrown millions of women out of work, though many would have clung successfully to factory jobs in automobile, machinery, and electrical plants. Unless unions somehow had reversed their male chauvinism, however, it is difficult to guess how many women would have persisted in hostile work places. The impact on white-collar employment patterns of these hypothetical reforms would have been nil, unless the early motivations and training of women changed drastically or the people of the 1940s had somehow managed to envisage and implement an "equal-worth" standard of pay for women in predominantly female occupations. Structural reforms such as those imagined here would have had, at best, a small impact on the lives of women, if, indeed, women were motivated primarily by internalized, private goals and ambitions.

But what if women's attitudes toward childbearing and family life had changed, and men's too? Then we would not be dealing with history, but with a utopia set in the past, or perhaps the 1980s magically transposed four decades back, and the history books would tell us more about ourselves than about the people of the 1940s. Women of the decade did not seek to break barriers or change their own values; rather, women sought and fought for companionship, and security within the home. A remarkable number achieved their goal. Eleanor Roosevelt said it best: "The circumstances that surround women as a rule force most of them into certain channels . . . The best she can do is to use the opportunities that come to her in life to the best advantage, according to her abilities. This is a little less true today than it was in the past, but nevertheless it still holds true, since women, or the greatest number of women, must subordinate themselves to the life of the family."

The circumstances to which Roosevelt alluded were not unique to America, but were shared broadly in other lands, most notably Britain and Canada. Those nations recognized the urgency of mobilizing womanpower early in the war, and in the case of military service both Canada and the United States studied and replicated the British model. Similar debates about women in factories, equal pay, and day care were played out in each nation. Yet there were differences. In Britain, for example, women members of Parliament caucused to present feminist views. They pressed for equality in the rates of compensation to which civilians would be entitled if injured by enemy action. Surely the human worth of the female equaled the man's, even if she was paid less! No, the government said, for it would lead to equal pay, which both the unions and the traditionalists opposed. But the feminists finally won over the War Cabinet in 1943. They pushed on and in 1944 defeated the government by a vote of 117 to 116 in Parliament to require equal pay for teachers. It was the first and only defeat the coalition suffered during the war. Winston Churchill, the Conservative Prime Minister, and Labourite Ernest Bevin, the Minister of Labour and National Service, immediately threatened to resign unless the vote was reversed. It was, and the principle of equal pay would languish in Britain for another generation. Nothing so dramatic happened in the United States, for the government adopted a policy of equal pay with so many loopholes that opposition was muted. It was a commentary on the state of feminism that no women's caucus emerged in Congress or the state legislatures.

It is difficult to argue that World War II, in itself, constituted a watershed in the experience of American women. During the short term of the war years, women responded to new challenges on the basis of their identities as women, as members of families and communities, that had been forged before the war and would persist after it. An insignificant proportion of American women seized upon the opportunities for new occupations that the war proffered as a permanent break with their past commitments, sense of themselves, and expectations. For the majority of American women, the war years may have altered some specific activities, but they did not change their interpretations of their primary roles. Gender roles—and, even more, gender identities—change in the long, rather than the short, term. For the majority of American women, the war years constituted one more installment in a series of events that shaped their lives. To be sure, the impact of those years on a woman's life depended in some measure upon her age, the moment in her life cycle, the cohort or generation to which she belonged. A married woman in her fifties, a married woman in her thirties, a late adolescent, a child—all experienced the war differently, not merely because of their age per se, but also because of the other events that had already influenced their identities and values. The vast majority of women who lived through those years were doubtless more profoundly marked by the secular changes that were slowly modifying women's experience than by the war itself.

Perhaps the principal impact of the war on women derived from the changes in American society as a whole that the war crystallized or accelerated. The recovery from the depression, the shifting balance between rural and urban populations, the greater equality in distribution of income among the population, among other tendencies, had important consequences for women as well as for men. The social patterns and values of the fifties as well as of the sixties can legitimately be traced to changes that had their seeds in the forties. The growing importance of peer groups in the decisive years of adolescence that was evident during the war years would have important repercussions in each succeeding generation. An array of social, economic, and political changes in American society that can be traced at least from the 1920s were slowly altering the conditions of women's lives in all classes and ethnic groups, albeit at different rates. The ideology of separate spheres and women's special moral mission proved an early casualty of the transformation of American society. But other ideas about gender roles and gender differences did not disappear so fast. In most walks of life and in most organizations, men vigorously warred against equality for women. In this respect, women's occasional access to men's jobs and men's pay rates proved a temporary expedient of wartime exigencies. But men were not alone in their commitment to returning women to women's proper place. Women themselves indisputably placed their highest priority on a family life that could only be sustained by their own special efforts. It would take more than the war for them even to begin to think of their own independence and full equality as a goal that might justify the sacrifice of the "traditional" values of home, husband, and children.

This assessment should not be taken to imply that women did not have personal ambitions and dreams, that they lacked self-respect, that they would not have preferred equal opportunities for jobs and careers, or equal pay for their work. We cannot easily judge what women may have wanted in the abstract. We can better judge the choices they made. If they wanted personal fulfillment in many areas, they clearly judged that personal fulfillment—not to mention economic security—was more likely to result from a solid family life than from independence, and that a solid family life was more likely to result from acceptance of, than from war against, the norms of inherited values. The challenge for the historian remains to recognize that even as the appearance of the conventional relations between men and women persisted, changes in society as a whole were eroding its foundations. When, in 1945, American women of various generations, classes, and races withdrew from choice positions in the labor market, picked up life as usual, and benefited from growing prosperity to devote time to their homes and families, they were not, in fact, returning to the world of their foremothers, but—consciously or not—reinterpreting it as a legacy for their daughters and granddaughters.

Further Reading for Part V

Anderson, Karen Sue. *Wartime Women*. Westport, Ct, 1981.

Blum, John M. *V Was for Victory: Politics and American Culture during World War II*. New York, 1976.

Calder, Angus. *The People's War: Britain, 1939–1945*. New York, 1969.

Campbell, D'Ann. *Women at War with America: Private Lives in a Patriotic Era*. Cambridge, MA, 1984.

Drinnon, Richard. *Keeper of Concentration Camps: Dillon S. Myer and American Racism*. Berkeley, Ca, 1986.

Hartmann, Susan. *The Home Front and Beyond: American Women in the 1940's*. Boston, 1982.

Havens, Thomas R. H. *Valley of Darkness: The Japanese People and World War Two*. New York, 1978.

Koonz, Claudia. *Mothers in the Fatherland: Women, the Family, and Nazi Politics*. New York, 1987.

Linz, Susan J., ed. *The Impact of World War II on the Soviet Union*. Totowa, NJ, 1985.

Marwick, Arthur. "People's War and Top People's Peace? British Society and the Second World War," in Alan Sked and Chris Cook, *Crisis and Controversy: Essays in Honour of A.J.P.Taylor*. London, 1976.

———. *War and Social Change in the Twentieth Century*. New York, 1974.

Milkman, Ruth. *Gender at Work: The Dynamics of Job Segregation by Sex during World War II*. Urbana, 1987.

Milward, Alan S. *War, Economy and Society, 1939–1945*. Berkeley, CA, 1979.

Polenberg, Richard. *War and Society; the United States, 1941–1945*. Philadelphia, 1972.

Rupp, Leila. *Mobilizing Women for War: German and American Propaganda, 1939–45*. Princeton, 1978.

Shillony, Ben-Ami. *Politics and Culture in Wartime Japan*. Oxford, 1981.

Summerfield, Penny. *Women Workers in the Second World War: Production and Patriarchy in Conflict*. Dover, NH, 1984.

Terkel, Studs. *The Good War: An Oral History of World War Two*. New York, 1984.

Wynn, Neil. *The Afro-American and the Second World War*. New York, 1976.

Part VI

How Grand Was the Grand Alliance?

The term "the Grand Alliance," the title of the third volume of Winston Churchill's monumental history of the Second World War, helped mold all subsequent thinking about wartime diplomacy and coalition fighting among the Big Three: Great Britain, the United States and the Soviet Union. In emphasizing a "special relationship" between himself and American president Franklin D. Roosevelt, and between their respective "Anglo-Saxon" peoples, the prime minister launched a second theme with great appeal to Anglo–American public opinion during the early years of the cold war. Both ideas contain kernels of historical truth, but both also disguise deeply rooted differences in interests and goals within the alliance. Realistically, this should be expected for great nations respond to their own peculiar historic developments; each has its own perceptions and requirements.

Given Hitler's reckless determination to have a war, his strategic miscalculations, and his underestimation of his opponents' will to survive, the combination of powers arrayed against Germany after 1941 seems inevitable. The coalition of the United States of America, the British Empire and Commonwealth, and the Union of Soviet Socialist Republics and their dozens of allies, however, was not inevitable. Though the troubled times of the late thirties led many to believe that war was very likely, nothing would have struck even well-informed people as more improbable than the Grand Alliance. Their conflicting interests drove them apart. Hitler was not alone in ruling out their international cooperation. But he was nearly alone in making the impossible happen (see Part I above).

What brought the alliance together was not resistance to aggression and tyranny. Of the Big Three, only the United Kingdom (the accurate, though less-often used name, since it includes both Great Britain and Northern Ireland), along with France and some members of the Commonwealth, came to Poland's defense in early September 1939. Stalin, in fact, invaded Poland shortly after the Germans in order to claim the eastern half of the country promised in the Nonaggression Pact the month before. Roosevelt, as he had so often done in the years before, offered only words. Congress did amend the neutrality acts to permit France and Britain to buy war materials, but still required them to pay in cash and to carry their purchases away in non-American ships.

The United Kingdom desired nothing more than to keep what it already had, an empire and a commonwealth with extensive territories on every continent except Antarctica. Admiral Sir Ernle Chatfield privately wrote with unusual candor in 1934, "We are in the remarkable position of not wanting to quarrel with anybody because we have got most of the world already, or the best parts of it, and we only want to keep what we have got and prevent others from taking it away from us."[1] Germany was only one of several threats. Japan's aggression in China, isolationist tendencies in Australia and New Zealand, Indian demands for independence, restlessness and rebellion among Arabs, and American economic competition all challenged London's interests as well as taxed its diplomatic ingenuity.

What Stalin wanted is not so clear. The speed with which he reversed Russian policy toward Germany in August 1939 sacrificed two decades of staunch opposition to fascism by the Communist International. It drove many leftists from their national communist parties, and lent strong support to the judgment that Stalin wanted to avoid war at almost any cost. He signed far-reaching trade agreements with the Third Reich to deliver oil, food and other raw materials. The annexation of the Baltic states and portions of Romania in 1940, however, suggest a Soviet desire to guard against a future German attack.

The United States felt safe with three thousand miles of ocean between it and the factious Europeans. Most Americans were determined to avoid being drawn into a foreign conflict as, they thought, had happened in 1917. The Great Depression continued to hang like a millstone around the economy's neck. Neither war nor new territory was the solution. An expansion of commerce through the lowering of trade barriers appealed to Secretary of State Cordell Hull and other administration policy makers as the best cure for unemployment and underutilized factories. That these ideas ran counter to British, French, and other European imperial interests, and counter to the ambitions of the Japanese in Asia, only underscored for Americans their own rightness in abjuring war and political domination in favor of economic competition. That their large domestic market and access to raw materials, skilled labor, and high levels of technology gave them advantages others did not have, did nothing to undermine confidence in their convictions (see Part III above for Anglo-American differences over decolonization).

American involvement in the European conflict began ineluctably.

---

[1]Cited by David Reynolds, "Competitive Cooperation: Anglo-American Relations in World War Two," *The Historical Journal* 23(1980):244–245.

Charge of isolationists and pacifists in the America First movement that Roosevelt was pushing the country into war is not supported by the evidence. Indeed, it is not easy to establish that Roosevelt did everything he could short of war to support the British in their lonely contest with the Nazi juggernaut. After the Fall of France in June 1940 Churchill pleaded for immediate aid. Fifty World War I destroyers, then mothballed, could help repel a German invasion and patrol Britain's vital sea routes. For two months the President waited, pressured by both military advisers and members of Congress not to grant the request. When the ships were finally offered, Roosevelt wanted ninety-nine-year leases on eight British bases in the western Atlantic and Caribbean in return. The British cabinet balked at this wholesale transfer of naval power, but had no alternative except to yield.

A similar story surrounds the more famous lend-lease arrangements of 1941 and after. When Churchill reported to Roosevelt that London could no longer pay for its American arms purchases in late 1940, the president quickly proposed and gained congressional approval to sell, lend, lease or otherwise dispose of American arms to the government of any country whose security he deemed vital to that of the United States. This came none too early to a grateful Churchill, but he found that the Americans raised new demands for concessions in negotiating the precise arrangements of lend-lease after the passage of the act. Many Americans, believing in an opulent British empire, had no desire to win the war for Britain and preserve its prewar world economic and political position.

This attitude spilled over into colonial issues as well. As a former colonial country itself, the United States sympathized with the aspirations of African and Asian nationalists. American officials, though often not well-informed about British colonial affairs, took frequent opportunity to condemn the evils of empire. When Roosevelt and Churchill met for the first time off the coast of Newfoundland in August 1941, they displayed an inspiring unity of purpose against aggression, tyranny and oppression. But the eight point Atlantic Charter also referred to their "wish to see sovereign rights and self-government restored to those who have been forcibly deprived of them"

---

[2]Hans-Adolf Jacobsen and Arthur L. Smith, Jr., *World War II. Politics and Strategy; Selected Documents with Commentary,* p. 156. ABC-Clio, Santa Barbara, CA, 1979.

(Point Three), and to "access, on equal terms, to the trade and to the raw materials of the world" (Point Five).[2] Churchill later stated that Point Three did not apply to the Empire; Point Five was also hedged to allow an interpretation in favor of continuing imperial preference, by which the Commonwealth members extended lower import tariffs to one another.

Anglo-Russian relations also ran hot and cold. German access to Russian resources after the autumn of 1939 undermined a key leg of British strategy, that of blockading the Third Reich and denying it the raw materials needed for modern warfare. Soviet annexations and the Winter War (October 1939–March 1940) with Finland further undermined the prospects of a common front. For nearly two years, Moscow served as Berlin's faithful ally. Hitler himself came to Britain's rescue when his armies crashed across Russo–German borders in the first days of Operation Barbarossa after June 22, 1941. Elated, Churchill broadcast to the British people that though Nazi Germany was "indistinguishable from the worst features of communism ... the past with all its follies and its tragedies, flashes away."[3] He would sign a pact with the devil if Hitler invaded Hell, he told Parliament. Reaching a treaty with Stalin proved most difficult, since the Soviet dictator demanded recognition of his recent annexations. He also demanded economic and military aid from the United Kingdom and the United States. From the start he also insisted on the opening of a second front, by which he meant an Anglo-American invasion of the western European mainland—the naval battles, the conflict in North Africa, and the strategic air offensive did not count.

In May 1942 London and Moscow concluded a twenty-year treaty of alliance (that ignored the issue of postwar borders). Washington avoided treaty commitments altogether, since treaties constitutionally required Senate ratification. Roosevelt preferred to handle such matters informally, waiting until the end of the war to open a public debate on the terms of the peace. Meanwhile, he successfully wooed former isolationists into supporting his project for international postwar coopera-

---

[2]Hans-Adolf Jacobsen and Arthur L. Smith, Jr., *World War II. Politics and Strategy; Selected Documents with Commentary,* p. 156. ABC-Clio, Santa Barbara, CA, 1979.

[3]Martin Kitchin, "Winston Churchill and the Soviet Union during the Second World War," *The Historical Journal,* 30 (1987); 418.

tion and American participation in the United Nations. Although the U.N. has not realized its founders' dreams, that it included the United States and the entire anti-Axis coalition when it came to life in San Francisco in April 1945 was due in no small measure to Roosevelt's energetic backing.

As for Roosevelt's relations with Stalin, they have been variously assessed as foolish, naive, and perhaps perfidious on the one hand, and generous, conciliatory, and farsighted on the other extreme. Indeed, the Soviet Union and the United States had few real conflicts, certainly nothing to match the century-long differences Russia had with the British in Iran, Afghanistan and China. Anticommunism was a perennial and corrosive theme in American domestic politics and Washington's military intervention in the Russian Civil War against the Bolsheviks is still remembered. On the other hand, a Soviet Union whose legitimate security interests were satisfied posed no threat to American economic ambitions. And at least until near the end of the war, Washington had no plans for retaining a postwar military presence overseas.

For these reasons, Roosevelt could play the role of mediator between imperial Britain and Communist Russia at Tehran and again at Yalta. At the Tehran Conference in late 1943, the first summit meeting of the Big Three governmental heads, all the sticky issues which surfaced afterwards at Yalta to plague the alliance were discussed and guidelines for future decisions laid down: the future of Poland, the treatment of postwar Germany, reparations, Soviet participation in the war against Japan, the organization of the United Nations, and, until Churchill protested, the future of European overseas colonies. It was the high point of Allied unity. Soviet resistance to Nazism was hailed and its "democracy" extolled as the western Allies celebrated their victories over the German armies in Africa, the surrender of Italy, and the Red Army's rout of the Germans at Stalingrad. Churchill and Roosevelt firmly promised a second front in Western Europe for the spring of 1944. Whatever the circumstances of its birth, at mid-point during the war the Grand Alliance seemed to foretell a new age of peace and justice. Two years later Allied soldiers linked arms and danced on the ruins of the thousand year Reich. Later that summer the Soviet armies invaded Japanese-held Manchuria as promised. The Grand Alliance had won the war. Soon, however, the euphoria of victory turned sour. What went wrong?

13

Robert M. Hathaway

The Economics of Partnership

In the past two decades historians have looked more closely at relations between Winston Churchill and Franklin Roosevelt than ever before. The publication of the complete correspondence between the two wartime leaders, edited with commentary by Warren F. Kimball, enables us to see full-bodied, three-dimensional personalities conducting a unique and extraordinary coalition global war. Of course, we can also examine their differences, both of style and of substance. A special relationship there was, but that does not mean that the prime minister and the president merged their own national goals and visions of the postwar order into one. Though Churchill and Roosevelt often agreed, or appeared to agree, conflict persisted among the lower officials charged with implementing policy. That this was true within the two nations' military establishments has been a commonplace in histories of the war. It also extended, however, to international economic cooperation and decolonization.

One part of the United Kingdom's response to the worldwide depression of the 1930s was to strengthen its links with Commonwealth countries and the Empire. In 1931 they reached agreements in Ottawa, Canada, referred to as imperial preferences, which functioned so as to close nonmembers out of each other's markets. As a result, United States trade with Britain, its best commercial partner, began to decline. Free traders feared that in supporting the British in the war against Germany, Americans would be financing an inequitable commercial arrangement for their own factories and workers. They also thought restricted markets were a primary cause of war.

Even after lend-lease, American policymakers fostered their

Reprinted from Robert M. Hathaway, *Ambiguous Partnership: Britain and America, 1944–1947*, pp. 16–35. Copyright © (1981) Columbia University Press.

vision of postwar multilateralism and free trade. The Bretton
Woods conference of 1944 looked forward to the establishment
of an International Monetary Fund (IMF) and an International
Bank for Reconstruction and Development (World Bank), all
along American liberal principles. When war ended, President
Truman abruptly cut off further lend-lease funds to London.
Britain's devastated economy hinged on its acceptance of the
Bretton Woods agreements. The imperialism of free trade, it has
been called. This was possible, not because the United States was
among the victors, but because the United States, alone among
the major belligerents, ended the war with a full-employment
economy producing most of the world's manufactured goods and
enjoying a standard of living fifty percent higher than before the
war.

In the following selection, Professor Hathaway analyzes both
sides of this Anglo–American conflict. How are we to assess the
right and wrong of the positions? Did American interests incorporate larger global benefits? Or were they naively and narrowly
expressions of an American desire to profit from the misfortunes
of others? While details have changed, many of the issues de-
bated in the 1940s resurface in later decades when international
economic interdependence runs deeper than ever before.

For senior officials in the American Department of State, the Second
World War represented at once a humiliation and an opportunity. In
matters of a political or strategic nature, Roosevelt repeatedly circumvented his foreign policy advisers, employing instead a variety of
personal envoys and relying upon the military for much of his counsel.
In addition, the war spawned a proliferation of independent agencies
which intruded into areas heretofore considered the exclusive pre-
serves of the State Department. On the other hand, the hostilities provided a singular occasion to further some of the objectives which the
American Secretary of State, white-maned Cordell Hull, had long
cherished. With a proper utilization of the great economic strength of
the United States, Hull and his associates reasoned, they might be able
to use the tragedy of global conflict to create a new international structure that would substantially reduce the likelihood of a third world war.
In so doing, moreover, they would be insuring America's own well-
being and spreading the blessings of a free and prosperous world order
to other peoples.

Unfortunately, the implementation of this new global structure did not depend upon American efforts alone. Because Hull's project involved major alterations in the conduct of international economic affairs, other nations, with highly different systems and needs, would have to be persuaded to accept his ideas. Great Britain in particular appeared to be the key, for prior to the war the United Kingdom and its Commonwealth and Empire associates accounted, along with the United States, for nearly one-half of the world's total trade. If Britain and America could agree between themselves on a design for the conduct and regulation of international financial transactions, the remainder of the world would have little choice, short of embracing virtual autarky, but to accept this system. But suppose the British chose not to participate with Hull in his grand undertaking? Here, then, was the challenge for American diplomacy: to convince the United Kingdom that its interests would best be served by embracing the American vision of the postwar order.

Hull eagerly accepted this challenge—indeed, found solace for his exclusion from any policy-making role during the war years by immersing himself in planning for the economic arrangements which were to accompany the peace. A true Wilsonian in virtually every sense of the term, the Secretary was a devoted advocate of his political mentor's belief in a liberal capitalist world order of commercial expansion and free trade. Over the course of four decades in public life, he had developed a distinctive set of ideas concerning the proper nature of international economic relationships, a philosophy that came dangerously close to becoming an obsession. By the early 1940s this body of concepts had gained almost universal acceptance in the State Department bureaucracy, providing a backdrop upon which extensive blueprints for the postwar world were drawn.

Two distinct but interrelated strands of thought ran throughout all the planning which Hull superintended. One concerned itself with the establishment and maintenance of worldwide peace, the other with the narrower question of American prosperity. Hull and his colleagues viewed these two issues as essentially opposite sides of the same coin. To work for one while ignoring the other was self-defeating. There was no conscious hypocrisy in this linking of national interest and lofty idealism. As easy as it is in a more cynical age to ridicule such logic, the evidence appears conclusive that virtually all senior officials in Washington sincerely believed that neither could be attained unless supported by the other.

Put most baldly, the men and women who drafted these detailed plans reasoned that if soldiers were not to cross international borders, then goods must do so. The "chief underlying cause" of the First World War, Secretary Hull had written one of his predecessors, lay "in the strenuous trade conquests and bitter trade rivalry" which had characterized the years before 1914. Similar contention, fueled in part by excessive Republican-sponsored tariff walls in the United States, had resulted in the formation of two antagonistic blocs in Europe in the years preceding the Second World War. Only by preventing the recurrence of economic warfare, the Secretary argued, could one avoid the attendant political frictions which led to war. Assistant Secretary of State for Economic Affairs William L. Clayton put it pithily: "Nations which act as enemies in the marketplace cannot long be friends at the council table." This being the case, the economic aspects of the peace were at least as important as the political aspects. Economics, Hull observed, "should be the spear point of the approach to peace." More specifically, in what was the central tenet of Hull's whole *Weltanschauung,* "unhampered trade dovetailed with peace; high tariffs, trade barriers, and unfair economic competition, with war." This conviction that unrestricted trade was a necessary ingredient for peace had by 1944 become an unquestioned assumption governing American thinking in international affairs.

At the same time, unimpeded trade promised material benefits for America's own producers. While the American economy depended upon foreign markets to a much lesser extent than those of Great Britain and many other countries, exports had become, for large segments of American agriculture and industry, the difference between prosperity and depression. In the two years before the war, the United States had sold abroad 31 percent of its raw cotton, 30 percent of its leaf tobacco, 54 percent of its refined copper. By 1945, moreover, with the economic expansion stimulated by the war itself, the United States possessed an industrial plant with a capacity nearly twice as great as before the hostilities. Postwar exports, the Director of War Mobilization and Reconversion told the House Ways and Means Committee, would have to be double the prewar level if prosperity and full employment were to be attained.

Hull's long years of isolation from the center of foreign policy decision making had afforded him ample time to reflect upon the best methods for encouraging this expansion of international trade. The

United States, the Secretary repeatedly insisted, should do everything in its power to encourage the creation of multilateral, nondiscriminatory trade relations. Gradually this goal of multilateralism, indeed the word itself, came to be seen as the very essence of Hull's—and America's—program. And as befitted a policy of global cooperation, the idea of eliminating all forms of discriminatory treatment in international commerce and of reducing tariffs and other trade barriers established itself as the one unalterable principle of United States policy. In a subtle and perhaps unconscious manner many American leaders came to equate economic freedom in the Gladstonian sense with political freedom.

The international financial institutions erected at the Bretton Woods conference in July 1944 nicely illustrate the prevalent thinking within Hull's State Department—and indeed, throughout the American government. Tucked away in New Hampshire's White Mountains, representatives of forty-four nations gathered to establish an International Bank for Reconstruction and Development (more popularly known as the World Bank) and an International Monetary Fund. The World Bank was designed to make funds available for reconstruction projects requiring large sums of capital, a function which by stimulating sound international investment would automatically promote world trade. The Monetary Fund was to provide nations with liquid reserves to assist in maintaining stable currencies without resorting to restrictive exchange practices. In both instances the predominant assumption was that only economic stability and continual development, fostered to a large extent by an ever-increasing world trade, could stave off a third and perhaps fatal global war. At the same time these arrangements could be defended as completely in the national interest. The arguments used to sell the program to Congress and the public emphasized the aid which it would render in increasing American exports. The nation's second largest labor union predicted that Bretton Woods would create five million American jobs because of its stimulus to overseas trade. There was "not one single element of Santa Claus philosophy" in the Bretton Woods agreements, Clayton assured congressional doubters.

Quite clearly then, American postwar objectives for the world economy consisted of a careful amalgamation of visionary concern for the maintenance of world peace and a determination that the nation avoid any repetition of the disastrous economic experiences of the 1930s. Both aims, Washington officials believed, could be best achieved in a multilateral world of freely flowing, constantly expanding trade. The enthusiastic diplomat who likened multilateral, regional, and bilateral trade to using the elevator, the stairway, and the fire escape was merely reflecting this conviction.

American planners devoted long hours to considering how Great Britain fit into this picture. Of one thing they were certain: London's partnership would be every bit as necessary in winning the peace as it had been in winning the war. Anglo-American economic cooperation, observed one of the senior officials overseeing the American wartime economy, could "influence the entire world's pattern of trade" and make it possible to "remove most of the economic frictions that generate wars." The means of obtaining that cooperation, however, and the concessions which the United States might be willing to make in return, were not nearly so apparent. On the one hand, administration policy makers were determined not to be outsmarted by the wily British, as it was widely believed they had been after the previous war. On the other hand, these same officials possessed an uneasy awareness that in the interests of partnership the British would need substantial aid in reconstructing their economy from the ravages of six years of total warfare. To perplexed American authorities the former seemed to preclude the latter, and Washington bureaucrats anguished for many months trying to develop an approach which would enable Great Britain to become a strong partner in a multilateral world while at the same time mollifying fears at home that American tax dollars were being used to bail out profligate Englishmen.

Hull and his colleagues recognized, of course, that the British might simply choose not to go along with all this careful planning. Great Britain had abandoned free trade in 1931, only shortly before the United States under Hull's tutelage began to move in the direction of fewer trade restrictions. At the Ottawa conference in 1932, the nations of the British Commonwealth had established a system of imperial preferences which served to stimulate trade among the member nations, but which placed severe obstacles in the path of American trade not only with Britain itself, but with Australia, India, South Africa, and a number of lesser nations. The embittered Hull termed the creation of this system of imperial preferences "the greatest injury, in a commercial way, that has been inflicted on this country since I have been in public life" and spent much of the 1930s attempting to persuade the

British to relax these restrictions. Congressional approval of the Lend-Lease Act in 1941 provided the Secretary a diplomatic lever with which to press the British, and Article 7 of the Master Lend-Lease Agreement signed the following year committed the two nations to do everything possible to promote the expansion of trade and "the elimination of all forms of discriminatory treatment in international commerce," and to reduce tariffs and other trade barriers. Here, so Washington believed, was a concrete promise by the Churchill government to abandon imperial preference and open the Empire to American commerce.

The British for their part wondered if the Americans were not being a bit hasty in demanding an end to London's system of supports and restrictions. Neither Hull nor anyone else in Washington had been able to convince key officials across the ocean that Great Britain could recover its economic balance simply by accepting the American program of multilateralism. It had taken nearly a year of negotiations after enactment of the lend-lease law before the two sides could complete the agreement extending this aid to the beleaguered British. These difficulties indicated the gap which separated the two countries in their ideas on the future of the imperial preference system. Furthermore, Whitehall harbored well-founded doubts as to the willingness of the United States to accept a large volume of imports, an absolute essential if the British were to have any chance of rebuilding their shattered economy. American manufacturers themselves were worried as to how they were going to dispose of the huge quantities of goods which their plants were able to produce, and neither business nor labor was likely to be enthusiastic about sharing the domestic market with foreign competitors. What was much more probable was that fierce rivalry for overseas markets would place an additional burden on Anglo-American relations. Long before the end of the war American missions around the world were warning of increasing British propaganda efforts and preparations directed toward expanding postwar commerce. The prospects of a potentially bitter competition for foreign markets lent credence to the arguments of those within the Churchill government who warned against any precipitant acceptance of the American scheme for achieving a workable, mutually advantageous economic arrangement between the two Atlantic democracies. This caution surfaced, for example, during a 1944 meeting between Henry Morgenthau, the American Secretary of the Treasury, and Sir John Anderson,

Britain's Chancellor of the Exchequer. If the difficult financial problems facing the two nations were to be tackled effectively, the ebullient Morgenthau declared, "we should practically have to sleep together." Perhaps so, Sir John primly replied, but he for one would keep his eyes open.

This brief exchange points out a fundamental distinction in the moods prevalent in each of the two national capitals. One of the most remarkable aspects of the American vision of the postwar economic order was its buoyant optimism, its easy acceptance of the idea that with proper planning and skillful management, both largely American of course, the people of the world could enter an era of peace and prosperity where want and insecurity would be abolished. The roots of much of this confidence undoubtedly lay in the nation's past, stretching back to the country's earliest days when it did appear that the land was sufficiently abundant to provide for all who were willing to work hard and live frugally. The more immediate experience of the war years reinforced this optimism, for in contrast to Great Britain, the United States emerged from the hostilities relatively unscathed and infinitely more powerful than it had been in 1939. Defense spending had finally lifted the country out of its decade-long depression and had acted as a stimulant not only for the war industries but for the economy as a whole. Between 1939 and 1944 the nation's gross national product rose from $91 billion to $210 billion. Manufacturing volume nearly tripled; raw material output increased by 60 percent. Moreover, despite the immense war production, the United States was still able to provide the civilian sector of the population with a greater amount of commodities and services than it had enjoyed in 1939; there was no need to substitute "guns for butter." "The American people," War Mobilizer Fred M. Vinson reported shortly after the Nazi surrender, "are in the pleasant predicament of having to learn to live 50 percent better than they have ever lived before.

Such words rang hollow to the inhabitants of Great Britain. The war for them had been a searing experience. Even as late as the end of March 1945, the fiendish V-weapons, the buzz bomb and the still more indiscriminate rocket bomb, devastated their cities and checked the elation which the daily bulletins from the various fronts might otherwise have occasioned. Four million houses were destroyed or damaged by the enemy. After an inspection of London shortly following the Japanese surrender, the new American Secretary of State, James F.

Byrnes, concluded that no fewer than fifteen years would be needed to rebuild the smitten city. A White Paper on the British war effort presented to Parliament in November 1944, reported that the country's meat consumption was down nearly one-fourth from prewar levels; butter consumption was off two-thirds; fruit, tea, eggs, and sugar all significantly lower. Perhaps the illustration offered by an Englishman best explains the differing experiences of Britain and the United States: "When you in America hear a plane overhead," he remarked, "you look up into the sky. You are thrilled. An airplane flying is a symbol of progress to you. When we in England hear a plane overhead, we don't look up. We look for the nearest air raid shelter."

Nor did peace promise better conditions. Within days of the German surrender, Britons were warned to expect not an easing of wartime rationing, but further cuts in the quantities of food which each family would be allowed to purchase. By the end of May the amounts of fats, soap, milk, bacon, and meat which an individual could legally buy had all been reduced. It was the prospect of these conditions that had led Churchill long before V-E Day to tell Henry Morgenthau that after the war he, Churchill, would be the most unpopular man in England because it would then become evident that Britain's strained economic condition would prevent the government from providing the amelioration in living standards which the people would inevitably demand.

The Churchill government, in fact, confronted a whole register of difficulties arising from its participation in the war. Raising the austere levels of civilian consumption and rebuilding the miles of drab, scarred, uninhabited streets into usable homes and factories constituted only part of the problem. The allied victory would also bring new obligations: occupation duties in Europe and the Far East, and some degree of responsibility for insuring that the peoples of Europe, who were even more devastated than Britain, did not starve before the economies of the various nations could be reestablished. Equally important, the government faced insurmountable pressures for new domestic programs: an extension of social insurance, a public health service, advances in education, and a guarantee of full employment. If he defied these demands, the Prime Minister knew, he risked political suicide.

Most knowledgeable Britons realized that they could not blame the war alone for the sorry economic plight in which they found themselves by the end of 1944; thirty years of relative economic stagnation prior to 1939 had also played their part. The interwar period had seen a continual downward trend in the volume of the export trade and an increasing dependence on the earnings of overseas investments and shipping, banking, and insurance services. In the three years before the war, the value of British exports was only 55 percent that of British imports. Income from investments abroad paid for another 24 percent of these imports, while most of the remainder were purchased with monies derived from shipping, insurance, and banking. Such a delicate juggling act could not indefinitely sustain a nation as dependent upon imports as was Britain.

The long years of fighting, moreover, had caused a dangerous decline in revenues from these increasingly important "invisible" assets. Net income from foreign investments was less than 40 percent of its prewar value, as many overseas assets had been liquidated in order to pay for essential imports and military supplies from abroad, particularly during the eighteen months before the United States made lend-lease available. The British merchant marine had been decimated by German submarines and was in no condition to compete with the larger, more modern American fleet. Similarly, the war had completed the shift of the financial center of the world from London to New York, and the British Exchequer could anticipate only greatly reduced income from banking and insurance services. In addition, Britain had incurred overseas debts of vast dimensions, approaching nearly 10 percent of the country's total prewar national wealth, and had consumed most of its gold and dollar reserves. Thus, having begun the war with a net creditor position of approximately £3,500 million, Britain would end it as a debtor with liabilities of roughly £2,000 million. [£3.5 billion and £2.0 billion are roughly equivalent to $105 billion and $80 billion respectively, based on the 1945 exchange rate and the U.S. rate of inflation since 1945.] Though little appreciated by the average Britisher, these stark figures foreshadowed the frustration of many of his hopes, both for himself and for his nation.

Simple logic seemed to dictate that, given this new debtor status and the loss of much of its income from invisible assets, Britain would in the future have to export more and import less in order to earn the revenue needed to pay off its liabilities. Yet, reducing imports would be difficult at best, for prior to the war nearly two-thirds of the food consumed by the British people and virtually all the basic raw materials except coal used in British industry had been obtained from foreign sources. To cut back on these levels, the United Kingdom would either have to reduce its population, or depress its standard of living still further. Not only would the British have to find a way to pay for their normal imports; they would also need a considerable amount of goods and equipment from abroad to rebuild their damaged cities and factories and to modernize outmoded, inefficient plants, notably in the textile, mining, and electrical equipment industries. Raw materials for industry were required in substantially greater numbers to sustain full employment. American officials estimated that in the 1945–48 period, the British would need to import from the United States alone 319 percent of the agricultural products and related manufactures which they had bought in the equivalent prewar period; 364 percent of the metals and manufactures; 393 percent of the machinery and vehicles. Despite Britain's indebtedness, the British Treasury announced in the spring of 1945, the country would have to incur over the succeeding three years a further trade deficit of £1,500 million, or $6 billion. In part, this increase in imports of industrial and construction materials would be offset by reductions in purchases of luxury and other nonessential goods. Still, by the end of 1944, it was axiomatic in both London and Washington that the British would need to expand their export trade by 50–75 percent after the war merely to maintain their prewar standard of living. This figure did not begin to take into account any new domestic social programs which the British government might feel constrained to undertake.

Many, however, ridiculed this proposed increase as virtually unattainable. Indeed, formidable obstacles lay in the way of any expansion at all. For one thing, some questioned whether British industry could effectively compete in the world market. Even before the war most British manufacturers had failed to modernize their equipment and improve their methods of production sufficiently to keep pace with advances in the United States and other progressive industrial countries. As a consequence output per worker in the United Kingdom lagged far behind that of its chief competitors. In 1938, output per man-shift in coal mining was only about one-fourth as great in Britain as in the United States; in the iron and steel industry, less than one-half; in radio and automobile manufacturing, less than a quarter.

Most doubts, however, as to Britain's ability to raise its export levels so dramatically centered not on the productivity of the British worker, but on the availability of markets where British goods might be sold. Many of the countries which would most need British wares, those in central and eastern Europe for instance, would have no money to pay for them. Other potential markets, such as the Dominions and Latin America, already had sterling balances acquired during the war, so that exports to these nations would only be paying off old debts. Even more alarmingly, the British export trade during the war had, like so much else in British life, been severely curtailed. Exports from the United Kingdom at the end of the war comprised barely one-third of their prewar volume. The United States, in comparison, had during the war years actually maintained the value of its cash exports at their prewar level, in addition to its enormous lend-lease shipments. British textile exports, to give one example, had dwindled to about one-fifth of their prewar level, whereas American textile sales abroad (aside from lend-lease) almost doubled. This disparity reflected the wholesale displacement of British firms by American exporters in a number of markets which had traditionally been theirs in Latin America, the Middle East, and even Australia. Unless the United Kingdom could win back these markets, prospects for any significant increase in exports looked bleak.

Great Britain, in signing the lend-lease agreement with the United States, had promised not to export anything constructed with lend-lease materials or even things substantially similar to materials supplied by lend-lease. Rather than a ploy to limit British exports and thereby move into British markets, this provision was merely a condition the Roosevelt administration deemed necessary to insure domestic support for its program of aid to the United Kingdom. British businessmen, however, complained bitterly that these restrictions were destroying the British export trade and pointed out that the United States, even though it received raw materials under reverse lend-lease, did not have any such limitations on the type of goods it could export. Some industries, particularly those manufacturing steel products, began pressing for cessation of lend-lease imports of their raw materials long before the war's end. In fact, British exports were being curtailed for reasons that had nothing to do with restrictions imposed by the Americans, but which stemmed directly from the great demands placed on the country by the hostilities. Nonetheless, serious doubts existed about the ability of British manufacturers to find postwar markets for their goods.

The Churchill government attempted to counter all these factors with extensive preparations in planning for industrial reconversion, reorganizing the Department of Overseas Trade, and developing informational and other administrative aids for exporters. A White Paper issued early in 1945 urged parliamentary approval of an equivalent of the American Webb-Pomerene Act to enable industry-wide export organizations to canvass the United States in an effort to discover new markets for British goods. Within days seventeen leading companies had banded together to create the British Export Trade Research Organization, a unique research and promotional agency designed to expand postwar export markets. That this new body had the blessings of the government was commonly understood. Yet, despite this recognition of the necessity of increasing sales abroad, British exports continued to run at only a fraction of the 1938 volume.

At the most elementary level, the British leadership faced two alternatives in attempting to resolve the export crisis. On the one hand, it could accept the principles of the American program of multilateralism, thereby hoping to profit from an expanding world economy in which the British share might be relatively smaller than before the war even though larger in absolute terms. Or Britain could use its position as the world's largest market for food and raw materials to conclude bilateral agreements with as many nations as possible. By the end of 1944 most thinking at the expert level in London favored the first option, in principle at least, but the Cabinet had been unable to reach any consensus.

Proponents of the second, more restrictive approach advanced formidable arguments. Britain's technical backwardness and the demands of British labor for a higher standard of living and greater social security, they insisted, had ended Great Britain's reign as a low-cost manufacturer. Rather than attempt to compete solely on the basis of cost, the United Kingdom must depend upon "arranged trade"—that is, the creation of a sterling bloc which might include not only the Dominions but even Africa, the Middle East, and western Europe. Operating behind frozen sterling and most-favored-nation clauses, such a bloc could be virtually self-sufficient. Best of all, British firms, protected by preferential tariff agreements, quotas, licensing controls, and other government-sponsored restrictions, would not have to worry about being undersold by more efficient competitors. Those who endorsed this position maintained that the attraction of this bloc would be so great that a large part of Latin America might even be lured into it.

The very mention of such a plan created tremors of apprehension among American officials. If Whitehall established such an economic grouping, countries that wished to sell to Great Britain would have to take payment in British exports. The nations to which the United Kingdom owed billions of dollars arising from wartime purchases would be compelled to take British goods as payment for these debts. Trade inside the bloc would be encouraged through preferences and licenses, and trade outside the bloc severely hampered by discriminations and controls. In the three years before the war nearly one-half of the total United States trade was with the countries of the sterling area. These nations purchased 88 percent of American leaf tobacco exports before the war; 59 percent of American meat, grain, and other food exports; 49 percent of American raw cotton exports. To lose these markets through the formation of an exclusive economic grouping would be, in the words of the American Secretary of the Treasury, a "body blow to our whole economy."

Such an idea found favor in Britain with an unlikely coalition of socialists and conservative imperialists, including one of Churchill's closest friends and political allies, Lord Beaverbrook. Portions of the Left, mindful of the massive unemployment suffered by the British worker almost from the moment of peace in 1918, opposed any international scheme that might subject the British economy to external influence, particularly to economic fluctuations in the United States. More influential than these leftists were the financial interests of the City of London, the old-line industrialists who desired protection from newer, more rationally organized competition. But the group which carried the most weight with the British Prime Minister personally consisted of those traditional defenders of the Empire who saw in America's economic designs another clumsy attempt at dismantling Great Britain's imperial domain. Almost unobtrusively, financial arguments became mixed with those of a different nature; advocates of imperial preference came to believe that the elimination of financial restrictions meant the death of the Empire and Britain's decline as a world power.

More moderate opinion as well had reservations about the advisability of tying British fortunes too closely to American ideas for the postwar world. Both Britain's leading daily, the *Times,* and one of its most respected weeklies, the *Economist,* ran a series of articles describing how the benefits of multilateralism might be obtained among a group of countries by means of bulk-purchasing agreements, quantitative import controls, and a comprehensive system of discrimination against goods from the United States. Quite clearly, resistance to the American vision of expanding trade and diminishing barriers to the free exchange of goods was not simply going to evaporate on its own accord.

British observers also complained that American practices often seemed to bear little resemblance to the fine words mouthed about free trade by Hull and his disciples. The Department of Agriculture, for instance, often pushed schemes involving price-fixing and wholesale bulk-purchasing, directly at variance with a policy of multilateralism. In the Middle East, American oil companies entered into cartel agreements with British firms, with Washington's obvious concurrence. Repeatedly, American officials insisted on the economic benefits which a multilateral world would bring to the United States. These statements, though intended only to insure adequate congressional and public support for administration policies, served to frighten the British as well. What, they pointedly asked, did "free trade" and "equal opportunity" mean in a world in which the United States had no economic peers?

American tariff practices also made the British skeptical of United States designs for free trade. Washington officialdom believed that in securing renewal of the Reciprocal Trade Agreement Act in the summer of 1945, it was striking a strong blow for multilateralism and that its actions deserved some significant British concession in return. The perspective from across the ocean could not have been more different. The British viewed this legislation as little more than a token reduction in the American tariff wall and only further reason to resist the elimination of imperial preference and other protective devices. President Truman, they undoubtedly knew, had promised members of the Senate Finance Committee that he did not contemplate wholesale reduction in tariff rates under the new act and that any agreements negotiated under his administration would be neither as extensive nor sweeping as those being proposed by some of the more enthusiastic supporters of free trade. Moreover, America's assertion that Britain's preference system was inherently more offensive than its own trade barriers rankled London. Washington viewed preferences as repugnant because they were discriminatory. Tariffs should be lowered, but they were not in the same category with preferences, even though they too hampered trade, because they discriminated equally against all. Whitehall officials, not surprisingly, placed far less emphasis on this distinction between tariffs and preferences. Why, they asked, should they be compelled to work for the *elimination* of British preferences but only for the *reduction* of American tariffs?

Public discussion in the two nations also demonstrated that each had very different conceptions of the role of the Bretton Woods institutions and the responsibilities which this program placed upon the individual national governments, a condition which could only lead to further misunderstandings and friction. Robert Boothby, chairman of the Monetary Policy Committee in the House of Commons, wrote the *New York Times* complaining that Americans had "been led to believe that the Bretton Woods proposals take us all back along the road to a gold standard, currency stability, non-discrimination and multilateral trade." The British, on the other hand, "have been assured, that they constitute the exact reverse of a gold standard, that exchange rates will be flexible and that reciprocal trade agreements involving discrimination will be permissible." The institutions erected at Bretton Woods, charged the London Chamber of Commerce, failed to deal with the essential problem blocking achievement of a satisfactory international trade: the refusal of certain economically powerful nations to buy as much from other countries as they wished to sell to them. Though no names were mentioned, it did not require much acuity to see that the United States was felt to be the principal culprit.

Given these differing perceptions as to the best means of obtaining national and international prosperity, and given the suspicions which were almost inevitably fostered in the minds of many Britishers by American economic might and the contradictions in American policy, it is hardly surprising that irritation and acrimony crept into the transatlantic dialogue. The chairman of one of England's largest banks chided the British government for "excessive tenderness" toward the United States in discussing commercial matters. Reports that American businessmen had traveled to France and China in military uniform to get a head start in the contest for postwar trade circulated extensively and created widespread alarm. The top official of a large British manufacturing company charged that unnamed foreign suppliers were offering electrical plant equipment and machinery abroad at prices below their production costs. American businessmen filed similar complaints. Motion picture executives protested that the British government was deliberately squeezing them out of the United Kingdom. Representatives of

Detroit's auto makers pointedly noted that British cars could enter the United States but that American automobiles were barred from British markets. Such accusations merely served to underscore the basic distrust which influential elements in each nation harbored toward the intentions of the other.

Throughout Britain one heard whispered fears of trade war with the United States, or of large-scale dumping on world markets by American firms eager to prevent unemployment at home. One M.P. called for assurances by the United States that it would not engage in a "phoney" export trade financed by credits that could not be repaid in goods because of high American tariff barriers. Another, admitting that Britain was frightened by United States economic might, suggested that Americans deliberately curb their exports after the war to "leave some leeway" for other countries. Foreign trade, the British Ambassador to Washington told a gathering of bankers, was "the most vexing question of all" separating the two nations. The crux of Anglo–American relations, he added, was how to adjust America's need for export markets with Britain's need to obtain the wherewithal to buy imports vital to its national existence.

But while serious obstacles impeded the establishment of any long-term economic partnership between the two, equally potent forces in Great Britain worked in favor of cooperation. At the abstract level practically all important British leaders tended to support the idea of international collaboration. Britain's wartime dependence on the United States for the achievement of its military and political objectives as well as its economic solvency also tended to push Whitehall toward a policy of cooperation. Perhaps most fundamentally, Britain's overwhelming need for overseas supplies of foodstuffs and raw materials and for foreign markets for its manufactures encouraged acceptance of some sort of multilateral world vision. London's desire to retain its place as a leading financier, carrier, and insurer of the trade of other countries provided a further stake in a free and extensive international commerce. In a typically perceptive editorial, the *Economist* seemed to have caught much of official thinking when it observed that as a matter of plain economics, the American vision of the postwar financial order presented serious pitfalls to the British nation. It went on to add, however, that "as a matter of politics or (if the word is taken to imply something sinister) of amicable relations between Governments, there is almost everything to be said in its favour." In concluding it asked, but could not answer, "How much economic hazard is a reasonable price for continued American generosity and friendship—or at least for the avoidance of American disappointment and resentment?"

One further idea permeated official British thinking on the subject: the absolute necessity of retaining the nation's financial independence and power of initiative. "In spite of their genuine good-will and magnanimous aid to us," John Maynard Keynes warned at the end of 1944,

> financial independence of the United States at the earliest possible opportunity should be a major aim of British policy. . . . There are very few objects of policy beyond the demands of victory over the enemy to which that should be subordinated. A might[y] Empire in financial leading strings to others will not be mighty at all, and we shall have sacrificed real power to show and sham.

As a consequence, while the British were blind to American sensitivities and sought ways to avoid irritating their powerful ally, they also recognized the imperative need to regain their own economic equilibrium, even if this at times created difficulties in relations with the United States. They would have to stand firm on those issues affecting essential British interests and the future prosperity of the nation. At the same time, a Foreign Office paper cautioned, "We must do so in such a way that we do not provoke the United States to withdraw from international economic collaboration; otherwise all our tasks will be rendered infinitely more difficult." The manner in which British relations with the United States were handled, this paper then continued, "will be a key factor in allowing us the freedom we need to go our own way, without giving the impression that we are sacrificing world interests to our own selfish designs."

Brave words, no doubt. Yet it appeared that the British position was more accurately summarized by the succinct if blunt observation of the group of English manufacturers who commented: "Everything depends upon the extent to which the Americans are prepared to cooperate." In late 1944 this question remained unresolved. The economic aspects of the relationship provided indications that could be interpreted in either fashion. The objectives of world prosperity and an expanding international trade were common to both Great Britain and the United States, and there were influential voices in each nation calling for a continuation of the wartime collaboration into the postwar era. On the other hand, there existed powerful disruptive forces and clashing interests that contained the potential for creating much bitterness in relations between the two, frictions which would inevitably spill over into the political and military spheres. In some cases these disputes had already erupted into the public forum and themselves contributed to an exacerbation of ill feelings. Just how much Americans would be prepared to cooperate with their British cousins remained to be seen. The answer, moreover, rested as much on emotion and irrationality as on any cold-blooded calculation of the national interest.

14

Melvyn P. Leffler

Adherence to Agreements: Yalta and the Experiences of the Early Cold War

Much American historiography on the fortunes of the alliance immediately after the war became caught up in the mounting Cold War. Within two years of the end of the war Europe was divided between a Soviet dominated East and an American led West. The Cold War quickly spread to Asia and consolidated the partitioning of Korea. For the next generation it polluted international relations throughout the globe. The Soviet Union, under the obsessive, tyrannical dictatorship of Josef Stalin, was viewed as reneging on agreements made at Tehran, Yalta, and Potsdam. An

Reprinted from *International Security* 11,1(1986):88–123 by permission of the MIT Press. Copyright © 1986. Cambridge, Massachusetts.

expansionary Soviet foreign policy and a steamrolling Red Army had to be contained, if not rolled back. Some traced the origins of the Cold War to the Bolshevik Revolution of 1917 and Lenin's call for world revolution. Those with a longer view found it in an abiding Russian drive for conquest rooted in czarist times, while more present-minded observers located it in Moscow's immediate experiences of German invasion (the second in one generation). Critics of interpretations that found the Soviet Union at fault for the Cold War grew more vociferous as American archives opened new documents, and as diaries and memoirs of American participants were published. Revisionists turned the tables, found responsibility for the Cold War rested primarily with the United States, and usually related it to the American capitalist drive for profit and expansion and to anticommunism.

From the beginning, the debate centered on the Yalta conference of February 1945 and the events subsequent to the agreements reached there. Yalta, along with Pearl Harbor, achieved mythic proportions as a symbol of American failure. This is ironic, since most of the issues agreed upon at Yalta had been discussed and bargained over at Tehran fourteen months earlier. Nonetheless, the Yalta conference produced public communiqués and raised more postwar hopes. It also stood closer in time to the rapidly changing realities of Central Europe. It absorbed the public's attention. In addition, Roosevelt died two months after the conference ended. His Vice President, Harry S. Truman, with whom Roosevelt shared none of his ideas or decisions in foreign affairs, took over the presidency. Determined to follow Roosevelt's policies, Truman found Roosevelt's advisors were not agreed or clear among themselves as to what the policies were.

Yalta, as the following essay by Professor Leffler shows, has continued relevance in American political discourse. With the collapse of Soviet military power in Central and Eastern Europe in 1989–90 we may at last be entering a post-Yalta era. Above all, however, Leffler shows that judgments on responsibility for adherence to international accords are far from easy. Even the most iron-clad agreements are subject to interpretation. This is no more true than in times of abrupt shifts in power relations. At the conclusion of the war in Europe, new interests and opportunities thrust themselves forward. Perhaps this is a key to the historical significance of the fate of the Yalta agreements.

On April 23, 1945 President Harry S. Truman had a stormy meeting with Soviet Foreign Minister V. M. Molotov. In what many historians consider the first round of the Cold War, Truman denounced Soviet violations of the Yalta agreements. When Molotov sought to defend Soviet actions, Truman bluntly retorted that the Soviets would have to adhere to their agreements if cooperation were to continue.

During the next year Truman lost faith in the Kremlin. He grew frustrated with the tedious deliberations among the foreign ministers; he became alarmed by the Soviet consolidation of power in Eastern Europe; and he was frightened by the sociopolitical turmoil throughout much of the world. In July 1946 he ordered two White House aides, Clark Clifford and George Elsey, to write an assessment of Soviet compliance with wartime and postwar agreements. If the Kremlin did not adhere to past accords, it made little sense to try to reach new agreements. Knowing the Chief Executive's wishes, Clifford and Elsey solicited the views of top officials in the Truman Administration and wrote a devastating critique of Soviet adherence to wartime and postwar agreements. Interpreting their assignment very broadly, they went on to attribute Soviet actions to Marxist–Leninist ideology, to claim that the Soviets sought world domination, and to recommend adoption of a series of measures to assist prospective allies, augment American strength, and redress the balance of power.

Taking another look at these early Cold War developments seems appropriate at a time when influential policymakers are using allegations of Soviet duplicity and non-compliance to extricate the United States from the SALT II and ABM treaties, to thwart progress toward new arms control agreements, and to help justify the Strategic Defense Initiative (SDI). On the eve of the 1985 Geneva summit, Secretary of Defense Caspar W. Weinberger denounced the Soviet record of adherence to recent accords. He urged President Ronald Reagan to resist any new commitments that would obligate the United States to observe the SALT II agreement, that would limit SDI research, development, or testing, or that would obscure the pattern of Soviet arms control violations. According to Assistant Secretary of Defense Richard Perle, one of Weinberger's closest advisers, it is "a great mistake" for the United States to honor past accords when the Soviets disregard their key provisions. Although the Administration thus far has been reluctant to renounce the SALT II and ABM treaties formally, the temptation to do so will mount as new nuclear submarines are deployed, as "Star Wars" research generates new demands for testing and development, and as additional B–52 bombers are converted to carry cruise missiles.

In effect, Weinberger and Perle are claiming that Soviet noncompliance constitutes a threat to vital American interests, justifies unilateral measures to enhance American security, and obviates the utility of negotiation. This line of reasoning closely resembles the arguments of Clifford, Elsey, and Truman at the onset of the Cold War. Accordingly, it is worthwhile to look at the historical events surrounding the disintegration of the great wartime coalition in order to clarify the records of compliance of the United States and of the Soviet Union. In fact, the Soviet pattern of adherence was not qualitatively different from the American pattern; both governments complied with some accords and disregarded others. American policymakers often exaggerated Soviet malfeasance and disregarded the strategic calculations that may have influenced Soviet actions. Driven by the need to safeguard vital American interests and impelled by a sense of power afforded by the atomic bomb, Truman Administration officials themselves sometimes violated key provisions of wartime agreements. And these transgressions could be construed as endangering vital Soviet interests just as Soviet violations may have imperiled critical American interests.

Of course, Clifford, Elsey, and Truman did not see things this way. They were convinced of Soviet duplicity and American innocence. Their self-deception could serve as a lesson to contemporary officials. By their very nature, great power agreements demand compromise and are wrapped in ambiguities. Pressures to interpret provisions, even unambiguous ones, to comport with national self-interest are relentless on both American and Soviet officials. Leaders of both countries tend to act opportunistically yet demand punctilious behavior from their adversaries. Their sense of expediency and self-righteous hypocrisy endanger efforts to regulate competition through international agreement. If competition is to be channeled into construction avenues and conflict contained, both great powers must abandon the temptation to use the issue of adherence to agreements as a morality play or a propaganda ploy; both sides must wish to define their security in terms of compliance and accommodation rather than in terms of other priorities that compete with and may take ascendancy over a cooperative relationship.

The Transition from Roosevelt to Truman

During World War II, the major allied governments—the United States, the United Kingdom, and the Soviet Union—signed agreements with one another and with many less powerful governments regarding postwar military, political, and economic developments. The most controversial of these were the agreements signed at the Yalta Conference in February 1945 by Franklin D. Roosevelt, Winston Churchill, and Joseph Stalin. Because the Yalta accords have assumed almost mythic proportions in the history of the Cold War, they shall receive primary attention in this analysis. But what can be observed in the record of adherence to the Yalta accords can be reconfirmed by carefully scrutinizing the pattern of compliance with other wartime agreements. In this respect, the treaties obligating Britain and the Soviet Union to withdraw from Iran six months after the war and similar ones calling for American withdrawal from advance bases in the Azores, Iceland, and elsewhere are of particular interest. Finally, because the Potsdam accords on Germany gave rise to so many recriminations, it will be worthwhile to look at them, if only in a cursory fashion.

The Yalta agreements have received much scholarly and popular attention. During the McCarthy era, partisan critics charged that alleged communist advisers, like Alger Hiss, were instrumental in undermining the American bargaining position and extending unnecessary concessions. Even sympathizers of President Franklin D. Roosevelt acknowledged shortcomings in the Yalta accords and attributed these flaws to Roosevelt's declining health. After the Department of State published many of the confidential papers and memoranda regarding Yalta in 1955, a number of scholars put together a collection of essays on the Crimean meeting. John Snell, Forrest C. Pogue, Charles F. Delzell, and George A. Lensen provided a careful scholarly assessment of the negotiating trade-offs at Yalta and emphasized the constraints on American actions. The desire for Soviet intervention in the Pacific War, the reality of the Soviet military presence in Eastern Europe, and the hope for postwar cooperation within a United Nations circumscribed the options available to American officials.

The Snell volume constituted a first-rate assessment of Yalta by a group of eminent scholars whose reputation for objectivity was beyond dispute. Their analysis led to the conclusion that the Yalta agreements were not inherently flawed. These accords reflected power realities in Eastern Europe and wartime exigencies in the Far East. What went wrong, they concluded, was subsequent Soviet violation of these agreements.

However, as scholars have probed more deeply into the immediate post-Yalta period, the meaning of the agreements has become ever more difficult to assess. During the last twenty years, historians have come to emphasize the reciprocal concessions made by Roosevelt and Stalin at the Crimea Conference. These concessions were dictated by the realities of the military situation and by Roosevelt's complex aspirations for the postwar era. The President realized that the Kremlin had legitimate interests in Eastern Europe that had to be accommodated if there were to be any hope for postwar cooperation. He desired a cooperative relationship not because he was complacent about Soviet intentions, but because he was altogether well aware of the imponderables that lay ahead. He thought accommodation of legitimate Soviet objectives might enable him to safeguard at less cost more vital American (and British) interests elsewhere around the globe. But Roosevelt also desired to preserve the nation's atomic and financial leverage should the Kremlin prove recalcitrant on matters of critical importance to the United States.

In his dealings with the Kremlin, however, Roosevelt felt it imperative to cloak his concessions in the ambiguous language of the Declaration on Liberated Europe. In this way he hoped to satisfy Stalin without disappointing domestic constituencies whose support he still needed for many legislative enactments, including American participation in the United Nations, the International Monetary Fund, and the World Bank. Paradoxically, then, Roosevelt's carefully concealed concessions were prompted by a desire to cooperate with the Kremlin, by a recognition of Soviet preponderance in Eastern Europe, and by a desire to ensure active American participation in world affairs, which, if necessary, could take the direction of the containment of Soviet power. Roosevelt evidently hoped that Yalta might allow Stalin to safeguard Soviet strategic interests without too overtly violating American principles. Elections in Eastern Europe were promised, but they were to be held without allied supervision and under the aegis of provisional governments that were for the most part the creation of Soviet occupation forces. Democratic forms would be adhered to, thereby satisfying American predilections, but the results would comport with the Kremlin's need for friendly governments. In return, the Soviets would be expected to restrain their ambitions elsewhere and to respect Anglo–American interests.

Roosevelt's goals were difficult to implement. Scholars have shown how Roosevelt refused to acknowledge his Yalta concessions to the American public lest he trigger a wave of cynicism and a return to the isolationism of the interwar era. Moreover, when he died on April 12, 1945, he left his foreign policy in the hands of Vice President Harry S. Truman, a man with whom Roosevelt almost never discussed foreign policy. Truman, by his own repeated admissions, had absolutely no idea of the intricacies of the Yalta agreements and knew very little about the motivations that lay behind Roosevelt's diplomatic and domestic posturing. The new President had to rely on Roosevelt's advisers to explain to him the meaning of the Yalta agreements and the objectives of Roosevelt's diplomacy. Yet because of the improvised way in which Roosevelt used his advisers, because of the bureaucratic morass and the wartime subordination of the State Department, and because of Roosevelt's own deceptive behavior, no one could convey to Truman the full meaning of Roosevelt's concessions and aspirations. Although historians have made substantial progress in putting together a picture of Roosevelt's intentions, few of his contemporaries grasped the multifaceted dimensions of his policies.

During his first months in office, Truman received a set of explanations and advice from one group of advisers, including Secretary of State Edward I. Stettinius, Ambassador to the Soviet Union W. Averell Harriman, Secretary of the Navy James Forrestal, and Admiral William Leahy, the President's chief of staff. He often received contrasting opinions from Secretary of War Henry L. Stimson, Army Chief of Staff General George C. Marshall, Secretary of Commerce Henry C. Wallace, Anna Boettinger, Roosevelt's daughter, and Joseph Davies, former ambassador to the Soviet Union and prominent Democratic fund-raiser. Ironically, Truman came to rely heavily on James F. Byrnes, former senator, supreme court justice, and wartime director of mobilization and reconversion. Although Byrnes had been spurned by Roosevelt as a vice presidential candidate at the Democratic convention in 1944, he reluctantly agreed to accompany Roosevelt to Yalta and to serve as public salesman of the Crimean accords before retiring to his native South Carolina. As Robert Messer has shown, Byrnes was not privy to all the discussions at Yalta partly because he had to rush back to Washington to lead the domestic media blitz before the final settlements were reached between Roosevelt, Stalin, and Churchill. Nevertheless, Truman looked to Byrnes, who had had little previous familiarity with Roosevelt's foreign policy, for the most definitive explanation of the meaning of Yalta. His dependence upon Byrnes was revealed by his decision to designate him secretary of state as soon as Stettinius completed work on the founding of the United Nations at the San Francisco Conference.

The above depiction of events is well known to historians who have examined the closing events of World War II and the succession from Roosevelt to Truman. The implications of these developments, however, have not been fully explored. Although recent historians like John Lewis Gaddis and Robert Messer fully acknowledge the chasm between Roosevelt's concessions at Yalta and the information disseminated to the American people, they focus attention on the American public's growing disillusionment with Soviet behavior. But the purposeful misrepresentation of the Yalta compromises, the unilateral interpretation of some of the Yalta provisions, and the clear abrogation of others had an important bearing on Soviet–American relations because these developments represented American efforts to extricate the United States from commitments and restraints that were no longer considered desirable. At the same time, the unqualified American denunciations of Soviet compliance with the Yalta accords and with other agreements constituted American efforts to define permissible Soviet behavior in as narrow a way as possible in order to circumscribe Soviet influence in Europe and Asia.

Differing Interpretations of the Yalta Accords

The Yalta agreements addressed five important topics: Poland, liberated Europe, Germany, the Far East, and the United Nations. Initial rancor revolved around the provisions for Poland and liberated Eastern Europe. With the definition of Poland's eastern border pretty well resolved at Yalta, the post-Yalta dispute focused on the procedures for establishing and the composition of the provisional government for Poland. When Soviet armies advanced through Poland in late 1944, the Kremlin put together and recognized a government of pro-communist Poles at Lublin as the Provisional National Government; the British and the Americans, however, still carried on wartime relations with the Polish government-in-exile in London. The State Department favored the establishment of a "fully representative" government inside Poland, to consist primarily of non-Lublin Poles from outside and inside Poland. When British Prime Minister Winston Churchill advocated this position at Yalta, Stalin was obdurate. Emphasizing the need for a Polish government friendly to the Soviet Union in order to guarantee future Soviet security and to safeguard lines of communication to Soviet armies in Germany, he wanted Churchill and Roosevelt to recognize the Lublin Poles.

Wisely or unwisely, Roosevelt mediated the Churchill–Stalin dispute. The final agreement stipulated that "the Provisional Government which is now functioning in Poland [i.e., the Lublin Government] should therefore be reorganized on a broader democratic basis with the inclusion of democratic leaders from Poland itself and from Poles abroad." There was no mention of this government becoming "fully representative." Although there was a reference to the holding of free elections, it could not conceal the critical importance of acceding to short-term Lublin control and of eliminating language calling for supervised elections. Roosevelt had made a critical concession which he understood at the time and which he again acknowledged, however unhappily, in a letter to Churchill on March 29, 1945. "You will recall," Roosevelt wrote,

> that the agreement on Poland at Yalta was a compromise. . . . The wording of the resulting agreement reflects this compromise, but if we attempt to evade the fact that we placed, as clearly shown in the agreement, somewhat more emphasis on the Lublin Poles than on the other two groups from which the new government is to be drawn I feel we will expose ourselves to the charges that we are attempting to go back on the Crimea decision.

In other words, the language of the Yalta agreement did concede Lublin predominance in a provisional government, albeit a reorganized one.

Notwithstanding this admission, Roosevelt assented to efforts to try to dilute the meaning of his Yalta concession. Churchill and many American officials sought to regain what had been given away by underscoring the importance of the post-Yalta talks in Moscow. The Crimean accord authorized Harriman, Molotov, and British Ambassador Archibald Clark Kerr "to consult in the first instance in Moscow with members of the present Provisional Government and with other Polish democratic leaders from within Poland and from abroad, with a view to the reorganisation of the present Government along the above lines [that is, on a broader democratic basis]." Churchill, under great criticism in Parliament for the Yalta provisions on Poland, sought to use these deliberations in Moscow to circumvent the Yalta language. Our goal, he wrote Roosevelt, is "to promote the formation of a new reorganised Polish government sufficiently representative of all Poland for us to recognise it." Harriman, too, struggled tenaciously to narrow the preeminence of the Lublin Poles. He demanded that consultations take place with leaders from outside Poland, and that the Lublin government have no veto over who could participate in these talks. Molotov argued that conversations should be held initially with representatives of the Lublin government and that Poles who opposed Yalta should not be consulted. Whatever the merits of the Anglo–American and Soviet positions on the procedural matter, the real dispute was over the composition of the reorganized provisional government. Harriman and Clark Kerr sought to establish a new government "broadly representative of Democratic elements of the Polish State," while Molotov sought reaffirmation that the Lublin government would constitute the "basis" for the reorganized government.

The deadlock on the formation of the Polish provisional government was complete when Roosevelt died. Harriman immediately rushed to Washington to brief Truman on Soviet perfidy and treachery in Poland and Eastern Europe. Before the ambassador reached Washington, the new President took his first look at the Yalta agreements and expressed shock and disappointment that they were not more clear-cut. On the very morning of the President's acrimonious interview with Molotov, Truman's advisers discussed the meaning of Yalta regarding Poland. Admiral Leahy, the chief of staff to the President, although well known for his tough-nosed, conservative, and anti-Soviet views, acknowledged that the Yalta language on Poland was susceptible to contrasting interpretations. Previously he had told Roosevelt that the language was so vague that the Soviets "could stretch it all the way from Yalta to Washington without ever technically breaking it." Thus when Truman met with Molotov later that same day, the President knew that the Soviet position was not an unreasonable interpretation of Yalta. But fearful of the Kremlin's growing strength and the emerging vacuum of power in central Europe, Truman unqualifiedly accused Molotov of transgressing the Yalta provisions on Poland. "The United States Government," Truman insisted, "cannot be party to any method of consultation with Polish leaders which would not result in the establishment

of a new Provisional Government of National Unity genuinely representative of the democratic elements of the Polish people." By focusing on results and calling for a new and "genuinely representative"
government, Truman shifted attention from the procedural issue of the
Moscow consultations, on which the United States position was reasonable, to the substantive question regarding the make-up of the provisional government, on which the American interpretation was
unfounded.

Soviet leaders were angered by the American interpretation. Before
Roosevelt's death, Stalin charged that the American position amounted
to a claim for "the establishment of an entirely new government." This
thesis, Stalin argued, was "tantamount to direct violation of the Crimean Conference decisions." The day before Molotov listened to President Truman's dressing-down, he met privately with Joseph Davies.
Molotov explained that Poland was an absolutely vital interest to the
Soviet Union, and expressed dismay that Roosevelt's subordinates and
successor were seeking to reverse and redefine the meaning of Yalta.
From the Soviet perspective, Truman's attempt to force Soviet acceptance of the American interpretation reflected America's failure to
adhere to the substantive concessions accepted by Roosevelt. At the
Crimea Conference, Stalin wrote Truman on April 24, 1945, we agreed
that the government now functioning in Poland "should be the core,
that is, the main part of a new, reconstructed Polish Government of
national Unity." American abrogation of the understanding, Stalin insisted, manifested American indifference to Soviet strategic imperatives: "Poland is to the security of the Soviet Union what Belgium and
Greece are to the security of Great Britain."

Davies agreed with Molotov's and Stalin's viewpoint. Moreover,
during the next two months, Davies spent many hours with Truman at
the White House seeking to explain how the Soviets viewed their vital
interests in Eastern Europe. Meanwhile, Byrnes, too, endeavored to
ascertain more information about the last minute concessions made by
Roosevelt at the Crimea meeting. By early June, Byrnes confidentially
admitted to Davies, "There was no justification under the spirit or
letter of the agreement for insistence by Harriman and the British
ambassador that an entirely new Government should be created . . . ."

When Harry Hopkins visited Moscow at the end of May and listened to Stalin's strenuous defense of the Kremlin's Polish policy, the
American emissary did not seek to justify the American position with a

legal or textual analysis of the Yalta accords. Instead, Hopkins alluded, rather lamely, to the sensibilities of American public opinion. In effect, Hopkins conceded that the Soviet position on the preponderant role of the Lublin Poles in any new provisional government comported with the substantive compromises worked out at Yalta. Truman acquiesced to this bitter reality.

The recognition of the Lublin Poles meant acceptance of predominant Soviet influence in postwar Poland. This point Roosevelt had conceded at Yalta, but he hoped to elicit at least minimal Soviet adherence to democratic forms. The Soviets, however, had little tolerance for such symbols, as reflected by their arrest and imprisonment of anti-fascist leaders inside Poland. Nor did the Kremlin ever show any willingness to support free elections or tolerate basic freedoms. The resilience of the anti-Soviet Polish underground and the persistent American pleas for open trade, economic data, and Polish coal (for Western Europe) helped to perpetuate Soviet suspicions about the future orientation of postwar Poland and reinforced the Kremlin's determination to have a friendly government susceptible to Soviet influence notwithstanding the democratic trappings of the Yalta provisions. Neither Moscow nor Washington, then, demonstrated much inclination to adhere to the meaning of Yalta regarding Poland, but American policymakers paid almost no attention to the significance of their own desire to disengage from one of the most significant aspects of the Yalta accords, that is, the provision on the composition of the Polish provisional government.

After the Yalta Conference, rancorous disputes also emerged over the implementation of the Declaration on Liberated Europe. The Declaration contained no mechanisms for the enforcement of its lofty principles on self-government and self-determination. Indeed, during the discussions at Yalta, Molotov inserted language that weakened even the implication of great power collaboration in the enforcement of the declaration. The Yalta agreement simply obligated the signatories to "consult together on the measures necessary to discharge the joint responsibilities set forth in this declaration." And this consultation would occur only "When in the opinion of the three governments, conditions . . . make such action necessary." Nothing Roosevelt said or did at Yalta suggested that he had much concern for developments in Eastern Europe except insofar as they might influence the political climate in the United States. With no language to implement its rhetorical flourishes, the Declaration on Liberated Europe did little to dispel the sphere of influence arrangements that had been incorporated into the armistice agreements and that had been sanctioned in the Churchill–Stalin percentages agreement of October 1944.

The armistice accords denied the Soviet Union any significant influence in Italy and gave the Kremlin the preeminent role in Rumania, Finland, Bulgaria, and Hungary. For all intents and purposes, Soviet officials had a legal claim to run things as they wished in Rumania and Finland until peace treaties were completed and in Bulgaria and Hungary at least until the war was over. The Churchill–Stalin deal complemented the armistice accords and assigned the Kremlin 90 percent influence in Rumania, 80 percent in Bulgaria, and 80 percent in Hungary, while allotting the British predominant influence in Greece and allaying British apprehensions over Soviet support for the leftist partisans in northern Italy. Notwithstanding its inspirational language, the Declaration on Liberated Europe never received much attention at Yalta and never superseded the clarity of the armistice agreements or the realpolitik encompassed in the Churchill–Stalin accords. And despite Churchill's self-serving disclaimers in his magisterial history of World War II, the documents now demonstrate beyond any reasonable doubt that the percentage agreement was neither designed as a temporary accord pending the end of the war nor contingent upon American acceptance.

Yet shortly after the Yalta meeting, Churchill sought to renege on the meaning of these previous concessions and to circumscribe Soviet domination. By the spring of 1945, British forces had put down the insurrection in Greece. Stalin said nothing. He even withdrew Bulgarian troops, now under Soviet tutelage, from Thrace and Macedonia. But when Stalin's emissary, Andrei Vyshinsky, forced the Rumanians to reshuffle their government and sign a bilateral trade agreement with the Kremlin, Churchill remonstrated and the State Department protested. Roosevelt, however, cautioned Churchill to tread carefully because "Rumania is not a good place for a test case. The Russians have been in undisputed control from the beginning, and with Rumania lying athwart the Russian lines of communication it is moreover difficult to contest the plea of military necessity and security . . . ." Although Roosevelt had not signed the percentages accord and was not obligated to abide by it, he knew that Soviet actions could not be construed as incompatible with the armistice agreement, especially while the war against Germany was still being waged.

After Roosevelt died, however, Truman sought to constrict Soviet predominance in Eastern Europe. American policy was more circumspect but no less intent than the British on reversing the real meaning of the Churchill–Stalin agreement, the armistice accords, and the Yalta compromises. Pending Soviet retrenchment in Eastern Europe, the State Department initially decided to refrain from discussing a postwar loan to the Soviet Union and to stiffen the conditions of lend-lease assistance. Truman refused to recognize the provisional governments set up by the Kremlin in Rumania and Bulgaria until they were reorganized and made more representative. At Potsdam, Byrnes endeavored to enlarge the influence of Anglo–American officials within the Allied Control Commissions in occupied Eastern Europe. After Potsdam, American diplomats pressed the Bulgarians to postpone their impending and obviously rigged elections. While rejecting proposals to monitor elections in Eastern Europe and disregarding pleas from American diplomats to intervene more directly in internal Rumanian affairs, Byrnes nonetheless continually prodded Molotov to reorganize the Rumanian and Bulgarian governments, to hold free elections, and to accept self-determination in Eastern Europe. At the London Conference of Foreign Ministers in September 1945, Molotov bluntly told Byrnes that the Kremlin interpreted his requests as efforts to establish unfriendly governments in Rumania and Bulgaria and to jeopardize Soviet security.

Byrnes disclaimed any such intention. From his perspective, he sought no more than Soviet adherence to the language of the Yalta Declaration on Liberated Europe which emphasized "the right of all peoples to choose the form of government under which they will live . . . ." Byrnes did not dispute the Soviet claim to a sphere of influence. Prodded by Charles Bohlen, one of the ablest Kremlinologists in the State Department, Byrnes publicly declared that the United States sought neither to impose hostile governments on the Soviet Union's periphery nor to encourage behavior unfriendly to it. Indeed, Byrnes proclaimed a willingness to accept the notion of an "open sphere," wherein Eastern European governments would conduct their foreign and defense policies within parameters set by the Kremlin (much like Latin American nations had to mold their policies within the confines established by Washington). The caveat, however, was that the Kremlin had to refrain from intervention in the strictly internal affairs of these countries and to accept the principles of open and non-discriminatory trade, free elections, and the unimpeded movement of Western journalists.

In abstract, this orientation constituted a means of reconciling the Soviet interpretation of Yalta as mandating a Soviet sphere with the American claim that Yalta underscored the principles of self-determination and personal freedom. But throughout Eastern Europe, except perhaps Bulgaria, free elections portended the emergence of anti-Soviet governments; open trade meant the eventual influx of Western capital, goods, and influence. Indeed the planning documents for the Yalta meeting reveal that American officials conceptualized the open door and self-determination as means to exercise leverage and to maintain some influence within a Soviet sphere. Harriman, for example, advocated free elections as a means to circumscribe Soviet predominance. Likewise, U.S. State Department officials championed the right of journalists to travel in Eastern Europe because they anticipated that reports of Soviet repression might generate public support in the United States for a more sustained diplomatic effort to achieve American objectives.

Although Eduard Mark has made a persuasive case for the view that American policy was designed to support an "open sphere," it was an illusion to think that the conflicting interpretations of Yalta could be reconciled through this concept. Wartime ravages, historical experiences, and traditional ethnic rivalries confounded the notion that free elections could lead to governments friendly to the Soviet Union. "A freely elected government in any of these countries," Stalin acknowledged at Potsdam, "would be anti-Soviet, and that we cannot allow." At the Moscow Conference in December 1945, the Soviet dictator reminded Byrnes that Rumanian troops had marched to the Volga, Hungarian armies had reached the Don, and Nazi naval vessels had moved unhindered through Bulgarian waters. Nor was Stalin unaware of the potential political leverage inherent in the principle of equal commercial opportunity. The open door was no different from a foreign military invasion, Stalin told Chiang Kai-shek's son. And unlike Truman, who suspected that German power was unlikely to revive very quickly, Stalin anticipated a German economic resurgence and expected another conflict within ten or fifteen years.

Leaders in Moscow and Washington, then, had reason to feel exasperated with one another's actions and attitudes toward Eastern Europe. However restrained might have been the use of American leverage on behalf of an open sphere and the Yalta Declaration on Liberated Europe, the constant American allusions to free elections, self-government, and open trade, the American eagerness to conclude peace treaties, and the American desire to expedite the withdrawal of Soviet troops cast doubt on the American commitment to accept a Soviet sphere, as defined in the Kremlin. But at the same time, Moscow's refusal to ensure free elections and to establish representative governments constituted clear-cut violations of wartime agreements and engendered legitimate consternation in Washington.

While officials in Moscow and Washington could charge one another with violations of the meaning of Yalta in Poland and Eastern Europe, the situation in Germany was initially less ambiguous. At Yalta, Stalin and Churchill argued heatedly over the amount of German reparations. Ultimately they agreed to create a Reparation Commission in Moscow. The commission was to apply the principles under which Germany was obligated to "pay in kind for the losses caused by her to the Allied nations in the course of the war." The United States and the Soviet Union concurred that the "Moscow Reparation Commission should take in its initial studies as a basis for discussion the suggestion of the Soviet Government that the total sum ... should be 20 billion dollars and that 50 percent of it should go to the Union of Soviet Socialist Republics." Churchill still refused to accept this compromise, but Roosevelt supported it. Based on the discussion at Yalta, Stalin had good reason to believe that the American government sympathized with his desire for large reparations, so long as they were not paid in cash. Moreover, American officials knew that Stalin expected metallurgical and other capital goods factories from the western zones. These reparations in kind would help rebuild the Soviet Union as well as guarantee Germany's postwar emasculation. Indeed throughout the Crimean deliberations Roosevelt did not contest the amount of reparations with Stalin; the ambiguity of the final agreement represented an American–Soviet attempt to accommodate British objections.

In the months between Yalta and Potsdam, however, American priorities changed significantly. In February, Roosevelt still sought Soviet cooperation to guarantee Germany's defeat and to perpetuate the wartime coalition into the postwar era. By July, Truman sought to revive Germany's coal production as a means to resurrect Western Europe and to contain the forces of revolution, even if it meant jeopardizing Soviet–American relations. Between February and July, the war in Europe ended and American officials became fully aware of the prospects for chaos, famine, and upheaval. In April, Assistant Secretary of

War John McCloy visited Germany and Western Europe. When he returned, he talked to Secretary of War Henry L. Stimson and President Truman. "He gave me a powerful picture of the tough situation that exists in Germany," wrote Stimson, "—something that is worse than anything probably that ever happened in the world. I had anticipated the chaos, but the details of it were appalling." During the following weeks, Under Secretary of State Joseph Grew as well as Acheson, Clayton, and Byrnes became alarmed by portentous signs of revolutionary upheaval. On June 24th, Truman wrote Churchill, "From all the reports that reach me, I believe that without immediate concentration on the production of German coal we will have turmoil and unrest in the very areas of Western Europe on which the whole stability of the continent depends." A few days later it was decided that the President would issue a directive to ensure the export of 25 million tons of coal from Germany by April 1946. This objective was to take priority over all other considerations except the health and safety of occupation troops and the redeployment of Allied forces to the Pacific.

These considerations decisively shaped American attitudes at Potsdam and impelled American officials to distance themselves from the position taken by Roosevelt at Yalta. Byrnes sidestepped proposals for four-power control of the Ruhr industries, rejected the $20 billion reparation figure, argued that the Soviets should take reparations from their own zone in Germany, and proposed a settlement that safeguarded the potential resources of the Ruhr, Saar, and Rhine for Western European recovery. Molotov and Vyshinsky went to see Joseph Davies, whom Truman had invited to Potsdam as one of his closest advisers, and expressed disbelief at the overt violation of the meaning and spirit of the Yalta compromises. Neither Davies nor Byrnes nor Clayton really disputed Soviet claims. From the perspective of the State Department, however, new circumstances dictated new priorities and a reinterpretation of Yalta. It was now evident that Germany could not pay $20 billion without risking economic chaos and revolution throughout Western Europe and without imposing a permanent drain on American financial resources. Nor could the Soviets be allowed to use their claim for reparations as a means to gain leverage over economic developments in Germany's industrial heartland. So a new formula had to be devised that entitled the Kremlin to reparations primarily from their own zone in eastern Germany rather than "from the national wealth of Germany . . . ," as stipulated in the Yalta accord. Transfers from the western zones to the Soviet Union were made contingent on a number of variables that the Kremlin had little means of controlling.

Stalin grudgingly accepted these conditions in return for Truman's equally grudging acquiescence to the Kremlin's position on the western border of Poland. Unlike the Soviet concession on reparations, which represented Soviet acquiescence to American backtracking both on the amount and the sources of reparations, the American acceptance of the Oder–Neisse line did not constitute any capitulation to a new Soviet demand or to a reversal of the Yalta language. Indeed the Crimean accord "recognise[d] that Poland must receive substantial accessions of territory in the North and West." The question at Potsdam was where to draw the new lines. Although Truman did not like the Soviet position, he could not claim that the Soviets were repudiating a previous commitment. On the other hand, Soviet feelings about the reversal of the American position on reparations would remain a sore point because that issue was so integrally related to Soviet reconstruction needs and to Soviet fears of a revitalized Germany. A year later, taking advantage of a very rare moment when Molotov seemed cordial and communicative, Byrnes inquired, "what is really in your hearts and minds on the subject of Germany?" Nothing more than had been asked at Yalta, Molotov responded: ten billion dollars in reparations and four-power control of the Ruhr.

Apprehension that revolutionary forces in Western Europe might bring Soviet influence to the Atlantic and Mediterranean impelled American officials to repudiate the Yalta agreements on Germany just as fear that democratic forces might bring Western influence and unfriendly governments to the Danube impelled the Kremlin to ignore the principles in the Yalta Declaration on Liberated Europe. And both sides perceived that the actions of the other constituted threats to national security interests. The Americans saw Soviet domination of Eastern Europe as a means to abet Soviet recovery, set back rehabilitation in Western Europe, and lay the groundwork for revolutionary advances in Western Europe and the Mediterranean, thereby enhancing the Kremlin's long-term economic potential and strategic capabilities to wage war against the United States, should it choose to do so in the future. In turn, the Kremlin suspected that the Anglo–Americans might be trying to absorb Germany's industrial heartland into an anti-Bolshevik coalition.

The Eastern Asian provisions of the Yalta agreements also generated recriminations and ill will on both sides. During the Crimean meeting, Roosevelt secretly negotiated a Far Eastern protocol with Stalin. Almost no one but Harriman was privy to the details of the Stalin–Roosevelt discussions. Roosevelt wanted a Soviet pledge to go to war against Japan shortly after Germany's capitulation. Stalin agreed, provided that the United States recognized the status quo in Outer Mongolia, Soviet annexation of the Kuriles and southern Sakhalin, a Soviet naval base at Port Arthur, and preeminent Soviet interests in the port of Dairen and on the Manchurian railroads. Roosevelt worried about making a deal behind Chiang Kai-shek's back. He agreed to Stalin's conditions, however, provided the Kremlin recognized Chiang, offered no support to the Chinese communists, and accepted Chinese national sovereignty over Manchuria. Stalin concurred. Significantly, Harriman warned Roosevelt that he was giving away too much and that the Soviets could easily interpret the language to mean Soviet domination of Manchuria. But the President felt that he was getting much of what he wanted if he could secure Stalin's support for Chiang, if he could tie down Japanese armies in China with Soviet forces, if he could devote American attention to the occupation and control of the Japanese mainland, and if he could secure formal Soviet recognition of Chinese sovereignty over Manchuria.

As soon as Roosevelt died, Harriman pressed for a reevaluation of the Yalta protocol on the Far East. Although few officials knew exactly what it contained, there was widespread disaffection with the prospect of Soviet gains in East Asia. During May and June, the highest level officials in the War and State departments continually discussed options for constraining Soviet gains in East Asia, including repudiation or renegotiation of the Yalta provisions. Stimson, Marshall, and Army officials cautioned against repudiation because they realized Soviet armies would be able to march into Manchuria and do as they pleased unless restrained by some accord. Abrogating Yalta would not contain the Kremlin in Northeast Asia; indeed outright repudiation might alienate Soviet leaders and whet their appetite. Instead Harriman and the State Department sought to define the language Roosevelt accepted at Yalta in ways that would promote American self-interest and that would circumscribe postwar Soviet influence in Northeast Asia.

In this respect, the successful testing of the atomic bomb on July 16 exerted an important influence on American policy. During the spring of 1945, top military officials gradually revised their view on the need for Soviet intervention in the Pacific War. Prior to the Trinity test, however, Truman sought Soviet participation. He traveled to Potsdam with this objective among his foremost concerns. But once the President received a comprehensive account of the atomic test's huge success, his attitudes changed. He checked with Stimson and Marshall on the need for Soviet participation in the war against Japan. Reassured again that intervention was not a military necessity, Truman immediately sent a telegram to Chiang Kai-shek, encouraging him to pursue further negotiations with the Soviet Union until the Chinese secured an interpretation of the Yalta accords acceptable to them and compatible with American interests. Since the Soviets had stated that they would not go to war until the Chinese accepted the substance of the Yalta agreements, Truman and Byrnes now hoped that a stalemate in the Chinese–Soviet talks would delay Soviet intervention and would allow the atomic bomb to end the Far Eastern war before the Soviets could consolidate their Yalta gains. Byrnes "determined to outmaneuver Stalin on China," noted the secretary of state's closest aide. "Hopes Soong [the Chinese Foreign Minister] will stand firm and then Russians will not go in war [sic]. Then he feels Japan will surrender before Russia goes to war and this will save China."

While Leahy thought this strategy was naive, Truman and Byrnes were intent on bringing the war to a rapid conclusion and containing Soviet power in East Asia. Much to the chagrin of Stalin and Molotov, the American and British governments issued the Potsdam ultimatum to the Japanese without consulting Soviet officials. Moreover, when high level Soviet–Chinese talks resumed in Moscow after the Potsdam Conference, Ambassador Harriman again urged Soong to contest Soviet privileges at Dairen and Soviet controls over the Manchurian railroads. Although the Yalta accords called for the restoration of Soviet rights in Manchuria as they had existed prior to the 1904 Russo–Japanese War, Harriman made a tenacious effort to define the "preeminent interests" of the Kremlin in as narrow a way as possible. Stalin was willing to accept numerous concessions, yet remonstrated that Harriman appeared to be seeking to reverse the meaning of the Crimean accords, especially as they related to Soviet security rights around Dairen. At the very least Harriman's actions contravened the American obligation, as specified in the Yalta accords, to "take measures in order to obtain [Chiang Kai-shek's] concurrence" with the provisions on

Outer Mongolia and the Manchurian ports and railroads.

In fact, Truman and his closest advisers often acted as if the United States had never entered into any secret agreement on the Far East. At the first cabinet meeting after he returned from Potsdam and after the atomic bombing of Hiroshima and Nagasaki, Truman denied the existence of any agreement relating to Manchuria. At almost the same time, the President sent a message to Stalin asking for American base rights in the Kuriles. The Soviet dictator replied with a stinging rebuff, causing Truman much embarrassment and prompting him to redefine his request. Notwithstanding this development, Secretary of State Byrnes still refused to acknowledge the concessions made at Yalta, and Under Secretary of State Acheson publicly intimated in January 1946 that the Kremlin had no right to the Kuriles. In response, the Kremlin released a statement quoting the exact language of the secret protocol signed at Yalta. The equivocation of American officials was partly due to Truman's ignorance of the terms of Yalta and partly due to Byrnes's fear of facing a domestic political debate over the Yalta provisions. But whatever their motives, American circumlocution could not have but triggered doubts in the Kremlin about American willingness to adhere to the Yalta language that called upon "The Heads of the three Great Powers [to ensure] . . . that these claims of the Soviet Union shall be unquestionably fulfilled after Japan has been defeated.

Soviet actions in East Asia, of course, did not always encourage American confidence. Much to the disappointment of the Truman Administration, the Soviets dismantled and carried off Japanese factories in Manchuria. On several occasions, Soviet commanders relinquished Japanese arms to Chinese communist partisans and allowed them to consolidate their hold in several localities. Furthermore, Soviet troops remained in Manchuria several weeks beyond the February 1946 deadline for their withdrawal, and Chinese communist propaganda often resembled that emanating from the Kremlin. The difficulty was in reconciling the Soviet pledge to respect Chinese sovereignty over Manchuria with the Yalta language which also recognized the Soviets' "preeminent interests" on the two key Manchurian railroads and in the port of Dairen. Yet Russian officers often collaborated with Chiang's forces, a fact that was dramatically underscored when Chiang repeatedly requested that Stalin delay Russian troop withdrawals. In so doing, the Soviets completed their Yalta commitments "to render assistance to China with its armed forces for the purpose of liberating China from the Japanese yoke." The Kremlin certainly wished to enhance its influence in China, as did the United States, but according to Walter Robertson, the American Chargé in China, there was no proof of collusion between Chinese communist and Soviet forces in early 1946. In fact, General George Marshall, who spent most of that year in China seeking to mediate the internal strife, held the Nationalists, rather than the Communists, more responsible for the persistence of civil conflict and for the initial breakdown of his peacemaking efforts.

Recriminations over Other Agreements

Neither America's own lackluster commitment to Yalta nor the ambiguity and tentativeness of Soviet actions caused Truman to reassess his initial conviction that the Soviets were violating their agreements. If any doubts persisted, the Soviet failure to withdraw Russian armies from northern Iran by March 2, 1946 appeared irrefutable proof of the Kremlin's nefarious intentions. No one could question the clarity of the 1942 agreement between the Soviet Union, Great Britain, and Iran that called for the evacuation of British and Russian troops from Iran six months after the end of hostilities. At the Potsdam, London, and Moscow conferences, Byrnes inquired whether the Kremlin would adhere to its commitment to withdraw. When Stalin and Molotov equivocated and talked of Soviet strategic concerns in the Caucasus, American officials sneered at the implication that Soviet interest could be endangered in an area where there was no formidable adversary, present or potential. When Soviet troops did not depart in February and when Soviet leaders entered into negotiations with the Iranian government over prospective concessions in northern Iran, American officials were infuriated. In dramatic moves underscoring the rift in the grand alliance, the United States prodded Iran to bring charges against the Kremlin before the United Nations; Byrnes made a tough public speech; and George Kennan presented a formal diplomatic note to the Kremlin calling for an explanation of the Soviets' failure to adhere to agreements.

The public sanctimoniousness of the American position nicely concealed the considerations that were prompting American officials in Washington to make some of the same decisions that their counterparts were making in Moscow. In January and February 1946, American policymakers faced the fact that their own wartime agreements with many countries, including Portugal, Iceland, Equador, Denmark, and Panama, called for the evacuation of American troops from bases established during the war against the Axis. Several of these governments were pressing for American withdrawal and resented any infringement on their sovereignty now that the wartime emergency was over. American officials fretted as they contemplated the prospect of withdrawing from critical bases in the Azores, Iceland, and Greenland (and from not-so-critical ones in Galapagos and the environs surrounding the canal zone in Panama). In April the Joint Chiefs of Staff (JCS) resolved that "There are military considerations which make inadvisable the withdrawal of U.S. forces from overseas bases on the territory of foreign nations in every instance in strict accordance with the time limitation provision of the existing agreement with the foreign government concerned." State Department officials concurred in this viewpoint.

Secretary of State Byrnes, Secretary of the Navy Forrestal, and Secretary of War Robert P. Patterson often discussed this issue at their meetings. They were embarrassed by the prospect that American actions in areas of strategic importance to the United States might contradict the high moral tone taken by the American government over the Soviet presence in Iran. Since Galapagos was not so essential, Byrnes, Patterson, and Forrestal agreed to withdraw, provided it was understood that if trouble arose, American troops would be reinserted with or without an agreement. As for the Azores and Iceland, temporary agreements were quickly negotiated that paid obeisance to Portuguese and Icelandic sovereignty and that nicely camouflaged the retention of many American base privileges, sometimes with the use of military personnel dressing in civilian garb. Yet when the Kremlin worked out a deal with Iran that provided for an oil concession to the Kremlin in return for the evacuation of Soviet troops, American officials ridiculed it. They pushed for the total excision of Soviet influence lest Soviet leaders use the concession as a cloak for furthering Soviet military goals or for retaining Soviet troops disguised as civilians.

The ironic parallels, of course, went unnoticed by American officials. While American actions and contraventions of agreements were ennobled by national self-interest and the strategic imperative of defense in depth, American officials would not attribute similar motives to the Kremlin. Although the considerations prompting both the retention and then the belated withdrawal of Russian troops from Iran still remain obscure, one suspects that Soviet military planners were eager to capitalize upon the presence of Soviet troops in Iran to safeguard their strategic interests, especially to help protect their petroleum fields and refining industry. They certainly must have known, as did American planners, that in 1940 the British and French contemplated bombing Soviet oil fields in the Caucasus in order to deny petroleum to the Nazis. Soviet planners, having observed the functioning of the Persian Corridor during World War II, must also have been wary of its future use in wartime if it should be controlled by an adversary. If they were not, they would have been remiss because the initial (and tentative) plans of the United States for waging war against the Soviet Union envisioned, among other things, an air assault from the south (from bases at Cairo–Suez). These war plans also denoted a route through the Balkans or through Iran as one of the few likely avenues for a land invasion of the Soviet Union, should it ever become necessary. If such ideas, however preposterous they may now seem, turned up in American war plans, it is not too improbable that Soviet leaders may also have been worrying about these contingencies, especially as they would have impinged on Soviet vital interests.

Just as the Iranian crisis was ebbing in May 1946 and the Soviets were completing their belated troop withdrawal, General Lucius Clay formally and unilaterally suspended delivery of reparations from the American occupation zone in Germany. The Soviets protested but to no avail. Clay's action was in response to the failure of the four occupation powers to agree on the economic unification and administration of Germany, as provided for in the Potsdam agreement. Indeed, a few months after Clay's decision, Clifford and Elsey cited the Soviet Union's actions in Germany as one of the litany of items demonstrating Soviet perfidy and untrustworthiness. Yet Clay himself did not blame the Soviet Union for the impasse in Germany. Nor did his superiors in Washington. In June 1946 Secretary of War Patterson and Assistant Secretary Howard C. Petersen, the officials responsible for the implementation of occupation policy, wrote the President that however much the Soviets might benefit from economic unrest and chaos in the western zones of Germany (and in Western Europe), it was the French, not the Soviets, who were the source of the problem and who were most egregiously disregarding the Potsdam accords.

The Potsdam agreements were imprecise and provided ample opportunity for self-serving interpretations. Two of the most knowledgeable historians dealing with occupation policy refrain from assigning any special responsibility to the Kremlin for the breakdown of allied unity in Germany. The policies of both the United States and the USSR were beleaguered with contradictory impulses; each government tried desperately to define Potsdam in ways that promoted its own interest. By the summer of 1946, for example, the United States had determined that the reconstruction needs of Germany and Western Europe meant that no reparations from current production could go to the Soviet Union. Since Potsdam did not explicitly mandate such transfers, State Department officials argued that the Kremlin was not entitled to them (even though they had been explicitly mentioned in the Yalta agreements). Most foreign governments, including the British, did not share the American view. Yet the Americans were reluctant to modify their position—not because the legal case was unassailable—but because they were much more concerned with the "first charge" and economic unification principles, also incorporated in the Potsdam provisions.

The "first charge" principle meant that reparations should not be paid until German exports were sufficient to finance German imports (thereby reducing U.S. occupation costs and abetting economic reconstruction in Western Europe). Yet the "first charge" principle was of little importance to the Kremlin, whose representatives continually insisted that the Western powers should comply with the reparations obligations spelled out at Yalta and Potsdam. Their argument was well founded because section 19 of the Potsdam agreement on economic principles explicitly exempted the transfer of equipment and products from the western zones to the Soviet Union from the application of the "first charge" principle. Notwithstanding the legitimacy of their position, Soviet leaders' contempt for the "first charge" principle and their tacit support of French opposition to the economic unification of Germany provoked Byrnes in mid-1946 to threaten a reconsideration of Poland's western border. Since the boundary had been the key Soviet achievement at Potsdam and the trade-off for Soviet acceptance of Byrnes's reparation formula, the American threat must have prompted Soviet officials to wonder who indeed was adhering to agreements.

Assessments of Compliance

The record of adherence to agreements at the onset of the Cold War is not a simple one to assess. Truman and his advisers correctly emphasized substantial shortcomings in the Soviet performance. Soviet leaders violated the Declaration on Liberated Europe in the Balkans and never carried out their pledge to hold free elections in Poland. They meddled in the internal affairs of Iran and were slow to withdraw from that nation. They interpreted "preeminent interests" in Manchuria broadly. They placed more emphasis on the extraction of reparation payments than on the economic unification of Germany. Notwithstanding these facts, the indictment of Soviet compliance written by Clifford and Elsey and articulated by Truman grossly simplified reality. The Soviet understanding of the Yalta provision on the Polish Provisional Government, the Soviet view of the Yalta and Potsdam provisions on Germany, and Soviet expectations in Manchuria were not inconsistent with reasonable interpretations of those agreements. And prior to the proclamation of the Truman Doctrine and the announcement of the Marshall Plan, the Kremlin's actions in Eastern Europe did not consistently contravene Yalta's democratic principles. However much American officials remonstrated about Soviet perfidy in Poland, Rumania, and Bulgaria, they acknowledged that free elections initially occurred in Hungary and Czechoslovakia and that acceptable governments were established in Austria and Finland.

By citing Soviet violations, however, American officials excused their own departure from wartime accords and rationalized their adoption of unilateral measures to safeguard American national security interests. But these American initiatives were not simply responses to Soviet transgressions; for the most part Soviet violations did not trigger and cannot be said to have legitimated America's own record of non-compliance. Most Soviet actions in Eastern Europe during the winter and spring of 1945, for example, were legally permissible under the armistice agreements and were compatible with a host of Anglo–Soviet understandings. However reprehensible was the imposition of a new government on Rumania, the Soviets were acting within their rights. Since the war against Germany was still underway, since Rumania was governed by the armistice agreement of September 12, 1944, since the Soviet High Command was authorized to act on behalf of the Allied powers, and since the Declaration on Liberated Europe did not supplant the armistice accord, the Soviets were not behaving illegally. Likewise, the Soviet position on the composition of the Polish Provisional Government, the issue that more than any other at the time engendered acrimony, was well within the bounds of any reasonable interpretation of the meaning of the Yalta compromises.

The officials who encouraged Truman to talk tough to Molotov in April 1945 were not motivated by legal niceties. Harriman, Leahy, and Forrestal were frightened by the great vacuums of power that were emerging as a result of the defeat of Germany and Japan. They recognized that the Kremlin would be in a position to fill those vacuums. Although they did not seek a rupture in the great wartime coalition, they were convinced that Soviet power had to be limited. If it were not, and if Soviet leaders proved to have unlimited ambitions, they might use their predominance in Central and Eastern Europe to project their influence into Western Europe, the eastern Mediterranean, and the Middle East. Prudence, therefore, dictated a policy of containment. The Yalta agreements provided a convenient lever to try to pry open Eastern Europe and to resist Soviet predominance, a predominance that temporarily (and regrettably) had been accepted in the armistice agreements (and, for the British, in the percentages deal) because of wartime exigencies.

But by April 1945, the European war was in its concluding weeks, and American officials were reassessing the need for Soviet intervention in the Far Eastern struggle. The factors that had demanded compromise and concession at Yalta were no longer so compelling. Prodded by General John R. Deane, the head of the United States Military Mission in Moscow, the JCS formally reevaluated American dependence on Soviet assistance and concluded that however desirable Soviet military aid might be, American foreign policy should not be governed by this consideration. On the very day that Truman lectured Molotov on Soviet compliance, Admiral Leahy wrote in his diary, "It was the consensus of opinion ... that the time has arrived to take a strong American attitude toward the Soviets, and that no particular harm can now be done to our war prospects even if Russia should slow down or even stop its war effort in Europe and in Asia." At the same time, Under Secretary of State Joseph Grew and other high level foreign service officers repeatedly emphasized that the Soviet Union was incomparably weaker than the United States. If Washington asserted itself and acted with determination, the Soviets would retreat and perhaps even accept a "genuinely" representative government in Poland. This way of thinking prompted Truman's bellicose approach to Molotov on April 23.

A curious mixture of fear and power, not legal considerations, impelled American policymakers to disengage from their own commitments at Yalta. With the war ending in Europe, officials in the White House, the State Department, and the War Department looked at the prospects for postwar stability and were appalled by what they saw. The magnitude of economic dislocation and sociopolitical turmoil was frightening. "There is a situation in the world," Assistant Secretary of State Dean Acheson told the Senate Committee on Banking and Currency in July 1945, "which threatens the very foundations, the whole fabric of world organization which we have known in our lifetime and which our fathers and grandfathers knew." In liberated Europe, "You find that the railway systems have ceased to operate; that power systems have ceased to operate; the financial systems are destroyed. Ownership of property is in terrific confusion. Management of property is in confusion. Systems of law have to be changed." Not since the eighth century, when the Moslems split the world in two, had conditions been so portentous. Now again, the situation was "one of unparalleled seriousness, in which the whole fabric of social life might go to pieces unless the most energetic steps are taken on all fronts . . . ."

Acheson never mentioned the Soviet Union in his testimony; it was not to blame for the conditions he described. But Soviet leaders *might* exploit these conditions to enhance their power. Hence action had to be taken to cope with these circumstances. While Acheson pleaded for Senate ratification of the Bretton Woods agreements, his colleagues struggled to safeguard German coal, to boost German productivity, and to circumscribe the availability of reparations from the western zones, even if this meant a reversal of some of the understandings reached at Yalta. Likewise, State Department officials remonstrated over Soviet controls in Poland and Hungary not simply because the Yalta provisions on self-determination were being violated but because Polish and Hungarian natural resources, if left open to the West, could aid European recovery.

If fear of revolutionary turmoil inspired an autonomous reevaluation of American interests and of American commitments under the Yalta agreements, the atomic bomb stimulated an autonomous reconsideration of American military and diplomatic capabilities. No one was more enamored of the bomb as a diplomatic lever than was Secretary of State Byrnes. From the day in early May that Stimson first briefed the secretary-designate on the Manhattan Project, Byrnes could not resist thinking that the bomb would be his trump card. On the one hand, it might precipitate a quick Japanese capitulation, thereby preempting Soviet intervention in Manchuria and obviating the need to make good on the concessions accorded Stalin in Yalta's secret protocol on the Far East. On the other hand, Byrnes also felt that "our possessing and demonstrating the bomb would make Russia more manageable in Europe." Just how this would occur, Byrnes never made clear, but American possession of the bomb certainly boosted his (and Truman's) initial determination to seek the revision of the reparation provisions of the Yalta agreement, to extricate the United States from the Far Eastern protocol of the Crimean accords, and to elicit Soviet compliance with the American interpretation of the application of the Declaration on Liberated Europe to Bulgaria and Rumania. In his diary, Davies noted that Byrnes felt the "Bomb had given us great power, and that in the last analysis, it would control."

Roosevelt's death catapulted Byrnes to the forefront of American diplomacy. Since Truman depended on him for a correct interpretation of Yalta, Byrnes's mistaken understanding of the provisions regarding Poland and the Declaration on Liberated Europe initially contributed to the President's erroneous impression that the Soviets were violating the meaning of Yalta. But by the time of the Potsdam Conference in July 1945, Truman and Byrnes certainly grasped the fundamentals, if not all the details, of Yalta's provisions on Germany and the Far East. Their efforts, then, to safeguard the open door in Manchuria and to limit reparations from the western zones of Germany did not stem from ignorance of the Crimean decisions but from their estimation of American needs and capabilities. They were responding not to Soviet transgressions, but to the real and prospective growth of Soviet power. By seeking to backtrack on concessions granted at Yalta, however, they stimulated legitimate queries from Soviet leaders about their own compliance record.

In fact, after the capitulation of Germany, American officials assessed the risks and benefits of compliance and concluded that they had little to gain from adherence to many wartime agreements. On the one hand, compliance might allay Soviet suspicions, temper Soviet ambitions, and encourage Soviet officials to define their self-interest in terms of an interdependent relationship with the United States. On the other hand, compliance might lock the United States into a strait jacket while the Kremlin consolidated its power in Eastern Europe and Manchuria, capitalized upon economic chaos and political ferment in Western Europe, and exploited anti-colonial sentiments in Asia. Given the risks, American officials chose to define compliance in ways that sought to circumscribe Soviet power in Eastern Europe, maximize American flexibility in western Germany, and buttress Chinese Nationalist interests in China. This orientation meant that, from the onset of the postwar era, American officials were interpreting the wartime accords in ways that placed a higher priority on containing Soviet power and projecting American influence than on perpetuating the wartime alliance.

The Soviets, too, had to weigh the benefits of compliance. On the one hand, compliance might moderate American suspicions, elicit American loans, and reap large reparation payments from the western zones in Germany; on the other hand, compliance might lead to the establishment of hostile governments on the Soviet periphery, risk the incorporation of a revived Germany into a British (or Anglo–American bloc), and arrogate the Kremlin and Eastern Europe to a position of financial and economic dependency. Given these parameters, Soviet officials chose to define compliance in ways that maximized their authority in Eastern Europe, circumscribed Western power in eastern Germany, and enhanced the Kremlin's flexibility in China. These decisions meant that Soviet officials preferred to place higher priority on unilateral safeguards of their security than on preserving a cooperative approach to postwar reconstruction.

As both Moscow and Washington were prone to see the costs of compliance greatly outweighing the benefits, they began to take tentative steps to jettison or reinterpret key provisions of wartime accords. Each such step magnified the suspicions of the potential adversary and encouraged reciprocal actions. Before long, wartime cooperation was forgotten, the Cold War was underway, and a new arms race was imminent. Neither side was innocent of responsibility; each side felt vulnerable, maneuvered to take advantage of opportunities, and manipulated or violated the compromises, loopholes, and ambiguities of wartime agreements.

Lessons for Contemporary U.S. Policy

It is worth remembering the past when contemplating the future. The Weinberger/Perle thesis, like the Clifford/Elsey report, offers a beguilingly simple approach to the conduct of American diplomacy with the Kremlin. Briefly stated, their thesis is that Soviet violations of agreements constitute a threat to national security; hence the United States should free itself from constraints and take unilateral action to safeguard its vital interests. Before accepting this view, its premises and conclusion deserve careful scrutiny. The history of compliance at the onset of the Cold War can be instructive.

Although charges of Soviet malfeasance in the fulfillment of their international obligations ring true because of the noxious nature of their internal regime, these allegations should be investigated carefully. The Kremlin's pattern of compliance with wartime agreements in the immediate aftermath of World War II appears no better or worse than the American record. American disillusionment was great because American leaders misled the American public about the real meaning of wartime agreements. American policymakers hesitated to discuss their concessions; hence Soviet officials and the American public possessed contrasting expectations about what constituted acceptable behavior. Deception created neither understanding at home nor trust abroad.

Allegations of Soviet violations, therefore, need to be checked against the negotiating history of the agreements in question. The records of the Yalta Conference make clear, for example, that the Soviet expectation for Lublin predominance in the Polish Provisional Government was a reasonable interpretation of the Crimean agreement. Likewise, the Soviet belief that the United States conceded a sphere of influence in Eastern Europe was a reasonable inference for the Kremlin to draw from Roosevelt's acquiescence to the deletion of enforcement provisions from the Declaration on Liberated Europe. Stalin never concealed his view that free elections and self-determination had to be reconciled with his determination to have friendly governments on his borders.

The temptation to make unqualified allegations of Soviet duplicity should be resisted because unsubstantiated charges can distract attention from more fundamental threats to national security. In 1945 and 1946, socioeconomic strife and revolutionary nationalist ferment constituted a much graver danger to the core interests of the United States than did Soviet violations of wartime agreements, numerous though they were. Alleged Soviet violations of the Yalta accords in Manchuria, for example, hardly accounted for the real problems in Northeast Asia. Likewise, Soviet infractions of the Yalta and Potsdam provisions on liberated Europe and Germany hardly constituted the source of

Europe's travail in the aftermath of depression, war, and Nazi domination. But policymakers in the Truman Administration, including Clifford and Elsey, felt they could evade ambiguities, clarify options, and mobilize domestic support most effectively by dwelling on Soviet behavior rather than on indigenous unrest. The result was to confuse cause and effect: Americans were educated to view Soviet transgression as the cause of postwar turmoil and as the principal threat to American national security rather than to see the Kremlin as the primary beneficiary of socioeconomic unrest and revolutionary nationalist upheaval.

The result was that Americans never really grasped the reasons for and the extent of their own government's disengagement from the wartime agreements. The United States backslided on its own commitments and moved toward a policy of unilateralism because American officials believed that the capitulation of Germany and Japan and the spread of postwar unrest jeopardized the entire balance of power on the Eurasian land mass. From the time Truman took office, which nearly coincided with the end of the European war, his advisers sought to extricate the United States from many wartime commitments in order to buttress democratic capitalism in Europe and to contain communism and revolutionary nationalism in Northeast Asia and elsewhere around the world. Finally, in the spring of 1947, claiming that the Soviets had not abided by a "single" agreement, Truman insisted that he had to resort to "other methods" and embarked on a policy of unrestrained competition. Unilateralism produced benefits, but one should not minimize the costs. The total clampdown on Eastern Europe followed, rather than preceded, the Truman Doctrine and the Marshall Plan; the blockade of Berlin followed rather than preceded the decisions to suspend reparations, boost the level of German industry, and carry out the currency reforms in the western zones. In other words, unrestrained competition helped expedite the recovery of Western Europe and Japan, but it also contributed to the division of Europe, the American conflicts in Korea and Vietnam, and the dissipation of trillions of dollars on the arms race.

Yet Weinberger and Perle, like their predecessors in the Truman Administration, still wish to use allegations of Soviet noncompliance as a smokescreen to legitimate the lifting of restraints on American actions and to justify a policy of unilateralism. The advantages and disadvantages of a policy of unrestrained competition merit discussion.

But the proponents of unilateralism commit a disservice and engage in historical distortion when they unqualifiably charge Soviet treachery in the implementation of agreements and when they exploit Americans' self-image of wounded innocence. The experiences of the early Cold War reveal that wartime agreements were violated not by the Soviets alone but by all the signatories and not necessarily because of evil intent but because of apprehension and expediency. Moreover, the greatest threats to American security emanated not from Soviet actions but from exogenous factors. Such knowledge should not cause despair. Notwithstanding the tarnished record of compliance in the past, there is still hope for the future if officials in Moscow and Washington can resist the temptations of unilateral advantage and if they can remain vigilant in the enforcement of their own behavior as well as that of their adversary.

Further Reading for Part VI
(See also Further Reading at the end of Part VII)

Anderson, Terry H. *The United States, Great Britain, and the Cold War.* Columbia, MO, 1981.

Barnett, Corelli. *The Collapse of British Power.* London, 1972.

Buhite, Russell D. *Decisions at Yalta: An Appraisal of Summit Diplomacy.* Wilmington, DE, 1986.

Clemens, Diane S. *Yalta.* New York, 1970.

Dimbleby, David. *An Ocean Apart: The Relationship between Britain and America in the Twentieth Century.* New York, 1988.

Divine, Robert A. *Roosevelt and World War II.* Baltimore, 1969.

———. *The Reluctant Belligerent: American Entry into World War II.* 2nd ed., New York, 1979.

Dobson, Alan P. *The Politics of the Anglo–American Economic Special Relationship 1940–1987.* New York, 1988.

Douglas, Roy. *From War to Cold War.* New York, 1981.

Eubank, Keith. *Summit at Teheran: The Untold Story.* New York, 1985.

Gaddis, John L. *The United States and the Origins of the Cold War 1941–1947.* New York, 1972; 2nd ed. 1976.

Gallicchio, Marc S. *The Cold War Begins in Asia: American East Asian Policy and the Fall of the Japanese Empire.* New York, 1988.

Harbutt, Fraser J. *The Iron Curtain, Churchill, America and the Origins of the Cold War.* New York, 1986.

Hathaway, Robert M. *Ambiguous Partnership. Britain and America, 1944–1947.* New York, 1981.

Herring, George C. *Aid to Russia 1941–1946. Strategy, Diplomacy, the Origins of the Cold War.* New York, 1973.

Kimball, Warren F., ed. *Churchill and Roosevelt: The Complete Correspondence.* Princeton, 1984.

Kuniholm, Bruce. *The Origins of the Cold War in the Near East.* Princeton, 1980.

Lash, Joseph P. *Roosevelt and Churchill, 1939–1941: The Partnership that Saved the West.* New York, 1976.

Loth, Wilfried. *The Division of the World 1941–1955.* New York, 1988.

Mastny, Vojtech. *Russia's Road to the Cold War: Diplomacy, Warfare, and the Politics of Communism, 1941–1945.* New York, 1979.

Reynolds, David. *The Creation of the Anglo–American Alliance, 1937–41: A Study in Competitive Cooperation.* Chapel Hill, 1982.

Sainsbury, Keith. *The Turning Point: Roosevelt, Stalin, Churchill, and Chiang Kai-Shek, 1943: The Moscow, Cairo, and Tehran Conferences.* New York, 1985.

Yergin, Daniel. *The Shattered Peace: The Origins of the Cold War and the National Security State.* Boston, 1977.

Part VII

What Was Needed for Allied Victory?

In hindsight the outcome of complex historical developments often appears inevitable. The logic of cause and effect suggests that since the Allies won the war, they must have also had what was needed to win it. Perhaps they did.

If the results of war depended on population and raw materials alone, certainly the Grand Alliance after 1941 had overwhelming advantage. The Soviet Union, the United States, and the United Kingdom had populations totaling 350 million people compared with less than 200 million for the Axis. When the other participants of both sides are added in, the balance is tipped much further in favor of the Allies. As for raw materials, the Allies had many times the sinews of war in coal reserves, iron ore, rubber, copper, nickel, lead, arable land, and oil. Except for Germany's coal mines, the Axis countries had scarcities of each of these. They also fell short in most other raw materials needed to engage in modern warfare.

The Axis powers also lacked access to world markets. They did not have the monetary reserves to make purchases abroad unless they could sell their products. Given, however, their relative weakness in manufacturing and the efforts of most countries to restrict imports during the depression, they could not buy what they lacked. The United States, France, the United Kingdom, and the Soviet Union produced 51 percent of the world's manufactured goods in 1938 to the 20 percent of Germany, Italy and Japan. By 1944 the Axis were further behind. American arms production soared from less than two billion dollars in 1939 to more than ninety billion by 1944, a forty-five-fold increase. German arms production, after its acceleration in 1942, grew by only five times between 1939 and 1944.

Wars are not lost and won by a calculus of addition and subtraction. The numbers of recruits and factory workers, weapons, ammunition, and stockpiles by themselves are only potential. War at its base is a contest of wills. It involves a science, however imperfect, of designing and implementing military strategies, tactics, and training which match changing technologies, geographic conditions, psychology, and diplomatic skills. The variables are complex and beyond the capacity of any individual or organization to predict with certainty. If that were not so, rational, sane opponents would first calculate the likely outcome of war and then yield without sacrificing the lives which war inevitably requires.

That, of course, did not happen during the Second World War, except in the case of minor powers such as Czechoslovakia in 1939, Denmark, and the Baltic states. Even small powers like Belgium, the Netherlands and Norway resisted militarily until overwhelmed by greater force. And it did not happen for those powers which were not invaded. Sweden, Switzerland, and Spain, for example, did not yield to Germany. However compliant they might have been in some cases with Nazis wishes, the uncertainties of the war allowed them to retain their sovereignty.

Those same uncertainties, it is important to remember, are also why major powers which were not victims of aggression did not act to defend those who were. Only the United Kingdom and France declared war on an Axis aggressor, Germany, without themselves first being attacked. The Soviet Union was a virtual ally of Germany for the first two years of the European conflict. Stalin made good his pledge to deliver vital raw materials and agricultural products until the day of the German invasion. The United States, though slowly and perhaps inevitably being drawn into war in the North Atlantic, only went to war in response to an attack on its own territory by Japan and a declaration of war by Germany and Italy.

By then, of course, the Axis faced opponents with superior potential. Allied victory became predictable; new supporters flocked to the banner of the United Nations. The Allies had the material edge, but could they keep the alliance together? That is the question partially addressed in Part VI above. In the field of intelligence, there hardly seems to have been a doubt (see Part IV) though the Germans needed only one slip-up by the Allies for the Ultra advantage to end. But what of the military struggle? or of the war between scientists for new weapons? Before the Anglo–German war of June 1940–June 1941 broadened into an Eurasian and oceanic conflict of unprecedented scale, there were turning points in which a different outcome might have shifted the global balance of power as rapidly as the German resurgence of 1938–1939 had altered the European balance. Thus, even after December 1941, the worldwide maelstrom remained a contest of political wills. Strategists and generals might still have reversed the course of history in one short day.

Military turning points during the Second World War are numerous. The major ones are taken up by Professor Levine in the first selection below. Clearly, had disasters like the fall of France continued, Germany would have won the war. Its victory would have swept Italy and Japan toward their ambitions too. There is room for disagreement as to whether France had superiority in arms and men in May 1940, but beyond doubt Germany's victory over its longtime enemy derived from something other than Nazi material preeminence. On what that derivation was, there is no agreement but plenty of suggestions. Were other turning points similar? Or was the fall of France the exception, psychologically devastating to the Allies because so unexpected and near the beginning of the war? Historians often apply the same indeterminacy to the Battle of Britain, Operation Barbarossa, the Battle of the Atlantic, the Battle of Midway, the American assault on Guadalcanal, the Anglo–American invasion of North Africa, the defeat of the German Afrika Korps, the long string of Soviet and German offensives and counteroffensives in western Russia, the Battle of Stalingrad, American success in devising an atomic bomb, German failure to wedge the Allies apart, the introduction of new military technologies (jets, rockets, improved submarines, etc.), and on and on. Turning points and contingencies abound throughout the war. Disregarding hindsight, did the realities of 1939 determine the world of 1945? Could there have been a significantly different global outcome? Above, we have examined similar questions from largely nonmilitary viewpoints. In Part VII we will confront the military ones, though without forgetting that war is always a political act and must be evaluated as such.

15

Alan J. Levine

Was World War II a Near-run Thing?

Most of the selections we have considered examine a single aspect of the war and reflect both the posing of new questions and the availability of previously inaccessible material. The conclusions drawn are not likely to be the last word, but they have

Reprinted by permission from the eighth issue of the *Journal of Strategic Studies.* Copyright 1978 by Frank Cass Co. Limited, 11 Gainsborough Road, London E11, England. Copyright Frank Cass and Co Ltd.

advanced our understanding of the war. However, in spite of more than four decades of research and debate, many issues remained unresolved. Moreover, even when consensus is reached on the basic questions, there remains the task of integrating new knowledge into old analyses. For this reason, the challenge of writing a comprehensive, up-to-date history of the Second World War remains and will likely remain for years to come. The fiftieth anniversary of the outbreak of war in Europe brought on a spate of new works, but few went beyond recounting the course of military conflict and high level diplomacy. Critics of even the most successful histories have not been satisfied.

One source of the perpetual appeal of the Second World War lies in its Manichaean conflict between absolute evil and the forces of good. In spite of some recent attempts by a few German historians to find some redeeming value in the Third Reich,[1] the Nazi portrait gallery excels all others in villainy, brutality and inhumanity. The mind and body recoil from the prospect that Hitler's gang might have won the war.

In the following article Professor Levine bravely takes on both the whole course of World War Two military history in its largest sense and, by implication, the heroic scale it achieved in the minds of those who fought against the Axis. Accomplished military historians are not eager to pass judgments on the scene from such a height. The demands on knowledge and intellectual acumen are formidable. In addition, Professor Levine's essay borders on counter-factual history, that is, writing about "what might have happened if . . . ," rather than focusing on unraveling and understanding what did happen.

The result, however risky, is worth the effort. His question stimulates us to look at many issues in a new light. The reader should consider whether Levine's opinions are prejudiced by knowing that the Allies won. What are the implications of his ideas for evaluating the length of the war? And for appraising wartime diplomacy among the Allies? Could the war have been won with less cost in lives?

Nearly 40 years have passed since the end of World War II. To a remarkable extent, that war remains vivid and meaningful, in a way quite unlike World War I after a comparable period of time had

[1]See Richard J. Evans, *In Hitler's Shadow: West German Historians and the Attempt to Escape from the Nazi Past* (New York, 1989).

elapsed. Interest in the war remains great. Yet despite—or perhaps because of —the enormous wealth of books and articles on the subject, a large number of popular misconceptions remain, many of them hold-overs from the war years.

Perhaps one of the more remarkable of these misconceptions is the notion that the Nazis came very close to winning the war. One of the curious aspects of this belief is that it seems to be far more prevalent in the former Allied countries than in Germany. It is strange that the heirs of what would, on the face of things, seem to have been an enormously superior victorious coalition feel compelled to "scare themselves" by reflecting on how close they came to disaster. At least, that is true in the West. The Soviets, by contrast, as exponents of a deterministic ideology, seem to regard an Allied and Soviet victory as inevitable. For once, perhaps, the Soviets' views may be somewhat closer to the truth than the view popular in the Western democracies. Ironically, their complacency may well be wrong as far as the Soviet Union itself is concerned, for the Nazis may well have come very close to defeating the USSR. But as far as the war as a whole is concerned, the Soviets are right: the chances of a complete Nazi triumph were certainly ex-tremely small, and probably non-existent. Even in 1940, Nazi Ger-many had inserted itself in a cul-de-sac. It may be impossible to prove a negative—that Germany could never have won the war—and it would certainly be wrong to be dogmatic on this speculative subject. If, however, this article is provocative of investigation and discussion, it will serve a useful purpose.

A number of reasons seem to account for the prevalence of a differ-ent view. For one thing, portraying World War II as a narrow escape (or a series of narrow escapes) from total disaster undoubtedly makes more interesting reading than showing it as tedious effort to deal with foes who, however terrible, were taking on a task that was just too big for them. Still, the notion is a curious one. It is not as though most of the revelations about Nazi leadership and planning since 1945 have been flattering. It is now clear that in many ways German preparation for war was ill-judged, that Hitler failed to mobilize the German econ-omy for an all-out war effort until 1942, and that not only Hitler's judgment but that of the professional heads of the armed forces was erratic in the extreme. The strength, or resolution, or both, of Germany's three principal foes was almost continually underestimated. A better, or more understandable, reason for the popular assumption may be the failure to separate the examination of the war itself, and especially the early German victories, from the disastrous *political* prelude to the war. This is highly understandable—to contemporaries, and to an observer looking backward, the French defeat of 1940 was just the horrible culmination of seven years of uninterrupted defeats the West had suffered at the hands of the Nazis. It could easily be seen as just another phase of seemingly endless suicidal bungling by the democracies since 1918.

The validity of such ideas, however, should not prevent us from recognizing that World War II was a military conflict, decided by the military strengths and weaknesses of the two sides. And, despite all the follies of the era between the world wars, Germany was never strong enough to win it.

In retrospect, even some of the German victories early in the war look less impressive, and they were not due to overwhelming superiority in numbers or weapons. Even in weapons and technology, the German forces were greatly superior only to their weakest and most backward foes, i.e., Poland, Norway and the Balkan countries. Generally speaking, Germany's victories were due to good leadership, training, and the revolutionary *use* made of tanks and tactical airpower. Against the Western European powers, the Germans enjoyed no qualitative edge in military equipment, and had a small superiority in numbers only in the air. It was doctrine, organization and leadership that enabled the Germans to defeat the French with a speed and ease they themselves never expected. Only the idiocies of a French leadership that had "learned nothing and forgotten everything" since 1918 made it possible to cut off the bulk of the French army and the British Expeditionary Force at one blow. Even in Poland and Yugoslavia, the blunders of the opposing military leaders made a considerable contribution to an admittedly inevitable German victory. Both armies tried to defend practically the whole frontiers of their countries, instead of pulling back to defensible positions. They let themselves be cut off by the Germans at the very start of the campaign. Once the Germans came up against stronger foes, who had had a chance to observe the tactics of blitzkrieg and learn from others' fatal mistakes, things were likely to be different. And, at least for offensive purposes, Germany was not ready for anything but a blitzkrieg.

A number of questions—military and political—must enter into any retrospective examination of Germany's chances to win the war after the defeat of France. The British Empire, almost alone, fought on against Hitler, but it could never have defeated a Nazi Germany controlling all of Europe. Much stronger forces had to be brought to bear. But what was the likelihood of such forces being assembled? Was American intervention inevitable, or a chancy thing due to clever manipulation by President Roosevelt, or even to Hitler's blunder in declaring war in December 1941? If American intervention was inevitable, could the Germans have defeated Britain before the U.S. came in or could bring its strength to bear? Could the Germans ever have defeated the USSR quickly enough to help them in their war with the Western powers? This article will examine these problems.

The above analysis is premised on one point: namely, that the entry of the United States, if it could use Britain as a safe and reliable base, would have meant an eventual German defeat. Without the bulk of the German army being tied down in the east, it is hard to see how the Western powers could have invaded the European mainland. But the fact that a conventional land campaign depended on Germany's invasion of the USSR, and that that invasion was defeated, does not mean that the whole Western war effort depended on Russia. Even conventional strategic bombing, though belatedly, deprived Germany of vital fuel and brought about her total economic collapse by March 1945, before the Allied armies were deep in the Reich. The success of this effort would not have been affected much by events in the east, as the Soviets tied down only a fraction of the Luftwaffe. The enormous superiority in air warfare of the Western allies is suggested by just two facts. By 1943 the Western air forces in the *Mediterranean theater alone* outnumbered the whole Luftwaffe. And in 1944, after Germany had finally fully mobilized for war, it was outproduced in planes by more than two to one by the United States alone, despite the fact that many of the American aircraft were large, expensive bombers, while German production was almost entirely concentrated on interceptors. (While the Germans were ahead in jets, the Allies would soon have caught up with them, and recent research shows that, contrary to general belief, the Germans could not have acquired jet fighters any sooner than they did.) In any case, the development of atomic weapons was bound to give the Western powers an advantage that would win the war for them, whatever happened on the battlefields of Russia and the Mediterranean, an advantage the Germans could not duplicate. There was never any prospect of Germany getting the atomic bomb before the

West. Even if the German atomic bomb project had not remained stuck at the point it reached in 1942, Germany did not have the spare industrial capacity to devote to a Manhattan-type project.

Analyzing the war is complicated by an issue that has become apparent only in the last decade: the role of "Ultra," the Allied code-breaking effort, which some have depicted as decisive in winning the war. If the code-breaking effort was indeed vital, then Allied victory in the war was hardly inevitable. Ultra was a great and valuable achievement, but also a fragile one. There was nothing obvious or inevitable about the code-breakers' victory. The Germans could certainly have nullified the Allied effort if they had had less reckless confidence in their communications security and had correctly sifted the evidence suggesting that the Allies were reading their messages. They could, in fact, have prevented the Allied success completely if they had only used the Enigma coding machine correctly. As those involved in the code-breaking effort have affirmed, only weaknesses in the Germans' operating procedures and failure to monitor their communications gave the Allies their chance. As Gordon Welchman has commented, "The [Enigma] machine would have been impregnable if it had been used properly." Some changes in the design of the Enigma machine would have defeated the Allies completely despite the Germans' procedural mistakes.

However, it is doubtful whether the code-breaking effort was the determining element in any of the decisive *defensive* battles of the war. Contrary to some early claims, code-breaking was not important in the Battle of Britain. The role of the reading of enemy messages in the Battle of the Atlantic is a somewhat more complicated issue, and will be examined in more detail below. However, it is doubtful whether it was decisive, though it was certainly extremely valuable. The British official history of the intelligence effort cautions that it was but one of many elements. While stressing the value of reading the U-boat code, it stresses that it should not be concluded that "reading the U-boat Enigma from the end of 1942 actually played a decisive part in defeating the second great U-boat campaign against the convoys which was unleashed in December 1942 and called off in May 1943." No one will question that Ultra saved many lives and shortened the war. However, it seems to have been more important in North Africa and the Mediterranean—in other words, in the secondary theaters—than in either the decisive defensive battles or the final victory in Western Europe.

With the defeat of France, Germany was the dominant power in Europe, and had a military position and sufficient freedom of action to make Britain's defeat inevitable, if not quick and easy. Considering the enormously greater resources of a German-controlled Europe, Britain's position, without outside help, was hopeless.

However, Britain was not completely isolated. Within a very short time after the fall of France, the United States adopted a policy of all aid "short of war" to Britain, though at first it actually had little help to give. While such aid would not have accomplished a German defeat, and it is not quite clear when President Roosevelt actually concluded that the United States itself would eventually have to enter the war, it is quite clear that he was always determined to prevent a Nazi victory. It is also quite clear that a great majority of the American people consistently shared that viewpoint, even though they were reluctant actually to enter the war. (A majority, however, *expected* eventual war with Germany.) Approximately 30 per cent of the American people were hardcore isolationists or pacifists, and opposed interventionist measures, but even of this minority few bore any love for Germany, which had very few defenders indeed. The large anti-interventionist minority, while able to fight a delaying action, was unable actually to defeat any of Roosevelt's pro-Allied measures. Isolationists were unable even to obtain the nomination of one of their own as Roosevelt's opponent in 1940. As Manfred Jonas has commented, "however difficult the struggle [against isolationism] may have seemed, there was, in fact, a continuous and relatively rapid retreat from isolationism after the start of the Second World War." The far-sighted German Ambassador to the United States, Dieckhoff, warned his government as early as 1937 that even most anti-interventionists disliked Germany and "the jump from a policy of isolation to one of intervention will not be very great." Even most leaders of America First, the primary anti-interventionist organization, were sensible enough to hope that Britain would not be defeated. Some even favored limited aid, though far less than the Roosevelt administration realized was necessary.

The folly and illusions of the isolationist minority were agonizing and frightening to more far-sighted Americans, but their importance should not be overestimated. Though popular opposition to an actual declaration of war remained considerable, the United States moved fairly steadily, if in retrospect too slowly, toward war during 1941. Part of Roosevelt's Cabinet (Secretaries Stimson, Ickes, Knox and Morgenthau), and not a few historians, thought he was unnecessarily cautious in his approach to war. As early as March 1941, however, Roosevelt indicated to the Cabinet that he hoped and expected that the Germans would provide an occasion for going to war.

In August 1941, Roosevelt indicated to Churchill that the American escort of convoys to Iceland would shortly produce an incident leading to America's entry into the war. The United States' occupation of Iceland in July 1941 had already put American forces within the naval war zone previously declared by Germany, and made such a clash inevitable. A battle between the U.S. destroyer *Greer* and U–652 led Roosevelt publicly to order the U.S. navy to attack German vessels on sight on 11 September. American ships escorted British transatlantic convoys and attacked, and were attacked by German submarines. In November, American ships captured a German blockade runner in the South Atlantic. Admiral Stark, the Chief of Naval Operations in 1941, and General Arnold, the Chief of Staff of the Army Air Force, both agreed that for practical purposes a state of de facto war with Nazi Germany existed from the shoot-on-sight order—not from Hitler's declaration of war in December 1941. Most of the leaders of America First were reduced to despair by the shoot-on-sight order. Contrary to what is generally recorded in our textbooks, therefore, war with Germany began at least partly as a result of intelligent American response to danger, not as the product of helpless drift and the Führer's suicidal impulses. Moreover, there seems to have been a high degree of inevitability about America's entry into the war.

Given the magnitude of the forces that were ultimately to be arrayed against them, the Nazis' chances of victory were thus reduced to the possibilities of quickly invading Britain or strangling the transatlantic supply line by submarine attack before the United States could mobilize its strength. Britain was indeed the almost indispensable base for American intervention in Europe. It was the only base from which a serious land invasion, or strategic bombing with conventional weapons, could be launched. (The possibility may also be suggested that a successful and quick conquest of the Soviet Union, at an early date, might have permitted Hitler to build up a continental Eurasian bloc all but invulnerable to assault, even by an intact Anglo–American alliance; but this notion will be dealt with later.)

At any rate, it can be accepted that Britain's survival in 1940 was probably essential to an Allied victory over Germany. Britain was vital not only for the Anglo–Americans; its survival was also indispensable for the Soviet Union. When Hitler turned to invade the USSR in 1941, he left 54 divisions—a quarter of his army—and 1500 planes—40 per cent of the Luftwaffe—behind to guard occupied Europe against a somewhat overestimated British threat. Albert Seaton, the leading historian of the Eastern front, has confidently asserted that had these forces been largely released for operations against the Soviets, the USSR would have been defeated.

What were the chances of Germany's achieving an early defeat of Britain by invasion, and of defeating the Western powers in the Battle of the Atlantic?

The Battle of Britain

Superficially, three possible ways of defeating Britain appeared to exist after the fall of France: invasion, an air–sea blockade of her ocean supply routes (e.g., success in the Battle of the Atlantic), and an indirect approach, involving the conquest of the Mediterranean and Middle East area.

Only a successful invasion, however, could *quickly* defeat Britain. Though Hitler in 1939 had believed that Britain, if it tried to hold out at all after the conquest of the Western European mainland, would fall as a result of an air–sea blockade, he lacked the means to accomplish this quickly—if at all. The German surface fleet, small to begin with, had largely been crippled in the Norwegian campaign, and the U-boat fleet was as yet only about one-fifth the size its commander believed was needed to achieve a decision. And Germany had only a few planes (and those improvised airliners) with sufficient range to attack convoys out on the ocean. The Mediterranean approach, if effective at all (this point will be explored later), would also consume a great deal of time.

It is widely, though not universally, supposed that in 1940 Britain came close to quick defeat by a German invasion. Only victory in the Battle of Britain saved her. An outnumbered Royal Air Force, against great odds, prevented the Luftwaffe from establishing air superiority over England and the Channel. Given the impotence of surface warships in the face of air superiority, and the weakness of the British Army, it is generally thought nothing could have stopped the Germans from crossing the Channel, had the RAF lost. And defeat was avoided by a terribly narrow margin. On examination, these ideas would seem to be very far from the truth.

It is not, however, true, as is sometimes claimed, that Hitler was never willing to invade England, because of his supposedly ambiguous attitude toward that nation. (This is often linked with another myth, that Hitler deliberately allowed the British forces to escape from Dunkirk in order to encourage Britain to make peace.) Hitler did in fact hope that the British would make peace after the fall of France, thus avoiding the whole problem of defeating it. When it became clear that the British would not deal with him, however, he was quite willing to invade. He may have been unenthusiastic about the project, for he had doubts about whether the plan would work—doubts which, as we shall see, were well-founded. But there is ample evidence that he was determined to attack if the prerequisites for the invasion, notably air superiority, could be fulfilled. The collection of the invasion fleet, which gravely interfered with Germany's inland water transportation system, alone showed that Hitler was serious. But the prerequisite of securing air superiority was unlikely to be fulfilled.

Churchill, by contrast, was rather sanguine. In his memoirs, he commented that "even in the irresolute years before the war, the essentials of sea and latterly air defence had been maintained." He was sure the RAF could defeat the Luftwaffe, and realized that the Germans had no proper landing craft. Retrospectively, he deemed the German invasion plan a "bleak proposition," and was skeptical of the invasion threat at the time. As he wrote later, "Certainly those who knew the most were the least scared." As usual, Churchill was right.

Post-war research has more or less destroyed the contemporary image of the Battle of Britain. The British fighter pilots were not a heavily outnumbered small band, who won victory by superior flying qualities and better planes. The German forces did enjoy numerical superiority, but it was far smaller than was imagined at the time. The quality of each side's pilots was about equal, and, while the RAF started out with inferior fighter formations and tactics, it soon adopted those employed by the Luftwaffe. The main German fighter, the Me 109, was about equal in performance to the Spitfire. Though three-fifths of the British single-engine fighter force was composed of the inferior Hurricanes, the superiority of the Me 109 over the Hurricane was not great, and the British to some extent compensated for the Hurricane's relative weakness by concentrating Hurricane formations against the German bombers.

In the critical category of fighter aircraft, the Germans enjoyed a superiority of about four to three at the start of the decisive battle in August. This was far smaller than the superiority of the victor in most offensive air campaigns in World War II. The British were never short of good planes: rather they lacked pilots. (They could easily have put one to two hundred more planes in the air, if they had had the men to fly them.)

Many sources nevertheless still insist that the British came close to disaster in the "third" phase of the Battle of Britain from 24 August to 6 September, and were saved at the last minute by the gross German blunder, often wrongly blamed on Hitler, of shifting the weight of attack against London. It is generally admitted that in the first and second phases of the battle—the initial sparring over the Channel in July, and Göring's massive assault of early and middle August—the British did well. Beginning on 24 August, however, the Luftwaffe clearly adopted a more sensible approach. All single-engine fighters were finally concentrated in the Calais area, on airfields as close as possible to Britain. Assisted by skillful diversionary operations, the Luftwaffe sent out smaller, more heavily escorted bomber formations, which concentrated on attacking fighter Command's airfields and control installations, causing considerable damage. During this period Fighter Command unquestionably suffered its heaviest losses of the battle. The ratio of German to British losses became much less favorable to the latter. The surviving experienced RAF pilots were very tired, and not a few felt that they were losing. Replacement pilots were being rushed through training, and were not as well prepared as their predecessors.

Recent examination, however, shows that the conclusion that the Germans were close to winning at this time was not justified. As Telford Taylor has summed up the situation, Fighter Command was badly strained, but "still basically intact." The research of Roger Parkinson has shown a more optimistic picture than earlier accounts allowed. By comparing Fighter Command's own returns with the figures of the Air Ministry, he shows that the losses of RAF pilots were apparently exaggerated by the latter. No airfields were actually knocked out by the intense German attacks. German aircrewmen were at least as tired as the RAF pilots, and their morale also sagged. British replacement pilots were not as badly trained as has sometimes been claimed. Replacements of pilots as well as planes kept pace with losses. An examination of the record shows that the number of operational RAF fighters hardly dropped at all during the Battle of Britain, while the number of German operational aircraft, both fighters and bombers, dropped fairly steadily throughout. Interestingly, the number of sorties flown by the Luftwaffe fell off steeply during the first few days of September—before the RAF was supposedly "saved" by the German decision to bomb London. Parkinson concludes that "The Battle of Britain never came near to being lost by Fighter Command; the post-war belief that the 'few,' battling for Britain's very survival, came to within days of defeat, is totally false." Moreover, he stresses, no switch in tactics by Göring could have saved things for the Germans.

The evidence suggests that the causes of the Luftwaffe's defeat were many and "built-in" long before the battle began. The Luftwaffe was a tactical air force, not a strategic one comparable to the RAF or the U.S. Army Air Force. It was "flying artillery" tied to the support of the German army. It lacked a four-engine long-range heavy bomber. Moreover, though some of the more far-sighted founders of the Luftwaffe did foresee the need for such a plane, it seems doubtful that the German aircraft industry could have produced one in sufficient numbers given its other commitments. The medium bombers the Luftwaffe did have were slow and poorly armed. The Luftwaffe's intelligence was inadequate, and its officer corps lacked good mid-level officers. Production and pilot training were already strained to replace the losses suffered in the Battle of Britain. The Luftwaffe's long-range escort fighter, the Me 110, was a flop—it needed fighter escort itself. The Me 109 was not available in sufficient numbers, and had much too short a range. Its range was so short, in fact, that it meant that the Germans could *never* win complete domination of the air over southern England. Even had far greater losses been inflicted on Fighter Command, and its bases in the south become untenable, British fighters could have operated from bases outside the range of the German fighter escort, and thus remained immune to serious bombing. From such bases, the RAF could still have operated over southern England and the Channel.

Even if, by some fluke, the Luftwaffe had won undisputed control of the air over the Channel and the projected beachhead, an invasion would still have been impossible. It is usually assumed that, had the Luftwaffe gained air superiority, it could have prevented the Royal Navy from interfering with the invasion fleet. Experience during

World War II seemed to show that surface warships, unprotected by fighter cover, were helpless against planes. This was true, however, only against properly equipped attacking aircraft. The destruction of heavy warships, especially, was a specialized task requiring the use of heavy armor-piercing bombs or torpedoes. The Luftwaffe had neither in 1940. General Pelz, the Luftwaffe's dive-bombing specialist, later declared that even in the best conditions, with the weapons then available, the Luftwaffe could not have stopped the British fleet from annihilating the German invasion forces.

Given these facts, it is almost a waste of time to discuss the German invasion plan; but it should be noted that by September 1940 the British army was by no means the almost unarmed mob that had returned from the Continent in June. It had built up to a force of 800 tanks and might well have been able to push the Germans, who planned to invade with only 310 tanks, into the sea.

It is occasionally argued that the Germans' whole approach to the invasion problem was simply belated or misdirected. They should have struck right after Dunkirk, when the British air forces were weak and no serious defense on land could have been mounted. Moreover, it is argued (generally by the same critics) that it was a mistake to embark on a long drawn out battle for overall air supremacy. Instead, the Luftwaffe should simply have aimed at covering the invasion force, at winning an air battle at the very moment of the Channel crossing. However, neither an early assault nor an all-out concentration on "one single battle" would have dealt with the threat posed by the Royal Navy. Moreover, an invasion in June or July was never a possibility, aside from the fact that such a move would have had to be planned months in advance. (Before the fall of France the Germans had made only sketchy preliminary studies of the invasion problem.) The German historian "Cajus Bekker" (Hans Dieter Berenbrok) has commented that the Germans found virtually no seaworthy craft in the Channel ports, and this alone "makes nonsense" of the idea of an early pursuit of the British across the Channel. Barges and other craft for the invasion had to be tediously brought from Germany to the Channel ports, which had been heavily damaged by British demolition parties. In any case, the Luftwaffe, too, had suffered heavily in the French campaign. In fact, its exhaustion and losses were partly responsible for the escape of the BEF from Dunkirk. Many bomber units had less than half their nominal ("establishment") strength of planes serviceable. In short, there was no "lost opportunity" for an early German conquest of Britain—or any conquest at all in 1940.

The Battle of the Atlantic

Many historians who have never felt that the threat of an invasion of Britain in 1940 was a serious one have nevertheless maintained that the Western powers did come close to disaster in the Battle of the Atlantic. The oft-quoted view of S. W. Roskill, the official British historian of the war at sea, is that Britain had a very narrow escape from defeat by the U-boats in the spring of 1943. Roskill wrote of the British naval leaders that "They must have felt, though none admitted it, that defeat stared them in the face." Churchill wrote that nothing worried him more during the war than the U-boat threat.

The U-boats were clearly a great threat to the Western Allies' war effort. They caused enormous damage and tied up considerable resources in a defensive effort. It is doubtful, however, that they came close to breaking the transatlantic supply line.

The question is a complex one, for the Germans could almost certainly have built up their U-boat force more quickly. U-boat construction had a low priority in 1939–40, and appears to have been halted altogether for a time. In the first year of the war, replacements only balanced losses to the small U-boat force. Göring, who then controlled the war economy's priorities, was hostile to the navy, and the naval high command emphasized heavy warships at the expense of U-boats. Nor was the employment of the submarine force optimal. Hitler on several occasions in late 1941 and 1942 diverted a considerable part of the U-boat strength to the Arctic and the Mediterranean. There, though they caused considerable losses, they on the whole achieved less than they would have in the Atlantic. Part of the effectiveness of the Allied anti-submarine effort, in 1941 and after December 1942, depended on the delicate foundation of the reading of the German navy's codes. Had the German navy's signals specialists been a bit less arrogantly confident of the security of their codes, a major source of information would have been lost to the Allies. (It should be noted, however, that during the most intense period of the Battle of the Atlantic, the Germans were reading the British merchant ship code, and the cryptographic efforts of the two sides may have effectively neutralized each other.) However, as we shall see, the Allies had considerable resources only belatedly thrown into the Battle of the Atlantic. The tide could probably have been turned far earlier.

Partly thanks to the naval high command's obsession with big surface ships, Germany started the war with only 57 U-boats, many small and short-ranged. Admiral Dönitz, commander of the submarine service, estimated that he would need a strength of *300* ocean-going boats, one-third at sea at any one time, to defeat the British convoy system—a number reached only in 1942.

Only in the second half of 1940, when French bases became available, did the Battle of the Atlantic really begin in earnest. The French bases increased the effective strength of the U-boat force by up to 40 per cent, and enabled the Germans to inaugurate wolf-pack tactics, in which groups of U-boats were concentrated in attacks on British convoys. (The British, at this point, missed a good opportunity to cripple or delay the growth of the threat; they failed to bomb the concrete shelters at the new bases while they were under construction and vulnerable. Once they were finished, they were immune to any bombs available before 1944.) The effectiveness of the German U-boat in World War II, it should be noted, depended on its ability to operate on the *surface of the ocean*. A submerged submarine, operating on batteries, was very slow—slower than a convoy of merchant ships. It could rarely count on more than one shot at a convoy, and was vulnerable to sonar detection. But a surfaced U-boat, operating on diesel engines, was faster than the great majority of merchant ships and even some escort vessels. It was almost invisible to sonar. The U-boats inflicted most losses on convoys by attacking on the surface at night. Quick transit to and from the operational areas also depended on the freedom to stay on the surface. This freedom was menaced by the airplane, and later by radar.

Almost from the start of the Battle of the Atlantic, the U-boats' freedom of action on the surface began to ebb. Even in 1940, British land-based air patrols began forcing the U-boats to operate farther westward. During 1941, the U-boats were finally forced into the American patrol area, which President Roosevelt was pushing eastward, producing the incidents mentioned earlier. During 1941 the Allied merchant marine suffered losses greater than the number of ships being built. But the U-boats met stiffening resistance as the Allied escort strength grew and escort was extended right across the whole Atlantic, and anti-submarine tactics became more efficient. By late 1941 the

U-boats lost most of the limited help long-range planes and surface warships had previously given them. A fuel shortage tied the surface navy to harbors. In June 1941, the British began reading the German naval code, which helped them divert many convoys clear of danger. (This first period in which the German naval code was broken lasted until January 1942, though with increasing gaps and delays in decoding messages.) However, while evasive routing, which was greatly aided by code-breaking, was important, the British intelligence history strongly implies that a more important way of reducing losses was the decision to reduce independent sailings of fast ships, which had provided the U-boats with sitting duck targets.

As Donald Macintyre has commented, already in late 1941, "The writing was on the wall" for the U-boat. In late December 1941, a heavy attack on convoy HG76, which was escorted by a well-led escort force and one of the first escort aircraft carriers, proved a notable reverse for the Germans. Though the Germans managed to sink the escort carrier, they lost nearly half their attacking force for otherwise small results. HG76 made it clear that the counter to the U-boat—trained escort groups of ships that had worked together, and a combined sea-and-air escort—already existed and, as Allied resources were brought to bear, would win. The staff of the German submarine service concluded that the U-boats were no longer in a position to combat the convoy system. Admiral Dönitz disagreed with his staff, but, as Macintyre points out, the successes the Germans continued to achieve in 1942–43 were due only to the Allies' inability to profit by the example of HG76.

The final decisive phase of the Battle of the Atlantic was postponed for six months after Pearl Harbor. Due to the stupidity of the American naval command, the U-boats found it enormously profitable to operate in American coastal waters and the Caribbean. No preparations for defense there had been made, and, lacking escorts, the Americans mistakenly postponed the introduction of convoys in these areas, wrongly thinking that weakly escorted convoys would be worse than none at all. The result was a massacre. However, with the creation of the convoy system there, "the most successful period of the U-boat war against Allied supplies was now over," as the German historian Jürgen Rohwer later commented. When the U-boats returned to the main theater in the North Atlantic—which lay in the mid-ocean "air gap," now only 600 miles wide, where no land-based air cover was yet available—they found the going increasingly tough, though they inflicted very heavy losses. By late 1942, even Admiral Dönitz was not optimistic, feeling that the Allies had already gained the upper hand tactically. The Allies, however, were very worried. Their diversion of warships to escort the North Russia convoys and the invasion of North Africa gravely weakened the defense of the Atlantic supply lines, though this was a temporary affliction.

In March 1943, the supreme crisis of the Atlantic battle appeared to develop. In several convoy battles in the first three weeks of the month, the Allies suffered extremely heavy losses, provoking the fears noted by Roskill. Shortly afterwards, however, the situation was dramatically reversed. In April–May 1943, the Allied losses dropped, while a massacre of U-boats occurred in the battles around the convoys. Shortly afterward, Dönitz actually had to withdraw the U-boats from the Atlantic for a time. The Allies had won the Battle of the Atlantic. A number of measures were responsible for the victory. Most important, perhaps, was the closing of the air gap and the provision of air cover for all threatened convoys by the allotment of escort carriers and very long-range land-based planes. New "support groups" of teams of escort vessels trained to work together were available to reinforce the escorts of convoys under attack. (The allotment of escort carriers and support groups would have occurred earlier but for the North African operation.) The U-boat code, "Triton," was cracked by the British in December 1942—though arguably this simply countered the Germans' own cryptographic efforts. New equipment for escort vessels became available, notably ten-centimeter microwave radars, high-speed high-frequency direction finders, improved depth charges and "ahead-throw" weapons.

The nature of the crisis of March 1943, however, has often been misunderstood. The losses suffered in 1942–43, though serious, did not threaten Britain with starvation and immediate defeat. There was more than enough shipping to sustain the British people and war production. Rather, what was in danger was the collection of enough shipping to sustain future offensives. Actually, sinkings of Allied merchant ships by all enemy causes during 1942 only slightly exceeded the total of Allied merchantship construction for that year. The curve of construction actually passed that of U-boat sinkings alone in 1942. (Thus, the situation in the Atlantic even at its worst was not truly comparable to the situation in the Pacific, where American submarines caused a continual shrinkage of the Japanese shipping pool almost throughout the war.

Nor was the 1943 crisis truly a narrow escape and the culmination of a situation worsening steadily throughout the war. Rather, as Macintyre says, in March 1943, "a setback on one part of the battlefield was being unreasonably looked upon as a herald of general defeat." Nor were the losses absolutely unbearable; even the convoys attacked suffered losses of 11 per cent, while many convoys passed unscathed. And the Germans found, in the winter, that only strong concentrations of U-boats produced results—and that only in the air gap. The severe convoy losses of March 1943 were due to such concentrations being achieved against individual convoys. Moreover, the pessimism Roskill attributed to the Admiralty staff was not felt by those immediately responsible for the fight against the U-boats. Macintyre, himself an escort commander, remarks that "Those closer to the fighting, however, such as the C-in-C Western Approaches, and his staff at Liverpool, the captains commanding the escort bases and the escort commanders themselves were by no means dismayed." They appreciated that the Allies were taking the measure of the U-boat threat. The staff of the Admiralty's operational intelligence effort was also confident.

The crisis was very much the enemy's last desperate effort before the air gap was closed. As Martin Middlebrook and others have pointed out, it was also an unnecessary crisis, though it was partly the result of the Allies' taking a chance with their supply lines to support their early offensive efforts. The escort forces were often composed, not of the latest and best-equipped vessels, but of "cast-offs and surplus ships." The force needed to close the air gap was rather small; the number of very long-range planes in the North Atlantic had to be increased only from 10 to 40. In fact, many such aircraft were available, some elsewhere in the Atlantic, and to some extent the air gap was merely the result of the maldistribution of available planes.

It would appear that the closure of the air gap and the arrival of the new microwave radars were the most important elements in the turn in the Atlantic battle. Given the density of the U-boat concentrations in the Atlantic and the Germans' own code-breaking successes, "Ultra" was probably not decisive. Knowing the location of the areas where the U-boats operated, and the evasive routing this permitted, were no longer very valuable to the Allies. There were too many U-boats in the North Atlantic in March–May 1943. The vital problem that had to be solved was the tactical location of the U-boats in actual contact with the convoys and close-in defense against them. Planes and radar were the prime factor in supplying this, though "Ultra" did help the Allies rush reinforcing elements to attacked convoys. And, after the U-boats were beaten in the convoy battles, "Ultra" helped the new escort carrier groups wreak a veritable slaughter of U-boats and their supply craft by guiding the Allies to their refueling rendezvous.

While it is impossible to be certain that Germany could never have won the Battle of the Atlantic, there is good reason to think that its chances of doing so were very slim. As "Cajus Bekker" has commented, even in the worst period of the Battle Allied shipbuilding nearly kept pace with losses, and if the Germans ever had any chance to win, it was only in the first two years of the war. Jürgen Rohwer affirms that the U-boat fleet simply reached Dönitz's minimum of 300 too late. It seems questionable whether, even given higher priorities, the fleet could have been built up fast enough. As in the case of the Luftwaffe, the defeat of the German navy seems to have been largely pre-determined by pre-war mistakes in planning made by the military service itself, and ensured by Germany's failure to mobilize her resources properly once the war began.

The Russian Campaign

It is widely believed that the decision to invade Russia was Hitler's fatal mistake. On the other hand, it is often thought, had the Russian campaign resulted in a German victory, Germany would have won World War II as a whole. It is noticeable that a number of German and other authorities who feel that there was no real chance of Germany defeating the Western powers, do regard a complete German defeat of the Soviet Union as having been within the realm of possibility. The German generals, in their post-war writings, have been happy to heap all the blame for both the Russian campaign and its failure on Hitler.

Putting aside the problem of whether or not the defeat of the Soviets would have meant a German victory in the war as a whole (it should be noted that neither the British nor the American leaders at that time thought it would), let us examine whether the Russian campaign was an avoidable mistake—and whether it could have been won.

An examination of Hitler's decision to invade the Soviet Union suggests that it was not a result of some specific contingency, narrow tactical solution or an avoidable mistake. Rather, it flowed quite directly from Hitler's world-view and ideas he shared with most other Nazi leaders. The need for *Lebensraum* in the east, and the supposed ease of acquiring it, and the need to destroy "Bolshevism," which Hitler regarded as the prime expression of the Jewish world conspiracy, were Hitler's most deeply held beliefs. The notion of "Jewish Bolshevism" tied the Russian campaign in his mind to the destruction of the Jews, who he hated more than anything else. The planning of the "Final Solution" was closely correlated with the development of the attack on the USSR, and it is no accident that the destruction of the European Jews began in occupied Soviet territory. It would have been hard indeed for Hitler to forego an attack on the Soviets once he felt at all free to initiate it.

It may be objected that this does not explain the immediate decision to attack Russia in 1940, which involved Hitler in the two-front war that he and all other Germans rightly feared. In 1939, after all, he managed to restrain his hatred of the Soviets long enough to sign a pact with them. It is also true that Göring, Admiral Raeder, and many German generals were unenthusiastic about the decision to invade the Soviet Union. Though they were not as strongly opposed to war with the Soviets as they later pretended, it is probable that had either Göring or the professional military been in a position to decide, the invasion of the USSR would not have taken place, at least not in 1941.

An examination of Hitler's statements in June–July 1940, however, suggests that after the fall of France he considered the destruction of the USSR the logical next move no matter how things developed in the near future—whether Britain made peace, was conquered, or fought on. Even before the end of the French campaign, he indicated to a number of generals that if Britain made peace (as he then expected) the stage would be set for the destruction of Bolshevism. When it became clear that Britain would not make peace soon, Hitler simply continued to push toward war with the Soviet Union, and initiated actual military planning. This continued steadily during the period when Hitler hoped Britain could quickly be knocked out of the war, and after it had become apparent that this was not possible. He then argued that Britain was continuing the fight because of the hope of Soviet help. Moreover, there was a grave danger that if the war in the west lasted a long time, this would invite economic blackmail by Stalin. Germany was dependent on the Soviets for oil and other important materials. Should Germany suffer serious defeats in the west, Stalin might actually attack.

Moreover, maintenance of the strong ground forces needed to defend against a move by Stalin would hinder the war effort against the British and the Americans. Should the Soviet Union be destroyed, however, Germany would be permanently assured of all the materials its war economy required, and would be free to develop her naval and air strength as needed for a war in the west. By demonstrating German power and increasing Japan's strength in the Far East, the defeat of the Soviets might deter the Americans from entering the war. Even if they did, an alliance of the European Axis, controlling a vast Eurasian continental bloc, and Japan could face this prospect with confidence. While some of Hitler's arguments, especially that the Soviets were a threat, smack of rationalization, and appear to have been designed to pacify his generals, he seems to have consistently assumed that the conquest of the USSR was the solution to his problems. *Lebensraum* was both a broad goal of policy and a panacea in grand strategy. Hitler apparently reasoned that though Britain was still fighting it was not really a "two-front" war, since that country was not capable of opening a serious land front against Germany, though the considerable forces left in Western Europe and the Balkans suggest that he was not really secure about this conclusion.

Hitler's plans and the construction of the allegedly impregnable Eurasian bloc depended on an early and complete victory over the Soviet Union which would secure its economic resources for Germany's use. The events of 1941 and 1942, however, showed that this was never in the cards.

This is not to say that a Nazi defeat of the Soviet Union was inherently impossible—as a conquest of Britain in 1940 was impossible. Had the Germans followed a logical and consistent strategy, they might indeed have won the war with the Soviets. (This has nothing to do with one's judgment of Soviet virtue or the lack of it. It is simply a fact that Nazi Germany was primarily a land power and the Soviet Union was thus more vulnerable to it than the English-speaking world.) However, a *quick* victory was not possible, nor would any victory the Germans were in a position to win have improved their economic position.

The Germans' battlefield failures were deeply embedded in their pre-invasion planning and intelligence (or rather the lack of it). Not only Hitler but virtually all his military planners gravely underestimated Soviet military strength, skill and industrial power. In August

1941, the shaken Chief of the General Staff, Franz Halder, admitted that he had counted on meeting 200 enemy divisions in Russia—but they had identified 360 by that date. After the easy defeat of the French army, which most German officers feared and respected, it seemed a comparatively simple task to beat the Russians, who had been a far less impressive opponent than the French in World War I. German intelligence was ignorant of the most elementary facts about Soviet military organization, order of battle, and equipment. The appearance of the Soviets' T–34 and KV tanks, the best in the world, came as a great shock in July 1941. The Germans had no agents at all inside the Soviet Union's pre-1939 frontiers. There was no sound picture of the Soviet economic structure. The Germans were unaware of the extent of Soviet industrial development in the Urals and the Far East. They wrongly assumed that the Ukraine and the Baltic States were economically vital to the Soviets, and they concluded that the Red Army would thus have to stand and fight to hold on to those areas at all costs, leaving it vulnerable to flanking thrusts launched from the central front to the Baltic and Black Sea coasts. The Germans did not even have up-to-date maps. There was, therefore, little guidance, and even less foundation, for the German assumption that they could count on defeating the Soviet Union in a single summer campaign, and reach the Archangel–Volga line.

The planning itself omitted vital provisions. The priorities given to some objectives was not clear; nor was the timing of certain moves, such as the switch of forces from Army Group Center to Leningrad. The question of what to do if the enemy escaped the planned decisive encirclement west of the Dnieper and Dvina was not examined. Certain disputes between Hitler and the army planners were not resolved.

Few criticisms of the German plans would command such universal agreement as the judgment that victory in a single year's campaign was always out of the question. The very assumption that it was possible to win without winter fighting led straight to disaster in the winter of 1941–42.

The failure to prepare the army for a winter campaign was undoubtedly an easily avoidable one. (It was, incidentally, the fault of the General Staff, not Hitler: the SS and the Luftwaffe were ready for winter.) The course of the campaign, however, revealed many "built-in" German weaknesses that could not have been readily corrected, even with greater wisdom or information. There were fundamental weaknesses in the German army's supply system. German tank and vehicle production was quantitatively and qualitatively inadequate. Neither the German-built trucks and horse wagons, nor those confiscated in the west, were suited to the poor Soviet roads. Neither enough replacement tanks nor enough spare parts were produced. Even the Germans' tracked vehicles (their treads were too narrow) found it hard to keep going in the rainy season; wheeled vehicles were completely halted. But the capacity of German industry was so stretched that fully tracked vehicles, which could have kept the German spearheads going even during the muddy season, could not have been produced in sufficient quantity even if the need for them had been foreseen. The Luftwaffe did not have enough transport planes to make up the difference. Nor did the Germans have adequate means to make use of the Soviet railroads. Their own locomotives were unsuited for the Russian winter.

Hitler's direction of the campaign has drawn much criticism, and a good deal of this is certainly justified. The primary criticism of Hitler is that he directed the German effort to the flanks of the front, emphasizing the conquest of Leningrad and the Ukraine, instead of driving on to Moscow, a strategically far more important objective which would have brought the main Soviet armies to battle. Further, having diverted his forces to Leningrad, Hitler then cut short the campaign there at the end of August, when a brief persistence would have captured the city. Hitler's final decision to capture Moscow, after Leningrad was besieged and the Ukraine overrun, was just too late in the year. Many Germans, and some foreign critics, notably B. H. Liddell-Hart, have argued that the initial German encirclement drive was too shallow. The armored pincers of Army Group Center, at the start of the campaign, should have pushed on to the Dnieper, or even further east, instead of Minsk, and the task of rounding up the encircled Soviet forces should have been left to the infantry, freeing the armored forces to resume the eastward drive. Some of these judgments, however, are highly questionable, and in general it seems doubtful whether more than marginally better results could have been achieved.

Had the German forces tried a deeper encirclement at the start of the campaign, they would only have found it even harder to close off the bigger pocket or pockets this would have created. The infantry units required to prevent the Soviet troops from breaking, or even severing, the German supply lines would have been left even further behind. (It must be remembered that the German infantry divisions were dependent on horse-drawn transport.) Nor did Panzer Group 4 actually have enough infantry to capture Leningrad quickly in August and September 1941. Any attempt to do so would have entangled the German forces in a battle of attrition in a city far bigger than Stalingrad. There is little question that the German army was right in favoring a drive on Moscow, and had this course been pursued resolutely and without any diversions, the city could have been taken. However, this would not have led to an immediate collapse of the Red Army, nor could the Germans have occupied all of European Russia before winter. The Germans would have been left to hold a vast salient with strong Soviet forces holding out to the north and south. As Barry Leach has pointed out, a drive on Moscow in August and September 1941 would have had to be carried out with one less Panzer Group than became available for the belated drive in October. An encirclement battle at that time would probably have bagged fewer Soviet forces than those destroyed in the actual battles in the Ukraine and at Vyazma in the fall. "Even if Moscow had been placed first instead of last in Hitler's list of priorities, the Germans would still have fallen short of complete victory." By late 1941, the Germans had run out of steam. The Soviets went over to the offensive and very nearly managed to cut off and destroy a large part of Army Group Center. During this time, even Hitler may have begun to doubt the possibility of victory, though he was careful to confess his fears only to the utterly subservient General Jodl.

Despite the losses suffered during the Soviet winter offensive, the Germans may still have had a chance of winning the war in the east in 1942, though again they had no chance whatever of achieving a *quick* victory. Despite the need for a quick victory in the east before the British and Americans could ready a decisive blow in the west, Hitler actually chose a plan of campaign that meant that victory in the east must be long in coming, if it came at all.

Instead of seeking to force a decisive battle on the Red Army and capturing Moscow, Hitler decided to seize the oilfields of the Caucasus, which were vital for the Soviet war effort. The capture of the oilfields had originally been planned as a follow-up to the completion of Operation Barbarossa on the main front; now it was to substitute for victory there. (Göring's economic experts had warned before the invasion of Russia that the Caucasus oilfields would have to be taken, apart from any other considerations, just to power the economy of the conquered Soviet Union.)

There has never been any lack of critics of Hitler's approach, which violated Clausewitz's fundamental rule that the proper objective of a campaign was the defeat of the enemy's military forces, and that the seizure of political and economic objectives must follow, not precede, this. In South Russia in 1942, the approach Hitler took seemed dubious even from a narrowly pragmatic standpoint. To reach the main Soviet oilfields the Germans would have to advance nearly 1,000 miles and cross a rugged mountain range. All their lines of communication—which were likely to be inadequate—would run through a vulnerable bottleneck at Rostov-on-Don, exposed to an attack by the undefeated mass of the Red Army from the northeast. Precisely because Hitler was evading a confrontation with the bulk of the Soviet forces, they would be in a position to launch a counteroffensive and force a decisive battle when it was least convenient for the Germans. Hitler's decision to make the Caucasus the target was thus fundamentally bad strategy.

Apart from his fears of a big battle, Hitler undoubtedly felt forced to this course, since Germany was already suffering from a fuel shortage. The German and Italian surface fleets were already suffering from a shortage of fuel oil, and the shortage of gasoline was already restricting the Luftwaffe's training program, which had already been disrupted by the demands of the winter airlift to encircled German forces in Russia. The fuel shortage alone, by this time, would have prevented the renewal of an offensive air effort on the scale of the Battle of Britain. Given the inevitable requirements of a major sea and air war in the west, fuel was desperately needed. On 1 June Hitler told the assembled senior officers of Army Group South, which was to conduct the coming offensive, that "If I do not get the oil of Maikop and Grozny, then I must end this war."

Whether the Caucasus could have been taken and held will never be known with certainty. The Germans did capture Maikop, the least important oilfield, but their efforts petered out in the foothills of the Caucasus range. During the offensive, Hitler's leadership became increasingly erratic. Most of the Soviet forces in South Russia escaped the planned encirclement west of the Don river. Hitler constantly weakened the decisive drive toward the oilfields. He transferred two panzer divisions from the southern attack to Army Group Center and, unnecessarily anxious about a cross-Channel attack, sent an SS division from South Russia to France. Most of the German forces in the Crimea, which had been scheduled to cross the straits to the Caucasus and intercept the retreating Soviets, were sent north to capture Leningrad instead. Hitler then developed his fatal fascination with Stalingrad. Originally, the city had not been an important objective. Now Hitler split his offensive in the south, ordering simultaneous offensives against both Stalingrad and the Caucasus. As the campaign proceeded, Hitler transferred more and more of the effort to the Stalingrad area. He imagined that he was destroying the Red Army in a battle of attrition in the city. In reality, he had merely tied down most of his offensive power against a fraction of the Red Army, which was free to prepare its devastating winter counteroffensive.

Even if the oilfields had been captured, it is doubtful that the results would have been satisfactory to the Germans. It would have taken many months for the fuel shortage to cripple the Soviet economy and the Red Army, for the Soviets had considerable reserve stocks, which, according to German and British calculations, would have kept them going until at least mid-1943 had they lost the oilfields in 1942. As for securing the oilfields for the German economy, this was probably never possible. The Maikop oilfields were thoroughly demolished before the Germans arrived. Even had the oilfields been taken intact, this would not have benefited the Germans much. Before the invasion of Russia, a report by General von Hannecken, an Assistant State Secretary in the Armament and War Economy Office, warned that only 100,000 tons of oil a month could be brought overland from the Caucasus to Germany, only enough to make up about one-third of Germany's deficiencies. The river tankers on the Danube were already working to capacity carrying Romanian oil, so further shipments from the Caucasus would require the use of a sea route through the Black Sea and the Turkish Straits, so that Caucasian oil could be brought to Mediterranean ports. To secure this route, the Germans would have had to eliminate British air and seapower from the eastern Mediterranean. As it was, the Axis merchant fleet in that sea was hard put to supply the German–Italian forces in North Africa, and was rapidly being wiped out by British submarines and planes in 1942–43. As will be noted later, it is possible that the Axis could have conquered the Mediterranean area before, or even concurrent with, the Russian campaign—but the requirements for making use of Russian oil were thus still enormous, being complete military successes, some improbable, and scarce means of transport in *two* different and competitive theaters!

Even had the Germans defeated the Red Army and caused the collapse of the Soviet regime in 1941–42, occupying the whole of European Russia, they could not have exploited Russia successfully in the near future. Their treatment of the conquered population, which was inseparable from the basic elements of Nazi ideology, was admirably suited to inspire desperate resistance. "Pacification" of the conquered territory would have taken years; use of the most vital resource of all, oil, was not really in prospect. The notion of a Eurasian bloc using the resources of a conquered Soviet Union to fend off an Anglo–American assault was a mirage, even disregarding the effects of Western nuclear weapons. Had the Western powers left the Nazis free to conquer the Soviet Union, they could indeed have eventually welded into a conquered Eurasia into a deadly threat to the West. But in a situation where the Nazis were at war both in east and west, there was never a chance that they would have the time and freedom of action to do this.

The Mediterranean Theater

The Germans have often been criticized for failing to perceive the importance of the Mediterranean and Middle East, and the possibilities for a German victory. It has been held that if Hitler had launched a serious offensive there, instead of attacking the Soviet Union, a deadly blow might have been struck at the British. It has been argued that the Germans could probably have defeated the British in the Mediterranean theater in 1941–42 even while they were engaged in Russia, had readily available resources been used to support Rommel.

Hitler's actual policy in the Mediterranean was basically defensive, at least in the short run. Admiral Raeder strongly favored a major campaign against the British to the south, and Hitler and the General Staff did give some tentative support to such an idea for a time in 1940. The army staff seems to have preferred a Mediterranean campaign to one against Russia. But Mussolini did not want German help for his invasion of Egypt, nor was General Franco disposed to join the war and cooperate with a German attack on Gibraltar unless Germany had already virtually won the war elsewhere and agreed to pay him off at the expense of the French. Hitler was not sufficiently interested in or worried about the Mediterranean to force Mussolini or Franco into line or solve the problem the latter's ambitions would pose for Hitler's policy toward Vichy.

Only when Mussolini met disaster in Africa and in his imbecilic attack on Greece did Hitler move. (He had thus wasted much of the interval between the cancellation of the invasion of Britain and the invasion of Russia, which he might have used for a decisive blow in the south.) Hitler's policy in the Mediterranean in 1941 was defensive. The Afrika Korps was sent to Libya, not to conquer Egypt, but to prevent a total British victory in North Africa. The conquest of the Balkans and the airborne invasion of Crete were designed to prevent a British bridgehead in the Balkans that would threaten the Romanian oilfields and the southern flank of the Axis forces moving into the Ukraine. After the conquest of Russia, however, Hitler did envisage a major offensive into the Middle East from both the north and the west. Rommel's successes, and the weakening of the British position in the Middle East after Japan's entry into the war, did cause Hitler to become more interested in the Mediterranean in 1942. It was decided to take Malta, to secure the Axis supply lines to North Africa, and then Egypt. Rommel's campaign in North Africa was envisaged as the weaker arm of a pincer movement into the Middle East; the major thrust was to be made from the Caucasus once that region was captured. After the fall of Tobruk, however, Hitler, who had always disliked the Malta operation, in effect postponed it indefinitely and allowed Rommel to gamble on a continued advance into Egypt.

In any case, Malta was very nearly starved into submission—the success, with heavy losses, of the vital convoys of June and August 1942, was a near thing. Rommel at one point came close to victory in Egypt in July 1942— though perhaps not as close as is often thought, for his force was greatly weakened by previous fighting and had a very long and tenuous land supply line. Had Rommel been given more support, however, he could almost certainly have overrun Egypt. Additional forces could almost certainly have been provided to him without any diversion of units from Russia, for considerable German forces (29 divisions) were idle in Western Europe, which was not in danger of attack. As Rommel later noted bitterly, after Alamein and the Allied invasion of North Africa, his masters suddenly found it possible to throw considerable forces into the futile defense of Tunisia. These units would have been an invaluable aid to his offensive if they had been available earlier. It should also be noted that the British forces attacking his supply lines across the Mediterranean were dependent on "Ultra" to an unusually high degree for their effectiveness—perhaps more so than any other major striking force in the war. They were even able to single out specific ships with cargoes of unusual value for special attention. British survival and success in the Mediterranean were thus unusually dependent on the valuable but fragile achievement of "Ultra" and the German blundering that this depended on.

If Rommel came close to victory in 1942 with very limited resources, it seems certain that, had Hitler acted promptly and decisively in 1940–41, he could have overrun the Mediterranean–Middle East area, probably without any damage to the Russian campaign. The prompt seizure of Malta and the dispatch of sufficient armored forces to North Africa would have inflicted a serious blow to the British, made the invasion and occupation of the Balkans, which later proved such a nuisance, unnecessary, and might have secured valuable oil supplies for Germany. Hitler's failure to launch a timely offensive in the Mediterranean in 1940–41, or to support Rommel later, was a classic case of being penny-wise and pound-foolish. As a result, the Allies were able to destroy an entire German army in North Africa, knock out Italy, and ultimately tie down over 50 German divisions in Italy and the Balkans, a force almost as great as that defending Western Europe in 1944.

However, there is little reason to think that the loss of the Mediterranean and the Middle East would have meant the defeat of the Western powers. The Cape route, not the Mediterranean, as is widely supposed, was the true "lifeline" of the British empire. In any case, the Mediterranean was closed to British shipping from 1940–43, as it had been during part of World War I, without this being more than a nuisance to the Allies. The Middle East was an underdeveloped region that did not contain any major Ally or indispensable source of military power. (The Jewish settlements in Palestine, which could have been a valuable source of manpower, were hardly exploited by the British.) Nor did the Middle East lead obviously to any place else. As von Manstein pointed out, the Middle East for logistic reasons would have been a good base for an attack on either the Soviet Union or India. Nor was there a prospect of a serious juncture of the European axis and the Japanese. Even the faction of Japanese naval planners oriented toward a "westward"— Indian Ocean—strategy, contemplated at most the capture of Ceylon, not a major invasion of India or a drive into the Middle East. In any case, given the threat posed by the American Pacific Fleet and MacArthur's forces in the Southwest Pacific theater, there was never much possibility of the Japanese feeling free to throw their forces into a major Indian Ocean campaign. Nor could the Italian fleet, which proved unable to stand up to the British even in the middle sea, have operated successfully in the Indian Ocean, since it lacked the aircraft carriers and the supply ships needed for oceanic operations.

Oil was the only substantial thing in the Middle East of great value to the Allies. But in those days the developed world was not yet dependent on Middle East oil. Britain's own supply during World War II came not around the Cape but from the Americas. The oil of the Middle East was vital, not for the Allied war effort in general, but as the only nearby and convenient source of supply for the British forces in the Mediterranean and Indian Ocean areas. Loss of the oil would probably have paralyzed any Allied threat to Germany from the southeast or to Japan from the Southwest; but the decisive blows against Germany and Japan were not launched from those directions. The Americans were so unruffled by the prospect of the loss of the Middle East that on several occasions in 1941 they urged the British to abandon the area lest they sink too much of their military power there. President Roosevelt himself, though not going so far, suggested to Churchill that the loss of the area, or indeed anything else, could be withstood as long as the Allies retained command of the Atlantic. Loss of the Mediterranean and the Middle East would have been a most serious blow, but a far from fatal one.

In short, the only victories Germany might reasonably have hoped to achieve would not have vitally affected the outcome of the war. In most respects Germany was not strong enough to affect, nor within range of, the vital spots of the major Allied powers. The Nazis had failed to prepare for the war intelligently enough, and capped this by not mobilizing properly for war until 1942. All German successes were tied to one form of warfare, the blitzkrieg. When the Nazis embarked on war with enemies who were geographically immune to it, or had the space and resources to survive the initial blows, the results were inevitably disastrous for them.

16

Lawrence Freedman

The Strategy of Hiroshima

For generations to come, Hiroshima and Nagasaki will be seared into human consciousness. The vast majority of Americans approved the use of the bomb and supported dropping even more atomic bombs, according to a Gallup poll of August 1945. As the enormity of the cost in lives and destruction became known, and as Americans lost their short-lived monopoly on the weapon and entered the missile age, Hiroshima took on a new significance as a precursor of the fate of the whole earth. And, though race has not been shown to have been a consideration in employing the bomb, the fact remains that its first use was by white men against another race.

The real prospect of nuclear energy as an instrument of war became known to physicists throughout the world on the eve of the war. Though it was uncertain exactly how powerful such a weapon would be or how it might be deployed, no doubt existed about the potential. In the event, the United Kingdom, Germany, the Soviet Union, Japan, and the United States all initiated research to find out. In 1941 the British, for security and financial reasons, joined the American effort. The day before the attack on Pearl Harbor, Washington decided to fund a mammoth, two billion dollar secret Manhattan Engineering Project to research and manufacture the bomb. Antifascist physicists, mathematicians and engineers from all over Europe joined the undertaking, many believing they were in a race with Germany. Winning would determine the future of all humanity. German physicists and leaders, unaware of any race, fell behind and failed. Only America had a working bomb in 1945.

Reprinted by permission from the first issue of the *Journal of Strategic Studies* published by Frank Cass and Company Limited, 11 Gainsborough Road, London E11, England. Copyright 1985 Frank Cass and Co. Ltd.

Meanwhile, the dynamics of war brutalized leaders on all sides. All Europeans feared war in 1939, especially the thought of bombs raining from the heavens. Hitler restrained the Luftwaffe in 1939 and early 1940. Only during the Battle of Britain did both sides begin deliberate bombing of civilians. In 1942 the bombing campaign against Germany accelerated, first with thousand-plane RAF raids on west German cities, then a merciless attack on Hamburg in 1943, followed by saturation bombing throughout the Reich in 1944. In February 1945, combined forces of the British Bomber Command and the United States Eighth Army Air Force leveled Dresden with no clear military objective. Germany was near to defeat. Did the tens of thousands of deaths save lives and bring the war to a quicker end?

Devastation from the air reflected a slowly accelerated harvest of death on the ground. More Americans were killed in armaments factories before November 1942 than in combat. German casualties only reached 85,000 by the end of May 1940. They quadrupled by the next May, but doubled each year thereafter to reach 3,285,000 in 1944. The air war against Japan only opened in the fall of 1944, by which time racist fever rendered few Americans able to identify anything Japanese as human. War, especially "total war" creates its own psychosis.

In the following article Professor Freedman examines what at first appears to be a minor issue relating to the decision to drop the bomb, that is, the "Administration's thought processes on the operational use of the first atomic bombs." In doing so, however, he examines a wide range of issues relating to the employment of atomic weapons to end the war. A major exception is the argument that by using the bombs, the United States saved a half-million lives. That myth has been convincingly laid to rest by the historian Rufus E. Miles. The figure of a half-million emerged after the event, perhaps as unconscious justification for what many leaders around Truman came to see as an act of questionable morality. Pentagon estimates of 1945 had been that it would cost 20,000 American lives or less to invade and defeat Japan.[1]

Professor Levine considered the possibility that the outcome of the Second World War was determined by the end of 1941. Are we to conclude from Professor Freedman's argument that the defeat of Japan is an example of a grossly overdetermined event?

---

[1]Rufus E. Miles, Jr., "The Strange Myth of Half a Million American Lives Saved," *International Security* 10(1985):121–140.

Were there no alternatives to the using the bomb? That none were actually considered still leaves open the question of whether Japan would have surrendered without the "strategy of Hiroshima."

Introduction

The circumstances and considerations which led to the creation and use of the first atomic bombs have been thoroughly examined in an extensive literature. The literature has been influenced by two important post-war observations. The first is that initially made by the U.S. Strategic Bombing Survey in 1946: If the bomb had not been dropped, "certainly prior to 31 December 1945, and in all probability prior to 1 November 1945, Japan would have surrendered even if Russia had not entered the war, and even if no invasion had been planned or contemplated." The second observation is that as the Second World War drew to a close a cold war between the United States and the Soviet Union began, a key feature of which has been the competitive accumulation of large stocks of ever-more sophisticated nuclear weapons. The feeling has grown that the atom-bombing of Hiroshima and Nagasaki was an unnecessary evil, particularly as it served to stimulate a Soviet–American arms race. Many writers have thus been anxious to search the consciences of the U.S. policy-makers involved in order to see (a) whether any serious thought was given to means of avoiding A-bomb use in the effort to secure a satisfactory conclusion to the Pacific War; and (b) whether the citizens of the two unfortunate Japanese cities were sacrificed in order that the U.S. could demonstrate its strongest military card to the Soviet Union in preparation for the coming struggle over the destiny of Europe.

Momentous and far-reaching actions are not necessarily preceded by comparable deliberations. Alternatives that appear blatant afterwards are often only dimly perceived or rejected as impractical at the time. Problems that loom large after the event appear only as hypotheses and speculations before. A sort of scholarly consensus has now developed that the decision to drop the bomb was inherent in the whole project to build the weapon in the first place. The politicians and military chiefs were mainly interested in ensuring that the most effective use was made of the weapon when it became available. No other considerations intruded sufficiently to result in questioning the wisdom of its use. Indeed, all discussions of the problems and possibilities opened up by the bomb assumed its employment against Japan. The only people who were both well informed and alarmed at the dangerous consequences of this early employment, the Chicago scientists, were isolated from the centres of power. "It was not," as Barton Bernstein notes, "a carefully weighed decision but the implementation of an assumption. The Administration devoted thought to how, not whether, to use [the bomb]."

This article is concerned to follow the Administration's thought processes on the operational use of the first atomic bombs, a matter that has received far less attention in the literature than the weightier questions connected with whether it ought to have been used at all. Given the assumption that the atom bomb was a weapon of war for use against America's enemies, why did its employment take the form it did? In answering this question some of the secondary issues connected with this episode might be illuminated: the choice of a predominantly civilian rather than a predominantly military target; the rejection of the option of a non-lethal demonstration; the lack of warning given to the Japanese of the horror that was to be inflicted upon them; the bombing of Nagasaki so quickly after Hiroshima; the relationship linking the atom-bombing of the two cities to the conventional campaign of strategic bombardment underway at the time and to the developing tension with the Soviet Union; the influence of the desire for full information on the character and capacity of the bomb on the manner of its use.

It will be argued that:

(i) Though the instinctive understanding of the bomb's military value was as a destroyer of cities, its employment in this way was only confirmed by the lack of significant military targets available by mid-1945.

(ii) The experimental value of the attack as a means of discovering more as to the full potential of nuclear weapons was virtually ignored in the choice of targets.

(iii) Considerations of strengthening U.S. military power *vis-à-vis* the Soviet Union were not involved. If they had been the result could well have been to cancel the detonation.

(iv) As more thought was given to the most effective use of the bomb, the strategy evolved from a simple one based on a maximizing the impact of the bomb's destructive power to one aimed at maximizing its shock value. To achieve this it became necessary to distinguish the use of this new weapon from conventional strategic bombing.

(v) There was no separate decision to bomb Nagasaki. It was not part of a carefully controlled strategy, but the logical extension of the decision to use the bomb in the first place.

The Most Terrible Weapon

The impetus behind the atom-bomb project in Britain and America came from a fear of the consequences of a unilateral German success in the military exploitation of atomic energy. This fear motivated many scientists, especially those who were refugees from Nazism, to lobby for and devote themselves to a project that they might otherwise have considered an atrocious militaristic debasement of science. The fears of a Nazi programme, which were not without foundation, were successfully communicated to political leaders.

Coincident with the start of the European war in 1939 had been the publication of a series of important discoveries in nuclear physics, with some of the most important coming from Germany. Almost four months before the August 1939 letter from Einstein to President Roosevelt drawing attention to the recent advances in nuclear physics and the possibility that "extremely powerful bombs of a new type may . . . be constructed," a Professor Paul Harteck was pointing out to the German War Ministry "the newest developments in nuclear physics." These could lead to "an explosive which is in many orders of magnitude more effective than the present one. . . . The country which first makes use of it has an unsurpassable advantage over others." As late as 1942 the Germans were still up with their adversaries in the theoretical aspects of atomic bomb development. Thereafter they fell behind, delayed by false starts, the general deterioration in conditions and lack of resources, plus the limited enthusiasm shown by both the scientists and the military. The German leadership was unimpressed by the lack of quick returns promised by the atomic project at the time when key decisions had to be made. There was little readiness to think of a prolonged war, rather of speedy victory through lightning strikes.

The German atomic threat did not materialize. What would have happened had it done so is by no means clear. Hitler presumably would have viewed atomic bombs in the same manner he viewed the "V" weapons: as an instrument of counter-terror which, if produced and delivered in sufficient quantities, might well turn the tide of the war. It was this prospect that made the British and Americans nervous. There does not, however, appear to have been much serious thought undertaken into the dynamics of deterrence and retaliation. In November 1942 General Groves, the head of the Manhattan project, in explaining the need for the bomb, pointed out that there was no known defence against such a bomb but the fear of counter-employment. How a system of mutual deterrence could have been established in the midst of a bitter war in which restraints on the use of force were being eroded all the time is hard to imagine. All the problems which we now associate with nuclear deterrence—of communicating a credible retaliatory threat and resisting temptations to pre-empt—would have been exacerbated, especially as it is highly unlikely that two separate projects would have reached fruition simultaneously.

It may be that the nuclear scientists, who later became so anxious to prevent the bomb's use, originally saw it purely as an insurance against a successful German project. Those in charge of the project had no doubt that when and if the bomb became ready it was "a weapon to be employed against the enemies of the United States," whatever these enemies had available in their own arsenal. Henry Stimson, the Secretary of War from 1940 to 1945, has made it clear that the

> common objective throughout the war [was] to be the first to produce an atomic weapon and use it. The possible atomic weapon was considered to be a new and tremendously powerful explosive, as legitimate as any other of the deadly explosive weapons of modern war. The entire purpose was the production of a military weapon; on no other ground could the wartime expenditure of so much time and money have been justified. The exact circumstances in which that weapon might be used were unknown to us until the middle of 1945.

He might have added that it was not until late in the project that there was any clear idea as to exactly what sort of weapon had been created. The expectations as to the likely character and capabilities of the bomb evolved during the project. At the start it was not known whether or not the finished project would be sufficiently manageable to be delivered to its target by existing means, nor was it known what sort of explosive yield could be anticipated on detonation.

The first problem concerned the amount of Uranium or Plutonium that would be needed to form a critical mass so as to get a chain reaction underway. Einstein's letter to Roosevelt had indicated that an atom bomb might have to be so large and cumbersome that it would "prove too heavy for transportation by air." Instead it might have to be "carried by boat, and exploded in a port," so destroying that port and the surrounding territory. At the same time in Britain Sir James Chadwick noted that, according to the data used, estimates of the amount of Uranium needed for an explosion varied from 1 ton to 40. The Smyth report, the first official history of the Manhattan Project, reported that in 1940 it had "seemed not improbable that the critical size might be too large for practical purposes." By the time of Pearl Harbor (December 1941) this doubt had been dispelled, but even as late as 1943 the limits of error remained large.

As to yield it had been estimated from early on that explosions equivalent to that produced by a few thousand tons of TNT were possible, but there was uncertainty as to how far the chain reaction within the bomb would go before the device was blown apart. It was not until the New Mexico test of July 1945 that it was realised that the Plutonium implosion bomb could produce explosions of the order of twenty thousand tons of TNT (20 Kilotons). General Groves later commented: "As late as May 1945 the responsible heads of Los Alamos felt that the explosive force of the first implosion type bombs would fall somewhere between 700 and 1,500 tons [of TNT]." Robert Oppenheimer has confirmed this: "Our estimates of the yield [prior to the New Mexico test] were quite uncertain and for the most part quite low." There had always been more confidence in the Uranium gun-type bomb. By December 1944 an estimate of a yield of five thousand to fifteen thousand tons (5–15 KT) had been attached to it and the mean of 10 KT served as a basis for planning until the first detonation over Hiroshima. When it became apparent that the bomb's effectiveness would exceed that of the most destructive conventional weapon its use became "subject to considerations of high level policy." However, Arthur Compton notes that: "If we could have made such a bomb the equivalent of, say, 500 tons of TNT, it would have been made available for military use without restriction."

Once it was certain that yields such as this had become available then the qualitative difference of atomic weapons compared with anything that had gone before was underlined. Up to this point the military and political leaders, while suspecting and hoping that the bomb would be of monumental importance, had to take the scientists' word of its eventual success. The sorts of results to be expected had been presented to them with a mixture of excited superlatives tempered with due scientific caution. It is an interesting question as to how much they actually comprehended the awesome nature of the scientific and technological achievement over which they were presiding. In August 1941, after being informed by the MAUD Committee that a weapon equivalent to 1,800 tons of TNT could be produced, Churchill minuted his contentment with "existing explosives" before recognizing that "we must not stand in the path of improvement." Compare this with his apocalyptical exclamation to Henry Stimson on hearing of the successful test at New Mexico: "Stimson, what was gunpowder? Trivial. What was electricity? Meaningless. This Atomic Bomb is the Second Coming in Wrath."

To Truman the bomb was a revelation, brought to his notice only after he became President in April 1945. Stimson described the undertaking to him in the following terms: "Within one to four months we shall in all probability have completed the most terrible weapon ever known in human history, one bomb of which could destroy a whole city." Truman later told an interviewer that the first comparison that had come into his mind was with the shells the large German gun "Big Bertha" had sent into Paris in the First World War. It was the power of the bomb in the July test, less than a month before its first operational use, that underlined its significance. Stimson himself has noted, in the context of hopes that the bomb would mean that Russia would not need to enter the Pacific War, that: "The bomb as a merely probable weapon had seemed a weak reed on which to rely, but the bomb as a colossal reality was very different."

Whether or not there was any notion that atomic weapons were in a class totally by themselves, deserving of special treatment in every respect, is to be doubted. Nor was it simply "just another weapon." What it could do could be done by other means—but not with the same awesome and spectacular efficiency. Furthermore, the manner of its production was wholly unique and the future promised even greater advances in destructive power. It was still a weapon of war, the use of which was legitimate as the use of any other weapon, but it was a weapon with implications and ramifications far beyond those which had ever accompanied the introduction of a new piece of military equipment.

The Elusive Surrender

The eventual strategic use of the bomb was determined by the conditions prevailing at the time at which the first bomb became available.

By 1944 it had become unlikely that the bomb would be ready in time to influence the war against Germany. In a way this was almost a relief for those Americans, such as General Groves, who wished to keep the British role in the whole project to a minimum. Staging an attack against Japan would be easier and, though there is no evidence at all that there was a racist preference for atom-bombing Asians rather than Europeans, it might have been felt that there was an element of fanaticism in the Japanese war effort that could only be dampened by a spectacular display of allied strength. In the Hyde Park Aide-Memoire, initialled by President Roosevelt and Prime Minister Churchill following discussions on the atom bomb project, the choice of Japan was confirmed: "when a 'bomb' is finally available, it might perhaps after mature consideration, be used against the Japanese, who should be warned that this bombardment will be repeated until the surrender."

By the middle of 1945 Japan was a spent force, unable to project her strength beyond her boundaries. Having lost command of both the sea and the air she was being starved of resources through blockade and being subjected to a regular and unmerciful burning and battering by waves of B–29 bombers. The problem for the Americans was how to turn this defeat into surrender; the problem for the Japanese, once they recognized that there was no path left to victory, was how to surrender under the most favourable conditions.

It is a feature of total war that once the full resources of a nation have been mobilized behind the war effort the military machine becomes difficult to stop until an unequivocal result has been achieved. War-aims move beyond a prevention of the execution of the enemy's most objectionable policies and a return to the *status quo ante,* to a transformation of the enemy's national identity in the belief that the particular structure of power and the character of the ruling ideology constitute the real cause of the war. The demand for "unconditional surrender" is a demand for complete control over the future destiny of the enemy nation.

The Japanese leadership's unwillingness to surrender in 1945, despite the blatant hopelessness of the position, was not based so much on a lingering sense of glory and honour as on a deep sense that the constitutional essence of Japan, embodied in the Emperor, was at stake. The Japanese continued to fight in the hope that the further costs they could impose on the Americans during the course of an invasion would be sufficient to encourage the United States to modify its war aims. This hope rested on sufficient resilience in the face of blockade and bombardment to force the United States into an invasion and then an ability to make this invasion as bloody as possible. There was also a false hope that the Russians, neutrals in the Pacific War, might be able to act as mediators.

Leading figures in the U.S. Administration were not averse to giving the Japanese some guarantees on a future constitutional role for the monarchy; they recognized that this might lead to an early Japanese submission and saw the Emperor as the focal point for the future reconstruction of the country. However, the total war atmosphere of the United States, inflamed by memories of Pearl Harbor, reports of atrocities and the popular image of the Emperor as a Hitler-like figure were not conducive to clear and unambiguous statements of moderation. The attempt to communicate to the Japanese that the Emperor's position in Japanese society would be respected was muted out of regard for American domestic opinion and turned out to be rather cryptic. Unfortunately, the Japanese Cabinet's attempts to indicate their willingness to consider surrender were equally cryptic owing to a desire to avoid provoking the powerful and fanatical faction who favoured war to the bitter end.

A successful invasion which would lead to the physical occupation of the key decision-making centres in Japan would settle the matter for the U.S. But the calculations of possible allied losses, fortified by the experience of the heavy fighting over Okinawa, led to estimates of casualties approaching the million. The military alternative was to continue, through blockade and bombardment, inflicting so much punishment on the enemy that this would lead to a reconsideration of the obstinate refusal to unconditionally surrender.

It was in this context that General Groves, in April 1945, set down criteria for a committee he had appointed to choose appropriate targets for the bomb:

> I had set as the governing factor that the targets chosen should be places the bombing of which should adversely affect the will of the Japanese people to continue the war. Beyond that, they should be military in nature, consisting either of important headquarters or troop concentrations, or centres of production of military equipment and supplies. To enable us to assess accurately the effects of the bomb, the targets should not have been previously damaged by air raids. It was also desirable that the first target be of

such size that the damage would be confined within it, so that we could more definitely determine the power of the bomb.

Before discussing the first of these criteria, some points can be made concerning the second and the third.

Military Targets

There was not any serious discussion from April 1945 onwards of the bomb being used against a wholly military target. General Marshall had wondered to Stimson before the key meeting of the Interim Committee that decided on the most appropriate use of the bomb whether or not a wholly military target, for instance a naval installation, should be bombed but did not press the view. One explanation for this lack of interest is that, by this time, Japan had ceased to function as a serious military force.

In an early meeting, in May 1943, to discuss the future use of the bomb the Japanese fleet concentrated at Truk was recommended as the most suitable target. This target would presumably have had an added attraction as a form of retribution for Pearl Harbor. Two years later the fleet was no longer in existence.

By mid-1945 the only major military engagement facing the allies was an invasion of Japan. If the bomb was to play a supportive role, preparing the ground for the invasion, it would have been used to attack the sort of military targets listed by Groves. But as the aim of the bomb's use was to render an invasion unnecessary, these targets could only have been of secondary importance.

Tactical use does appear to have been considered by the U.S. Chief of Staff General Marshall when developing plans for the invasion of Japan. Marshall was concerned about the "appalling cost" in American lives liable to be claimed by the anticipated ferocity of the Japanese resistance. Reminiscing in 1947 he told David Lilienthal:

> We knew that the Japanese were determined and fanatical, like the Moros [sic; the Moros, a South Filipino Muslim people who fiercely opposed American rule after 1902; Marshall served in the Philippines at the time], and we would have to exterminate them, almost man by man. So we thought the bomb would be a wonderful weapon as a protection and preparation for landings.

Lilienthal recorded a figure of "12" in his diary for the number of bombs to be employed, though in a later interview of Marshall a figure of "9" was mentioned. The manner of employment was to attack defences in the early stage of the invasion with remaining bombs being saved for the Japanese reserves.

How firm an intention this was is hard to say. Herbert Feis writes that in "none of the memos or directives about these strategic plans [for the invasion] is there any mention of the atomic bomb as a tactical weapon to be used in connection with the landings." It is by no means clear with whom Marshall could have discussed this, other than with Groves, Stimson or the President, because of the secrecy surrounding the project. Nor, as Lilienthal observed, did Marshall appear to have considered how "the radioactivity would affect our own forces," though this was a problem Groves and others were well aware of.

It appears that whatever schemes were tentatively hatched they did not survive 1944. The first invasion plans were under consideration in the summer of 1944. Marshall described the "tactical" use of atomic bombs as being in the "original" plans, and considered at a time when "we didn't know the real potential of the bomb." Furthermore, the only time when fulfilling an order of 9–12 bombs for the fall of 1945 could have appeared conceivable was mid-1944. In April 1944 General Groves had reported to General Marshall that several of the implosion bombs with the smaller, anticipated yield (0.7–1.5 KT), and thus more suitable for "tactical" use, would be available between March and the end of June 1945. Presumably several more could have been made available in a further few months. By the end of the year Marshall had been informed that these hopes had been "dissipated by scientific difficulties which we have not as yet been able to solve." Even if the bombs used at Hiroshima and Nagasaki had been spared, production would not have reached the necessary levels by the time of the planned invasion.

Military facilities were located in both of the targets actually bombed. The addition of this component served as a sort of insurance against the main objective of stimulating an immediate surrender failing, and also for cosmetic purposes. In his announcement of the dropping of the bomb on Hiroshima Truman described it as "an important Japanese Army base."

Experimental Use

The third of the Groves's criterion has been less discussed in the literature. With the operational use expected to be limited, such knowledge of the effects of atomic bombs as could be gained was considered by the military invaluable, on the presumption that these bombs would form a key component of the U.S. arsenal in the post-war years. Nevertheless, this experimental aspect carried little weight in the choice of targets. Thus Groves favoured Kyoto as a target because, amongst other things, it was large enough for the damage from the bomb "to run out within the city" and so provide a "firm understanding" of its destructive power. But this was not sufficient to override Stimson's strong political objections to Kyoto as a target. General Farrell, Groves' deputy, recalls reservations on putting Nagasaki on the target list:

> On the ground that the city was not a proper shape and dimension for the large bombs. It was long and narrow and was confined between two ranges of hills that would deflect the blast effect of the bombs. Also it had been very seriously bombed on several occasions before and it would be difficult to measure the effects of the atomic bomb in view of this previous damage.

Strategic Bombardment

To appreciate the primary role seen for the atomic bomb it is necessary to understand the context in which it was chosen. Without the bomb, the only alternative to an invasion was a war of attrition, with blockade and bombardment being used to starve and pound the Japanese into submission. The initial presumption was that the bomb would be an additional instrument of pressure. This can be detected in the Churchill–Roosevelt aide-memoire cited earlier. Given the means of the weapon's delivery and its effect on the ground the obvious comparisons to be made were with strategic air power. The growing experience and associated doctrine of air power provided the foundation for the evolution of a particular strategy appropriate to the new weapon.

It is doubtful whether the Air Force leadership responsible for executing the A-bomb strategy ever moved far beyond the conventional wisdom of strategic bombardment when considering the role of the bomb. It was seen as a supplement to the campaign of conventional bombing being waged at the time by the Air Force under General Curtis LeMay. These conventional raids did not stop as a prelude to the introduction of the bomb; they continued up to the very moment of Japan's surrender. The Air Force leadership's opinion was that Japan would soon collapse as a result of the strategic bombardment and that a couple of A-bombs would not, by themselves, take the Japanese over the threshold of pain. General Arnold wrote in his memoirs:

> The abrupt surrender of Japan came more or less as a surprise, for we had figured we would probably have to drop four atomic bombs or increase the destructiveness of our Super Fortress missions by adding the heavy bombers from Europe.

The Air Force felt quite capable of completing the task it had set for itself without resorting to novel weapons. Those Army and Navy chiefs aware of the bomb preferred more traditional forms of warfare and viewed atom-bombing with the same distaste with which they viewed the conventional bombing of civilians. In mid-1945 the then General Eisenhower told Secretary of War Stimson that he was against the use of the bomb on two counts. "First, the Japanese were ready to surrender and it wasn't necessary to hit them with that awful thing. Second, I hate to see our country be the first to use such a weapon."

The crucial decisions were not taken by military commanders. General MacArthur, Supreme Commander of Allied Forces in the Pacific, who also saw little necessity for the bomb, only heard about the weapon shortly before its use. As already noted there was little doubt amongst the key policy-makers that this expensive new weapon was to be used. The remaining questions on the manner of its use were taken by Stimson, Marshall, those such as Vannevar Bush and James Conant who had been concerned with atom bomb issues since the start of the project, and some of the key figures associated with the Manhattan project, particularly Oppenheimer and Groves. Serious strategic discussion concerning the atom bomb appears to have taken place in the Target Committee, made up of Manhattan Project Scientists and ordinance specialists, set up by Groves, and the Interim Committee set up by Stimson to consider the wider implications of the bomb which discussed, almost by the way, its employment.

The starting point was the current theory and practice of strategic bombardment. In Europe strategic bombardment had become accepted as an important instrument of attrition, even though it had not been as decisive as the pre-war proponents of air power had hoped. In the European theatre the U.S. Army Air Force had preferred to use its heavy bombers in a precise manner, against discrete economic targets. This was in contrast to the RAF's preference for an indiscriminate area bombardment, directed as much against the "morale" of the civilian workforce, as against factories and fuel depots. Because of the RAF's belief in the value of area bombardment, and also because it was easier and less hazardous to accomplish than precision bombing, by the end of the European war precedents had been set for the use of air power for mass destruction.

The U.S. distaste for area bombing vanished in the Pacific war. Japan seemed particularly suitable for area raids: industry was dispersed rather than concentrated and the people were crowded into wooden structures and consequently extremely vulnerable to incendiaries. After limited fire-bombing raids in January and February 1945 the Army Air Force embarked upon a remorseless campaign, beginning in March with an all-out attack on Tokyo that left nearly 300,000 buildings destroyed and over 80,000 dead. In April General Curtis LeMay, who was in charge of this campaign, wrote:

> I am influenced by the conviction that the present stage of development in the air war against Japan presents the AAF for the first time with the opportunity of proving the power of the strategic air arm. I consider that for the first time strategic air bombardment faces a situation in which its strength is proportionate to the magnitude of its task. I feel that the destruction of Japan's ability to wage war is within the capability of this command.

The particular contribution to be made by the atom-bomb could only be judged by reference to this campaign. Groves, who had managed to get himself responsible for choosing appropriate targets for the bomb as an extension of his responsibility for ensuring it got produced, shared the objectives of LeMay's campaign. In the same month that LeMay was writing the comments cited above, Groves was drawing up his criteria describing the primary mission of atom-bombing as being "to adversely affect the will of the Japanese people to continue the war." This was similar wording to that customarily used by the Air Force to explain the purpose of terror-bombing.

The bomb was not, however, to be seen purely as an intensive form of strategic bombardment. To get full benefit of the massive investment and scientific advances exploited in the Manhattan project it was necessary to emphasize the unique and awesome properties of the bomb. After it had been noted in the Interim Committee that the effect of one bomb would not be that different from "any Air Corps strike of current dimensions," Oppenheimer pointed out that: "the visual effect of an atomic bombing would be tremendous. It would be accompanied by a brilliant luminescence which would rise to a height of 10,000 to 20,000 feet." It was on the basis of this spectacular quality that those considering the use of the bomb began to move away from the previous, implicit, strategy of cumulative pressure to one of maximum shock.

The theory of the strategy of cumulative pressure was similar to that of a torturer: to force compliance with wishes by demonstrating a capacity to inflict sanctions beyond the victim's threshold of tolerance. There is, however, a difference between deterring conceivable adversary actions through threats of severe and indeterminate pain, and the compellance of termination of action through a process of intensifying pain. A prospect of future pain is liable to be more influential than a prospect of continued suffering, so long as this suffering has thus far been endured and resistance offers a chance of strategic reward. In discussing the value of air power Liddell Hart noted that "so long as the process is gradual" human beings can accommodate to degradation of their standard of life. "Decisive results come sooner from sudden shocks than long-drawn out pressure. Shocks throw the opponent off balance. Pressure allows him time to adjust to it." To throw the enemy off balance was precisely what was required. Stimson wrote in 1947: "I felt that to extract a genuine surrender from the Emperor and his military advisers, they must be administered a tremendous shock which would carry convincing proof of our power to destroy the Empire." The atomic bomb "was more than a weapon of terrible destruction; it was a psychological weapon." He notes that Marshall was "emphatic in his insistence on the shock value of the new weapon."

A Strategy of Shock

The report of the Interim Committee records how:

> After much discussion concerning various types of targets and effects to be produced, the Secretary expressed the conclusion, on which there

was general agreement, that we could not give the Japanese any warning, that we could not concentrate on a civilian area, but that we should seek to make a profound psychological impression on as many Japanese as possible. At the suggestion of Dr. Conant the Secretary agreed that the most desirable target would be a vital war plant employing a large number of workers and closely surrounded by workers' houses.

The lack of warning was the key to the whole strategy. A shock requires an element of surprise. Here there is a contrast with a strategy of cumulative pressure. If the aim is to convince the enemy of the horror ahead if resistance continues then a declaration of intent to devastate the enemy's homeland is a natural part of the strategy. Surprise will only follow a warning when the warning was either not credible or not properly comprehended.

Warning was, in fact, given in the Potsdam Declaration when it was stated that a failure to accept unconditional surrender would result in "prompt and utter destruction." It did not need the mention of a new bomb to make this a grim and credible threat. Apart from the added horror of radiation, there was little to choose between being fire-bombed by a few hundred B–29s or atom-bombed by one. With or without the atom bomb there was a capability for the obliteration of the socioeconomic infrastructure of Japan, and the Japanese were well aware of this. Before Hiroshima LeMay was already expecting to run out of targets by October when "there wouldn't really be much to work on except probably railroads or something of that sort." Furthermore it is not altogether clear what a mention of atomic bombs would have meant to the Japanese. Even after Hiroshima some of the Japanese military were ready to dispute Truman's claim to have dropped an atom bomb, insisting that this was just a "scare tactic." Initial reports from Hiroshima minimized the effects of the bomb.

Specific warning of the means of destruction, rather than the fact of destruction was ruled out because of the need to ensure psychological shock. General Marshall explained "It's no good warning them. If you warn then there's no surprise. And the only way to produce shock is surprise." In addition there was concern over the counter-productive consequences, in terms of morale, of a new weapon, heralded as a spectacular destroyer of cities, turning out to be a dud.

Nevertheless it is to be regretted that no way was found, or even sought, to provide the citizens of Hiroshima with some warning of an impending attack. The tactics of this attack involved distracting the attention of any Japanese air defences by carrying out other air raids on the same day and by using a single, unescorted plane on the assumption that the Japanese would take no notice of a lone plane flying at high altitude. If anything it would be taken to be a reconnaissance plane. Given the unique nature of the load it is not surprising that LeMay wished to draw as little attention to the delivery plane as possible. Unfortunately, this tactic worked too well. When the bomber appeared over Hiroshima, despite some tentative instructions over the local radio, there was no rush for cover. An all-clear had recently sounded and most people were embarking on their daily work. The presence of so many people in the open or in vulnerable buildings vastly increased the amount of death and mutilation suffered. Robert Oppenheimer had estimated prior to Hiroshima that some 20,000 would die. In fact the actual total was four times as great. "It was not anticipated that when the attack was made practically no one would have sought shelter."

Similar arguments to those used against a warning applied to the suggestion that a demonstration of the bomb's power might be provided for the Japanese. The execution of such a demonstration would have been difficult enough. The Japanese might not have been prepared to sit and watch. Instead they might have been tempted to interfere with the display by shooting down the delivery plane or placing allied POWs in the target area. If the bomb was a failure then the Americans would look foolish with the Japanese determination to resist reinforced. Conferring before the New Mexico test, the scientific advisers to the Interim Committee found that "the difficulties of making a purely technical demonstration that would find its way into Japan's controlling councils were indeed great." They eventually decided that they were too great. An unimpressive demonstration would be worse than none at all. A "precious" bomb would have been used up, and there were not many available, and the element of surprise would have been lost.

The prevailing view was that the message of the bomb would be most effectively communicated by exposing as many Japanese as possible to its effects, hence the detonation close to workers' homes. To emphasize the message it was also felt necessary to distinguish atom-bombing from conventional bombing. When it was suggested at the Interim Committee that several strikes could be attempted at once, one of the objections raised by General Groves was that the effect of this "would not be sufficiently distinct from our regular Air Force bombing program." In order to do this the cities chosen for targetting—Hiroshima, Kokura, Niigata, Nagasaki—were placed on a reserve list. They were spared from strategic bombing so that the destructive capacity of a single atomic bomb would be much more notable. On 6 June 1945 Stimson explained his objection to area bombing to Truman:

> First . . . I did not want to have the United Nations get a reputation of outdoing Hitler in atrocities; and second, I was a little fearful that before we could get ready the Air Force might have Japan so thoroughly bombed out that the new weapon [the atom bomb] would not have a chance to show its strength.

Stimson wished to emphasize to the Japanese the novelty of America's new weapon. The A-bomb would make less of an impact if conventional bombing was already making the flattening of cities the norm.

The one major disagreement over targetting was over the preference of Groves for the ancient capital Kyoto. The cultural and religious influence of Kyoto, Groves argued, would make the Japanese feel the bomb's impact even more, while it had the additional advantage, noted the Target Committee, "of the people being more highly intelligent and hence better able to appreciate the significance of the weapon." Whatever the role of the Kyoto intelligentsia in determining Japanese attitudes as a whole, Stimson did not feel that this justified the attack on such a sacred city. The logic of a strategy of cumulative pressure points to attacks on targets of high social value, but this was not thought necessary, at least by Stimson, for a strategy of shock. The greater the loss the greater the residual bitterness after the war, and Stimson already sensed that a revived Japan in the post-war years would be of importance to the United States.

The Second Bomb

No separate decision was taken to use the second bomb. On 25 July 1945 Groves had directed General Carl Spaatz that: "Additional bombs will be delivered on the above targets as soon as made ready by the project staff." The intention was to keep on producing A-bombs and delivering them on to Japan until the enemy capitulated. Groves himself stated an expectation that no more than two would be needed; "One bomb would show the Japanese what the bomb was like and the second would show them that we had more than one."

Obviously a shock effect does not last for many days. After a while adjustment to the new situation begins. So long as the bombs were spaced far apart in time then the effect would be only of pressure. However, if one followed the other in quick succession then, as Groves noted, "the Japanese would not have time to recover their balance." This would reinforce the initial shock, though whether or not this reinforcement would be necessary would be unclear. It precluded waiting to ascertain the political results of the first bomb.

In fact the governing factor determining the speed of the second bomb's use was not strategic concepts but the actual availability of the bomb. At one point this bomb was not expected to be ready until 20 August. If fact it became available some ten days earlier. The decision on when to use had been left with the local commander who hurried the bomb to its target in order to catch good weather. (Aiming relied on visual observation to ensure maximum accuracy.)

Political Considerations

The most eloquent statement in favour of a technical demonstration was the Franck report, an unofficial production of some of the concerned nuclear scientists based in Chicago. This report did not contradict the essence of the U.S. strategy. It agreed that "important tactical results can be achieved by a sudden introduction of nuclear weapons." The objections to such a "sudden introduction" were based on wider considerations:

> If the United States were to be the first to release this new means of indiscriminate destruction upon mankind, she would sacrifice public support throughout the world, precipitate the race for armaments, and prejudice the possibility of reaching an international agreement on the future control of such weapons.

The property of the bomb that made it so attractive as a means of winning the war might lose the peace. Not only would the Japanese be shocked but "Russia and even allied countries which bear less mistrust of our ways and intentions, as well as neutral countries may be deeply shocked by this step." Franck and his colleagues were more concerned with the spectators than the victim.

Others, including some in the higher policy-making echelons, were aware of these problems. Though the use of the bomb would inevitably be primarily a military decision, serious political objections to its use were taken into account. It is unlikely that those in policy-making positions feared the "wave of horror and revulsion" following the dropping of the bomb. If the military objective was attained the over-whelming reaction would be one of relief at the end of the war; if it failed then the atom bomb would be added to the horrors of war without stimulating any special reaction. By 1945 moral sensibilities had taken too much of a battering for that. The impact on Soviet–American relations was of more concern.

The worst that could be done here would be to add to a deteriorating situation. But Russia would be alarmed only if the Americans attempted to direct the bombs, in some way, against the Soviet Union. The Russians argued in the days after Hiroshima in favour of the bomb's use. What they did come to object to was the Administration's rather clumsy and ill-considered attempts to brandish atomic bombs as a bargaining counter in negotiations with the Russians over the shape of the post-war world—so-called "atomic diplomacy." They did not mind the bomb being dropped on the Japanese. They did dislike the implied threat of it being dropped on them.

The matter of avoiding an arms race revolved around the question of whether or not other powers received their first notice of the atom bomb with its first use. The Franck report had one "realpolitik" comment following logically from the premise, which it hoped was invalid, that it might be hard to get international control on the military exploitation of atomic energy. "If this [arms] race is inevitable, we have every reason to delay its beginning as long as possible in order to increase our head start still further." In the deliberations of the Interim Committee General Marshall raised a similar objection to the bomb's early use:

> General Marshall stated that from the point of view of the postwar safety of the nation he would have to argue against the use of the bomb in World War II, at least if its existence could be kept secret. Such use, he said, would show our hand. We would be in a stronger position with regard to future military action if we did not show the power we held.

The reply to this was twofold. First, there was little chance of the work on the atomic bomb being kept secret; the theoretical possibility was already well-known in the outside world. Second, the prospect of ending the war with the minimum further losses in allied troops was of greater value than "the possible advantage of holding a powerful secret weapon." Thus, if the military challenge of the Soviet Union had been considered an overriding factor, the result would have been not to encourage the visible use of the bomb, thus giving the Russians early warning of an important new weapon, but to preserve the secret for as long as possible.

Both Britain and the Soviet Union were in fact well aware of the capacity to release atomic energy. Britain had promoted and participated in the project and the Soviet Union had been kept informed through sympathizers working on the bomb as well as the studies of its own nuclear scientists. It should be noted that the American success was a challenge to Britain as well as to the Soviet Union and a source of strain in her relations with them both. Such a unilateral acquisition of a powerful military novelty creates a vacuum at the top of the armament inventories of other nations with great-power pretensions, even allies. It also, inevitably, introduces tensions into an alliance. The successful party, having made the effort, resents the desire of others to be let into the secret, whilst the allies start to become jealous and suspicious. The reaction was most marked in the case of Soviet–American relations because these relations were getting into a parlous state independently. But the bomb also developed into a considerable irritant in Anglo–American relations, both during and after the war.

The clearest political benefit the United States saw in the use of the bomb lay in its capacity to finish the war with Japan before the Russians had time to play a significant role in the war, thus limiting the role she would be able to play in the peace. Without the bomb, the American military considered a declaration of war by the Russians as a vital step in achieving victory over Japan. The bomb did not, in fact, become available quickly enough to force a Japanese surrender before Russian entry into the war; this came on 9 August 1945, three days after Hiroshima. It remains a moot point whether or not it was Hiroshima or the Russian advance that served as the catalyst for Japan's surrender.

A Strategy of Shock

This study has shown that though responsible military officials did see atomic bombs primarily as a means to extending and intensifying a campaign of strategy bombardment, key U.S. policy-makers felt that the weapon's terrible and spectacular efficiency was a unique quality which might have an immediate impact on the Japanese ruling group.

With the prompt surrender of the Japanese following Nagasaki the impression has been left that the strategic concepts that guided the use of the bomb were valid. The accumulation of evidence since the war has suggested that the bomb was less important than it appeared at the time in terminating the war. Surrender is a political decision, usually controversial, and so may require a shift in the power structure before it can take place. It was the movement of this shift, dependent on the delicate handling that the hard-line militarists required and a hope that surrender terms might be negotiable, that determined the date of the Japanese surrender. The drift had begun in 1944 and was showing results by April 1945 when Admiral Suzuki became Premier. By June the peace faction had already enlisted the critical support of the Emperor, though the cabinet remained deadlocked. The main question at issue preventing an early surrender was the position of the Emperor. It was not until the cabinet had satisfied themselves that this was secure that surrender could be contemplated. Even after the dropping of the bomb, the cabinet still reserved the right to continue resistance if a threat to the throne was renewed by the allies.

If the bomb did have a role it was in accelerating and intensifying the process of political change. But even here caution is due. The dropping of the bomb was not the only shock that the Japanese received in the four days starting 6 August 1945. Combined with the atom bomb was the introduction of the Soviet Union into the war. This dashed any lingering hopes that there might have been of Soviet support in mediating for more favourable conditions for surrender. It was this, as much as the bomb, that led the cabinet to take the unprecedented step of calling upon the Emperor to make the decision to surrender as a means of breaking their own deadlock. Kecksemeti's suggestion that the bomb, "far from being the 'controlling' factor, cause[d] no significant reorientation of attitudes, no manifest change in views," is too extreme. Leading figures in the Japanese cabinet have cited the bomb as, at least, one cause of the surrender in August 1945. According to Butow the dropping of the bomb had resulted in the sort of dislocation that the administering of strategic shock is supposed to bring:

It was not that the military men had suddenly become reasonable in the hours following the Hiroshima and Nagasaki disasters; it was rather that they . . . had momentarily been caught off balance. They were also at a loss for words which could make any lasting impression upon the end-the-war faction. Prior to the dropping of the two A-bombs they had been able to pledge their belief in their ability to meet effectively any action taken by the enemy, but now whatever they said made them look foolish and insincere.

Even assuming that the bomb was the major source of surrender the lessons that could be drawn from the minimal operational experience were limited. It was like administering poison on the death-bed. The target was a fragile one and not able to resist or withstand this sort of attack. The "command of the air" had been won. There was no danger of retaliation. Finally, because the dropping of the bomb was not simply the climax of an ongoing campaign of strategic bombardment but a distinct operation to maximize the shock caused by the sudden appearance of a major new means of destruction, it was based on advantages, surprise and unpreparedness, that would not necessarily be present in the future.

Further Reading for Part VII

Alperovitz, Gar. *Atomic Diplomacy: Hiroshima and Potsdam.* New York, 1965.

Bernstein, Barton J. *The Atomic Bomb, the Critical Issues.* Boston, 1976.

Boyer, Paul. *By the Bomb's Early Light: American Thought and Culture at the Dawn of the Atomic Age.* New York, 1986.

Butow, Robert J. C. *Japan's Decision to Surrender.* Palo Alto, 1954.

Feis, Herbert. *The Atomic Bomb and the End of World War II.* Princeton, 1961; 2nd ed., 1966.

Harrison, John A. "The USSR, Japan, and the End of the Great Pacific War," *Parameters* 1984:76–87.

Herken, Gregg. *The Winning Weapon.* New York, 1980.

Hersey, John. *Hiroshima.* New York, 1946; revised ed. 1988.

Milward, Alan. *War, Economy and Society 1939–1945.* Berkeley and Los Angeles, 1977.

Rhodes, Richard. *The Making of the A-Bomb.* New York, 1986.

Sherwin, Martin J. *A World Destroyed: The Atomic Bomb and the Grand Alliance.* New York, 1977.

Sigal, Leon. *Fight to a Finish. The Politics of War Termination in the United States and Japan, 1945.* Ithaca and London, 1988.

Index

Loyd E. Lee is professor of history with the State University of New York, the College at New Paltz. He is the author of *The War Years: A Global History of the Second World War*, published in 1989. Professor Lee's research interests also include modern German and world history and the impact of military institutions on social life. He has taught a course on the history of the Second World War for two decades.